The Cooperstown Symposium on Baseball and American Culture 2000

The Cooperstown Symposium on Baseball and American Culture

2000

Edited with an Introduction by
 William M. Simons

<small>Series Editor: Alvin L. Hall</small>

McFarland & Company, Inc., Publishers
Jefferson, North Carolina, and London

To the memory of Zelda Kahan

ISBN 0-7864-1120-1 (softcover : 50# alkaline paper)

British Library cataloguing data are available

Library of Congress cataloguing data are available

Manufactured in the United States of America

McFarland & Company, Inc., Publishers
  Box 611, Jefferson, North Carolina 28640
  www.mcfarlandpub.com

Table of Contents

PART 2: BASEBALL AS HISTORY

PART 3: THE BUSINESS OF BASEBALL

PART 4: RACE, GENDER, AND ETHNICITY IN THE NATIONAL PASTIME

Acknowledgments

Alvin Hall created the Cooperstown Symposium on Baseball and American Culture. Jim Gates, Tim Wiles, Scot Mondore, and the superb staff at the National Baseball Hall of Fame and Museum provided invaluable research assistance. Sharon Corna contributed much appreciated secretarial support. Colleagues and friends Tom Beal, Mark Boshnack, Dora Dumont, Joe Fodero, Gerrit Gantvoort, John Hurley, Bob Jackson, Armand LaPotin, Gene Obidinski, Dave Richards, Bob Russell, and Denny Shea read manuscripts and offered insightful criticism. State University of New York College at Oneonta Provost F. Daniel Larkin and Interim Dean Marguerite Culver offered institutional support. Fawn Holland produced the index.

— WMS

Preface

Alvin L. Hall

The Cooperstown Symposium on Baseball and American Culture has taken on a life of its own. Well, almost. When it began in 1989, we thought of it as a one-time event held in conjunction with the National Baseball Hall of Fame's Fiftieth Anniversary. Yet, here we are at the beginning of a new century, completing the Twelfth Cooperstown Symposium. Who would have thought there were that many men and women with solid academic credentials committed to the serious, scholarly study of the national pastime? In these 12 years, well over a hundred authors have presented nearly three hundred first-rate papers on baseball's impact on American culture. The papers have covered a full range of disciplines as diverse as art history and women's studies. They have been presented by faculty members from prestigious universities and obscure community colleges and secondary schools, by undergraduate and graduate students, and by freelance scholars. The rich mixture has included three original stage plays, a screenplay, and original poetry and fiction.

The papers have not been the only attraction. We have been exceedingly fortunate in attracting some of the most outstanding keynote speakers one could imagine. In the second year, Harold Seymour, generally acknowledged as the individual most responsible for making the serious study of baseball acceptable in the academic world, provided an outline of his soon-to-be-published *The People's Game.* In the summer before the last major league strike, Donald Fehr, executive director of the Major League Baseball Players Association, told those in attendance what their bargaining position would be and why he thought they would win. Just

1

before PBS released his opus on *Baseball,* Ken Burns provided a rough-cut preview and told those present that Buck O'Neill was the most outstanding individual he had met during the filming. Stephen Jay Gould, whose scholarly interests lie elsewhere but who writes eloquently about baseball, as he does about virtually everything else, used classical evolutionary theory to dispel some of baseball's hoary myths. W. P. Kinsella, author of *Shoeless Joe* and *The Iowa Baseball Confederacy,* read from his works and then listened as undergraduate students in advanced architecture class at the University of Miami described their designs for the baseball stadium in Big Inning, Iowa, a figment of Kinsella's imagination. Others have included Jim Vlasich, author of a book on the origins of the Hall of Fame; Marty Appel, former director of publicity for the New York Yankees; David Q. Voigt, Seymour's heir as the definitive historian of baseball; Peter Levine, a student of sport and ethnicity in America; G. Edward White, a constitutional and Supreme Court historian whose book on the origins of modern baseball caused his friends to worry that he might compromise his reputation as a serious scholar; Eliot Asinof, author of *Eight Men Out;* and Leonard Koppett, the only sportswriter in both the National Baseball and the National Basketball Halls of Fame. This year, they were joined by Roger Kahn, who regaled us with tales of being a young reporter when the Dodgers were at their height and still in Brooklyn and Jackie Robinson broke the color barrier. And, the beat goes on.

In 2001, the Thirteenth Cooperstown Symposium on Baseball and American Culture will meet at the National Baseball Hall of Fame and Museum on June 7, 8, and 9. For the triskaidekaphobes out there, we will take a special look at baseball superstitions, myths, and legends in addition to our usual multidisciplined and multiple topic approach.

I would like especially to acknowledge the continuing co-sponsorship of the State University of New York College at Oneonta and the National Baseball Hall of Fame and Museum, and to thank Dr. William Simons, Professor of History at SUNY–Oneonta, and one of the best baseball scholars I know, for his diligent effort as the volume editor.

Alvin L. Hall
The Union Institute
Cincinnati, Ohio

Introduction

William Simons

The Cooperstown Symposium on Baseball and American Culture constitutes an annual rite for serious students of the national pastime. Conceived in 1989, the Symposium provides a June summons for baseball acolytes to gather in the game's mecca. Historian and academic administrator Alvin Hall, the Symposium's founder, director, and series editor, elicits comparison with the late, great television impresario Ed Sullivan. Sullivan did not sing, dance, or tell jokes, but he consistently put on a great show. Al Hall does not engage in baseball teaching, research, or writing, but he consistently produces a great Symposium. Through his energy, enthusiasm, formidable charm, organizational gifts, and nurturing of talented scholars, Hall has rendered the Symposium baseball's preeminent conference, as the papers in this anthology, presented at the 2000 Symposium, attest.

Synergism marks the relationship between the National Baseball Hall of Fame and Museum and the State University of New York College at Oneonta, co-sponsors of the Symposium. For the dance team nonpareil, Fred Astaire gave Ginger Rogers class, and she provided him with glamour. The Hall of Fame brings to the Symposium the resources of its unrivaled baseball library, a meeting place within the game's shrine, an excellent staff, and celebrity. And the State University of New York contributes its reputation for academic excellence in teaching, research, community service, and publication.

Establishing the academic legitimacy of baseball history was no mean achievement. The first time I said to my dean that I wanted to teach a course on baseball history, he said with eyebrows raised, "What are you going to do—sit around talking about last night's game?" The excellent papers presented at past Symposia, inspiring a plethora of articles and books, contributed to the process that made it possible for baseball history to find a respected place in the academic curriculum.

Baseball can be used as a vehicle to stimulate intellectual curiosity in our history and culture. For several generations, baseball was the undisputed national pastime, making it a revealing mirror to the American past. As historian Christopher Lasch noted, "Games derive their power from the investment of seemingly trivial activity with serious intent." The symbolism attached to baseball casts it as a microcosm of American society. The focus of the Cooperstown Symposium is this symbiotic relationship between baseball and the larger culture, not parochial aspects of the game.

Philadelphia Inquirer sportswriter Frank Fitzpatrick once satirized the "more than 100 baseball-bleeding academics" who participate in the "brainy bliss" of the Symposia:

> Had there been an egghead detector outside the Hall of Fame's Grandstand Theater, it would have buzzed itself to a breakdown.
> Mismatched outfits, glasses, beards and the smiling, disoriented gazes that signify intellectual obsession branded the cerebral crowd waiting for the start of the recent ... Annual Cooperstown Symposium on Baseball and American Culture.

Quite clearly those who make the pilgrimage to the Symposium love baseball. But, despite Fitzpatrick's nerdy imagery, many of the participants played high school and college ball; a few rode buses in the minors; and several continue to suit up for competition in senior leagues. Surrounding the conference's core activity, the presentation of rigorous academic studies of the national pastime, infatuation with baseball punctuates the fellowship and conversations of participants. Spirited town ball games enliven the assemblage. Original baseball plays, poems, and short stories have debuted at the Symposium. Anecdotes, vignettes, and reminiscences of the game enliven meals, informal gatherings, and nocturnal hours.

Nonetheless, the Symposium is an academic gathering of serious baseball scholars. Through the years, Symposium participants have included reputable students of the game drawn from history, literature, sociology, anthropology, political science, linguistics, business, economics, psychology, law, medicine, architecture, journalism, theology, and other disciplines. Institutional affiliations of participants have included Temple University, Massachusetts Institute of Technology, Barnard College, Hofstra University, Kenyon College, Boston University, the University of Rochester, the State University of New York, Yale, Southern Illinois

University, the University of Massachusetts, the University of Tennessee, Southern Methodist University, and numerous other noted colleges and universities.

What draws intellectuals to the Cooperstown Symposium on Baseball and American Culture? The main enticement is collaboration and fraternity with fellow students of the game. Symposium participants recognize the validity of Jacques Barzun's observation about the national pastime: "Whoever wants to know the heart and mind of America had better learn baseball." Americans invest their game with symbolism. An oasis of green in an industrial society, the bucolic baseball field evokes rural nostalgia. The broad expanse of outfield recalls an America without limits. Poet Walt Whitman observed, "It's our game, the American game. It will ... repair our losses. And be a blessing to us."

Another major appeal of the conference is its Cooperstown, New York, setting, crowned by the beauty of Lake Otsego. Cooperstown is home to two of America's great legendary heroes, James Fenimore Cooper's frontiersman and Abner Doubleday's baseball player. Some Americans still believe the myth that future Civil War general Abner Doubleday invented baseball in pastoral Cooperstown in 1839. Faith denies that our national pastime could have evolved from English games. The Doubleday myth attests American exceptionalism in the same way that historian Frederick Jackson Turner's frontier thesis proclaims our uniqueness.

Cooperstown is baseball's spiritual home. Mythology, the Hall of Fame, Doubleday Field, tradition, and belief make it so. Participants in the Symposium find inspiration in Cooperstown. Here they encounter baseball's most emblematic icon. Near the parking lot entrance to Cooperstown's Doubleday Field resides the *Sand Lot Kid* monument. It is he, the *Sand Lot Kid*, who is the true inventor of baseball. He symbolizes the millions of American youth who created their own version of the American game in backyards, empty lots, fields, city streets, and playgrounds. Exempt from the rigid rules of adults, sandlot kids decide the number of players per side, the composition of teams, the distance between bases, whether to call balls and strikes, and the other essentials that make the game their own. Dressed in bib overalls and farm hat, the barefoot *Sand Lot Kid*, proud of his homemade bat, personifies the Edenic innocence of youth. Baseball is America before the fall from grace. Reflecting upon the *Sand Lot Kid*, Symposium participants remember the words of *Field of Dreams'* Terence Mann: "Baseball ... reminds us of all that once was good and could be good again."

The title of the Symposium, "Baseball and American Culture," is telling. Baseball trivia is alien to the formal proceedings. The mandate of the conference is to illuminate American civilization from the vantage point of baseball. Serious students of the national pastime examine American history, the national character, the social fabric, intellectual currents, race, ethnicity, gender, business, economics, technology, urbanism, education, the arts, the media, architecture, and other components of culture.

Harold Seymour initiated the process of legitimizing academic studies of baseball. *Sports Illustrated* termed him "the Edward Gibbon of baseball history." And there is an intimate connection between Seymour and the Cooperstown Symposium. Teenage batboy for Wilbert Robinson's Brooklyn Dodgers, high school and college first baseman, and semipro manager, Seymour wrote the first Ph.D. dissertation on the national pastime, "The Rise of Major League Baseball to 1891" (Cornell, 1956). In 1960 Seymour's *Baseball: The Early Years* became the first book on the game to merit publication by an academic press (Oxford). More superb writing followed.

In 1990 Seymour, ill and aged, served as the keynote speaker at the Symposium. A memorable event, it was the last public presentation of the scholar who inaugurated academic study of baseball. Within a few years, Seymour died. His ashes made their way to Symposium director Al Hall.

As darkness descended on June 8, 1995, Symposium participants gathered at Cooperstown's Doubleday Field to honor Harold Seymour. Speakers read excerpts from Seymour's great baseball histories. Al Hall reminded the assemblage that Seymour, as the first academic historian of the national pastime, had paved the way for the Symposium's baseball scholars. Then Seymour's ashes were scattered around first base. With wry wit and affection, Hall noted, "Now we know who's on first."

Along with organizer Al Hall and indefatigable historian Tom Altherr, I have participated in each of the first 12 editions of the Symposium. Thoughts of conferences past elicit so many memorable moments, and, as with all participants, some of mine are personal. Thanks to the delivery of my taped remarks by State University of New York colleague and friend John Hurley, a painful 1991 case of chicken pox failed to snap my streak in its infancy. In 1992 I received an award for the best paper presented at that year's Symposium. A former student of mine, Scot Mondore, then senior researcher at the Hall of Fame Library, introduced several of my Symposia presentations. Six of my graduating seniors joined me as co-presenters at a 1998 panel on the teaching of baseball history. And one year I served as chauffeur to the keynote speaker.

Driving Mr. Kinsella: June 11, 1996

"Are you seeing a psychiatrist?" novelist J.D. Salinger nervously asked the stranger, baseball fanatic Ray Kinsella, who forced him, with a fake gun, into a Datsun for a 1,500-mile ride to a baseball field in Iowa.

The journey of Ray Kinsella and J.D. Salinger takes place in the novel *Shoeless Joe*, written by W.P. Kinsella. In 1996 I was instructed to take Kinsella, not the fictional Ray but his creator and namesake, W.P., on a trip. Ray's travel itinerary came from a supernatural voice; mine came from Symposium director Al Hall.

The night before Kinsella's keynote presentation to the Symposium I drove him from Albany County Airport to Cooperstown. My 11-year-old son Joe and our friend Bob Russell came along to meet Kinsella.

At 8:30 p.m. on Tuesday, June 11, 1996, Bob, Joe, and I waited at Gate 4 for Delta flight 2120 from Cincinnati. A photograph enabled us to recognize the tall, lanky, casually-dressed man with glasses, mustache, goatee, and theatrically long hair as Kinsella. A small book bag was his only luggage.

Kinsella's trip began at 5 a.m., three flights ago, in Vancouver, and he would return to his Canadian home directly after Wednesday's presentation at Cooperstown. After introductions, we guided Kinsella to my Camry, settled in and let him set the tone.

Kinsella and Bob chatted about the recent success of Mets pitchers. Sympathetic to my view that there had been too many home runs of late, Kinsella suggested a definitive scientific test to determine whether the ball was "juiced."

William Patrick Kinsella, then 61, grew up on a farm in rural Canada. In his youth, he was a solid hitter with a weak glove. An early marriage and two daughters detoured Kinsella's writing aspirations. Driving a cab, investigating insurance claims, and operating an Italian restaurant paid the bills. In the 1970s, Kinsella, as an older student, earned degrees from the University of Victoria and the University of Iowa.

Joe, sitting in back, leaned forward and asked Kinsella, "When did you begin to write?" Kinsella answered, "I started to write when I was 5. I just woke up one day and knew how to read and write." I suspect Kinsella's response, like his writing, was meant to convey mystery, magic, and humor.

Literary fame came slowly. Kinsella's initial publications about Canadian Indians brought critical praise but modest recognition. Sliding into middle age, he was unhappy teaching "Bonehead English" at the University of Calgary.

After years of obscurity, Kinsella found fame through his baseball fiction. Millions have seen *Field of Dreams*, the film version of Kinsella's *Shoeless Joe*, a novel about innocence, guilt, and redemption.

Kinsella employs baseball as a metaphor. His writing is of the game and transcends the game. Baseball, Kinsella once observed, "is timeless and the foul lines diverge forever, taking in the entire universe."

The Camry's muffler growled as our destination beckoned. Cooperstown's darkened Main Street was nearly deserted. Within sight of the Baseball Hall of Fame, we turned left onto Pioneer Street.

Parked in front of the Tunicliff Inn, I turned on the interior light. "Would you autograph this?" I asked Kinsella, handing him a pen and a paperback copy of *Shoeless Joe*. He wrote something and returned the book.

While Bob and Joe remained in the car, Kinsella and I walked into the small, dimly-lit lobby of the Tunicliff Inn. It was empty. Kinsella looked tired. Picking up the house phone, Kinsella said, "I have a reservation. I'd like to check in." Putting the phone down, Kinsella sighed, "It's 10:30, and she sounds like I woke her up."

Back in the car, I checked to see what Kinsella had written in the book. I read the inscription aloud, "Go the distance — Bill Kinsella."

I thought of *Field of Dreams*. The morning after Joe first saw the film he tiptoed into my room and woke me with the words, "If you build it, he will come."

Our car turned off Main Street into the parking lot that leads to Doubleday Field, the symbolic birthplace of baseball. With the *Sand Lot Kid* monument standing guardian and using car headlights for illumination, Bob, Joe, and I played catch.

Keynote Speakers

Kinsella and Seymour reflect the outstanding keynote speakers who have graced the Symposium. At the first gathering, convened in 1989 to commemorate the fiftieth anniversary of Cooperstown's baseball shrine, Dr. James A. Vlasich, a Southern Utah State College historian, discussed "Alexander Cleveland and the Origins of the Hall of Fame," and Marty Appel, then executive producer of New York Yankee baseball for WPIX-TV and a graduate of the State University of New York College at Oneonta, examined the contemporary game.

The 1990 Symposium also featured two keynote speakers. In addition to Seymour, whose presentation was entitled "Baseball: Badge of Americanism," David Quentin Voigt also appeared. Rivals, Seymour and Voigt both independently wrote magisterial three-volume histories of the game. Voigt discussed "Getting Right with Baseball."

Historian Peter Levine, author of *A.G. Spalding and the Rise of Baseball*, held forth "On Doing Baseball History" in 1991. Then, in 1992 Harvard paleontologist, man of letters, and cultural guru Stephen Jay Gould infused his presentation, "Keeler's Average and Buckner's Legs: Legends and Reality of a Not-So-Golden Past," with wit and wisdom. Donald M. Fehr, executive director of the Major League Players Association, followed in 1993 with a pragmatic analysis of "Organized Baseball at the Close of the 20th Century."

In 1994 documentary filmmaker Ken Burns showed and discussed excerpts from his *Baseball* series prior to its subsequent debut on PBS. Legendary sportswriter Leonard Koppett, a recipient of the J.G. Taylor Spink Award, discussed "Baseball as We Knew It — Never Again" in 1995. And in 1996 Kinsella provided an interpretive reading of his memorable baseball fiction.

To mark the fiftieth anniversary of the reintegration of major league baseball in 1997, Jules Tygiel, author of the brilliant *Baseball's Great Experiment*, insightfully analyzed "The Legacy of Jackie Robinson." In 1998 the University of Virginia's noted scholar G. Edward White elaborated on the themes developed in his valuable study *Creating the National Pastime: Baseball Transforms Itself, 1903–1953*. The next year, Eliot Asinof, author of *Eight Men Out*, the definitive account of the 1919 Black Sox scandal, gave a wonderfully entertaining and informative chronicle of his experiences as a minor league player and baseball writer. And, to inaugurate the new millennium, Roger Kahn delivered the 2000 keynote address.

For many baseball enthusiasts, the mere mention of Roger Kahn conjures up a series of indelible images. He is not simply a gifted sportswriter; Kahn is a great writer. Make no mistake — Kahn knows the game with an insider's familiarity, but his best writing employs sport to better understand the human condition.

The term sportswriter fails to convey the essence of Roger Kahn's work. A versatile author, his writings encompass literary, political, sociological, and philosophical concerns. He even wrote a children's book and two novels. Kahn covered sports for the New York *Herald Tribune*, served as *Newsweek* sports editor, and was on the staff of *Sports Illustrated*. He is the author of magazine articles and books on a variety of subjects. His books include *A Flame of Pure Fire: Jack Dempsey and the Roaring '20s* (1999), *Memories of Summer* (1997), *The Era* (1993), *Games We Used to Play* (1992), *Joe and Marilyn* (1986), *Good Enough to Dream* (1985), *The Seventh Game* (1982), *The Battle for Morningside Heights* (1970), *The Passionate People* (1968), and *Inside Big League Baseball* (1962). Kahn's best writing, however, always returns to his early interest in sports. Although he finds universal truths in the lives of men who play games, he also deftly illuminates those characteristics particular to the world of the athlete. At his best Kahn is both literary figure and sportswriter.

The Boys of Summer is Kahn's most important work. *The Boys of Summer*, perhaps the most widely read account of the reintegration of baseball, is, by turns, memoir of Roger Kahn's youth, chronicle of Brooklyn baseball during the Jackie Robinson era, and series of character studies focusing on the lives of former Dodgers. Kahn's poignant account of fathers and sons, men and time, discrimination and justice, always leads the reader back to Robinson and the lingering resonance he left for those who knew him. Kahn's Robinson — embattled, courageous, and proud — appears a tragic hero.

Kahn's keynote address at the most recent Symposium, "'When Homer Smote His Bloomin' Lyre': Some Observations on Sportswriting," was delivered on June 7, 2000, in the Grandstand Theater of the National Baseball Hall of Fame. Kahn's remarks were a celebration of great prose. His story of Big Ed Gilligan, the New York *Herald Tribune*'s rod and gun writer, turning to novelist Thomas Hardy for inspiration on the placing of a single star in a dark sky, was one of many memorable Kahn anecdotes:

> "But how to put it in the sky," Gilligan said. "Hanging? Twinkling? Shining? All terrible. Then I thought how would Hardy have put that star up there and it came to me. A single star was *candling* in the sky. I was so excited I screamed and my wife came down to the cabin where I write and found me at the typewriter, tears streaming down my cheeks, saying, 'Gilligan, you can write like a son of a bitch.'"

Kahn waxed eloquent over the great sportswriters of the 1920s and poignantly described his own mid-century apprenticeship in the craft. He lamented the recent descent of journalism into voyeuristic sensationalism, frequently devoid of fairness or literary merit. Amidst unctuous philistines, Kahn continues to uphold the tradition of Grantland Rice, Ring Lardner, Heywood Broun, Paul Gallico, and Damon Runyon. We are honored to include Kahn's keynote address in this volume.

Structure of the Anthology

This anthology containing the essays delivered at the most recent conference is divided into four parts: *Baseball and Culture, Baseball as History, The Business of Baseball,* and *Race, Gender, and Ethnicity. Baseball and Culture* analyzes the relationship between sport and the beliefs, values, intellectual currents, and social patterns that constitute American civilization. *Baseball as History* examines the national pastime's relationship to the past, both literal and mythic. *The Business of Baseball* concerns the entrepreneurial, economic, and labor components of the game. *Race, Gender, and Ethnicity* explores the human diversity within the extended family of baseball. Each part contains multiple essays, related by theme and topic. A guide to the papers follows.

Baseball and Culture

"When Homer Smote His Bloomin' Lyre": Some Observations on Sportswriting by Roger Kahn is quite appropriately the anthology's leadoff essay. Kahn, himself one of America's preeminent writers, offers an elegy to the rise and fall of great baseball prose. He chronicles sportswriting's Golden Age and its fall from grace.

Safe at Home: Forging Intergenerational Alliances by C. Oren Renick explores the "unintended consequences of a father and a son tossing a baseball ... back and forth." Drawing on his own extensive athletic background, Renick recounts baseball experiences that nurture familial and friendship bonds, transcending differences in age and background. Trained in the ministry and law, Renick, a frequent contributor to professional journals and conferences, is associate professor in the Department of Health Administration at Southwest Texas State University.

"Jesus Is Standing at the Home Plate": Baseball and American Christianity by Gregory Erickson analyzes the relationship between religion and the national pastime. Writing fellow at Medgar Evers College (former site of Ebbets Field) and instructor at the Brooklyn Conservatory of Music, Erickson observes, "Because American baseball and religion come out of a white/black, fair/foul, safe/out, and heaven/hell mentality, they find themselves in tension with an increasingly relativistic and postmodern world that is questioning our knowledge of such concepts as truth." Erickson, part-time color commentator for the Beliot Snappers Class A minor league team, has published on theology, literature, musicology, and television.

Physical Literacy in Baseball and Other Sports by Robert Ochsner contends that "baseball and literacy are good for each other." Ochsner, on leave from the University of Maryland-Baltimore County, is currently serving as chair of the Department of English and Foreign Languages at Fayetteville State University. Ochsner demonstrates that "baseball provides an especially apt analogue for the social changes, and more specifically the technological developments that have reshaped the nature of written language." Ochsner's publications include *Physical Eloquence and the Biology of Writing*.

A Flexible Metaphor: Baseball in the Classroom by Michelle Jones illustrates that "baseball is a flexible and accessible way of teaching a variety of academic subjects at the high school and college level." Associate professor of English at Muskingum College in New Concord, Ohio, Jones asserts, "Using baseball in the classroom can teach reluctant students the joys of contemplation and analysis." Jones' baseball poetry and prose regularly appears in *Elysian Fields Quarterly.*

"Walter Johnson" by Jonathan Richman: The Portrait of a Hero in Song by Richard J. Puerzer provides detailed content analysis and cultural context for a song about the legendary Washington Senators pitcher who won 417 games and recorded 110 shutouts. According to Puerzer, assistant professor of engineering at Hofstra University, the song "Walter Johnson," written and performed by musician Jonathan Richman, treats its subject as a hero yet retains a sense of realism. "This song," writes Puerzer, "is unique in that it exhibits a rare honesty and true exuberance for baseball and for how Walter Johnson played the game."

BASEBALL AS HISTORY

"This Town Isn't Big Enough for Both of Us": Politics, Economics, and Local Rivalries in St. Louis Major League Baseball by Roger D. Launius examines "the creation, rivalry, and eventual demise of all but one major league baseball team in St. Louis." Chief historian of the National Aeronautics and Space Administration, Launius investigates the strategies employed by Chris Von der Ahe, Branch Rickey, Bill Veeck, and other promoters of St. Louis baseball. Authors of numerous articles and books on diverse subjects, Launius' *Joseph Smith III: Pragmatic Prophet* won the Evans Award for biography.

Baseball During World War II: An Exploration of the Issue by Gerald Bazer and Steven Culbertson builds upon the pioneering studies of Richard Goldstein and William Mead concerning the symbiotic relationship between the national pastime and wartime America. Colleagues at Owens Community College, Culbertson, professor of communications, and Bazer, dean of arts and sciences, examine "the decision to continue baseball at all organized levels during World War II and the effects of doing so." The authors illuminate the "shared sacrifices" shouldered by baseball and the larger American society to facilitate the war effort.

Baseball in a Football Town: The Neighborhood Diamond, Heavy Industry, and High Attendance (1930–1949) by Peggy Beck examines the legacy of baseball in Canton, Ohio, a city better known as "the cradle of pro football." Former instructor of English at Stark College of Technology, Beck discusses the relationship between local industry and Canton baseball during the Great Depression and World War II. Her grandfather and father helped create the Canton field used by the Pennsylvania Railroad baseball team.

The Game in Sepiatone and Soft Focus: Nostalgia and American Baseball in Historical Context by Thomas L. Altherr explores the sources, manifestations, and significance of a nostalgia that fashions an idealized rendering of baseball's past. Altherr, professor of history at Metropolitan State College, writes of disciples of baseball nostalgia: "Some of this personal nostalgia may be inarticulate, inchoate, diffuse, inexpressible, but nevertheless powerful and on occasion empowering." A prolific author, Altherr is the editor of *The Cooperstown Symposium on Baseball and American Culture, 1998* (also to be published by McFarland).

The Business of Baseball

Major League Umpires and Collective Bargaining by Karen Shallcross Koziara analyzes the background and implications of the 1999 vote of the Major League Umpires Association "to use mass resignations as a tactic to pressure baseball management to negotiate." Professor of human resource administration at Temple University, Koziara concludes that labor "confrontation is a risky strategy, and its outcomes are unpredictable." Koziara has published in a number of journals and books on labor relations in various fields, including several articles on labor relations in baseball.

Customer Discrimination in Memorabilia: New Evidence for Major League Baseball by Rhonda Sharpe and Sumner La Croix examines the prices of "baseball memorabilia to determine whether baseball fans prefer the memorabilia" of white players to the artifacts of Latin or African-American athletes. Sharpe and La Croix investigate discrimination in the purchase of autographed baseballs, autographed photographs, gloves, and game jerseys. Sharpe is Carolina Minority Post Doctoral Fellow in the Economics Department at the University of North Carolina at Chapel Hill. La Croix is professor of economics at the University of Hawaii.

Despoiling the Sleeve: The Threat of Corporate Advertising Upon the Integrity of the Major League Uniform by Ken Moon considers, within an economic and historical context, the current debate over whether to allow commercial advertising on major league uniforms. Instructor of English and media at Indian Hills Community College, Moon analyzes the controversy surrounding the patches worn on the uniform sleeve of the New York Mets and Chicago Cubs in Japan during the opening of the 2000 major league season. Beyond baseball research, Moon nurtures his ties to the game by umpiring Little League games on Iowa's fields of dreams.

RACE, GENDER, AND ETHNICITY IN THE NATIONAL PASTIME

Houston's Latin Star Cesar Cedeno and Death in the Dominican Republic: The Troubled Legacy of Race Relations in the Lone Star State by Ron Briley focuses on the context and consequences of the 1973 shooting death of a young woman in the hotel room of Astros star Cesar Cedeno. Assistant headmaster at Sandia Preparatory School, Briley asserts, "The Houston Astros, based upon their experience with Cedeno seem to have ... on an unconscious level, bought into the racial stereotype that Latin ball players" lack the attributes "around which one should organize a team." Briley received the 1999 SABR/Macmillan Research Award for his article "As American as Cherry Pie: Baseball and Reflections of Violence in the 1960s and 1970s."

Comparative Ethnicity: Joe DiMaggio and Hank Greenberg by William Simons asserts that the Yankee center fielder and the Tiger slugger "were the most popularly celebrated members of their respective ethnic groups during the 1930s." According to Simons, "It is as ethnic standard bearers during a crucial era ... that Greenberg and DiMaggio share their most important similarity." Professor of history at State University of New York College at Oneonta, Simons is the editor of this anthology.

Baseball in the Ocean State: Rhode Island Black Baseball, 1886–1948 by Lawrence D. Hogan and Jeffrey L. Statts chronicles professional baseball, across the color line, in the nation's smallest state. Although numerous studies of black professional baseball followed the 1970 publication of Robert Peterson's seminal account, *Only the Ball Was White*, Hogan and Statts enlarge our knowledge of the subject through their investigation of state and local history. Lawrence D. Hogan is professor of history at Union County College, and Jeffrey L. Statts is professor of architecture at Roger Williams University.

"She Loved Baseball": Effa Manley and Negro League Baseball by Amy Essington relates the story of an extraordinary woman, white by birth and black by identity, who emerged as a major figure in black baseball. Co-owner and business manager of the Newark Eagles of the Negro National League during the 1930s and 1940s, Manley transcended conventional racial and gender roles in baseball and in her personal life. Essington, doctoral candidate in American history at Claremont Graduate University, is a former intern at the National Baseball Hall of Fame Library.

Black Players on the Field of Dreams: African American Baseball in Film by George Grella analyzes the relationship between racial practices in the national pastime and cinematic depictions of those protocols. Professor of English and film studies at the University of Rochester, Grella, sensitive to sociological and historical context, contends that baseball films "demonstrate some of the unchanging attitudes toward race, many of them entirely unpleasant and obnoxious." A longtime participant in the Cooperstown Symposium on Baseball and American Culture and the film critic for WXXI-FM, Rochester, a National Public Radio station, Grella is the author of numerous publications on baseball and film.

"*I Haven't Got Ballplayers. I've Got Girls*": *Portrayals of Women in Baseball Film* by Robert Rudd and Marshall G. Most examines depictions of women in cinema over the past six decades. "Despite the influential role of women in transforming the male hero" in baseball movies, Rudd and Most find that "these films serve not as expressions of feminist values or a challenge to traditional patriarchal gender definitions, but rather as reflections of those values." Professors in the Department of Communication at Boise State University, Rudd and Most are frequent contributors to the Cooperstown Symposium on Baseball and American Culture.

Part 1

BASEBALL AND CULTURE

"When Homer Smote His Bloomin' Lyre": Some Observations on Sportswriting

Roger Kahn

An eon or so ago, when Dwight Eisenhower presided and had sense enough to keep American soldiers out of Vietnam, I served some time at *Newsweek* magazine where John Lardner wrote a weekly column, mostly about sports. That writing would have made John's father proud.

John remarked across a Cutty Sark one afternoon that he was thinking of doing a piece parodying each of the six or seven New York power sports columnists.

Jimmy Cannon, we agreed, would be fairly easy. You may remember that Cannon used a conceit called "nobody asked me, but." Nobody asked me, but when I see someone wearing a green shirt, I figure that his laundry didn't come back. Nobody asked me, but if Howard Cosell was a sport, it would be Roller Derby. Those are real ones. A simple parody: Nobody asked me, but I never seem to see the Sixth Avenue El anymore. Or nobody asked me, but strangers who peek over my shoulder in public urinals make me nervous.

Arthur Daley, who wrote sports for *The New York Times*, had won a Pulitzer Prize for reasons no one understands to this day. Daley was a decent sort, but a flat writer. Typically, 800 words on Gil Hodges would end: "A fine fellow indeed is Gilbert Ray Hodges of Princeton, Indiana, and Brooklyn, New York." Since he has already told you six times that Hodges is a fine fellow, as he was, the tag line is not exactly chain lightning. Another easy parody.

Then we came to Red Smith, long my colleague at the *Herald Tribune*. When Smith had to write about a non-communicative subject, he worked a device: put a lot of information into the questions he asked. For Smith, Lardner's parody would be one very long sentence with compounds, admixtures and amalgams. The subject would then respond, "Yes."

I urged Lardner to go ahead with his parodies, but after a while he shook his head. He was a laconic fellow. He simply said, "Not worth it. One column makes seven enemies."

I've remembered that ever since. This afternoon I intend to speak with complete frankness and — life is so complex — make as few enemies as possible. I mean the parody tale to emphasize my great fortune. When I was learning the art and craft of sportswriting, as, of course, I still am today, I had Smith as a colleague at the *Herald Tribune* and Lardner as a co-conspirator at *Newsweek*.

Each man was fiercely proud to be a writer. That pride survives in me today.

My title comes from a poem Grantland Rice composed as Jack Dempsey and Jess Willard were preparing for their extraordinary heavyweight match that would take place in Toledo, Ohio, on the afternoon of July 4, 1919. Because boxing has so deteriorated over recent decades, we may forget that just like baseball, boxing possesses a rich history of literature and journalism. (I don't think any other sport is even close.)

The year 1919 was remarkable in America. Prohibition descended. It was suddenly illegal to buy a bottle of fine Bordeaux in the forty-eight states. Red-baiting began. The White Sox threw the World Series. And, not telling you anything you didn't know, Dempsey destroyed Jess Willard. Rice had covered trench warfare during World War I, along with perhaps 60 American foreign correspondents, and he was, to put it quietly, bemused that six hundred journalists now settled into Toledo. He wrote:

> When Homer smote his bloomin' lyre
> When Nero set his town on fire...
> They got their space between old jokes —
> But think of all the Itrrychure
> Now written on two simple blokes...
> A million words upon this fray!
> And when I see two low-browed men
> Grab all this space — I rise to say
> The Punch is Mightier than the Pen.

These lines presume some education. To understand them, you have to know that Homer is not something one better than a triple. You also have to know that lyre here is neither Bill Clinton nor Ken Starr.

I came across this verse in researching *A Flame of Pure Fire*, sending me to research libraries and through them on to the sports pages of the 1920s. We know the Twenties as a Golden Age of Sport. Dempsey. Babe Ruth. Big Bill Tilden. Bobby Jones. Red Grange. It was also a Golden Age of Sportswriting. Our language — what Lincoln Barnett has called "the treasure of our tongue" — came to a glorious flowering in Elizabethan England. Sportswriting, previously a mostly anonymous field, drab as a November meadow, flowered gloriously in the 1920s. Rice. Ring Lardner. Heywood Broun. Paul Gallico. W.O. McGeehan. Damon Runyon. They were all writing at once, producing an output that collectively has not since been equaled.

I grew up reading and re-reading *Pitching in a Pinch*, the enchanting 1912 work by Christy Mathewson with a little help from John Wheeler. After that I found Ring Lardner and such wonderful short stories as "Alibi Ike" and "My Roomy." I'd played a little ball, and it was a very happy day when Stanley Woodward of the *Herald Tribune* brought me into the sports department as a cub reporter in 1949 when I was 21.

I was assigned a desk and typewriter next to Al Laney, who was covering the Giants. In an earlier life he had worked for the Paris *Herald*. In France James Joyce asked Laney to type business letters for him, most of which Laney told me went to publishers and began, "Why has my royalty payment not arrived?" When Joyce's eye problems left him blind, as they did periodically, he asked Laney to read aloud novels in English and French. "Finally," Laney said, "he asked that I read a novel in Italian, and when I told him I couldn't read Italian, Joyce fired me, which is how I got fired from a job for which I was not paid." Late some evenings, Laney and I repaired to the *Tribune* cafeteria and there, amid clanging silverware and stale donuts, I heard all that Al remembered of James Joyce's commentary on writing.

The *Tribune's* rod and gun man, Big Ed Gilligan, admired Thomas Hardy, a novelist I shunned as clunky when I encountered him at the age of 16. Gilligan sold a novel of his own to MGM, which caught my attention, and said that for a climactic funeral scene along the Grand Banks of Nova Scotia he needed a single star visible through the mists. "But how to put it in the sky," Gilligan said. "Hanging? Twinkling? Shining? All terrible. Then I thought, how would Hardy have put that star up there and it came to me. A single star was *candling* in the sky. I was so excited I screamed, and my wife came down to the cabin where I write and found me at the typewriter, tears streaming down my cheeks, saying, 'Gilligan, you can write like a son of a bitch.'"

I loved associating with Laney and Gilligan. I knew some Joyce, but obviously I had better make another run at Thomas Hardy. To spin off Mark Twain, I was amazed at how much Hardy's writing improved between my own sixteenth birthday and my twenty-first.

The *Tribune* was intent on strong, individual reporting, to be sure, but it was equally intent on writing. John Lardner was talking once about W.C. Heinz, author of good books and some of the best magazine stuff I've read. "A good writer," he remarked.

"And a good reporter, John," I said.

Lardner nodded somewhat curtly. He had worked for the *Herald Tribune.* "The one presumes the other," Lardner said.

In 1952 the *Tribune* sent me out to cover the Brooklyn Dodgers, who were still recovering from Bobby Thomson's "shot heard round the world," a great hit off a very poor pitch by Ralph Branca. At that time, seven New York newspapers covered the Dodgers. The *Tribune,* the *Times,* the *Daily News* and the *Daily Mirror* were a.m.; the *Post,* the *World Telegram* and the *Journal American* published toward afternoon. Only the *Trib,* the *News* and the *Times* paid traveling expenses for their writers. The others accepted what was euphemistically called "the charity of the team." I can still see writers lined up in front of Lee Scott, the Dodgers traveling secretary, to pick up envelopes containing $56, a week's worth of $8-a-day. How can you criticize a ball club that is feeding you? With difficulty, mucho difficulty.

The *Times* sports sections then was soporific and the *Mirror* didn't seem to care much, but Dick Young at the *News* provided all the competition I needed. Young had never read Hardy, much less Joyce, but he typed with a forceful tabloid style. When he thought the Brooklyn pitching staff was choking, Young wrote this lead: "The tree that grows in Brooklyn is an apple tree and the apple is in the throats of the Dodgers." He disliked Jackie Robinson, who returned the sentiment. I admired Jack, we became friends and, in the matter at hand, I now had a baseball source that was closed to Young. Despite our rivalry, we stood together for access to trainers' rooms and everyplace else where a story might lie. We traveled together for half a year, and we often talked about our work.

Here is an issue: if someone says something that you are quite certain is false, do you print it? Today the answer is yes, if it attracts attention. Our reasoned conclusion was no. In a sense that made us judge and jury both, but isn't that better than reading, as I did on the Internet the other day, "I really feel bad for the guy. I feel bad for his family. It was not my intent to do that kind of story." That is the *Sports Illustrated* writer Jeff Pearlman on John Rocker and the tumultuous article he wrote about Rocker. I worked at *Sports Illustrated,* and I've known ambitious young journalists. As

Hemingway said of himself, "I have a built-in bull shit detector." I would not print Pearlman's quote. What did he think he was writing, a comic valentine? If he did, he should be fired for bad news judgment.

The Dodgers were televising and broadcasting all their games when I joined them, and Young worked out what I still think is the ideal formula for a newspaper story. Diagrammatically it goes like this. "In yesterday's 3-to-2 Dodger victory over the Giants, the most interesting thing that happened was..." Get the score in the first paragraph; in the first sentence, if possible. That imposes discipline and helps keep a writer from ambling formlessly. If I'd been covering that wonderful recent Red Sox-Yankee game, where Pedro Martinez beat Roger Clemens, 2 to 0, on Trot Nixon's ninth inning home run, here is the approach I'd pursue. Focus on the pitch that Nixon hit. Looked like a fast ball. Who called the pitch, Clemens, Posada, Torre? What's the Yankee book on Trot Nixon? Over to the other clubhouse. Talk to Nixon. What was he looking for? Check with Jimy Williams. Anybody tip Nixon to look for a fast ball in that spot? To do all this and make a deadline, you need good baseball sense, strong legs and good typing skills. Plus access. Nothing means anything if you can't get to Clemens, Torre, Nixon and the rest in a hurry. That done, you better know how to write lucidly into a deadline, without panic.

Here are two leads written into the teeth of a deadline. Red Smith on the Bobby Thomson home run. "Now it is done. Now the story ends. And there is no way to tell it. The art of fiction is dead. Reality has strangled invention. Only the utterly impossible, the inexpressibly fantastic, can ever be plausible again."

Shirley Povich on Don Larsen's perfect game in the 1956 World Series. "The million-to-one shot came in. Hell froze over. A month of Sundays hit the calendar. Don Larsen today pitched a no-hit-no-run, no-man-reach-first game in the World Series."

Neither lead has the score in the first sentence, but if you write like Red Smith or Shirley Povich, you can make your own rules and do just fine.

Where are we today? Robert Frost reminds us that the present is "too much on the senses, too crowded, too present to imagine." Indeed, but let us try.

Newspapers and magazines feel threatened by television, by the Internet and are increasingly willing to print nonsense so long as it attracts attention, readers and advertisers. That is a comment on the institutions. Tommy John asked me if I knew what has spoiled current sportswriting. I let him go on. "Woodward and Bernstein. They made so much money nailing Nixon that every young reporter today wants to nail somebody big and make a million."

Book publishers lust for celebrity books and controversial books, even if the celebrities are vapid and the controversy is mindless. You frequently hear about corporate baseball. We live in an era of corporate publishing. The man who runs Warner Books is an MBA. Such people may make money, but they don't often make good books. The man who rules Harper/Collins also rules the Dodgers. Rupert Murdoch. The jacket for the new millennium edition of *The Boys of Summer* arrived for my approval with an obscure term misspelled. What was the obscure term? Ebbets Field.

One can rage and ridicule, but all of us, even writers, live in the real world, and we are subject to the real pressures. As Wordsworth put it, "Getting and spending, we lay waste our powers." I sometimes say I've been unemployed since 1959, when I quit as sports editor of *Newsweek*. That's bravado. I have been writing and selling my writing ever since without missing very many meals.

I hope that dietary law continues, but twice in the last five years I have been presented with proposals that would more than pay off my mortgage. No names here, but each came from the representative of a Hall of Fame player. As it happened, each is a player whose company and friendship I enjoy.

With one, the advance bidding was edging toward a million dollars, with the proviso that the Hall of Famer make appearances in fifteen cities. Then it struck me. These fellows hitting fifteen cities could sell 300,000 phone books if they signed them. Why was I brought in? A little for my writing, perhaps, but mostly for my name. Twice I was seduced into composing celebrity books, once with Mickey Rooney and once with Pete Rose. Subsequently Rooney went bankrupt and Rose went to jail. I will never say never, notably while that mortgage sits out there, but I don't lust after further collaborations. As I said, that pride I saw in John Lardner and Red Smith, the pride in being a writer, in being one's own man, still burns strong.

We began with a poem. Let's end with one. As you may know, Christy Mathewson's most famous pitch was an early screwball, which Mathewson called his "fadeaway." When his arm began to go, John McGraw traded Mathewson to the Cincinnati Reds, so he could move on to managing. When that happened, Ring Lardner wrote:

> My eyes grow very misty
> As I pen these lines to Christy;
> Oh, my heart is full of heaviness today.
> May the flowers ne'er wither, Matty,
> On the grave in Cincinnati
> Which you've chosen for your final fadeaway.

For reasons which I hope are obvious by now, I think those six lines are more valuable than six dozen ghosted baseball memoirs.

Thanks for listening.

Safe at Home: Forging Intergenerational Alliances

C. Oren Renick

This paper is dedicated to Skip Bradley, Jack Lee, Nelson Wolff, and all the players of the Men's Senior Baseball League, San Antonio, Texas. When I finish, it will be your turn, as a reader, to reflect on your baseball alliances.

Playing Catch

There is profound symbolism in the simple, literal act of a father and a son tossing a baseball back and forth ... just playing a game of catch. The father and the son picture represents the parent-child relationship without regard for gender or disregard for the joy many mothers and daughters have for the game of baseball. The picture does not require that the father be the biological father of the son with whom he is playing catch. The picture depicts the binding of the generations — the forging of intergenerational alliances. This contribution of baseball to American culture is one that we intuitively know exists and typically recognize in the context of the one on one game of catch. The broader implications of the contribution of uniting the generations has not been adequately appreciated. The time has come to celebrate that unintended consequence of a father and a son tossing a baseball ... back and forth.

Like many, I have unresolved issues concerning a parent, my father, who died prematurely over 20 years ago. Yet this is the same man who introduced me to baseball as a game to be played and also enjoyed as a fan. My earliest recollections of the game are with him trying to teach me one fundamental ("Keep your eyes on the ball.") and endure my restlessness as a three year old at a Texas League game. I still have the souvenir bat he got me. Perhaps it was from him that I acquired my obligatory eating ritual at all baseball games — the biggest hot dog, a giant soft drink, peanuts, and, of course, Cracker Jacks. Tell me: Why do those humble, proletarian foods become such mouth watering delicacies at any baseball game?

My son and I have always had a good relationship. The same cannot be said for the relationship I had with my father. His death and the passage of time cannot erase those shadows, but writing, presenting, and discussing this paper has resulted in a personal catharsis of acceptance, understanding, and recognition that we were closer than I had been willing to acknowledge. Reflecting on baseball, my father, and the Sunday afternoons we shared playing the game all remind me of the common threads that ran between us ... and which I allowed myself to forget. Baseball has returned me to the wellsprings of those memories and repaired much of what separated the father from the son.

Others have observed how a parent and child can civilly discuss baseball, but virtually no other topic. I can recall a tense moment or two with my own son broken by an interjection about the extra inning thriller decided last night in the wee hours. Many might say we missed an opportunity to resolve our issues, but I suggest that our issues are small because of the game of baseball. You see, I contend that the game reminds us so subtly of all that we have in common and that which separates us is usually a short list compared to that which unites us. The circle shall not be broken. The center holds. For the first time, I realize that these messages of union *must* be referring to the game of baseball ... more specifically, the baseball itself.

The Greenest Green

He was the Rev. Dr. Frank Campbell, and he was my first, and probably most important, spiritual leader. He would later perform my wedding ceremony and my ordination service and share generously from his personal library upon his retirement. His death in 1977 was the first significant grief experience of my life. However, in the early 1960's, he and I formed an intergenerational alliance that was due far more to baseball than any of our other bonds.

For many years Dr. Campbell was afflicted with a chronic, degenerative, and terminal muscular disease somewhat similar to Lou Gehrig's Disease (ALS) except that its effects were cumulative over many years. It severely altered his gait, reflexes, vision, stamina, and occasionally, his speech. To see him, one would not realize that he had been a very good high school football player who loved sports and harbored the desire to be the next great sports journalist.

Until major league expansion, the St. Louis Cardinals were the South's team and St. Louis was 500 miles from my boyhood home in Jackson, Mississippi. Nevertheless, for the summers of '60 and '61, afflictions and all, Dr. Campbell, his son Bracey — my "adopted" younger brother, and I made pilgrimages to cities with major league teams — St. Louis and Chicago, followed by Washington, D.C., New York City, and Cincinnati.

Surprisingly, for a southerner of that time, I was a diehard Yankee fan. All of our stops in American League cities were to catch a Yankee series. We followed Mantle and Maris from city to city in '61 at the height of their chase after Ruth's record.

Those trips were 40 years ago, but for Bracey and me, they remain as fresh as yesterday. However, of all the good memories, the one that lingers most is the moment I topped a walkway at old Sportman's Park in St. Louis and saw for the first time the lights shine on the grass of a major league field. It was the greenest green I will ever see.

Going Home

For an adult of middle age and older, the game of baseball becomes largely one of memories and vicarious experiences. There are the opportunities to recall or read of pennant races won and lost and the current team standings and box scores, chances to coach a team or an individual player, occasions to watch or listen to a game, and participation in fantasy leagues. For a more mature adult, the chance to play the game as part of a team or in competition with other teams has gone away — or has it?

I was away from Home too many years. Home Plate that is. As a high school, American Legion, collegiate, and semi-pro baseball player, I had often felt the exhilaration of rounding third with a full head of steam, headed for Home. But my baseball experiences gradually came to exist only in the shadow of my memory. The years relentlessly passed, unavoidably marking my mind and body as clearly as the concentric circles of growth rings mark the passing seasons on the trunk of a tree.

Then suddenly and unexpectedly, I returned Home! After an absence of 15 or more than 15 years, I returned in 1997 to the baseball diamond as a member of the San Antonio Black Sox.

I had heard about adult men, even those over 40, playing baseball for pure love of the game. But I was unaware of the national scope of the Men's Senior Baseball League (MSBL), or of a MSBL league in San Antonio. The MSBL is an intriguing national movement about men returning to the game, including a number of former major league stars, but that story is for another time. Rather, it is returning to the game as a player that has stimulated a personal reflection on baseball's impact on American culture.

Our home in San Marcos, Texas, is only 45 miles by Interstate from San Antonio. My tryout with the Black Sox was arranged by my son, Scott, a law school student at the time residing in San Antonio. The Return of The Kid (that's me) began when, as a substitute in a regular season game (my tryout), I made two sparkling defensive plays at first base and was immediately added to the permanent Black Sox roster. (The team name means no disrespect to the Chicago White Sox or its 1919 team, eight members of which were paid by gamblers to "throw" the World Series to the Cincinnati Reds).

The Black Sox were a good team with an outstanding player-manager, Jack Lee; one superstar, Steve Harris, a former pro player; and a lot of good and enthusiastic players like Nelson Wolff, a former mayor of San Antonio. We won the San Antonio City Championship (40+ division). This was particularly gratifying since Steve was away on business and could not play in the series.

The Kid? I batted a consistent .400 and struck out only once. I made virtually no errors on defense (shades of my errorless senior year in high school), and I was only hampered by my bad left shoulder which limits my ability to throw hard (Renick 1998).

The Locality Rule

Playing the game again is a reminder that baseball is part of the glue that holds communities together. The backyard game of catch, the sandlot, the local team(s), a renewed appreciation of just how difficult it is to play the game well, the need to hone and improve skills, to maintain a level of fitness, to get better no matter what one's chronological age — these are all ingredients that make us recall how baseball is tied to the local fabric of communities.

It is probably "premature revisionist" (an oxymoron, perhaps) thinking, but the recent released film *Frequency* illustrates how baseball is part of the glue that holds communities together (New Line Cinema 2000). While the film violates the laws of physics, its premise is so attractive to us — the perfection of father-son, family, and extended family relationships —

that we accept its plausibility. In the film, a father and a son separated by the father's death 30 years before in 1969 are reunited by a ham radio and weather patterns that defy physics to solve and largely reverse crimes committed by a serial killer on the rampage in 1969. In the process, they radically transform events surrounding their own family history to void the father's death and maintain his active presence during his 30 year absence. Given such an involved excursion into science fiction, what event or events tied the film together and made the changing of history a reality? It was the Miracle Mets and, specifically, the 1969 World Series. It was a sequence of flashbacks and replays of that series that provides the glue that holds the film together. The film is largely about symbolism and miracles. If the Miracle Mets can happen, then miracles can happen that change the course of the past. Baseball has provided the miracle from which a continuum of miracles emulate to … perfect relationships within families, among friends, and entire neighborhoods. Is it any wonder that *Frequency* ends with the father, the son, the friends and neighbors, and the community playing a sandlot game?

Do I expect to see *Frequency* featured at the Hall of Fame's Bullpen Theater? Possibly, but not for a few years to come. Is *Frequency* a film symbolizing how baseball is part of the glue that holds communities together? Definitely.

Wellness

The game of baseball has played a positive and crucial role in the overall wellness, mental and physical, of American culture. It is a game for young and old and in-between alike. Talkin' baseball has long been recognized as something in which all ages can be engaged. With the national trend on wellness and prevention, models like the MSBL will increasingly find a participating audience to demonstrate the physically positive dimensions of the game for all ages. Golf and tennis and bowling and jogging will increasingly lose some of their potentially more active participants who will opt for the overall demands and challenge of the game of their youth — baseball. Increasingly, the gray heads of America playing baseball will recall Satchel Paige's words of wisdom, "Age is a question of mind over matter. If you don't mind, age don't matter" (Connor 1982).

A few years ago, I was asked to be the keynote speaker at the local high school's annual awards banquet for its baseball team and boosters. The address was entitled, "How Do You Play This Game, Anyway?" The four suggestions made to the players to improve performances were as follows:

- Prepare or practice;
- Compete or be aggressive and hustle;
- Relax or stay loose; and
- Enjoy or have fun because baseball is a game.

I contend that those suggestions remain valid, but an exception is now taken with the context in which the enjoyment suggestion was set. I said, "Take in the moment ... the panorama. Take time to enjoy the experience. You will not play forever" (Renick 1997). My MSBL experience, which was to begin a year later, now belies the mortality of one's moment in time to play baseball. In my short time as an MSBL player, I have played in the 30, 40, and 50 years old or older divisions. There is realistic talk by our League President, Skip Bradley, of a 60 years old and older division in a few years, and it should be a reality when I am ready to move to that next level.

Those high school players, most of whom thought they had played on their last baseball team, should never have been told, "You will not play forever." The MSBL says you can. The film *Field of Dreams* suggests that playing the game may be a forever, heavenly experience. I can wait, but baseball in the afterlife is a nice thought. It was, after all, the renowned writer Thomas Boswell who has observed like others that since baseball is not on the clock, a game could go on forever ... just do not make that last out (1984).

The other thing that's different is that my sports injuries do not make me a hero anymore. My wife Judy is supportive. But I can imagine her response if I choose to complain about my aches and pains. "So, you pulled a hamstring again playing baseball at your age. I'm real sorry. Don't forget to cut the grass."

My teammate's lack of sympathy is not hypothetical. "Why are you breathing so hard?" a teammate asked me in the dugout after I had run the bases. "I'm ... I'm just ... I'm just not back in playing shape yet," I gasped. "That's not it," replied my teammate. "You're old, just like the rest of us."

So, OK, I've got sore wrists and ankles, a special exercise program for the bad shoulder, and an icepack in the freezer. But I'm Home! And it's great to be back (Renick 1998).

Intergenerational Alliances

SCOTT AND GENERATIONAL ROLE REVERSAL

Baseball ties America's generations together, but when coupled with the reality of mature adults playing the game, a new paradigm emerges.

There are just a couple of small differences between my playing experience now and that of 15 years ago. For one thing, my son, Scott, and his girlfriend came to watch me play. They were impressed with the level of baseball played in the MSBL and became fans, cheering me on as I had cheered Scott's athletic efforts when he led his high school team to post-season play and was named its Most Valuable Player. And Scott gave me some advice when he noticed a flaw in my hitting technique. The generational reversal in this picture is very thick (Renick 1998).

JOHN THE BASEBALL PROFESSIONAL

After a number of years as a practitioner, I became a fulltime academic in the Fall of 1990. References to baseball soon emerged during class lectures, and this led to some after class discussions with students. John Almaraz was one such student. He disclosed that he had returned to campus to complete his bachelor's degree following a career as a player in the Cincinnati Reds organization. A right handed pitcher, John had risen to AAA affiliate Indianapolis before an arm injury, uncorrected by surgery, had permanently shelved his career. John adjusted well to his return to student life, but his love for the game was unabated, and it was apparent that, in some significant way, baseball still loomed large in his vision of his own future.

Having pitched a lot as a southpaw through the years in youth and adult leagues, I knew first hand that hitters can be retired through guile, finesse, and by throwing off their timing. In fact, after my own severe arm injury, I had survived (at least, occasionally) by staying low in the strike zone, on the corners of the plate, and using an assortment of off speed pitches. Surely John, with his major league potential, skill, and experience, could make the transition from thrower to pitcher. After all, he indicated that his post-surgery fast ball topped out in the low 80's (MPH). John Tudor came to mind as did Whitey Ford. This sage advice was offered to him. My first major lesson in intergenerational role reversals was soon made apparent.

John respectfully pointed out that the advice was coming from someone who fancied himself a left handed pitcher and that speed on the fastball was not as important for the southpaw as for the righty. Left handers often have a natural movement on their pitches, there are fewer of them, and so they are usually more deceptive for hitters. A lefty can be successful with a fastball in the low 80's. The pitchers cited were certainly examples supporting my advice, but both are southpaws and so underscored John's response. Right handed pitchers could not get away with a low 80's fastball and for the reverse of all the reasons why leftys have been successful with such a fastball. In short, John did not have a potential career as a major league pitcher. End of story and end of my first intergenerational role reversal baseball lesson.

Well into the semester, John came to me and shared that the Reds had contacted him about becoming a regional scout for them. It was obvious that he was interested, but was conflicted because, if he accepted a position, he could only enroll in school during the fall semester and then only as a part-time student. Indefinitely delaying graduation was the negative, but the opportunity was a good one and would get him back in the game. He was encouraged to seriously consider the offer, particularly if he could really pursue his degree part-time. By the end of the semester, John informed me that he and the Reds had reached an agreement and that he would be withdrawing from school in the spring with plans to return in the fall. This series of events positioned me to receive my next intergenerational role reversal baseball lesson.

As planned, John returned to campus to continue progress toward his degree during each subsequent fall semester. While his program major does not have him take additional courses from me, time is made for a couple of visits each semester to talk baseball. Typically, he gets the third degree about how the Reds rebuilding is progressing and what he thinks of this team or that player. Following my return as a player in the MSBL, the questions turned from "how they" play the game to "how to" play the game. For example, one of the last face to face meetings with John was after my son had noticed a hitting flaw, and no correction I made seemed to work. The problem stemmed from being overly aggressive, over striding, opening the front shoulder too soon, and hitting off the front foot. The result — ground balls to second base or not driving pitches that should have been hit hard and long. John asked for a simulated swing and then thoroughly diagnosed the problem and offered a series of solutions, including lengthening the stance, minimizing or eliminating the stride by only slightly lifting and then lowering the front foot, focusing on the top hand or back shoulder to drive through the ball, and swinging level to avoid pop ups to the infield.

In retrospect, the problem started years ago when a home park had an unusually short right field foul line. Its solution, while there to see based on John's coaching, was easy to see. However, its execution required unlearning some bad habits that could no longer be concealed by a short right field porch. Finally, after two inconsistent, hot and cold seasons, John's lesson had finally taken hold, and my confidence, concentration, and consistency were back.

So now the teacher gets the student to provide the lessons on how to play the game better. The student-teacher roles have been reversed.

CHAD THE STUDENT TURNED MENTOR

The John Almaraz role reversal relationship has been exceeded by that of Chad Southard, a former undergraduate and graduate student of mine. Chad was an outstanding Division 1A college baseball player. A pitcher, shortstop, or third baseman, Chad always hit in the middle of the order and was considered an extra coach on the field by his high school and college coaches. An arm injury requiring the Tommy John type surgical procedure permanently curtailed his potential as a professional baseball prospect.

My baseball comments in the classroom drew out comments by Chad about his love for the game and disappointment that an injury had ended his career after his junior year in college. An exceptional student, Chad continued his education by enrolling in graduate school, including two of my graduate courses. Because of my own rotator cuff problems, I could identify with Chad's painful injury. Sharing "war stories" and "aches and pains" experiences, I lamented about my own hitting inconsistency and working through chronic shoulder pain to perform at an acceptable level. Chad volunteered to workout with me and share some of his tips on hitting and relieving arm stress by improved techniques. Now we began a series of practices with the student teaching and the teacher trying to learn — how to hit better, pitch better, play better. Immediately, the tips paid off— particularly those about throwing — throwing harder, and more accurately, and most importantly, throwing with less stress and without pain. I actually returned to the mound for a few innings with mixed, but encouraging results. Realistically, the injury toll on my shoulder probably means my pitching days are over except for emergency situations, and that is O.K. by me. Chad is a seemingly natural coach and teacher, and his skill as a player-coach will take him far in his chosen career as a heath care administrator and executive. With Chad, the student-teacher roles have been transformed. The young man is teaching the older man.

Chad's father, Rick, a public school educator and administrator in Texas, is the foundation for Chad's love of the game. An expert collector of baseball memorabilia, Rick always saw to it that Chad was well coached and knew how to play and respect the game.

Chad's family and my family have become friends and visited in each other's homes. Rick and my son reside in the same area of Texas and will likely interact and network from time to time via their mutual love for baseball.

During summer 2000, I will conduct the wedding ceremony for Chad and his fiancée. I was not asked to do this because of classroom interaction with Chad. It all stemmed from the diamond and those late, hot afternoons in Texas when the student taught and the teacher learned. It was baseball that formed this friendship and this intergenerational alliance.

Bridges

ALFRED, MY TRANSITIONAL PERSON

Baseball ties the diverse elements of American culture together. As important as baseball is to intergenerational alliances, it also builds interracial alliances or bridges that may or may not be purely intergenerational. Such alliances should also be celebrated.

It was the summer of 1970 in New Orleans. Controversy surrounding the Vietnam War had taken center stage in the minds of America's collective citizenry. However, New Orleans is located in the deep South, and the Civil Rights Movement there remained turbulent and raw in the lives and hearts of most people.

I had just completed my graduate theological education and my wife, Judy, and I had just had our first child. We were considering our next stage — beginning a career, further graduate study, a combination of the two, to remain in New Orleans or relocate.

Judy had completed her teaching contract at a local preparatory school, and I had completed my theological studies while teaching at a local junior college. It was a time for change, but not quite yet.

I returned to Kingsley House to direct their summer recreation program as I had the previous summer. A United Way agency and the first settlement house in the South, Kingsley House had served the residents of the Irish Channel of New Orleans since before 1900. With programs for preschoolers to senior adults, a highlight was the all day summer program for an enrollment of 300 children and youth from the age of five through 18.

Staff for the program primarily consisted of college students and older teenagers secured through the Summer Job Corps Program. They were supplemented with permanent staff assigned to specific program areas.

Many of the children and youth enrolled in the summer program came from the nearby St. Thomas Housing Project. The Irish Channel was in transition and decline like much of inner city New Orleans. By 1970, probably eighty percent of the children and youth enrolled for summer were Black, ten percent were White, and ten percent were Hispanic.

A member of the summer staff was Alfred Gibson, a New Orleans native and a recent graduate of Grambling University, a predominantly Black college. I was told that Alfred had played baseball at Grambling and had been Captain of the team. A twin brother had also been a Grambling starting player. Both of them were playing that summer for an area semi-pro team called Jesse's All Stars.

Alfred and I had occasional conversations about our affection for baseball, but the start-up demands of the summer program did not allow for anything more.

Alfred exhibited intelligence, maturity, a disarming personality, and significant interpersonal skills with other staff and his group of 15 boys, ages nine and ten.

Kingsley House participated in a summer baseball program for its teenage boys. Home games were played at the Kingsley House field located on the premises of the facility. The opponents for a weekday home game had to cancel at the last minute. So as not to disappoint the team, summer staff were challenged to a game. Using a right hander's glove on the wrong hand to play, I participated. The game was close, but the staff team prevailed. Something was certain to me after that game. Alfred Gibson could play baseball, and he could play it very, very well. In fact, he could probably play better offensive baseball than anyone I had ever played with or against.

I had grown up in Jackson, Mississippi, during the era of apartheid and segregation in the South. I had played baseball at all amateur levels from Little League, high school, American Legion, and summer leagues to a very competitive college program. I had reluctantly stopped playing because of my college academic program and other extracurricular activities, but I always took the game with me. However, during all those years, I had never played on an organized team with or against an African American. A total of 23 years after Jackie Robinson integrated major league baseball in 1947, I played on my first integrated team — the emergency summer staff team — and played against my first integrated team — the Kingsley House baseball team.

Alfred and I were drawn together from that game, exchanged compliments, and began to play catch at Kingsley House after the work day ended. Alfred shared more with me about throwing the curve ball during one such exchange than pitching coaches on several teams had ever been able to do. Alfred made it make sense; and it suddenly dawned on me that he was the first Black man with whom I had ever played catch one on one.

After several pitching sessions, Alfred invited me to try out for his semi-pro team. As on his Grambling team, he was the Captain. There was only one catch. His team, Jesse's All Stars, was an all Black team.

So it was that after a brief tryout, I became the only White on a Black semi-pro team. Remember that it was 1970, it was the South, the turbulent progress of the Civil Rights Movement remained raw, open, and unhealed for most people — the murders in Philadelphia, Mississippi, the Civil Rights Act of 1964, the fire bombing of Black churches across the South, the Voting Rights Act of 1965, inner city riots in cities like Los Angeles and Detroit, the murders of Dr. King and Robert Kennedy, increasing Black militancy, and on and on…. In the face of such times, my days as a player for Jesse's All Stars was a unique, warm, and all too brief experience.

Most of Jesse's players were college players from predominantly African-American schools in Louisiana, Mississippi, and Alabama. At least two of the players were former minor leaguers, the most notable of whom had played in the Pittsburgh Pirates organization. He was something of a mentor to the other players, though as he approached 30, he obviously held out the hope of being resigned to a professional contract. It was from him that I came to better understand baseball as a game of skill and the importance of the professional contract to provide a place to play to constantly improve on skills. The amount of money was secondary to having a place to play and improve. Just to get noticed enough to be drafted and signed by a major league franchise was really all that mattered. The money, the location — they were all secondary to having a place to play and improve. Whether he was encouraging a player who made a mistake or speaking of the dream of playing professional baseball, his words of advice always seemed to come down to "You've got to work on your skills, you've got to work on your skills…"

A particular game that season remains fresh in my mind. It was a hot, muggy Sunday afternoon in New Orleans and the opponent was another Black semi-pro team. The game itself was played at a park on the West Bank, actually east of New Orleans, in a fairly isolated area which was unfamiliar to me. About the fourth inning, while we were batting, I took a moment to look around at the other team, the umpires, and the bleachers almost filled to capacity. And then it hit me. I was the only White person there. There was no vista beyond the park to even spot another White. In that moment I had some sense of what it must have been like for a Black child to be the first to integrate a White public school. Of course, there was a major difference. I was welcome and always made to feel that way. My moment of reflection past, it was back to the game.

The game was close and aggressively played. Emotions ran high and while we batted in the eighth inning, a brush back pitch caused the dugouts to begin to empty with players going onto the field. Recalling my surroundings, I smiled and said to a teammate, "I think I'll stay in here." He smiled back and nodded in agreement.

I do not know why Alfred was never signed by a professional team. He was drafted after his junior year, but never again. He could hit for average and with power, he ran very well, he was baseball smart, and a team player. He had good size and looked like a prototype baseball player. Perhaps it was his defense since he was a shortstop. Maybe he projected only as a middle infielder with insufficient range. I do not know why, but I believe that he was a professional offensive player who should have been signed so that he could "work on his skills."

Alfred and I remained good friends until I left New Orleans in 1974. He was the athletic director at Kingsley House for several years, and I continued my involvement there by doing volunteer work.

By the time I returned to New Orleans at the end of the 70's, Alfred had moved on to advance his career. Prior to my departure from New Orleans for good in the mid-80's, I had served on the Kingsley House Board of Directors and had gotten a message of best wishes to Alfred through a mutual friend. Though we both intended it, we never talked or got together. I should look him up. He was a transition figure for me. He meant a lot to me, and, obviously, he still does.

Stephen Covey speaks and writes eloquently of the transition figure who enables a culture, a community, a family, a person to overcome the negativity of the past. He or she is a wall against bias, prejudice, hatred — anything or that thing that denies effective living for the present and the future (Covey 1989). Quite unintentionally, Alfred Gibson was one of my transition figures.

Jose and Baseball's Universal Language

A house next to ours in New Orleans was vacant and had been so for several years. Its owner had moved closer to the Lake Front, but he kept it furnished and the yard immaculate. For us, he was probably the perfect neighbor.

At the end of one week, my wife noticed that a young man was in the house and periodically out in the yard and on the sidewalk. She had greeted him and understood enough to know that he was from Latin America, spoke little English, was there temporarily, and would be enrolled at Louisiana State University in a few days to initially take English language classes. He appeared lonely. We and our children decided to try and make him feel more welcome.

The opportunity quickly arose because he was soon back in our neighbor's yard. Invited into our home, he, my son of 11, and I became instant friends because of our mutual fondness for baseball. Jose had played on select teams in Colombia and hoped to continue playing while in the states for college.

He left briefly and returned with his photo album. Proudly he showed us pictures of his family, friends, and a prized photograph of his Colombian hero. It was a glossy, autographed picture of Tony Oliva. We recounted Tony's brilliant, but all too brief major league career. Now it was time to play.

Jose, Scott, and I walked down to the school park a block from our home to practice. Jose was very good, and we had much fun. Now for my ethical dilemma.

At the time, I played for and coached a men's sandlot baseball team in New Orleans. We had a Saturday afternoon game, and I invited Jose to attend the game and ... maybe even play. He was not on my roster; he spoke almost no English; in short, he was a ringer. He normally played third base and so my shortstop was assigned to help him through the game — deflect the umpires, the opposing team and coach, buffer his language barrier, and all else. It worked without raising too many suspicious eyebrows. We won, and we had a great time.

Jose spent as much time with us that weekend as possible. Perhaps the language barrier and our bond caused some inconvenience for our neighbor who was Jose's official host during his stay. However, Jose, my son, and I spoke the universal language of baseball those few days. It remains an intergenerational alliance to this day that was only made possible by the game of baseball.

A Celebration

We often celebrate the game of baseball. Far too often, we fail to celebrate its contribution to American culture as a great, and potentially greater, unifying force. We need to recognize and build on baseball's contribution to national unity, local community improvement, the wellness of America, as a unique tie between the generations, and as a way to build bridges of understanding and civility. Through the game of baseball, American culture can find a path that leads safely home.

The intent of this paper is to be more interactive with readers than words on a page. My intergenerational alliances, my bridges of racial and cultural understanding through baseball are unique to me, but they are not unique. In fact, they are quite common. They are merely representative of the shared experiences of countless others. Now, for you dear readers who have found your way to the end of my story, a few reflections posed as questions. Who were your baseball mentors? Will you thank them? Who have you mentored on the nuances of the game? How has baseball served you in building intergenerational alliances and bridges of interracial harmony? How have you kept the game close through the years and the transitions of life? Who will you tell?

References

Boswell, T. 1984. *Why Time Begins on Opening Day*. New York: Penguin Books.

Connor, A. 1982. *Baseball for the Love of It*. New York: Macmillan Publishing Co., Inc.

Covey, S. 1989. *The Seven Habits of Highly Effective People*. New York: Simon & Schuster.

Frequency (film). New Line Cinema, 2000.

Renick, O. 1998. "Going Home: Memoirs of a Black Sox Baseball Player." *Between the Lines* 4(4):3.

Renick, O. 1997. "How Do you Play This Game, Anyway?" Keynote Presentation: Baseball Team and Booster Banquet, San Marcos High School. Later reprinted in part by the *San Marcos Daily Record*, May 18: 12-A.

"Jesus Is Standing at the Home Plate": Baseball and American Christianity

Gregory Erickson

Jesus Is Standing at the Home Plate

On the CD of baseball music, *Diamond Cuts*, there are several light gospel and country songs that combine baseball and Christian themes.[1] The most up-beat and toe tapping is a version of a gospel song called "The Ball Game."[2]

There are several things I find interesting about this song, and its relationship to the spirit of both American Christianity and baseball. Set in a simple old-fashioned gospel style, the song consciously suggests a folksy and moral American past that both baseball and religion nostalgically desire to return to. "Everybody can play," proclaims our beloved democracy, an important concept in the formation of both American Christianity and baseball, although the word "can" suggests that some will not be involved. The metaphor of the perilous trip around the bases is one we will return to, and is a familiar one used to refer to everything from sacred journeys to mortal life to sexual conquest.

If we look a little deeper, the song also draws out attention to some contradictions in the sport and the religion: both are communal rituals but also intensely personal; both are democratic events that glorify cheating or have practiced exclusion based on race or gender; and, even as new pursuits, both were almost instantly infused with a sense of an "old-fashioned" morality.

40

Baseball continues to embody these contradictions. "You've got to play it fair," the song says. Yet hidden ball tricks, knockdown pitches, and spitballs have become a romanticized part of the game — even of its glorious golden age ("In the old days we wudda put him on his ass"). And no other sport has so developed and encouraged the "kill the umpire" anti-authority mentality that stretches from "Casey at Bat" to Earl Weaver.

Finally, the song portrays Christ as "standing at the home plate": in other words, a supportive teammate who will greet you as you score a run, give you a high five and pat you on the butt. This accurately depicts the American Christ, who is not a mysterious part of the Trinity, but a very tangible and human acquaintance. "We may converse with Him as one man converses with another," Joseph Smith preached.[3] If Christ greets you at the home plate, he must be playing the role of the on deck hitter, on your side from the start, cheering you out of the box, around the bases, and, if needed, ultimately given a chance to drive in your run.

The base runner, as the song says, must avoid pitfalls and danger as he works his way home. As the only member of his team in fair territory, always surrounded by the enemy, a base runner is a metaphorical symbol of the American Christian. For early American preacher Jonathan Edwards, "one that stands or walks in slippery Places is always exposed to fall."[4] Each American's spiritual trip around the bases is also made alone, however much teammates and fans can cheer you on; whatever base coaches tell you, the decisions are ultimately yours. This is something that is unique to and characteristic of American Christianity. Religious leaders in the early 19th century did not look to sages, history, or books for answers, but "espoused convictions that were essentially individualistic."[5] This attitude is shown in the 1820's by an unknown woman named Lucy Smith, who wrote, "there was not then upon earth the religion which I sought. I therefore determined to examine my Bible and ... to endeavor to obtain from God that which man could neither give nor take away."[6] This creative approach to interpretation and salvation was even more evident in her son, Joseph, who, as the founder of Mormonism, created a whole new sacred text in which he wrote of Christ's visit to what is today the United States. If Christ were to visit America, what better position for him then as some sort of permanent on-deck hitter, greeting each base runner as he crossed the plate, and threatening to come to bat himself.

Reading Religion and Baseball as Culture

We all remember the opening scene of *Bull Durham*, featuring Annie Savoy's incantation: "I believe in the church of baseball.... I've tried 'em all, I really have, and the only church that truly feeds the soul, day in, day out, is the church of baseball."[7] Or W.P. Kinsella's *Shoeless Joe*, where "A ballpark at night is more like a church than a church."[8] While many of us have had moments where we felt like this, my aim is to go behind that, to treat baseball as a text, not as a ritual or as a pastime, but to try to use the game as a window into part of our national psyche.

What I am interested in exploring in this paper is the way that America's different and unique religious epistemology manifests itself in the game of baseball. To try to look at one's own culture entails finding fresh ways to see what is most familiar, and, as Jacques Barzun famously said, "Whoever wants to know the heart and mind of America had better learn baseball." Furthermore, to understand America's subconscious, we need to understand that while situated within the Judeo-Christian tradition, our religion and our religious imagination is and has been different. American religion, as R. Laurence Moore says, is a "curious and somewhat unique national passion...quite like baseball."

What I will not be doing is discussing baseball *as* a religion. This has been done in various ways, seriously and otherwise, before. I have already cited examples of baseball as religion in literature or film, and there are numerous scholarly approaches to the idea of sport as religion or as religious ritual; the idea goes back as far as ancient Greece or the Mayan ballgame. But there is much to be learned by looking at sport *and* religion. Religion is perhaps most interesting where it is not expected, and by looking for it in the game of baseball, I am seeking different ways of understanding our cultural heritage. Moore says in *Selling God*, "The history of religion in the United States has suffered from being placed in a category separate from the general issue of understanding culture," and part of my intention is to put it back.[9]

If the study of religion, then, is necessarily a study of culture, and if we look at "popular" culture for what it reveals *about* a culture — essentially for *why* it is popular — then for the same reasons, we need to examine "popular" religion. By popular religion I mean not the stated theologies and creeds of institutionalized churches, but a religion that is communicated primarily in ways outside of these traditions. A religion not of churches and denominations, but of tents and summer camps, drugstore paperbacks, billboards, bumper stickers, and gospel songs. In other words, what do people really think and do in the name of religion? This, more than dialectical discussion between professional clergy or theologians, is how people use religion to make sense of their lives. And popular religious thinking is what finds its way into the population's subconscious, emerging, in disguise, in our buildings, our television shows, and our sporting events.

From a historical perspective, shifts in religious thinking are directly related to baseball in that the breaking from Puritanism in the 1800's allowed adults to play games. By 1888 Protestant minister Washington Gladden could say that he no longer believed that salvation "involved the sacrifice of baseball."[10] But to look at the relationship more from an anthropological perspective, we can paraphrase Clifford Geertz in saying that baseball is an American way of reading American experience, a story we tell ourselves about ourselves.[11] In *The Interpretation of Cultures*, Geertz characterizes sacred symbols as "function[ing] to synthesize a people's ethos ... the picture they have of the way things in sheer actuality are, their most comprehensive ideas of order."[12] This American idea of order is both determined by and inclusive of its religious epistemology. Ultimately, I want to see baseball as an example of, as anthropologist Claude Levi-Strauss says, "not how men think in myths, but how myths operate in men's minds without their being aware of it."[13]

Church and Game: 1800–1900

If, as many recent historians and religious scholars have stated, American religion really begins in the second half of the nineteenth century, then its development almost parallels baseball.[14] Calvinism and Puritanism are often cited as being the heart of the American religious consciousness, but it is the 19th century's radical refashioning of the Christian experience that spawned the unique forms of religion that are still prominent today. Both baseball and religion (primarily Christianity) developed together, inheriting certain values from Europe, but also self-consciously carving themselves into "American" institutions. What does each say about the culture from which it springs? If we see them as arising and developing together, does looking at them together give us any insight into their cultural relevance, and can it tell us anything about their future?

From their beginnings, American Christianity and baseball have looked back to some imaginary golden age when things were good and pure. American Christianity looks to an original primitive church of the early Christians, untarnished by 2000 years of history. Baseball has insisted upon an earlier untouched more honest version of the game that we need to get back to. As early as 1867, *The Ball Players' Chronicle* complained that baseball "seems to be no longer participated in for the mere pleasure of the thing."[15] Today the most respected baseball stars, ones we feel know and love the game (Cal Ripkin), are affectionately called "throwbacks"; our favorite parks (Camden Yards) are considered "old-fashioned." From a cultural studies perspective, the need for a rural Edenic past, and the controversy over the game's origin, are not so important as realizing that we have a need for such myths and such controversies. The "good old days" feeling that is in both baseball and American religion refers not to a former time, but to an essential part of the thing itself.

Americans in the first half of the 19th century, perhaps invigorated by their victory in the Revolutionary War, began creating a new type of faith and religious experience. Although rooted in European Christianity, it rapidly developed its own personality. "What makes the American Religion so American is that the Christianizing of the American people, in the generation after the Revolution, persuasively redefined what Christianizing meant."[16] Americans were infused with a spirit of individualism, a sense of rebellion against authority, and the faith and arrogance to create something new.

The American ideal of democracy, according to some scholars, was *the* defining force in 19th century religion. No longer was God brought to the congregation by an anointed and educated clergy, but both congregation and clergy looked to the common man to find God. True virtue was associated with "ordinary people," and an individual's spiritual convictions were not subject to clergy re-interpretation. As early as 1839, America's camp meetings were referred to as "festivals of democracy."[17] Not only could anyone define salvation in their own way, but anyone could become a religious leader. Despite complaints by traditionalists of "illiterate ministers," various new movements led by lay persons gained momentum throughout the century.

Baseball, arising in the same period, shares many of the same features. The concept of a batting order is profoundly democratic; no matter how good a hitter you are, you have to wait your turn. Michael Jordan will not always get the last shot; but the last out may come down to Bobby Thomson, with Willie Mays waiting helplessly on deck.

Keeping pace with apocalyptic predictions and camp meetings, 19th century baseball had the "snap, go, fling of the American atmosphere," as Walt Whitman said, and an early description of a team's roster is a Whitmanesque celebration of democratic ideals: "the pitcher was a former stonemason; the catcher, a postal employee; the infielders worked as compositor, machinist, shipping clerk, and compositor. Among the outfielders, two were without previous job experience and the other worked as a compositor. The team substitute worked as a glass blower."[18] Far from its English roots, and early fraternal organizations, baseball may have "begun as a gentlemen's game, but its demands proved to be democratic, the game insisted on conditioning and skill, not on social breeding."[19]

If early baseball is related to the free spirited, democratic, and somewhat coarse religion of the time, then its parentage, like that of Christianity, is a more reserved and refined European figure: cricket. British born journalist Henry Chadwick, an early baseball supporter and player, represents this American "conversion" from cricket to baseball. A former cricket player, he found baseball's pace more suited to the American psyche, "Americans do not care to dawdle over a sleep-inspiring game all through the heat of a June or July day. What they do, they want to do in a hurry. In baseball, all is lightning; every action is swift as a seabird's flight."[20]

Another advantage baseball had over cricket was its portability.[21] Baseball fields, unlike the carefully prepared grounds of cricket, could be set up anywhere: a backyard, an empty lot, even a Civil War battle ground. Whitman, a baseball fan and prophet of the American religion, comments on the effortless transformation of wildness to ball field and, at the same time, pays homage to his beloved democracy (no one piece of land is better or worse than another):

> I remember — it is quite vivid — a spot off on Long Island, somewhere in the neighborhood of our old home — rough, uncultivated, uncared for — choked with underbrush — forbidding: people coming would avoid it — it was that kind of place: put to no practical uses untouched.... I left the neighborhood — was away for years: wandering, seeing living: went back again: the whole face of it was changed: now a baseball ground, a park ... it had required but little work to effect the transformation — simply clearing away the brush: now it is a perfect spot of its kind — a resort.[22]

The baseball field was to the cricket field as the camp meeting was to the historical church. Like the baseball field, the camp meeting was a portable sacred space, not a temple in Jerusalem or a building in Rome, but Moses and the people in the wilderness.

Like the American churches and clergy, early baseball moved further away from its British roots by becoming more working class. The Atlantics, Brooklyn's dominant team in the 1860's, was one of the first organized teams to be predominantly working class. As in the churches, this resulted in battles of class and disparaging remarks about the unwashed or uneducated. Respectable Methodists in Philadelphia split from lay-led congregations, "the wealthy and respectable minority against the poor majority," according to a minister.[23] The Prince of Wales commented that American baseball "offended" the English "love of fair play,"[24] and in the churches this more confrontational style also offended visiting English Bishops and more traditional clergy in American churches.

In the 1820's, for example, Bishop Daniel Payne stepped in to stop a "singing and clapping ring" taking place after his sermon. His congregation refused to stop: "sinners won't get converted unless there is a ring," he was told.[25] The official English Methodist response to the American camp meeting was "It is our judgment that even supposing such meeting to be allowable in America, they are highly improper in England, and likely to be productive of considerable mischief; and we disclaim all connection with them."[26]

Like the American congregations who created their own worship that church leaders reluctantly allowed, baseball players bucked against genteel traditions of fair play to develop a game more suited to their taste. Faster pitches, curve balls, bunting, and stealing were all initially regarded as legal but morally dubious. Along with other traditionalists, Whitman was suspect of these changes, "In baseball is it the rule that the fellow who pitches the ball aims to pitch it in such a way the batter cannot hit it? gives it a twist — what not — so it slides off, or won't be struck fairly?"[27]

From the beginning, not only players but the baseball crowds were part of this "manly"[28] and rough style. Albert Spalding even said that the fan's harassment of umpires was part of a democratic right to protest tyranny. Like the "Shouting Methodists," the enthusiasm was initially regarded with a somewhat condescending air. George Bernard Shaw wrote,

> What is both surprising and delightful is that the spectators are allowed, and even expected, to join in the vocal part of the game. There is no reason why the field should not try to put the batsman off his stroke at the critical moment by neatly timed disparagements of his wife's fidelity and his mother's respectability.[29]

Both churches and ball clubs dealt with the question of whether to try and curb participants' excitement. "What ... can any club do?" a baseball executive complained,

> Can we restrain a burst of applause or indignation emanating from an assemblage of more than 15,000 excited spectators.... He who has witnessed the natural excitement which is ever the attendant of a vast miscellaneous assemblage knows full well that it is an utter impossibility to prevent the crowd from expressing their sentiments in a manner and as audibly as they please.[30]

In 19th century churches, as well, the enthusiasm that was originally regarded as vulgar became an essential part of Christianity. And as Moore points out, Christian enthusiasm was not that different from theatrical or sporting events: "Whenever people rush down aisles, fling themselves in the straw, and cry for salvation with mighty sighs and groans, other people become spectators."[31] These characteristics of both baseball and the American religion are what enabled them to become part of America and not imports from Europe.

In looking at cultural parallels like this, the inevitable but impossible questions are those of causality. Is the reason behind the aggressive, enthusiastic, democratic and individualistic developments the attitude fostered *by* the American Revolution? Or were the attitudes the cause for the Revolution itself? As Geertz says, religious attitudes are both models for, and models of, cultural processes. They both "express the world's climate and shape."[32] To try to arrive at an objective explanation is impossible.

America's Games: Heroes, Theologies, Statistics, and Pastorals

I don't know if there's a record-keeper up there or not. But even if there weren't, I think we'd have to play the game as though there were.[33]

As baseball and religion entered the 20th century they were wildly successful, both in America and abroad.[34] Figures from Babe Ruth to Billy Sunday became enthusiastic if somewhat uncouth ambassadors, and writers from Grantland Rice to William James proclaimed the uniqueness and "Americanness" of their respective subjects. To continue to trace shifts in the development, perception and participation of both in the 20th century is beyond the scope of this essay, but we can go deeper into an analysis of some areas.

Baseball, as has often been noted, is open to many mythical or religious analogies. The trip around the bases — a hero venturing forth from home to encounter and overcome dangers to victoriously return home again — embodies what Northrup Frye calls a U-shaped pattern which he sees as containing the entire Bible. A pattern "in which man ... loses the tree and the water of life at the beginning of Genesis and gets them back at the end of Revelation."[35] The hero can only be saved by returning from his Exodus or to his Garden of Eden.

More than just the archetype of a religious quest, baseball presents a quintessential American Hero on an American quest. Our opening song, with a trip around the bases of temptation, sin, and tribulation, captures baseball's metaphorical connection to the American quest. In Robert Coover's remarkable novel, *The Universal Baseball Association, Inc.*, his protagonist remarks on this aspect of the sport

> Motion. The American scene. The rovin' gambler. Cowpoke and train-man. A travelin' man always longs for home, cause a travelin' man is always alone ... like a base runner on the paths, alone in a hostile cosmos, the stars out there in their places, and him trying to dominate

the world.... Probably suffered a sense of confinement there in the batter's box, felt the need to strike forth on a meaningful quest of some kind.[36]

The American Hero is always a loner, a mysterious Shane rolling into town to deal with things alone. The American Christian, as well, is only truly religious when she is alone with Christ, her personal relation with Christ is primary. This claustrophobic American hero, striking forth on a solitary, self-inflicted mission, from John Wayne to Batman, also represents the American search for salvation. American religion, in some form or another, whether apocalyptic, Calvinist, Universalist, or Adventist, has been obsessively concerned with the specifics of salvation — how, who, when, how many — a salvation that is entirely personal. American salvation, as Bloom points out, is a "one-on-one act of confrontation," that cannot come through the community or the congregation."[37] Baseball reflects these modes of thought. Like the heroic confrontation, like the American Christian, baseball creates a constant one-on-one tension. The pitcher may have his team behind him, the hitter has a bench rooting for him, but all fades away into batter against pitcher, pitcher against batter. A contest that is no less than life or death.

Death, as Bloom and others say, is the father of all religion, and the fear of death is particularly part of American religion and culture. In baseball, the fear of death is unconsciously buried in the language and machinations of the game. In his journey around the bases, a runner must avoid being put out, or worse yet, being part of a "twin-killing." One way of avoiding this is being put out of danger by a teammate's "sacrifice." While other sporting events, like the Spanish Bull Fight and the Balinese Cock Fight, have been interpreted as being about sex and death, baseball is more about personal salvation and personal reflection: not about the reality or beauty of death, but about the ultimate defeat of it. Baseball's often mentioned unique time relationship is actually an opportunity to cheat death. As Westbrook says, the progress of the game is measured by deed, not by a clock, and it is potentially infinite.[38] If a team can just keep a rally "alive" the game is conceivably endless, and, in fact, each inning, each at bat, and even each play is theoretically endless ("If I can just stay in this run down forever...").

One paradox or tension in American Religion is its pull towards a simplification or domestication of complex thought, and its creative movement towards new religions at the same time. We can see the first half of this in the characteristic American anti-intellectualism and in the craving for a simple old-fashioned space. The association of this with baseball is demonstrated in a recent commercial for "Good Old Time Country

Lemonade," that uses "Take Me Out to the Ball Game" as background music. On the other hand, one thing American religion did was to open up the possibility of new religions, new prophets, and new Gods. This is the same contradictory thinking that make "same original formula," and "new and improved," two classically effective American marketing campaigns.

One way in which American Christianity domesticates its European models is to consciously make its theology less ambiguous. European Christianity, for example, has grappled and developed complex explanations and images of the Trinitarian character of the divine. The unfathomable nature of the concept is often cited as part of its mystery and ultimate truth. American Christianity, on the other hand, has developed as one of its characteristics, either a non-emphasis on the Trinity or a denial of the concept all together.[39] Rather than construct difficult questions, American Christianity often tries to offer basic answers to simplified problems. "Stop suffering," the sign in front of a Brooklyn church reads, "Today at 10 AM, 4 PM, and 7 PM." Necklaces and billboards across the southern United States read "W.W.J.D." (What Would Jesus Do?) as the answer to life's dilemmas. A t-shirt says simply, "Know God. Know Peace," a phrase that would make little sense to Thomas Aquinas or Soren Kierkegaard.

To extend our analogy, we can say that from the outset baseball has been a game of clearly drawn lines: safe or out, fair or foul, strike or ball. Like American Religion, it attempts to suggest simplicity and a democratic availability. Thomas Boswell speaks for American Christianity as well as baseball when he says, "Instead of celebrating mysteries, baseball rejoices in the absence of mysteries and trusts that, if we watch what is laid before our eyes ... we will cultivate the gift of seeing things as they really are."[40] The idea that it is possible to see things as "they really are" is central to American Christianity, most clearly in the claim to "read" the Bible and not "interpret" it. We can also a see parallel to the relationship between the mysterious Christ of Europe, who Augustine saw as "an enigma and as through a glass,"[41] and the American Christ who "walks and talks with you" and is a "friend." The American Jesus is indeed more like a teammate, "not a first century Jew, but a 19th or 20th century American, whose principal difference is that he already has risen from the dead."[42]

Americans, in their new found freedom and religious enthusiasm, came to think of their religion as a new original Christianity. Doing away with 2000 years of Western civilization, they had a blank slate and were the chosen people creating a fresh Christianity. The American struggle allowed them to see themselves as the New Jerusalem, and their battles as those of the original Christians. They used events from the Hebrew Bible to help them understand their situation: the camp meetings were Moses in the wilderness, and confronting the American Indian was Daniel in the Lion's den.

Baseball, as a sport of the book, does the same thing. The past is always part of the present; an event is made more meaningful by its relationship to a glorious, more perfect past. I was recently listening to a game where Andruw Jones was racing back to catch a line drive directly over his head. The radio announcer called the play: "back, back, back, Jones has a chance. Oh! Willie Mays!" Any true baseball fan knows with just the mention of the name that he made the catch, and that Mays caught the ball over his shoulder running away from home plate.

The American Christian, although he might not be able to cite the verse, knows that "Jesus loves me," because the "Bible tells me so," and American Christianity, although not a learned intellectual tradition, has often accepted the "book" at a level unique to Western culture. Unlike the European emphasis on exegesis and interpretation, a characteristic American take on the Bible is that it alone offers all that we need. Fundamentalism has been valued over interpretation, and American fundamentalist Christians claim not only that the Bible cannot be wrong, but that to *interpret* it is to warp the meaning. While I am not trying to draw too close a parallel here, baseball has come to accept its book and its numbers as a form of absolute "Truth." And while new statistical analysis and reinterpretations of baseball history may flourish among baseball scholars, the general public changes slowly. Like new complex theological arguments, modifications of the game's lore tend to remain in the hands of the professional. Two examples of this are the refusal to let go of baseball's myth of a rural origin, and the reluctance to accept new baseball statistics. A "runs created per 27 outs" statistic may define a hitter's value more than a batting average, but it won't get you recognized as a "batting champion" in the *Daily News*.

Baseball's "book" is best represented in its obsession with recording every play. As is often pointed out, how many other sports can recreate a whole game by looking at a sheet of paper afterwards? From its origins, baseball kept close records of its numbers. Chadwick was one of the first to get newspapers to publish baseball statistics, and he commented on the worth of them, "many a dashing general has 'all the gilt taken off the gingerbread,' by these matter-of-fact figures, and we are frequently surprised to find the modest but efficient worker, who has played earnestly but steadily through the season, apparently unnoticed, has come in, at the close of the race, the real victor."[43] In other words statistics were meant to show who *earned* what, who *worked* the hardest, who *deserved* the glory.

Baseball's numbers reveal its own mythology and belief system. "Numbers don't lie," we often hear, but of course they can and do. What is easy to forget is that the numbers we choose to record are by no means the obvious ones or the most important. By looking more questioningly at our everyday box score, we can examine what a psychoanalyst would call the structural unconsciousness of its language. For one thing, baseball statistics reinforce and reveal aspects of the game we have been discussing, like the focusing on the individual confrontation. Early baseball box scores didn't record pitching statistics, only hitting and fielding. But as the game progressed the pitching numbers became important and fielding statistics (except for errors) faded away. A pitcher's wins and strikeouts and a batter's average and home runs became significant measures. In another example, the game's obsession with recording "errors" and "earned runs" reflects a culture obsessed with one's own individual responsibility for his or her salvation. There is always a winner and a loser; there is always fault to be found. As Roger Angell points out, the game provides a perfect, finished balance. Each hitter's credit represents a pitcher's debit, and vice versa.[44]

On the other hand, a player's on base percentage doesn't include reaching base on an error. The point is to get on base, but if you reach on an error, you don't receive credit. Like the non-Calvinist Christianity, it must be personally earned. Yet, a six foot dribbler can count as much as a line drive single off the Green Monster. Again, like American salvation, it must be earned, but the process is unimportant: one's status changes, it happens instantly. Product is always emphasized over process. It is interesting to imagine what baseball statistics we would keep with a different religious orientation. Had we remained stubbornly Calvinist, for example, or if baseball had evolved (which it probably couldn't have) in a Buddhist country.

Baseball's language also reveals its unconscious epistemology, or as the poet Wallace Stevens says, "what we said of it became a part of what it is." As the language of baseball has developed, it has also increasingly emphasized the personal confrontation of the pitcher/hitter. Bradd Shore discusses the difference between "playing" and "being." One "plays" first base, but cannot "play" hitter, pitcher, or catcher. Frank Thomas cannot play batter, although he "plays first base." You have to "be" the batter.[45] The status changes instantly, a player can become what he does, and the real confrontation and salvation are personal.

The ultimate salvation in baseball is to score, to reach home. Bart Giamatti addresses the familiar topic of "home," by asking "why is it not called fourth base?" As he points out "home" is an English word that does not translate into other languages, and it creates a sense of not only returning to a promised place, but also of a sense of flux. Home, as he says, "is a concept and not a place…. Home is where one first learned to be separate and it remains in the mind as the place where reunion, if it were to occur, would happen."[46]

Much has been written about the shapes of baseball, but, as usual, they are contradictory. Westbrook sees in the field a "gigantic transformation of the mandala, one of the oldest and most ubiquitous metaphors for both cosmos and self, outer and inner space."[47] For Shore, "Baseball is the only American sport that does not use a symmetrical field, defined by sides and ends. The baseball park defines a tension between an ever narrowing inner point, called home, and an ever widening outer field."[48] Yet for Giamatti, "baseball believes in ordering its energies, its contents, around threes and fours. It believes that symmetry surrounds meaning, but even more, forces meaning. Symmetry, a version of equality, forces and sharpens competition. Symmetrical demands in a symmetrical setting encourage both passion and precision."[49] The idea that baseball's meaning is due both to its asymmetrical and its symmetrical organization is American contradiction at its best.

The shape of the field does offer a sense of the infinite; the foul lines extend outwards forever. In former rules, a ball that curved foul after it cleared the fence was a foul ball, so that theoretically a ball remained in play to infinity. In discussions of shapes and fields, baseball has been identified as having two centers. Depending on how you are reading, the center of the field is either the pitcher's mound or home plate. But linguistically the center of the field is home plate. A pitchers walks *out* to the mound but runs *in* to cover home plate on a wild pitch. A runner stealing is described, "there he goes," but stealing home is always, "here he comes."

For a Buddhist, there is no center; for St. Augustine, the Trinity forms a complex divinity that is not locatable; but for an American Christian, there is no doubt about the center. As baseball player turned superstar preacher, Billy Sunday put it, "All other religions are built around principles, but the Christian religion is built around a person, Jesus Christ."[50] Baseball's sense of a center from which all emanates is further enforced by the traditional TV view and the location of the press box. The game is perceived and written about from this angle. (My brother, a play-by-play announcer, notes that if the game were called from center field, home run calls would sound more like orgasms. "Coming, coming, coming. Here! Yes!")

A center always implies origin, and as we have seen both baseball and

American Christianity insist upon the idea of a rural and unspoiled Edenic origin. This is not, of course, unique to America. Unspoiled pastoral green meadows have been a part of the human imagination since Virgil's *Eclogues*, and Eden goes back to ... well, Eden. But baseball has one of the strongest modern day associations with the pastoral. "The green geometry of the baseball field [is] more than simply a metaphor for the American experience and character ... [it] is closer to an embodiment of American life."[51] For Giamatti, we can never underestimate the "power of an enclosed green space" on the American religious imagination.[52] While other sports have this as well, the pastoral is always tied up in beginnings, origins, and the myth of the garden, and baseball with its mythical rural beginnings and its long history offers that. Giamatti writes that the "enclosed green field of the mind" can offer solace to those who feel the "need to think something lasts forever."[53]

Yet how much of this is truly baseball, and how much is the imagination of a baseball loving Renaissance scholar? David McGimpsey is probably right when he says, "baseball fans generally watch games not to commune with the fields of green in a quasi religious way, but to see their team win."[54] And in the same vein, people go to church not to grapple with theological questions but to improve their chance for salvation or to talk to friends. American Christianity is not St. Augustine. Baseball is not Virgil.

The point here is not whether you associate baseball with the pastoral or not, but that we have needed it to be that. In his classic study of the American Pastoral, Leo Marx identifies two types of pastoral. The first is popular and sentimental (Whitman's baseball of parks and picnics), and the second imaginative and complex.[55] It is the second, of course, that is more interesting, and that we can see in American Christianity and in baseball. Marx develops the idea of the pastoral in 19th century America as something that rises out of the image of our country as the site of a new beginning (much as we have discussed religion and baseball). He demonstrates how the imaginative pastoral is never just peaceful, but must contain a "counterforce" in order to capture our imagination.[56] His central metaphor for this, and indeed for the contradictory American epistemology in general, is the *Machine in the Garden*. He points to examples of 19th century pastoral from Nathaniel Hawthorne to Thomas Cole, who introduce a train into a peaceful scene of nature. (The baseball metaphor for this could be its violently active infield surrounded by great expanses of grass.) Baseball and America's need to maintain a sense of rural old fashioned origins, at the same time that they are aggressively refashioning and denying origins, is an example of the pastoral garden planted with the seeds of its own destruction. And yet these are the very seeds that allow for continued growth and interest.

What Now? A Tentative Conclusion

So what now? Where does any of this lead, and does it tell us anything about the future of baseball, religion, or culture? If we were to somehow transport a game from 1900 to the present time, put everyone in modern day uniforms, and put it in Yankee Stadium, your average fan would probably not notice a difference. By the same token, if a local Methodist minister preached a sermon first delivered in 1900, using current language patterns and events, his congregation would hardly sit up. Does this mean nothing has changed?

Modern scholarship is more about asking questions than about making statements, and in this final section I want to use baseball and some of the connections I have made, to open up some questions about religion. Because American baseball and religion come out of a white/black, fair/foul, safe/out, and heaven/hell mentality, they find themselves in tension with an increasingly relativistic and postmodern world that is questioning our knowledge of such concepts as truth. From scientists like Albert Einstein to philosophers like Jacques Derrida, reality has become more dependent upon individual perception — on one's experience rather than on an objective "out there." While religion and baseball can appear to be in opposition to this epistemological and experiential shift, they have also, unavoidably, become part of it.

Experience has always been a definitive concept in American Religion. The unique American God is experiential, and is known to exist because he can be felt. If we are looking at baseball *and* culture — baseball *and* religion — we need to look most closely not at the objects themselves, but at how they are perceived and experienced. Although both baseball and American Christianity are often regarded as troubled institutions, 86 percent of Americans consider themselves Christian, and more people than ever before are watching and going to baseball games.[57] What is their experience?

In Robert Coover's novel, *The Universal Baseball Association, Inc., J. Henry Waugh, Prop.*, the protagonist creates a whole fictional world of baseball and life with dice and charts in his small apartment. The players in his league are rookies and veterans, they marry, retire, become managers, and they die. Henry lives a "real" life of loneliness and drinking, but his only pleasure is in the manipulating of his baseball league. At the end of the novel, Henry himself seems to disappear, but the players continue on, unaware of the death of their creator. Coover's book is an expression of our attempts to understand our own history, our alienation, and our questions as to origins and reality. The book creates a postmodern world where the boundaries between virtual and real, fact and fiction, and history and narrative are blurred or dissolved. The ending of the novel presents us with a society unaware that its creator no longer exists, and with no answer as to what they are doing there. It asks us, through the language of baseball, the existential questions of our time: Is there a God? Did we create Him? Are we crazy? Is He?

Does baseball produce fans or do fans produce baseball? And if the experience of God or of baseball is now one of blurred edges, no beginnings or endings, and no definitions, how do we proceed?

The experience of a 21st century baseball fan is one of a multi-layered reality. Baseball, and sport viewing in general, has become more complex, a network of connections, one leading to another with no logical flow. The game as a self-contained unit is no longer the typical experience. With radio, television, and the Internet one can follow a whole season by seeing only ESPN highlights, or only statistics, or only through the lens of a fantasy baseball team. The concept of "team" and "game" has become different. If a televised game is boring, viewers cut to another one. With rare exceptions, major league teams almost completely change their players within two years. The team is an empty symbol, a simulacrum; like many contemporary religious symbols, like information on the Internet, it stands for something that does not exist. A sign without a signified.

My experience of baseball is probably typical. I can sit in my living room and, using my remote control, flip back and forth between up to four games. If I miss a big play, I'll catch it on *Baseball Tonight* later. I can switch on my computer and listen to my brother broadcast a minor league game or listen to almost any professional game in the country. While my computer is on, I can go to a web site to check on the progress of my rotisserie team or look at the box scores of a 1976 simulation league that I am currently in. (I recently demoted John Hiller to middle relief and am giving Gene Garber a chance to close.)

The possibilities that the Internet offers to baseball are a model for new ways of thinking. It is already a cliché of this new century to define modes of thought by talking about the Internet, but as theologian Graham Ward points out the Net is the "ultimate postmodern experience ... the ultimate in the secularization of the divine ... a God who sees and knows all things, existing in pure activity and realized presence, in perpetuity."[58]

Contemporary baseball has not moved away from its connections with American religion, but has continued to develop along with it. The blurring of virtual and real is encouraged by a religion's thinking that has also become postmodern. Religion in cyberspace is represented by hypertext bibles and the *Idiot's Guide to Religion On-Line*, but it is also more complex than that. In a culture that has been open to new gods and new sacred scriptures, this new way of viewing the world goes straight to the core of American spirituality. American popular culture has developed into a Post-Christian one where the multitude of American Gods have begun to blur and erase each other.

I offer this not as praise or as critique, but as analysis. Like baseball and religion, I am torn between past and present. I can damn the designated hitter in an e-mail, and I can bring my laptop to Fenway without feeling the contradictions. Baseball and Christianity now exist in an ambiguous world of past and future and of truth and fiction. Jesus is still the on deck hitter, but in the sense of an anticipated messiah. He is a messiah that by definition can never arrive, just as an on deck hitter never comes to the plate. And in our imagination, present and absent, secular and divine, baseball and religion will continue to represent, change with, and determine our culture.

Notes

1. *Diamond Cuts: A Compilation of Baseball Songs and Poetry* (Washington DC: Hungry for Music, 1997).

2. Sung by Yvonne Hood. Words and music by Sister Winona Carr, 1953.

3. Joseph Smith, "King Follett Sermon," in *American Sermons: The Pilgrims to Martin Luther King, Jr.*, ed. Michael Warner (New York: Library of the Americas, 1999), 587.

4. Jonathan Edwards, "Sinners in the Hands of an Angry God," in *American Sermons*, 347.

5. Nathan O. Hatch, *The Democratization of American Christianity* (New Haven: Yale University Press, 1989), 6.

6. Quoted in Ibid., 43.

7. Ron Shelton, *Bull Durham*, 1988.

8. W.P. Kinsella, *Shoeless Joe* (Boston: Houghton Mifflin, 1982).

9. R. Laurence Moore, *Selling God: American Religion in the Marketplace of Culture* (Oxford: Oxford University Press, 1994), 8.

10. Quoted in Ibid., 153.

11. Clifford Geertz, *The Interpretation of Cultures: Selected Essays* (New York: Basic Books, 1973), 448.

12. Ibid., 90.

13. Claude Levi-Strauss, *The Raw and the Cooked* (New York: Harper and Row, 1969), 12.

14. See Hatch, Moore, and Jon Butler, *Awash in a Sea of Faith: Christianizing the American People* (Cambridge: Harvard University Press, 1990).

15. Quoted in Warren Goldstein, *Playing for Keeps: A History of Early Baseball* (Ithaca: Cornell University Press, 1989), 67.

16. Harold Bloom, *The American Religion: The Emergence of the Post-Christian Nation* (New York: Simon and Schuster, 1992), 28–29.

17. Hatch, *The Democratization of American Christianity*, 58.

18. Ed Folsom, "Whitman and Baseball," in *Walt Whitman's Native Representations* (New York: Cambridge University Press, 1994), 35.

19. Ibid., 35.

20. Quoted in Geoffrey Ward, *Baseball: An Illustrated History* (New York: Alfred A. Knopp, 1994), 8.

21. Ibid., 12.

22. Quoted in Folsom, *Walt Whitman*, 52.

23. Ann Taves, *Fits, Trances, and Visions: Experiencing Religion and Explaining Experience from Wesley to James* (Princeton: Princeton University Press, 1999), 95.

24. Ward, *Baseball*, 29.

25. Quoted in Taves, *Fits, Trances, and Visions*, 102.

26. Quoted in Hatch, *The Democratization of American Christianity*, 50.

27. Folsom, *Whitman*, 47.

28. If baseball needed to separate itself from cricket, and the class, authority, and intellectualism it represented, it also consciously separated itself from "rounders" and other "games" of the time. Baseball was going to be serious business, and it didn't descend from some children's game either. The concern for early baseball supporters like Henry Chadwick was that baseball, "this manly pastime," be separated from such "primitive and simple" games as rounders (Goldstein, 44).

29. Quoted in Ward, *Baseball*, 79.

30. Quoted in Goldstein, *Playing for Keeps*, 32–33.

31. Moore, *Selling God*, 15.

32. Geertz, *The Interpretation of Cultures*, 94–95.

33. Robert Coover, *The Universal Baseball Association Inc. J. Henry Waugh, Prop.* (New York: Random House, 1968), 239.

34. Just *why* American Christianity and baseball are such popular exports is another question for another paper.

35. Northrup Frye, *The Great Code: The Bible and Literature* (New York: Harcourt Brace Jovanovich, 1981), 169.

36. Coover, *The Universal Baseball Association*, 141.

37. Bloom, *The American Religion*, 32.

38. Deeanne Westbrook, *Ground Rules: Baseball and Myth* (Chicago: University of Illinois Press, 1996), 100.

39. Paul K. Conkin, *American Originals: Homemade Varieties of Christianity* (Chapel Hill: University of North Carolina Press, 1997), 316–318.

40. Ward, *Baseball*, 193.

41. St. Augustine, *The Confessions of St. Augustine*, trans. Rex Warner (New York: Penguin, 1963).

42. Bloom, *The American Religion*, 65.

43. Quoted in Ward, *Baseball*, 8.

44. Roger Angell, *The Summer Game* (New York: Popular Library, 1978), 12.

45. Bradd Shore, "Loading the Bases: How our Tribe Projects Its Own Image into the National Pastime," in *Applying Anthropology: An Introductory Reader*, ed. Aaron Podelefsky and Peter J. Brown (Mountain View: Mayfield Publishing, 1997), 125–126.

46. A. Bartlett Giamatti, *A Great and Glorious Game* (Chapel Hill: Algonquin Books, 1998), 100.

47. Westbrook, *Ground Rules*, 112.

48. Shore, "Loading the Bases," 125.

49. Giamatti, *A Great and Glorious Game*, 90.

50. Billy Sunday, "Food for a Hungry World," in *American Sermons*, 793.

51. Giamatti, *A Great and Glorious Game*, 42.

52. Ibid., 42.

53. Ibid., 8 and 13.

54. David McGimpsey, *Imagining Baseball: America's Pastime and Popular Culture* (Bloomington: Indiana Press, 2000), 3.

55. Leo Marx, *The Machine in the Garden: Technology and the Pastoral Idea in America* (Oxford: Oxford University Press, 1964), 5.

56. Ibid., 25.

57. Gallup Poll, 1999.

58. Graham Ward, "A Guide to Theological Thinking in Cyberspace," in *The Postmodern God: A Theological Reader*, ed. Graham Ward (Malden: Blackwell Publishers, 1997), xv–xvi.

Physical Literacy in Baseball and Other Sports

Robert Ochsner

More than any other sport, baseball provides an especially apt analogue for the social changes, and more specifically the technological developments, that have reshaped the nature of written language. These changes become immediately evident in the relationship between baseball and literacy, a linkage that subsumes other spectator sports as well, notably football and basketball. To demonstrate that relationship, I will examine one literacy trend in particular, the gradual transition in American society from a print-based literacy to an emergent electronic literacy, concentrating on a single feature of that literacy, its physicality. Furthermore, by placing physical literacy within the broader linguistic context of perceptual functions that are visual, auditory, and kinesthetic (eye, ear, and body-image), I will conclude with some preliminary observations about the future of baseball as a spectator sport and the relevant literacy skills invoked by other sports.

Introduction

The appeal of baseball as a spectator sport undoubtedly extends throughout American society. Like football and basketball, the two other professional sports with pervasive fan support, baseball represents something distinctive about our national identity, and arguably more than any other sport, baseball encompasses that identity in over a century of sports reporting, literary journalism, popular fiction, belletristic essays, and other artistic and intellectual representations of the game. Indeed, this refined cultural response warrants particular notice because it suggests an underlying congruence between baseball as a spectator sport and the cultivated sensibilities of those who are inclined to watch it. In more general terms, there appears to be a close link between baseball and literacy, between watching this sport and cultivating the ability to understand it.

Without question, baseball differs from other American sports to the extent it attracts professional writers and others who might be described as highly literate. A simple check of current book publications on our national sports indicates that far more writers of distinction — writers like George Will, Roger Kahn, David Halberstam, Bernard Malamud, among many others — have devoted themselves to topics about baseball rather than to football or basketball. In sheer volume, baseball literature is about ten times more common than literature of any other sport (cf., Amazon.com listings). Similar differences apply when one considers the number of traditional magazines and online e-zines dedicated to just one sport; in that regard, baseball titles prevail at a ratio of about 3 or 4 to 1. We might also infer that more readers gravitate to novels, essays, and related professional writing about baseball.

If we accept this preliminary observation that baseball appeals widely to people of literary or cultural refinement, then we might reasonably ask why this attraction exists for baseball but not nearly as much for other sports. Possible explanations include the pastoral appeal of baseball, its celebration of perseverance against inevitable failure, the challenge of mastering arcane traditions and complex rules of play, or similar reasons that invoke primarily social aspects of the game.

While each of these points warrants consideration, I have taken another approach to examining the distinctive appeal of baseball, one that shifts our attention from social to physical characteristics of experiencing a sport. Above all, I am concerned with *how* people experience a game, as a preliminary explanation for why someone would prefer one mode of perception rather than another. The choice of reading about a sporting event, or listening to it on radio, seeing it on television, or watching it live represents the essential range of possibilities that affect our decisions as spectators.

Just as important is our ability to derive a sense of satisfaction from reading a delayed summary of action to hearing a live broadcast on radio to watching a live or tape-delayed televised game or being physically present when the game is actually played. These perceptual options translate directly into equivalent literacy skills, or what I will refer to as the physical literacy of being a competent spectator.

Definition of Terms

The traditional form of literacy, often referred to as print culture, flourished during the first half of the 20th century, a period that roughly corresponds to the Golden Age of baseball. During this 50-year period the most obvious relationship between baseball and print culture appears in baseball journalism, with its remarkable and distinctive tradition of excellence. From Grantland Rice to Shirley Povich, we can trace an unparalleled history of professional sports writers who have clearly loved baseball, and just as clearly have recognized its cultural significance in defining the American experience.

Indeed, the shift of most sports coverage from newspapers in the first quarter of the century, then to radio and print in the second quarter, followed during the last 50 years by television and four-color sports magazines, and lately by the electronic print of Internet web pages, encompasses an almost self-evident transformation in the way Americans read, hear, view, and otherwise respond to baseball. In a more general sense, the history of sports journalism, broadly defined to include all media, coincides almost exactly with historical trends in literacy, at least in this country.

This brief reference to the social histories of literacy and baseball can be linked directly to the evolving media of sports journalism. Moreover, each type of reporting can be placed along a literacy continuum that begins with newspaper accounts and concludes with interactive sports programs (e.g., radio call-in shows or live Internet forums).

CHART ONE: CLASSIFICATION OF LITERACY SKILLS BY SPORTS MEDIUM

Newspaper Articles	*Radio Broadcasts*	*Television Broadcasts*	*Online Netcasts*
			→
Static Medium			Dynamic Medium
Single Channel		Mixed/multiple Channel	
Eye (or)	Ear	Eye/ear	Eye/ear/body
Unidirectional		Interactive	
Visual Literacy (or) Auditory Literacy		Kinesthetic Literacy	
Remote experience		Live attendance	

Chart One offers a simple but useful way to identify the literacy skills most closely associated with various sports media. The most salient distinction along the continuum from newspapers to netcasts is the degree to which a medium, like print or streaming Internet video, approximates a live performance. Newspapers and, to a lesser extent, radio broadcasts necessarily filter the live experience because we are removed either by time or distance (or both) from the actual event. Television and live Internet streaming, of course, bring us closer to the live experience as if we were physically present.

This difference in temporal and spatial experience has, I believe, a robust effect on literacy skills and subsequently on our choices as spectators of a sporting event. A sport like baseball, for example, allows artistic and even fanciful renderings in print because it is simply too complex to be encompassed by a live broadcast. The nuances and textures of baseball, the strategies and unseen action invite reflective interpretation. Why did the manager leave a struggling pitcher in the game as long as he did? Why did the clean up hitter swing away on a three and no count? Why did the number nine batter not lay down a sacrifice bunt at a critical moment of the game? Reconstructed in print, we can examine answers to these questions because the reporter has already had a chance to ask relevant questions of the players involved. In this respect, the delayed reporting of a newspaper article may actually enhance our experience of a game. The simultaneity of live experience, of course, minimizes this kind of sustained reflection. It also reduces our experience of a game to immediate kinesthetic reaction as one event follows another.

On the other hand, a live experience or the technological simulacrum of actually being there immerses us in the moment. In place of reflection, we learn to savor the intensity of spectacular play or the excitement of anticipation when a key pitch or defensive play or at bat occurs. Thus, imaginative reflection gives way to kinesthetic enthusiasm.

A printed text or radio broadcast, for instance, will normally be limited to a single literacy channel that is either visual or auditory. This limitation simultaneously elicits a projected imagination as we mentally visualize events in a game. By contrast, the more complex media of television merges sight and sound, and Internet broadcasts may provide an additional interactive channel for respondents. Radio call-in shows belong somewhere between relatively static print and virtually dynamic hypermedia, a continuum from single to multiple channels for communication. In effect, the one-way channel of traditional radio locks us into a narrow and impartial experience of the game that depends ultimately on our own mental recreation of events.

As channels of communication increase, however, the corresponding visual and auditory literacies merge, typically bundled with the interactive functions of kinesthetic literacy. This potential merging of literacy skills also promotes a more active role for an audience, one that radically alters traditional literacy because it establishes a direct physical link between communicators, whereas in print culture that link has characteristically been remote, indirect, at a distance, fundamentally a feat of imagination.

Kinesthetic Literacy

The shift from traditional literacy to kinesthetic literacy takes us from print to pixels, from static newspaper pages to electronic multimedia, from recreated and reimagined versions of events to simultaneous and supplemented experiences of the event itself. This shift thus introduces basic changes in the physical properties of language as words and images become interwoven in immediate reactions to events. As spectators we now respond to broadcasts of a live (or tape recorded) sporting event in ways that invoke eye and ear and more diffuse sensory experiences that rarely depend on our use of just one physical channel of perception or on surrogate channels of abstract imagination. We are, in other words, conflating eye and ear as if they were one physical (or neuro-physiological) property. The eye hears and the ear sees.

CHART TWO: PHYSICAL LITERACY

Visual Channel:	Symmetry of Images, Linear Print, Frames of
(EYE)	Reference in Television, Computers, Video Games
Auditory Channel:	Rhythmical Properties of Sound, Narrative Frames
(EAR)	in Telephones, Radio, Popular Music
Kinesthetic Channel:	Immediate Experience of Events, Streaming Frames
(BODY-IMAGE)	of Live Performance

The term physical literacy refers to a matrix of eye, ear, and non-specific kinesthetic sensation, or body-image. I use this term physical literacy with some reservation as it implies too sharp a distinction between body and mind; nevertheless, when literacy is regarded as a biological or physical activity, the representation of how one uses language becomes much more apparent as a co-determinant of how one might respond as a spectator seeing, hearing, or otherwise experiencing a sport.

In a more familiar sense, physical literacy might also be understood as the fine motor skills — eye/hand coordination, for example — that regulate an athlete's ability to perform effectively. Similarly, the physicality of writing a text reduces to neuromuscular hand/eye movements that result in discrete activities such as handwriting, keyboarding, clicking a mouse, and so on. Once again, I want to avoid too simple a dichotomy, in this case separating athlete from spectator, or writer from reader. In both instances, significant overlap blurs these distinctions. An athlete, for example, simultaneously performs in a game while observing himself and others in action, albeit as a highly personal observer of events. In key respects, a writer also reverses roles to become a reader, especially when editing a text; and a reader always to some degree actively (re-)creates the text by selecting and then interpreting what the author has presented.

These overlapping roles become even more indistinct as we move towards less traditional forms of text production or newer forms of athletic competition. Body image perhaps best represents this change as players become bigger, stronger, taller, and therefore more distinctively separate from ordinary spectators. The attraction of this god-like athlete is that fans can see themselves in their surrogate heroes. This projection is not, however, an imaginative transference but instead a more literal replacement, as in the sympathetic magic that entails wearing the star's jersey or buying his endorsed products.

The oddity of kinesthetic literacy is that body image paradoxically disembodies the spectator. In other words, the way a spectator projects himself or herself into the events of a game roughly corresponds to the fan's immediate identification with the player (or self-dissociation). In traditional literacy, this identification differs crucially because the fan creates and therefore subtly controls the imagined hero. The offended child's apocryphal response to Shoeless Joe Jackson's transgression, "Say it ain't so," expresses precisely this difference between imagined heroism and actual behavior.

The ability and willingness of someone to project themselves into the events of a game, essentially to read potential and actual game events as they would read and interpret a text, is a literacy skill that fundamentally affects how a sport is experienced. Perhaps more than any other sport, baseball invites and even requires this imaginative participation, which directly ties it to traditional literacy. Listening to football or basketball on the radio is less of a kinesthetic experience than watching it on television. In contrast, baseball does not suffer nearly as much from being reconstructed on radio or recorded in the newspapers. That is because each pitch, each at bat provides us with physical sequences of activities that are relatively discrete, individuated, and easy to imagine. A ground ball to the shortstop plays out as a stereotyped routine with physical movements of fielding and throwing to first that are simple to recreate in our minds. Other sports do not allow this narrow visual or auditory reconstruction, at least not regularly or in predictable movements.

In football, too many people act simultaneously for most plays to be replicated with any imaginative accuracy; even a touchdown pass from quarterback to wide receiver involves essential blocking schemes of the down linemen and variations in passing routes that no one can reconstruct mentally with much consistency. Basketball adds a geometrical imprecision as players move in almost intertwined patterns of collective action. We can mentally visualize a play resulting in a ten foot jump shot, a three point shot, or a slam dunk, but the complex ballet of movement that precedes this temporary result is not readily imagined, just assumed. Of course, baseball has complex sequences of action too, but they occur with much less frequency, and the relatively slow pace of the game allows us to embrace greater complexity.

Another way of explaining body image in kinesthetic literacy is to stress body rather than image. In traditional literacy, we learn to see or hear physical action by projecting it as mental images; radio and print augment the development of this literacy skill. Electronic media like television and computers suppress and essentially displace this imaginative projection of physicality by substituting immediate reality. I know of no one, for example, who turns off the volume of a televised football or basketball game in order to listen to the radio broadcast. However, I will routinely choose to hear a baseball game on the radio supplemented by a muted broadcast on television, a variant of two channels of communication. In Baltimore, where I have lived the last twenty years, the radio station that broadcasts Orioles' games markets itself as the alternative "voice" of a televised game. In this respect, the radio offers a better account of the game because the announcers obviously cannot rely on the camera to supplement or supersede commentary.

The reason this marketing strategy works is that people like me, and presumably others made literate for print culture, respond best to the single channel of traditional literacy. We interpret events eye foremost or ear foremost; we prefer foreign films with subtitles rather than dubbed voiceovers; we avoid interactive sports talk programs; we read newspaper accounts of baseball games for informed observations and disdain the manufactured controversies of shock journalism; we are also outdated literati of a print culture that has devolved from its Golden Age to the Technological Age of electronic literacy.

Frames of Interpretation

As we focus on physical literacy in eye, ear, and body-image, the temporal/spatial experience of any sport can be framed in at least two ways, as auditory rhythm or as visual symmetry. Other variables include a whole panoply of mental constructs, social functions, and linguistic processes, far too many to be reviewed in this brief study. However, to note some broader applications of this study, I will conclude with a few general comments about physical literacy as it affects the future of baseball as a national sport.

The cumulative temporal rhythm of a game like baseball simply does not compress well into a few highlighted events, at least not with much dramatic flair, except of course for the relatively rare events like game-winning home runs or perhaps spectacular defensive plays. In comparison, basketball and football have a more frenetic, improvised, or maybe even atonal rhythmicality, which paradoxically is heightened by interruptions of time, by the sporadic temporal pace established by a game clock. As one consequence, the experience of watching these games is less imagined and much more physical, a simplistic but useful distinction between mind and body.

This mind/body dichotomy roughly corresponds to the old and new forms of literacy and the relative popularity of sports like baseball versus football and basketball. Like the older traditional print literacy, baseball maintains a rather strict adherence to linear reading of events. Most action occurs in the straight line from pitcher's mound to home plate; base runners are required to follow a rectangular course around the bases within narrow limits of being outside the base paths. Sports like basketball and football are also somewhat linear, especially in the rectangular shape of courts and fields (in this latter respect baseball parks are anomalous). But action within these defined areas differs significantly from baseball.

In its most reductive sense, baseball has been described as 80 percent pitching, and certainly most of the game's action occurs in a narrowly focused area stretching 60'6" from the pitcher's mound to home plate. Reading the game as a visual text, however, requires an almost impossible ability to scan the entire field of play. That is one reason why higher levels of play will have as many as four umpires, each attending to areas of the field that would not be readily visible to an umpire behind the plate. But the key issue is perspective.

While other sports will also use multiple umpires (or referees), the action of the game is framed differently. The area of competition in football, for example, will nearly always bring all players to a central locus: a huddle, offensive and defensive lines facing each other, piles of tacklers, and so on. The long pass establishes a contrast to this clustering activity, but even that play is usually seen as a small cluster of receiver and defender. Significantly, the entire field of play is strictly limited too: a pass that goes beyond the end zone has no obvious value, in part because offensive players must at all times remain within fair territory or be ruled ineligible until the next play. Basketball has similar constraints that frame the action in clusters.

Baseball enacts a remarkably different visual game. In baseball, the field of play, of course, extends beyond fair territory for defensive purposes; this transition to foul territory becomes literally an imagined line as umpires determine whether a line drive is a hit even though the ball may first touch foul ground. I suppose the home run, because it goes completely beyond the field of play, ultimately distinguishes baseball from all other sports, at least for the visual framing of significant action. In all other major sports, we can keep in sight a touchdown pass, a slam dunk, a soccer goal. Baseball, however, memorializes events that transcend the field of play, notably home runs out of the ballpark.

This contrast in spatial framing explains, in part, the relative popularity of sports now as opposed to ones favored by earlier generations. Above all, the rhythm of action in baseball corresponds to the visual symmetry of its framing, and this congruence has special implications for how the game is observed. Before television, people who did not attend a baseball game could listen to play on the radio or read delayed narrative accounts in newspapers.

During the last half of the twentieth century, television was probably the main factor explaining the ascendancy of basketball and football. Certainly these sports are optimally framed by a television lens. As I have already noted, the action in both sports occurs in "clusters," with rich visual opportunities for dramatic highlights that are largely self-evident in a frame or two. In contrast, the rhythm of baseball subsumes our awareness of actions that have already occurred — that's why a late-inning single to drive in the winning run resonates differently than a game-ending score in other sports. The game-winner in basketball has a dynamic effect based on almost immediate changes in focus from offense to defense. In tight games, there may be repeated lead changes, or opportunities to take the lead. The temporal frame of a game clock also heightens the significance of a last second shot. The potential winning score in football also gains urgency as time is running out.

In a temporal sense, baseball is a much more textured, nuanced experience, one that is played out in our imagination as we anticipate a panoply of options or remember a complex sequence of events leading to the moment of each pitch and play. Certainly the game can be viewed in a much more superficial manner, analogous to how most of us watch basketball or football. I want to quickly add that these other sports are enriched too by careful, informed observation. Nevertheless, we probably derive more pleasure with less effort by watching sports like basketball and football that can be framed temporally by the importance of a last-second action.

To explain this difference in temporal response, I want to supplement the effect of television with the emergence of electronic literacy as a primary influence on popular tastes, ultimately reflected in viewers' preferences for major sports. Like traditional print, the temporal experience of baseball is static because the game exists in key respects independent of time, obviously without a clock but even more crucially without the need for "action" to confer significance. The decision not to steal a base, not to swing at a pitch, even not to pitch to a hitter, in each case constitutes a meaningful delay of action. On this last example of inaction, a pitcher may temporarily stop pitching as a tactic to freeze the batter; when this happens a hitter will usually reciprocate by stepping out of the batter's box until the umpire intervenes to have play resume. The official rules of baseball require that a pitcher initiate play within 15 seconds after the umpire has signaled he is ready. However, no stopwatch is officially part of the umpire's gear; in this sense time remains essentially a matter of judgment, a subjective approximation of "real" time.

It is worth noting that basketball and football have the opposite temporal frame. In both sports, play clocks/shot clocks are used to supplement the game clock. Part of the reason for this extra time keeping is to prevent tactical slow downs of a game, a strategy that can radically diminish scoring but more importantly also suspend action. Clearly, it is the physical action of these sports that matters most, symbolically represented by the high numbers conferred for scores (two and three points for baskets, three and six points for field goals and touchdowns). In contrast, baseball remains decidedly timeless — all sorts of delays interrupt play, and entire games are suspended to allow for inclement weather. Moreover, the physical action of a baseball game can essentially bypass some defensive players (the American League's designated hitter, for example, but also any fielder who has no defensive plays to make during a game).

The complaint that baseball is a boring sport makes perfect sense if someone views the game entirely in a temporal frame. Most of the time players stand around with apparently nothing to do while the pitcher and catcher toss the ball back and forth. The whole framework of the game reduces to very few people going through repetitive motions. This temporal perspective is remarkably akin to the reaction of some people — especially young people in my experience — to spending their time reading, an even more inactive suspension of time. In some respects, watching a baseball game, or more aptly listening to a game, requires that a person must engage the text or the entire act of reading or listening becomes dull and unrewarding. Even the most literate person will occasionally experience this soporific effect while reading a text without mentally engaging it. The mind wanders. Words are read without understanding. Time stands still.

The perceptual frame that enables productive reading depends in large part on our ability to exclude nonvisual input. In effect, traditional literacy restricts us to one physical channel of communication — the eye, just as the telephone or radio forces us physically to rely on just the ear. As technology has evolved, however, newer media such as television and more recently the computer have expanded our sensory channels for remote communication. With television, sight and sound obviously merge, and with computers even denser mixtures of sensory input are possible.

So far I have deliberately avoided the issue of attendance at games since watching any sport in person immediately combines sight and sound. Yet the spectator's experience of attending a baseball game also differs significantly from observing other sports. For instance, basketball and football almost never have simultaneous action occur in widely separate areas of play; yet in baseball a play in one part of the field, say a sacrifice fly to right field, can initiate a nearly simultaneous response in the opposite side of the field as a runner tags up to score from third base. In fact, when the bases are loaded, almost any action elicits complex and varied reactions elsewhere: as warranted, runners must decide to advance one or more bases, and depending on what happens, fielders must be ready to change positions and complete or back up different plays. These interrelated actions differ from all other sports because the defense in baseball controls the ball at all times except for the moment a hitter puts a pitch in play — if he actually hits the ball.

The complexity of baseball arises from its fundamental dyadic linkage between offense and defense, a relationship that almost exactly recreates the basic exchange between writer and reader (or speaker and listener). A reader, for example, must depend on the writer to generate text; without that initial text production there is no communication. Similarly, the offensive player in baseball must wait for the pitcher to initiate the action of the game, without that action nothing happens. In this crucial sense, a baseball game is essentially an old fashioned literacy event, a text produced by the defense as writer and reacted to by the offense as reader. The hitter's attempt to "read" a pitch conveys the basic point of this traditional print relationship.

By contrast, in other sports, the offense controls its own actions; in theory, a football or basketball team could score on every possession, as if the defense were not present or otherwise involved in play. In this sense, the defense assumes an entirely passive role as a respondent to the offense. Baseball, however, reverses this relationship, at least initially, so that the offense is more controlled, more narrowly channeled according to the type of pitch thrown, the position of fielders, and related adjustments in defensive strategy.

In traditional literacy, the writer is presumed to control the text, limiting a reader's responses as much as possible within narrow ranges of interpretation. More recent theories of literacy have expanded the reader's role in shaping meaning, in some cases by making the text and the writer almost irrelevant. But these relatively modern views of literacy essentially conflate traditional print literacy with emergent, nonstatic forms of visual and auditory literacy — in electronic texts, television programs, and many of the interactive electronic games that children now play.

Physical Literacy and the Future of Baseball

The history of baseball depicts masculinity for an entire century in heroic, celebratory, and greater-than-life public figures such as Babe Ruth, Jackie Robinson, Joe DiMaggio, Willie Mays, Mickey Mantle, Satchel Paige, Bob Gibson, Sandy Koufax, Ken Griffey, Jr., and Mark McGwire among many others. This history also ultimately depicts the progressive end of traditional masculinity, a decline that corresponds in significant respects to changes in acceptable stereotypes. Until recently, stereotypes of gender emphasized clear differences between the sexes, with well known and fairly rigid social roles assigned to each gender. The newer stereotype reverses that ideal, with Mia Hamm tearing off her shirt in celebration of the United States women's team victory in the World Cup, or Mark McGwire showing his sensitivity about abused children by unashamedly crying during an interview. The general opprobrium directed at John Rocker for his comments in a *Sports Illustrated* interview signal yet another change in social values, one that stands in immediate contrast to fellow Georgian Ty Cobb, whose expressions of racial intolerance and bigotry were essentially tolerated 70 years ago.

Physical literacy assumes a major significance for sports as social values transform what is acceptable for fans to hear and see. That is, what we perceive becomes embedded in how we perceive it as a cover picture on *Sports Illustrated*. Rather than being represented as immodest, as would almost certainly have been the reaction in prior generations, Hamm is valorized as an icon of exuberance. In the same magazine, Rocker is vilified for what he says, not for what he does. Words thus subsume action, just as images replace banner headlines. Whether Rocker is treated fairly or not does not matter today — rather, he clearly did not understand the new literacy that decontextualizes experience by reducing it to a blend of sight and sound bites. In another era, when traditional literacy still prevailed, he would probably have been ignored or considered foolish, but what he said would not have been so readily equated with how he actually behaves, or who he is. Like channels of communication, these channels of identity would have remained relatively separate.

The Roberto Alomar spitting incident of several years ago demonstrates a similar but opposite conflation of words with action. In this case, Alomar spit on umpire John Hirschbeck after a very heated argument that allegedly had the umpire refer to Alomar as gay, a grievous cultural insult to a Hispanic male. However, the argument really never factored into the media response to this event, which focused on the act of spitting almost exclusively. As in Rocker's case, context was reduced to a single point of reference, viewed from multiple camera angles and then selectively framed in print and auditory channels of communications.

The difference between traditional and emergent literacy is this immediacy of experience. Nuance, complexity of circumstances, imagined reconstruction of events — these are old-fashioned concomitants of traditional literacy. In the new literacy, what matters is excitement, personal investment, and as much as possible the impression of being actually present at an event. Thus, multiple channels of communication paradoxically reduce experience to momentary highlights. Conversely, in traditional literacy a single channel of communication forces us to experience events in sequence, removed from the events, dependent on our own ability to interpret and understand what has transpired.

The complexities of baseball essentially require a highly developed ability to understand symbolic action. A sophisticated fan of baseball understands the game beyond the narrow frames of literal or immediate action; that's partly why some people much prefer listening to baseball on the radio rather than watching it on TV. Unlike football, the action of baseball is dramatization, embedded in linear scenes literally played out in our imaginations. It is the genuine fan's intellectual projection that anticipates the selection and placement of each pitch, the consequences of each ball put into play, and the potential effect on the game of every action, each scene of the play, all the layers of framed activity so far.

What I am describing is, of course, the traditional form of print literacy, one that enables us to hold time in abeyance as we reflect on past, present, and future. It is also the literacy of print culture, essentially the static enactment of symbolic actions — or words read on a page. As I have also previously noted, this narrow channel of literacy is held separate from an audience because the exchange between writer and reader is more imagined and projected than immediate or dialogic.

The future of baseball as a spectator sport obviously entails far more than the literacy skills of those people who may potentially watch the sport. Issues of age, gender, race, and cultural heritage, for example, may have even more powerful effects than literacy, yet ignoring or otherwise minimizing the way that people are likely to watch a sport is almost certain folly. In the new literacy, perception overrides substance, excitement of the moment supersedes informed judgment, and those who fail to recognize these differences will risk becoming victims of their ignorance.

In noting features of the new literacy, I am not recommending that baseball adapt to become a more "modern" sport — that adding a game clock or juicing the baseball for more offense will somehow improve the game or enhance attendance at ballparks and draw higher ratings for televised games. I am suggesting that a society with strong traditional literacy skills will more likely gravitate to watching baseball. In that sense, baseball and literacy are good for each other.

A Flexible Metaphor: Baseball in the Classroom

Michelle Jones

"American intellectuals are crazy about baseball," wrote one analyst.[1] Academics ranging from Stephen Jay Gould, who uses baseball to explain biology, to Emily Vermeule, a Harvard professor of classics who sees classical themes of "heroism, the fickleness of fate and the gallantry of the loser"[2] in the game, to many high school and college teachers across the U.S., incorporate baseball into their classrooms. Baseball is a flexible and accessible way of teaching a variety of academic subjects at the high school and college level.

What are the advantages of using baseball over more traditional classroom approaches? One of the concepts most discussed in education courses is defining a "comfort zone" in the classroom; in other words, making students feel free to offer opinions and ideas and to ask questions. A college classroom can be an intimidating and hostile environment: students are uncertain of their abilities, self-conscious about venturing ideas, and their TV-trained attention spans don't allow for sustained concentration on an esoteric topic. Incorporating baseball addresses these problems. My discussion will include teaching baseball from historical, literary, sociological, psychological and scientific perspectives. I'll include references to baseball as a subject, illustration, model or reference, using the experiences of teachers in high schools and colleges to explore the potential of baseball as a classroom technique.

Margaret Atwood, in *Survival: A Thematic Guide to Canadian Literature,* described the frontier as "a flexible metaphor dear to the American heart."[3] Similarly, baseball is a mirror of American culture. Alterations in the game, such as the rise of African-American and Hispanic players, reflect larger changes in society. And like the frontier, baseball can function as a flexible metaphor for many teachers in areas as diverse as history, physics, and creative writing. William McGill of Lebanon Valley College suggests that baseball appeals on so many different levels because of "the variety of ways one can appreciate it (aesthetically, statistically, narratively, culturally)."[4]

The Joys of Analysis

The best way to delve deeper into a ball game and to find out more to think about and enjoy ... is to analyze the decision making and the execution of the pitcher and the hitter on each individual pitch and then to watch and analyze the resulting play with this understanding ... My motto: Pay attention. Pay attention to the nuances of the game.
— Keith Hernandez, *Pure Baseball*[5]

[Baseball fans] are spectators of a game that rewards, and thus elicits, a remarkable level of intelligence from those who compete. To be an intelligent fan is to participate in something.... [Being a serious fan] is doing something that makes demands on the mind of the doer.
— George Will, *Men at Work*[6]

Critical analysis: the bane of the composition teacher's existence. How does one insist that her students appreciate the nuances of a Shakespearean sonnet or a James Joyce novel? It does not work to start a lecture on critical analysis with a definition of symbolism, theme, tone or style; to most students, "critical" has a strongly negative connotation, and "analysis" sounds too scientific. But if the teacher begins, "Did you see the Reds' game last night?" everyone relaxes.

Using baseball in the classroom can teach reluctant students the joys of contemplation and analysis. When I have had difficulty explaining how "picking apart" a poem or story can lead to greater appreciation, I use a baseball analogy. One can watch a game without understanding all the nuances, but isn't it more enjoyable, doesn't one get more of an insider's thrill, when the pitch sequence or setup of the double play is clearly seen and understood? Similarly, students begin to see that understanding an author's tone, style, or structure leads to more enjoyment of the text overall. When baseball or softball players are students in my classes, I ask them to explain to the other students what is involved in preparation: months of conditioning, drills on plays, sprints, studying — in order to show that nothing worth having—whether it's a baseball game or a short story—is created out of thin air.

Much angst over why our children aren't reading could be remedied by baseball stories: John R. Tunis was frequently mentioned in my survey. Ron Sheasby, a writing teacher, assigned Tunis sports books to remedial-level and ESL college students (many of them athletes) in Chicago.[7] Where books on other topics may appear daunting, who could be intimidated by Schoolboy Johnson, Razzle, or the Kid? Another teacher uses baseball stories to show

> the meaning of myth, the importance of games, the roles of heroes and American culture ... In America, baseball can be a very real means of developing self-identity and a sense of self-worth, as part of the growing-up experience.[8]

Science and Math

Tim Suermondt, in a poem called "The Highest Math,"[9] writes:

> The boy who couldn't do school arithmetic
> had a field day computing batting averages,
> ERAs, won/loss percentages
> ....
> Billy McCool, Jim Maloney,
> Chico Ruiz, Vada Pinson ... an entire
> team and a boy badly in need
> of wins, kept alive and hustling
> by the often inelegant elegance of statistics:
> .238   5.56   .457

Good teaching builds on the familiar, and intimidating topics can be made less worrisome with the incorporation of baseball. Several teachers use baseball as a way of illustrating explanations about physics, statistics, and mathematics. Mark Schraf, a chemistry professor at West Virginia University, uses baseball examples to demonstrate the metric system, showing his students that Toronto and Montreal display both feet and meters on their outfield walls, and then asking students to calculate the outfield distances at Three Rivers Stadium. He will also ask students to figure out the distance in meters traveled by a McGwire home run, or the velocity thrown by a pitcher in meters per second. He wrote, "All of this is done in an attempt to use familiar concepts to illustrate and clarify difficult or unfamiliar ones. I can think of no more familiar concept than baseball."

Another area is physics: If an atom were the size of the Astrodome, Schraf tells his students, the electrons would be on the ceiling and the nucleus would be a pea on pitcher's mound. A teacher could use any number of overheads and chalkboard drawings to illustrate the shape of the atom, but I doubt any student would forget this vision of Astro physics.[10]

One of my colleagues has his beginning physics students use video analysis to show the effect of air drag on a baseball, along with the effect of the ball's spin on its trajectory — i.e., what makes a curve ball curve? Perhaps his physics training has made him the daunting whiffle ball pitcher he is today; science has let him understand the physics of moving objects (how to have a round ball and round bat and hit it squarely).[11]

Stephen Jay Gould, who weaves references to baseball into his Harvard biology lectures, has also used the sport to illustrate — in an accessible and appealing way — scientific concepts that would otherwise make one's eyes glaze over. He uses the "creation myths of Cooperstown" to explain the idea of human growth as a continuum ("Baseball evolved and people grow; both are continuua without definable points of origin"[12]). Or, to make complicated ideas about "the working of random processes and patterning in nature"[13] understandable, he employs a discussion of DiMaggio's 56-game hitting streak. The laws of probability — and the remarkableness of Joltin' Joe's achievement — are much clearer as a result. Similarly, his statistical analysis of the extinction of the .400 hitter (in *Full House*[14]), holds up Keith Hernandez's plea to "pay attention." But, in a statement that exemplifies baseball's marriage of practicality and mysticism, he concludes: "Every season features the promise of transcendence."[15]

Ethical Issues

Wes Westrum, a New York Giants catcher, commented that "baseball is like church: 'Many attend but few understand.'"[16]

Complex ethical issues can be raised and discussed in the context of sports. One professor of religion, in a class called "Faith and Ethics," uses sportsmanship issues in baseball as a way of discussing integrity and self-respect.[17] Mark Hodermarsky, who teaches a baseball literature course in a Cleveland high school, comments that "Both academics and baseball reflect man's innate desire to seek truth, order and wisdom in an oftentimes chaotic world. Both help to elevate the spirit and the mind." The connection between baseball and religion, of course, has been discussed elsewhere; suffice it to say that Hodermarsky's favorite fictional character is Eddie Scissons from *Shoeless Joe*: "Because of his evangelical fervor for the game of baseball, he is redeemed. He becomes whole again. He finds salvation through baseball."[18] The "redemption" angle, so prominent in the film versions of *The Natural* and *Shoeless Joe*, resonates especially well with students; even at their tender ages, they understand the desire to undo past errors (or, as Whitman would say, "repair those losses").

Regular readers of *Elysian Fields Quarterly* know that unethical behavior (Alomar's spitting, Rocker's tirade) incites some fine baseball writing. Of course, this is true for fictional characters too: what drives Roy Hobbs? Is he (as Malamud suggested) like Richard Nixon, or maybe more like Macbeth? Does he exist to show us our similarity; that if presented with such a temptation, we might too have given in? The liveliest discussion in ten years came in my course in postwar fiction. A student and former high school star gave a presentation on greed in *The Natural*, commenting that while we want to hold our heroes up as larger than life, "Greed is a part of baseball and always has been." Somehow there exploded a free-for-all on ambition, entitlement, capitalism; Bill Gates was mentioned, as were Alex Rodriguez, Curt Flood, and Shoeless Joe Jackson. This took place at a small and conservative college where students normally do not feel comfortable voicing opinions — especially male students in female-dominated literature classes. Yet several students remarked that it was the most enlightening discussion we'd had all semester. One doesn't have to look far to see topics with which students can connect: is the Cleveland logo racist? Is the John Rocker case about free speech? Should affirmative action be used in the hiring of front office staff and coaching staff? Why are girls pushed to play softball, not baseball, which limits their choices at the collegiate and professional levels? What is the best governing philosophy for coaching children? Some of these topics will elicit powerful memories and reactions from students.

Frank Rashid, former President of the Tiger Stadium Fan Club, teaches an interdisciplinary seminar in Detroit Studies. He uses "a discussion of stadium economics and the blackmail that major league sports franchises perpetrate on American cities," saying that in his classes "[w]e connect this issue to the same kinds of tactics employed by the auto industry, the casino gambling industry, and others who attempt to profit by means of public subsidies and exertion of their power over planning decisions." Though he is an English professor, he became interested in the political and economic side of baseball when getting involved in Detroit's stadium issue, saying, "I feel the way I do about the stadium scam because I am an English teacher, sensitive to the misuses of language and logic by the greedy beneficiaries of stadium subsidies, their political frontmen, and their media apologists."[19] He notes that almost all of his students have some knowledge of the stadium issue, and show great interest in it; his course in Detroit Studies incorporates literature, history, and economics.

American Studies

Much has been said and written about baseball as a mirror of American culture. When I taught in the former Soviet Union, baseball was a useful way to illustrate unfamiliar topics, among them sports as central to the American educational system. Excerpts from *The Natural* provided a way to launch a discussion on ambition, competition, and what my students mockingly called "Yankee hopefulness"— American idealism.

Post-Soviet students, while inundated with icons of American culture like MTV and McDonald's, still sometimes had difficulties comprehending the "foreignness" of baseball: though a team sport, it is beloved by capitalists and largely dependent on individual achievement. Baseball literature also pointed up the close tie between baseball and politics: Malamud's comment "Roy Hobbs is as American as the lawyers involved in Watergate," or a photo of Presidents (and now a First Lady) throwing out the first pitch illustrated my lectures about the links between sports and politics better than any theory could.

American Studies might sound redundant to American students, but in fact the opportunity to look at our lives and cultures with fresh eyes is increasingly valuable. One writing teacher said, "Baseball is an innate part of the American psyche. It is absolutely democratic, at least since 1948, and as such stands for what we wish our country was and hope it may some day become, an absolutely equal playing field with equal opportunity for all, a place where the humblest citizen can become the richest or most popular, no matter from what origin or social class.... In sum, then, baseball is a metaphor for the American way of life."[20]

To pick up on Atwood's comment about the frontier as a flexible metaphor, baseball similarly mirrors American culture: alterations reflect larger changes in society. As baseball coach and college teacher Ron Mazeroski (cousin of Bill!) commented, "most film periods included a baseball production that represented the themes of an era."[21] It's interesting to have students compare the cynical ending of *The Natural* (novel) with the Reagan-era pyrotechnics of the film version, or to look at the way Babe Ruth is heroized in 1948's *The Babe Ruth Story*. Certainly films like 1973's *Bang the Drum Slowly* and *Bingo Long Traveling All-Stars and Motor Kings* show a new sensitivity to prejudice, while 1990s baseball films like *Cobb* and *The*

Fan show a dark and paranoid side to American culture. The two most popular baseball films among college students, though, are *A League of Their Own* and *Major League*—the latter is traditionally shown before the opening of every Muskie baseball season.

Writing Courses

Incorporating baseball into the classroom also allows an instant rapport in uncomfortable situations. For example, a composition teacher, Ron Sheasby, will tell a student who is "overwriting, trying to sound scholarly" to "'[cut] back on the breaking stuff and [concentrate] on getting the ball over the plate,' that is, write shorter and simpler sentences which communicate more effectively."[22] Another teacher regards his own baseball writing as a model for students: "If I ask my students to write (as I do), I should be writing myself. And of course what I read and what I write about has a way of sneaking its way into lectures and discussions in the strangest ways."[23] Students enjoy knowing that their teachers struggle over their own writing and research, and it makes the atmosphere in class less like a sweatshop and more like a workshop.

In the early stages of writing this presentation, I asked my students for advice; later I showed them the outline (they loved the fact that it was scrawled, taped together, and in three colors of ink), the rough draft, and finally the finished proposal. This made them realize that writing is a *process* involving planning and revising. But maybe more than that, the chance to be regarded as "experts" in something was appealing and gave them confidence. Students who would never venture an opinion on Ginsberg's poetry or Wharton's novels felt perfectly assured analyzing Updike's essay on Ted Williams' last at-bat ("Gods do not answer letters").

Composition students invariably groan when I assign a descriptive essay; so many high school teachers wanted a description of a sunset, a park, or Wordsworth's field of daffodils. It snapped them to attention when I asked them to describe a baseball game with as much sensory detail as possible (quoting *Elysian Fields Quarterly*'s mission statement of "baseball for the mind, the heart, and all five senses"): we spent a happy class period pinpointing the exact words for the pungent aroma of Tiger Stadium: is it predominantly the hot dogs sizzling on open grills, underlaid by freshly cut grass with a suggestion of cigarette smoke and beer? Are bleacher seats splintery? What is the precise texture of the pebbly concrete underfoot?

The comparison/contrast essay is another old chestnut. But when students read Murray Ross' "Football Red and Baseball Green," they see for themselves what a valuable technique this can be. They are much more ready to analyze Ross' football as military, baseball as pastoral, and always have plenty of their own theories to offer. If I schedule this unit during the playoffs, we often compare two of the involved teams: breaking them down position by position, including managing, the ballpark, the strength of the bench, "intangibles," and so on. Students who have been silent in previous classes will become involved in passionate arguments about these comparisons — and I can relax, knowing they've gotten the point.

History

Two events that determined "the American century" — the labor movement and the civil rights movement — can be well explained to students by using baseball. Stories of individual players — Jackie Robinson, Larry Doby, Hank Aaron, Curt Flood — have a much greater impact on students, showing that sports are, as Brooke Horvath said, a "repository of cultural values."[24] Leslie Heaphy of Kent State University teaches history through sports: "how sports have affected the growth of America and how events in American History have influenced the growth of sports as a major industry."[25]

Jules Tygiel, author of *Baseball's Great Experiment*, uses *The Jackie Robinson Reader* to illustrate various points about African-American history in the 20th century in his survey courses at San Francisco State, and also incorporates baseball themes in his U.S. history courses. In a co-taught History and Literature of Baseball course, he examines the "industrial evolution" of baseball from 1876-1918, and the players' response to professional baseball gaining a new level of stability as a national institution. Using Roy Campanella and Jackie Robinson's experiences as case studies, he looks at the effect of integration on both black and white baseball and on the broader culture; students are asked to consider the effect of playing in "Jim Crow" venues. And students also examine the rise of free agency and the "empowerment of players" movement from the 1960s until now.[26] Here American history, instead of being a dreary succession of names and dates, has a face and wears a baseball uniform.

Gender Studies

Gender studies are relatively new to my campus. Since I'm a Gender Studies teacher and feminist, some students come into my classes with preconceived ideas of what my attitudes will be; others see the whole idea of scrutinizing gender roles as uncomfortable and revolutionary. But in Gender Issues in Literature, we first talk about gender identification in childhood. This inevitably brings up the topic of sports and baseball. When I talk about the effect of Title IX on women's sports or the (to them) astounding fact that I was not allowed to play Little League baseball, issues of equity and gender stereotyping become much clearer. When we study Charlotte Perkins Gilman's feminist utopia *Herland*, I circulate pictures of women's Olympic teams at the turn of the century so the students can marvel at the confining clothing and etiquette demanded of the women; many students mention the film *A League of Their Own* as having a big influence on their own athleticism ("There's no crying in *college!*").

Students also offer their own experience as support or evidence; they discuss inequities between women's and men's sports teams (in funding, uniforms, practice fields and transportation) and the benefits of athletics. These issues spark discussion, whereas a discourse on feminist theory or men's studies would incite blank stares. Sometimes I read from the Donald Hall essay,

> Baseball is fathers and sons ... Baseball is the generations, looping backward forever with a million apparitions of sticks and balls .... Baseball is fathers and sons playing catch, lazy and murderous, wild and controlled, the profound, archaic song of birth, growth, age and death. The diamond encloses what we are.[27]

Then I follow by a mention of Greg Lichtenberg's autobiography, *Playing Catch with My Mother*, which depicts "becoming a man when all the rules have changed."[28] We discuss how often in films, male bonding is done through baseball; it is an avenue of communication for fathers and sons (*Field of Dreams*, *The Natural*, even films like *City Slickers*, "When I was 18 and couldn't talk to my dad about anything else, we could talk about baseball"). But we also discuss the possibility that women, long denied access to the baseball mythology, may finally be allowed a piece of the dream. Silver Bullets player Michele McAnany said, "This thing's a one-day-at-a-time shot now. It's the American way. And the American way means male and female." A lecture on *The Female Eunuch* or *The Feminine Mystique* would not provoke anything like the discussion aroused by that comment.

Conclusion

Baseball can exemplify American culture: as in society as a whole, it can be a unifying force in the classroom. The teaching zone, like U.S. culture, is constantly reinvented with new members — some of whom are uncertain about where they might fit. In a place whose history is exceedingly new, baseball provides a common language and a common set of images. As Johan Huizinga, the writer of the classic analysis of play, *Homo Ludens*, observes: "Into an imperfect world and into the confusion of life it brings a temporary, a limited perfection." Baseball can do the same in our classrooms.

Notes

1. Barol, Bill. "Baseball: The Sport of Eggheads," *Newsweek* (October 20, 1986): 62.

2. Barol, 62.

3. Atwood, Margaret. *Survival: A Thematic Guide to Canadian Literature* (Toronto: McClelland and Stewart, 1972): 35.

4. McGill, William. Lebanon Valley College. Personal correspondence, February 2000.

5. Hernandez, Keith, and Mike Bryan. *Pure Baseball: Pitch by Pitch for the Advanced Fan* (New York: HarperCollins, 1994): 7.

6. Will, George. *Men at Work: The Craft of Baseball* (New York: HarperPerennial, 1991): 10.

7. Sheasby, Ronald. Assistant Professor of Writing, Loyola University Chicago. Personal correspondence, February 2000.

8. Hodermarsky, Mark. English teacher, St. Ignatius High School, Cleveland. Personal correspondence, February 2000; course syllabus for Baseball Literature class.

9. Suermondt, Tim. "The Highest Math," *Elysian Fields Quarterly* 17.2 (Winter 1999): 94.

10. Schraf, Mark. Visiting Assistant Professor of Chemistry, West Virginia University. Personal correspondence, February 2000.

11. Teese, Robert. Professor of Physics, Muskingum College. Personal correspondence, February 2000.

12. Gould, Stephen Jay. *Bully for Brontosaurus: Reflections in Natural History*. (New York: W.W. Norton and Co., 1991): 57.

13. Gould, 467.

14. Gould. *Full House: The Spread of Excellence from Plato to Darwin* (New York: Harmony Books, 1996).

15. Gould. *Bully for Brontosaurus: Reflections in Natural History*. (New York: W.W. Norton and Co., 1991): 132.

16. Will, *Men at Work*: 4.

17. Nutt, Rick. Professor of Religion, Muskingum College. Personal conversation, February 15, 2000.

18. Hodermarsky, Mark. English teacher, St. Ignatius High School, Cleveland. Personal correspondence, February 2000; course syllabus for Baseball Literature class.

19. Rashid, Frank. Associate Professor of English, Marygrove College. Personal correspondence, February 2000.

20. Sheasby, Ronald. Assistant Professor of Writing, Loyola University Chicago. Personal correspondence, February 2000.

21. Mazeroski, Ron. Director of Alumni Relations, Muskingum College. Personal correspondence, February 2000.

22. Sheasby, Ronald. Personal correspondence.

23. Chalberg, Charles. History Department, Normandale Community College. Personal correspondence, February 2000.

24. Horvath, Brooke. English Department, Kent State University Stark Campus. Personal correspondence, February 2000.

25. Heaphy, Leslie. http://www.stark.kent.edu/~lheaphy/sports/USsport.htm. Syllabus for U.S. Sport History, Spring 1999.

26. Tygiel, Jules. Professor of History, San Francisco State University. Personal correspondence, February 2000. http://bss.sfsu.edu:207/hist490/490page.htm Course outline for History 490, The History and Literature of Baseball, Spring 2000.

27. Hall, Donald. *Fathers Playing Catch with Sons* (New York: Laurel, 1985): 30.

28. Lichtenberg, Greg. *Playing Catch with My Mother: Coming to Manhood When All the Rules Have Changed* (New York: Bantam Doubleday Dell, 1999).

"Walter Johnson" by Jonathan Richman: The Portrait of a Hero in Song

Richard J. Puerzer

The song "Walter Johnson," a two minute and twenty second ditty written and performed a capella by musician Jonathan Richman, eloquently portrays the great baseball career and kind persona of pitcher Walter Johnson.[1] "Walter Johnson" is interesting both in what its lyrics describe and in its inspiration to its writer and performer. Like so much of the music, art, and literature inspired by baseball, this song is as much about a baseball player as it is about life. The goal of this paper is to investigate the claims put forth in the song and to explore how they serve as the basis for inspiration to the artist, Jonathan Richman.

Introduction

In extolling the many virtues of Walter Johnson in the song, Richman describes just why Johnson is a hero to the singer/songwriter. However, this is not your typical song of candy-coated idolatry and hero-worship for a great baseball player. Richman sings not in the voice of an awe-struck fan, but with a heartfelt expression of admiration. A song praising Johnson could easily be based on his strikeout records, no-hitters, or scoreless inning steaks. However, none of these are to be found in this song. Instead, the listener learns about what kind of person Walter Johnson was on and off the baseball diamond.

It is rare to find a baseball song such as this, addressing the subject of baseball players as heroes yet retaining a sense of realism. Other songs in this vain include Bob Dylan's bluesy "Catfish,"[2] concerning Jim "Catfish" Hunter, and Chuck Brodsky's jangly folksong "Letters in the Dirt,"[3] concerning Richie Allen. These songs express admiration for proclaimed heroes based primarily on true human virtues such as humility, mental tenacity, and grace under pressure. "Letters in the Dirt" looks at the hero worship of a young baseball fan towards the best player on his favorite team. The twist is that this player, despite his athletic prowess and accomplishments, was, for many reasons, far from being a fan favorite. Brodsky sings how he "never booed Richie Allen" when he was a kid. He goes on to explain that as an adult, he now understands the reasons behind the attitude towards and the booing of Allen by many Philadelphia Phillie fans. But he is thankful that in his childhood innocence he did not understand and he never booed, even when Allen did strikeout. He was too loyal to boo, and was glad to have a hero despite what others felt. He sings, "If back then you knew Daddy, why all those other people booed, thanks for letting me have my heroes as a kid." Brodsky was allowed to idealize Richie Allen as a hero, whom he stood by as a child, and whom he still respects today. "Walter Johnson," too, defines some of the qualities that its songwriter finds heroic. Like the point of view taken in "Letters in the Dirt," the qualities which are idealized are not so much based on athleticism as on virtue.

Likewise, the song "Walter Johnson" tells an intriguing story. Because the song is performed a cappella, and thus there are no musical distractions to draw the listener away from the lyrics, the impact of the story as told in song is impossible to miss. The lyrics intertwine several interesting tales about the career of Walter Johnson. Despite his undisputed preeminence amongst all pitchers in the history of baseball, the song describes two odd points, weaknesses perhaps, concerning the play of Johnson. First, it states that Johnson was afraid of hurting batters and thus would not throw a bean ball or even a brush-back pitch. The song then goes on to describe how he would let up on some opposing players and give up hits when he and his team had the game well in hand and were on their way to victory. Richman treats these observations on Johnson's actions as a baseball player not as weaknesses, but as an admirable attitude towards life, making it clear that Johnson was a man who felt no need for recognition in a record book and who, when given the proper situations, would treat his competitors as friends. These attitudes and their inherent humility are precisely what make Walter Johnson an ideal hero to Richman.

The Songwriter

It is interesting that Jonathan Richman chose to write a song concerning a player who had retired well over 50 years and was dead for 40 years before the song was written. At face value, the topic of a nice guy who was a baseball player seems unlikely for a rock musician considered to be one of the seminal influences on the punk rock movement of the early 1970s. Richman, like most of the musicians who influenced the punk movement, was himself influenced by the band The Velvet Underground. It was their music and its difference in both sound, unpolished, and attitude, not aiming for mainstream acceptance, from almost all of the rock music that was popular in the late 1960s and early 1970s that inspired Richman into performing. His songs have never exactly been radio friendly and have received little attention aside from the left side of the radio dial where college radio resides. Richman is similar in some ways to Woody Guthrie in that their songs are honest, honest to themselves and to their artist. Richman's songs are not fodder for the masses. Unlike the hollow sentiments of much of the popular music of the last 30 years, his songs are expressions of his life experiences, and his very real thoughts, feelings, and emotions. These differences from the norm in musical outlook and inspiration are what have made and continue to make the music of Jonathan Richman influential to a broad range of musicians, from folk to punk rock.

Richman's first album, released in 1977 with his band The Modern Lovers, was produced by Velvet Underground member John Cale.[4] A song from this album, "Roadrunner," was later covered by one of the original and most infamous punk rock bands, The Sex Pistols, in their last concert together as a band in San Francisco in 1978.[5] "Roadrunner," like "Walter Johnson," is a song about something Richman finds as both exciting and inspirational. In the case of "Roadrunner," this inspiration is of driving alone late at night on the highways around his hometown of Boston, listening to the radio, feeling lonely and yet feeling the thrill and exuberance of life itself. Topics such as these are what Richman has sung about his entire career, especially including songs on romantic and unrequited love, but also others on artists such as Picasso and Van Gogh, his gusto for eating, his love for the sound of his guitar, his warm feelings for his parents, and, of course, baseball.

At first glance, one may wonder why someone involved in the anti-establishment forces of rock and roll and, more specifically, punk rock music, would be inspired to write a song on mild-mannered Walter Johnson, let alone proclaim him as a hero. Johnson, after all, was an affable family man, a quiet and respected superstar, who after retirement from baseball ran for a Maryland Congressional seat. As staid and quietly dignified as Walter Johnson was, it was these qualities that attracted Richman to literally sing the praises of Johnson. Walter Johnson is a good topic to Jonathan Richman for good reason.

The Song

The lyrics of "Walter Johnson" go on to describe several of the reasons that Walter Johnson is a hero to Jonathan Richman. This description begins with the song's chorus, which asks whether Johnson felt any bitterness (presumably over the fact that Johnson toiled for the lowly Washington Senators for the entirety of his career). Despite this, he is often regarded as the greatest right-handed pitcher if not the best overall pitcher in the history of organized baseball.[6] He holds the twentieth-century records for most wins (417), complete games (531), and shutouts (110). His microscopic 1.14 earned run average (ERA) in the 1913 season was a major league record for 55 years. And of course, his 3508 career strikeouts were a major league record for 56 years until 1983, when Nolan Ryan surpassed that total.[7] Given his pitching prowess, it must have been at the least frustrating to Johnson for his pitching efforts to go for naught, primarily due to the weak offense of the Senators. Sixty-five of his 279 career losses came in games in which his team failed to score, including 27 instances in which he was on the losing end of 1-0 games. Yet, despite his dominance as a pitcher, the Senators finished within 14 games of the division leader only four times in his 21 years as a player in the major leagues. In fact, it took eighteen years in the majors before Johnson finally reached the World Series, the first of only two times in which he would see post-season play.

Johnson knew that he was a great and extremely fast pitcher and he knew what one of his fastballs could do to an opposing batter. The song goes on to discuss Johnson's reluctance to brush-back a batter much less to hit a batter with a pitch.

Now certainly Johnson didn't always throw the ball right down the middle. On the contrary, he is credited with hitting 203 batters in his career, including a league leading twenty hit batsmen in 1923.[8] This wildness existed in Johnson's pitching, despite, for the most part, unusually remarkable control. Johnson allowed slightly over two walks per nine innings in his career, a very small amount in any era of pitching. There are several documented instances of Johnson hitting batters and knocking out teeth or knocking the batter out cold. It is even reported that he ended the career of Chicago White Sox Lee Tannehill by breaking his arm with a pitch.[9]

Despite these numbers and facts to the contrary, there is a great deal of anecdotal information stating that Walter was not a purveyor of the brush-back or knockdown pitch. In his interview for the oral history book *The Glory of Their Times*, Jimmy Austin states that Walter was a careful pitcher and was "too good a guy, scared stiff that he'd hit somebody."[10] However, Johnson's grandson and biographer, Henry Thomas, describes there being but one instance in the career of Walter Johnson in which he threw intentionally at a batter. This occurred in a 1914 game against the Philadelphia A's, while facing slugger Frank "Home Run" Baker. Apparently urged on by his teammates, Johnson threw a pitch upstairs at Baker that did not hit him, but did send him sprawling. Johnson reportedly regretted throwing the pitch as soon as it left his grip. Although he was relieved that he did not injure Baker, he was obviously unnerved and was left ineffective for the remainder of his stay in that game. After that incident, Johnson vowed that this would be the last beanball he would throw in his life.[11]

The crafty Ty Cobb used this knowledge of Johnson's reluctance in throwing at a batter to his advantage against Johnson. Cobb, knowing that Johnson feared hitting him, crowded the plate when facing him, and hit .335 in his career against Johnson. "If I hadn't been able to read him, it would have been about .290," Cobb, with his .367 lifetime batting average, admitted after his career was over.[12]

The song goes on to describe how Johnson was such a good sportsman that he was not only afraid to hit the opposing batters, but actually at times made it easy for them to get a hit. This "easing up on the opposition" which Johnson was reported to have done went beyond the pacing of oneself or "pitching in the pinch" which was common among pitchers in the deadball era.[13] Walter Johnson was, in fact, charitable with easy fastballs thrown right down the center of the plate to certain hitters when his team was virtually certain to win. It is mentioned by Detroit Tiger Hall of Famer "Wahoo" Sam Crawford in *The Glory of Their Times* that Johnson allowed him to get hits when the occasion arose and it wouldn't affect the game. Contrary to what is mentioned in the song, Johnson's catcher, Gabby Street, was in on the plan as well, tipping Crawford off by telling him that "Walter likes you today." Johnson would then deliver a "nice half-speed fastball" that Crawford could belt. Of course, if the game were close, Johnson was the consummate competitor. It is no wonder then that Crawford describes Johnson as "warm, and friendly, and wouldn't hurt a soul." Oddly enough, Crawford states that Johnson would always bear down against Crawford's teammate, Ty Cobb. The aforementioned Jimmy Austin also admits that he too was the beneficiary of Johnson's friendly pitching. He describes one instance when the Senators held a large lead and Johnson gave him an easy pitch that he hit for a home run. "I don't know which one of us was laughing harder as I was going around the bases," Austin gleefully described.[14]

Obviously if Johnson gave up the occasional hit, or even home run, to the opposition, he wasn't terribly concerned about his personal statistics. Richman sings of this in the song:

Johnson's easy going nature did one time cost him a place in the record book. His 1913 season was perhaps his greatest and one of the best of all time. He won 36 games, including 11 shutouts, struck out 243 batters, and held the opposition to a .217 on-base percentage, all major-league leading totals for the year.[15] Going into the last game of that season, Johnson's Washington Nationals, as they were known then, were guaranteed a second place finish. Washington manager Clark Griffith made the last game a joke game; one that certainly would count in the standings but would be played with much more humor than seriousness. For almost the entire game Johnson played center field. This was the first time in his career he appeared in a major league game at a position other than pitcher. However, at the demand of the fans, Johnson did come in to pitch in the ninth inning. To clarify that this game certainly was not taken seriously, Johnson's battery-mate was 43-year-old coach Jack Ryan, who had made only one other appearance since the 1903 season, that in the previous year in a similar joke game. Lobbing the ball more than pitching, Johnson gave up two straight hits before ending his pitching appearance and retreating back to the outfield. The pitchers replacing Johnson on the mound gave up additional hits allowing the two runners he put on to score. Without knowing it at the time, and no doubt not caring, Johnson's ERA rose from 1.09 to the equally minuscule 1.14.[16] This ERA stood as a major league record until 1968 when Bob Gibson recorded an ERA of 1.12 for the season. Had Johnson been more concerned about his statistics than his love of the game, his record ERA of 1.09 would still stand today.

The Hero

In examining the history of the game of baseball, one can find men of all types exhibiting character ranging from basically good to basically bad, from the dishonest, misogynist, racist, self-important, and just plain mean to those exhibiting perseverance, humility, strength of belief, courage, and goodness. Certainly one can point to any number of men of character as "good" and exhibiting sportsmanship, honesty, courage, and fortitude as Walter Johnson. A short list would include: Jackie Robinson,

Hank Greenberg, Ernie Banks, Pete Gray, Jim Abbott, Cal Ripken Jr., Curt Flood; the list goes on and on. But it was Walter Johnson that Jonathan Richman chose to sing about, and for good reason. Certainly one could discount the statement of Johnson's heroic qualities made in the song by stating that it is based on nostalgia for a simpler time, both in baseball and society. Never in today's media saturated game would a player not be cognizant of their ERA at the end of the season and of their potential place in history and record books. Of course today there is far too much money at stake for a player to ever "ease up on the opposition." However, this does not diminish the character of Walter Johnson one bit. In his time the game was filled with cheats, vainglorious stars, and hateful men. One need only look at the segregation in baseball, the 1919 World Series scandal, the corruption of Ty Cobb and Hal Chase, and the death of Ray Chapman to a beanball to see that things were not so simple then. In his time, Walter Johnson stood out, not only as a great pitcher but also as a great man. And greatness, both in athleticism and in character, transcends time.

As staid, decent, and quietly dignified as Walter Johnson was, it was these qualities that attracted Richman to literally sing the praises of Johnson. Richman admires the fact that Johnson played the game of baseball unselfishly and as a gentleman. He admires that Johnson was not bitter about the years that passed in which his team, the usually mediocre Washington Senators, languished in the second division of the American League. He admires that Walter Johnson enjoyed baseball as a game which he had fun playing. Richman admires Johnson for his positive attitude, his humility, and for his goodness as a human being. But, most of all, Richman admires Johnson because he stands out from the crowd. It is clear then why Richman finds Walter Johnson not just an admirable athlete, but a great man of heroic character. Richman, like any good groundbreaking rock 'n' roller, respects Walter Johnson for standing out and breaking from the conformity and complacency of the norm. In singing of Walter Johnson, Jonathan Richman is singing of the idealism for which not only athletes but all people should aspire. This song is unique in that it exhibits a rare honesty and true exuberance for baseball and for how Walter Johnson played the game.

Notes

1. Jonathan Richman, *Walter Johnson* (Rockin' Leprechaun Music — Rounder Music, 1995). Originally found on the Jonathan Richman and the Modern Lover's 1985 album *Rockin' and Romance*, Twin/Tone label, catalog number TTR 8558. The album

also contains the song "The Fenway," native New Englander Richman's paean to the Fenway Park. It can be found on the recently issued compilation of baseball songs titled *Diamond Cuts — Triple Play*. *Diamond Cuts — Triple Play*, a compilation of baseball oriented music released in 1999 released on the Hungry for Music label. Hungry for Music is run by SABR member Jeff Campbell and has released several albums of baseball oriented music. They can be reached at 2020 Pennsylvania Ave. NW, Suite 384, Washington, D.C., 20006, or at 1-800-843-0933.

2. Bob Dylan, *Catfish*, can be found on The Bootleg Series, volumes 1-3 (rare & unreleased), 1961-1991 box set, Columbia Records catalog number 47382, or on the first Diamond Cuts release, *Diamond Cuts — Single*.

3. Chuck Brodsky, *Letters in the Dirt*, can also be found on *Diamond Cuts — Triple Play*.

4. Ira Robbins, editor, *Trouser Press Record Guide, Fourth Edition* (Collier Books, 1991).

5. For a discussion of the advent of punk rock and the connection from the Velvet Underground to Jonathan Richman to The Sex Pistols, see Greil Marcus, *Lipstick Traces: A Secret History of the Twentieth Century* (Boston, MA: Harvard University Press, 1989) and Clinton Heylin, *From the Velvets to the Voidoids: A Pre-Punk History for a Post-Punk World* (Penguin Books, 1993).

6. Bill James, *Historical Baseball Abstract* (New York: Villard Books, 1985), rates Johnson as the greatest right-handed pitcher of all time in terms of both peak and career value, the seventh best player and third best pitcher of all time (behind Lefty Grove and Sandy Koufax) in terms of peak value, and the twelfth best player and third best pitcher of all time (behind Grove and Warren Spahn) in terms of career value.

7. John Thorn and Pete Palmer, editors, *Total Baseball* (New York: HarperCollins, 1993).

8. Henry W. Thomas, *Walter Johnson: Baseball's Big Train* (Washington, D.C.: Phenom Press, 1995).

9. Ibid.

10. Lawrence S. Ritter, *The Glory of Their Times* (New York: William Morrow, 1984).

11. Thomas, *Walter Johnson: Baseball's Big Train*.

12. Al Stump, *Cobb: A Biography* (Chapel Hill, NC: Algonquin Books, 1994).

13. The practice is discussed in detail in Christy Mathewson, *Pitching in a Pinch: Baseball From the Inside* (Lincoln, NE: University of Nebraska Press, 1994). Basically, due to the deadball and the lack of the threat of home runs which might immediately change the face of a game, pitchers could pace themselves throughout a game and save their best stuff for situations in which they had to "make a pitch."

14. Ritter, *The Glory of Their Times*.

15. Thorn and Palmer, *Total Baseball*.

16. Thomas, *Walter Johnson: Baseball Big Train*.

Part 2

BASEBALL AS HISTORY

"This Town Isn't Big Enough for Both of Us": Politics, Economics, and Local Rivalries in St. Louis Major League Baseball

Roger D. Launius

Introduction

Even though professional baseball was born in New York, its roots and indeed its heart may be found in the American Midwest. And no place is more important to Midwestern baseball than St. Louis, Missouri. Indeed, the first reported baseball game to be played in St. Louis took place on July 9, 1860, and the sport was routinely covered in the city's newspapers thereafter. The city has been home to the *Sporting News*, the self-styled bible of baseball, since it began publication, and some of the earliest and most successful major league teams called the "Gateway to the West" home.

Beginning in 1876, St. Louis became a charter member of the newly formed National League, and St. Louis has never been the same since. In the more than 120 years since the rise of major league baseball in Missouri, eight major league franchises from seven different major leagues have played in St. Louis.[1] The Cardinals are by far the most significant St. Louis major league baseball team. A franchise renowned for its excellence on the field, the Cardinals have earned more pennants (fifteen) and more World Series championships (nine) than any other National League team.[2]

But the St. Louis major league baseball experience is not limited to

the story of the Cardinals. For much of the history of major league baseball in St. Louis, the Cardinals shared the city with alternative baseball
clubs. These included, especially, the American League's Browns, who
spent most of their existence in the first half of the twentieth century at
the bottom of the standings before fleeing to Baltimore in 1954.[3] There
were also the excellent but short-lived Brown Stockings, the city's first
entry into the National League; the virtually forgotten Terriers of the Federal League in 1914-1915; the Stars of the Negro American League; and the
Maroons of the pre-twentieth century National League. These teams, with
their colorful and highly skilled players and owners, combined to make St.
Louis one of the premier baseball towns in America.

The major issues noted above have informed many serious studies of
baseball history, but no one has explored them in the context of the history of St. Louis. This paper will trace briefly some of these major themes
associated with the creation, rivalry, and eventual demise of all but one
major league baseball team in St. Louis.

The Beginnings of Baseball in St. Louis

In 1870, the first truly professional league was formed, and in 1875 two
teams from St. Louis participated in the final season of this league, the
National Association of Professional Baseball Players. This marked the
debut of St. Louis in the major leagues. The thirty-year period from the
rise of the first professional team in 1869 to the end of the century was a
critical time for major league baseball. Teams struggled to establish themselves as major league franchises and leagues rose and fell, and the owners and players engaged in battles over salaries, contracts, and profits
(much as they still do today). During that period chaos reigned, but by the
end of the nineteenth century major league baseball as both a business and
as a spectator sport had been established in a form recognizable a century
later.[4]

While earlier efforts to create a major league had failed, on February
2, 1876, William Ambrose Hulbert of Chicago presided over a meeting at
the Central Hotel in New York City where representatives from eight cities
met to charter the National League.[5] The farthest west of the new league's
teams was located in St. Louis, a city of 330,000 at the time. The team's
owner, Charles Fowle, brought the Brown Stockings onto the field for their
first game on April 22, 1876. The city leaders desperately wanted a first class
professional team, for the city had slipped in status in business and commerce, culture, and population relative to many of its sister cities in the

Midwest. Perhaps this is no better demonstrated than in St. Louis' rivalry with Chicago, a city with the "broad shoulders" that had become the largest and most successful in the region since the end of the Civil War, and by 1900 was second only to New York City in the nation. Baseball became a symbol of post-bellum St. Louis' commitment to ensuring its place as among the best of all the American cities.[6]

When the St. Louis professional team beat the Chicago nine in the summer of 1875, the St. Louis *Republican* captured beautifully this rivalry with Chicago for prestige and rank:

> Time was when Chicago had an excellent base ball club, the best in West, but that was before St. Louis decided to make an appearance on the diamond field and there, as everywhere else, attest her supremacy ... St. Louis is happy. Chicago has not only been beaten at baseball, but the result only illustrates once more the old truth that bluster does not always win. In this, as other things, St. Louis proves stronger ... Chicago came, saw, and was conquered.[7]

This anecdote precipitates several observations about the importance of baseball for the city of St. Louis throughout its history. First, and most important, the competition of baseball operates at several levels to assist residents in feeling good about themselves and their homes and their lives. Especially in an environment in which a community feels inferior in other capacities a winning baseball team, particularly one that beats a rival community, helps to ease those feelings. Certainly that was true of many in St. Louis in relation to the economic and cultural powerhouse on Lake Michigan in 1875. The city has seen this repeatedly since that time. Second, and related to this first point, within the city itself certain groups defined by race, ethnicity, class, or a combination of all of these may adopt a particular team and trade on its fortunes in determining the boundaries of their status. In some respects, this identification allows fans to ignore, indeed to deny, the stark reality of any inferiority that might exist. Third, baseball in general — and certainly it was true in St. Louis — has saliency in that it readily translates into human understanding of who the winners and losers are on any given day in the season. One need not pour over economic analyses or understand obtuse and drawn out treatises. Baseball's simplicity ensured its grasp by even the densest of observers.

Fourth, baseball proved itself remarkably "scaleable" from the very beginning. While a team's won-lost record could serve at a fundamental level in a fan's ability to fix status, other less blatant measures of the game may be used to accomplish the same task. Individual player performance even on a losing team, for instance, may allow fans to enhance their self-worth. For all of the years between 1947 and 1963 that St. Louis fielded generally mediocre teams, many local fans still followed with excitement the exploits of Stan Musial. The same is true at present; even when the Cardinals play essentially .500 ball, they offer glory to their fans through the individual exploits of Mark McGwire. What else explains the hoopla associated with McGwire everywhere? The fact that fans will buy and wear Cardinals jerseys with his name and number on the back suggests a desire to transform oneself into the current king of the long ball and lose one's mediocrity at least for a period. Identification with one who accomplishes gargantuan exploits on the field allows the fan to bask in reflected glory and to escape the reality of inferiorities that exist.[8]

In 1876, that first year of the National League, the St. Louis Brown Stockings were an excellent team that won 45 and lost 19 games, finishing in second place and only six games behind the first place Chicago White Stockings. Following the 1877 season, four players from the Louisville Grays National League team were banned from baseball for life for throwing some of their games. The Louisville club dropped out of the league after this, its team decimated. John Lucas, the president of St. Louis's Brown Stockings, had planned to sign three of the expelled players for 1878. In protest over their expulsion, he withdrew the St. Louis club from the league. Thus ended the first foray into the National League by a team from St. Louis. It would be four years before another major league club played in St. Louis, and almost ten before another St. Louis club competed in the National League.[9]

TEAMS IN ST. LOUIS

Years	Teams (6 Total)				High Population
1875 — 2 teams	RS	BS			311,000 (1870)
1876–1877 — 1 team	BS				
1878–1880 — no teams					351,000 (1880)
1881–1883 — 1 team	B				
1884–1886 — 2 teams	B	M			
1887–1901 — 1 team	B				575,000 (1900)
1902–1908 — 2 teams	C	Br			
1909–1912 — 3 teams	C	Br	G		687,000 (1910)
1913–1915 — 4 teams	C	Br	G	T	
1916–1919 — 3 teams	C	Br	G		
1920–1943 — 3 teams	C	Br	S		773,000 (1920)
1944–1953 — 2 teams	C	Br			857,000 (1950)
1953–current — 1 team	C				750,000 (1960)
					339,000 (1998)

Legend: B-Browns; Br-Browns from Milwaukee; BS-Brown Stockings; C-Cardinals; G-Giants; M-Maroons; RS-Red Stockings; S-Stars; T-Terriers

Chris Von der Ahe and the Origins of the Cardinals

In 1880 business leaders in St. Louis reorganized the two main base-ball clubs that had been playing in St. Louis during the 1870s, the Red Stockings and the National League's Brown Stockings. Two of the princi-pal figures involved in this reorganization were Al Spink (co-founder of the *Sporting News*) and Chris Von der Ahe, both well-known St. Louis businessmen. Von der Ahe owned a beer garden and boardinghouse near the Grand Avenue stadium where the new club would play its games, and seeing that his bar business always picked up before and after baseball games played there, he understood that baseball fans would be good patrons for his business. Mustachioed, Roman nosed, and speaking with the Dutch accent that betrayed his birth in an obscure Germanic province in 1851, Von der Ahe was the prototype spotlight grabbing Major League Baseball team owner. He referred to himself, in his thick accent, as "der poss bresident," and the fans loved it. He spent freely, indulged his play-ers, and built an early baseball dynasty in the 1880s. Von der Ahe loved the celebrity his ownership brought him, for now he was not just a prosper-ous businessman but both a prosperous businessman and a public figure. It was an unbeatable combination, perhaps the real attraction for baseball ownership up to the present, and something repeated many times by many different owners since. In a city rich in baseball history, no one has been more significant in shaping the game in early St. Louis than Chris Von der Ahe.[10]

Von der Ahe offered the city's baseball fans a superb baseball team coupled with a circus-like atmosphere. Half a century before Bill Veeck, owner of several teams at different times and supposed pioneer of baseball promotions with giveaways and fireworks, Von der Ahe had horse races, merry-go-rounds, and shoot-the-chute boat rides from a tower into an artificial lake as attractions for his games. He hired the Silver Cornets, a marching band made up of 24 attractive young women, to provide music at the games. His goal was to make Sportsman's Park, where his team played, the "Coney Island of the West." He realized that he led the city's entertainment business, of which his baseball team was the centerpiece, and he meant to dominate that business.[11]

The organization Von der Ahe formed, the Sportsman's Park and Club Association, renovated the park where these earlier teams had played and renamed it Sportsman's Park. In 1881 they put on the field for the first time the St. Louis Browns, an independent team that played several exhibition games against other professional clubs, including a highly successful series against the Cincinnati Reds and the Philadelphia Athletics, both National

League clubs. Encouraged by the success of these games, O. P. Caylor, the leading figure in the Reds, and Horace Phillips of Philadelphia, organized representatives from St. Louis (Von der Ahe), Cincinnati, Philadelphia, New York, and several other cities for a meeting in Pittsburgh in November 1881 and formed the American Association.[12]

Beginning in 1882 Von der Ahe's Browns began playing in the American Association at old Sportsman's Park.[13] The Browns were an excellent team and dominated the American Association throughout the 1880s. It won the league's pennant each year between 1885 and 1888 under the leadership of manager-first baseman Charles Comiskey, later the owner of the American League's Chicago White Sox. During that four-year period when the St. Louis Browns were the rulers of the American Association, they played a post-season series with the winners of the National League pennant, although the term "World Series" had yet to be dreamed up. Although the American Association collapsed in 1891, four of its teams still survive in the National League (NL) today — including the St. Louis franchise — that transferred there with the 1892 season.[14]

The St. Louis NL franchise did not fare well in the 1890s, in part due to poor management by Von der Ahe. It was not entirely his fault, however. The combination of poor investing and economic depression as a result of the Panic of 1893 sent his resources into a downward spiral. This led to his drinking excessively and that, coupled with a succession of mistresses that infuriated his wife, prompted her to sue for divorce. By 1898 Von der Ahe was a hollow shell of what he had been a decade earlier. The final blow, and the other owners enjoyed levying it because of the animosity they had for Von der Ahe's lifestyle and his showmanship, happened when the league forced him to sell the club to more stable owners.[15]

Those new Browns owners, Frank and Stanley Robison, also owned the Cleveland Spiders in the National League, and they replicated the curious phenomenon of "syndicate baseball" that had been previously limited to the East Coast. Syndicate baseball involved the ownership of multiple franchises by a single ownership group. For instance, the owners of the Baltimore Orioles, which was the best team in the National League throughout the 1890s, had also bought an interest in the Brooklyn team. Brooklyn, which had recently become part of a five-borough greater New York, was a much larger and more lucrative market than Baltimore, and the owners made the business decision to send the best Oriole players to Brooklyn where larger profits could be had if a winning team could be fielded. Baltimore smarted from the loss, but as a small market city its fate seemed assured.

The same thing happened with the Cleveland and St. Louis franchises.

The Robison brothers proceeded to switch the best players from Cleveland to St. Louis prior to the 1899 season, including sending to St. Louis future Hall of Famers Cy Young, Jesse Burkett, and Bobby Wallace. At the time St. Louis was one of the top five U.S. cities in terms of population while Cleveland was in the second tier. The St. Louis baseball fans had a tradition of supporting the great Browns teams, and Cleveland had been lukewarm to the Spiders even when they have been competitive in the first part of the 1890s. The Robisons had an easy answer to this question: why let great players like Young and Burkett languish in Cleveland when they could go to St. Louis where a larger population base would appreciate and support a contender?[16]

Some decried the moves as "syndicate baseball" and charged the Robisons with creating a monopoly. They responded, of course, with "What's wrong with monopoly?" It was the epitome of big business in the nineteenth century, and the Robisons believed that baseball would become big business. Their ambitions were every bit as great and every bit as nefarious as those of Cornelius Vanderbilt and John D. Rockefeller and Jay Gould. The National League sought monopoly, and its owners believed it a good thing.[17]

The Browns: From Doormats to Dominance and Back

During its first two decades of existence, the National League withstood threats of competition from several newer professional leagues. Upon the formation of the successful American League (AL) in 1901, however, it went head to head with the National League for players and city loyalties in St. Louis and elsewhere.[18] The AL's St. Louis team was one of the most storied and least able teams ever to play at the major league level. The Browns, named to remind the St. Louis fans of Von der Ahe's legendary dynasty of the 1880s, were easily the most inept team in major league history, winning only one pennant in more than fifty years and finishing in the second division a record 40 times. Yet they have engendered more nostalgia than virtually any other team other than the Boston Red Sox and the Dodgers of Brooklyn. A long list of books about the Browns history grace the shelves of any researcher in baseball history, and more are published every year. Of course, anyone can love a winner, but it takes a certain masochistic love of baseball and gluttony for punishment to embrace a perennial loser. St. Louis had one in the Browns and, while from the mid-1920s second in allegiance to the Cardinals, the Browns had the quality of an incorrigible but lovable screw-up for most of the team's history. Their aficionados believe to this day that the Browns were the worst team in baseball; they say it loud, and they say it proud.[19]

The St. Louis Browns had finished last in the American League three times in its first decade and seemed well on their way to a legendary status as the worst team in the league. But in 1913 two very important events took place in their history that portended a change in their fortunes, at least for a time. First, although they were again last in the American League, losing 96 of 154 games, they were not the worst major league team in St. Louis that year. The Cardinals, who were woeful at this point in their history, were last in the National League, and they lost even more games (99 altogether).[20] The Browns at least had a reason to believe they were not as bad as their rivals. Second, the owner of the Browns, a St. Louis businessman named Robert Hedges, hired Branch Rickey as a scout. Rickey soon came to dominate the Browns, and later the Cardinals, and to build both teams into winners.

While a coach at the University of Michigan, Branch Rickey discovered left-handed first baseman George Sisler, the greatest Browns player of all. In a fifteen-year career Sisler compiled a .340 lifetime batting average, batted over .400 twice, led the league in stolen bases four times, and set a record at first base with 1,528 assists that stood for over sixty years.[21]

Within two years of starting work for the Browns, after a short and undistinguished stint as field manager, Rickey moved into the front office and began to build a winning team. His process for doing so involved the establishment of what he referred to as a "farm system." It represented essentially a form of vertical integration in professional baseball and its origination represented sheer genius. After all, what is major league baseball if not an attraction on a playing field that draws spectators? The attraction is the players — their quality and their likability — so the objective is to place as high quality a product as possible on the field for as little money as possible. Therefore, holding down the cost of acquiring the services of outstanding players reigns supreme as the objective of all team owners. But where can one find proficient players? The answer is in the minor leagues, the owners of which were pleased to sell the contracts of their players to the major league teams for a profit. That was the system in place prior to the development of Rickey's farm system. But Rickey found those prices too high for the Browns, so he decided to purchase a few minor league teams, stock them with promising players already under Browns contract, and give them excellent baseball instruction. As the best players rose in the system, the Browns already owning their contracts meant that the team need not put money out of pocket to acquire these players' contracts.

Players in the minors were referred to as being "down on the farm," hence the name for the system.[22]

Rickey's central point in taking this approach was that since it was exceptionally difficult to predict which players would be successful in the major leagues, the best means of ensuring success was to start with a large group of potentially good players and then to winnow them down until the cream rose to the top. Between the ages of 18 and 25, when this winnowing process took place for most ballplayers, a whole range of circumstances could arise to alter any prospect's actual development — injury, illness, life experience, character flaws, and the like. The farm system would discover those circumstances and produce, if operated properly, enough talent to stock both the Browns and to trade excess players to other teams. The farm system, from Rickey's perspective, reduced the very large gamble inherent in player development and allowed the Browns to receive, rather than to pay, top dollar for the best minor league talent.

During the years that Rickey was with the Browns, 1913–1917, he was only able to begin the process of developing a stable farm system, but his efforts resulted in a very good team that took the field in the early 1920s. Rickey's inability to complete what he started with the Browns resulted from a personality clash he had with the Brown's new owner, Philip DeCatesby Ball, who purchased the team in 1915. The Browns did not have a front office large enough to accommodate the inflated egos of both Ball and Rickey, and one had to go. Rickey went across town to the Cardinals, where he spent the next two decades establishing a full-fledged farm system and used it to turn the Cardinals into one of the best NL teams of all time.

But even with the departure of Rickey, the Browns made history in the "roaring twenties." In 1920 the team finished in the first division for the first time since 1908. George Sisler, Rickey's first important player signing, set the pace. He led the league with a .407 batting average, drove in 122 runs, and set the single season record of 257 base hits for the season that still stands. Ably assisted by outfielder Ken Williams, who hit 24 home runs and drove in 117, and pitcher Urban Shocker, who won 20 games and lost 10, the Browns made a run at the pennant. In 1921 they finished third, with the same cadre of players. This time Shocker won a league-high 27 games. It looked like 1922 would be the year of the Browns, and everyone in St. Louis was poised to take a championship.[23]

They nearly did. In 1922 the Browns won 93 games, the most ever in the franchise's history, but they finished one game behind the New York Yankees. Even so, it was probably the best team in Brown's history. Sisler had a career year, batting a league high .420, and Ken Williams hit a league leading 39 homers and 155 runs batted in (RBIs). Shocker, winner of 24 games, anchored the pitching staff. The Browns ran neck and neck with the Yankees all summer, and were in first place as late as July 22. But in the end the Yankees won the pennant by a game-and-a-half.

The 1922 season represented the high-water mark for the Browns. The next year, absent George Sisler who missed the season with an eye infection that nearly did him in, the Browns slipped to fifth in the league. When Sisler returned in 1924, the team improved its record and vied for the pennant, finishing fourth. It finished third in both 1925 and 1926, slipped to seventh in 1927, and then returned to third in 1928. Thereafter, in part because of the hard times of the Great Depression, the Browns began a collapse that lasted until their pennant-winning year of 1944.[24]

The Rise of a Cardinal Dynasty

If from the 1920s to the 1950s you were to ask almost anyone in the American Midwest, Great Plains, South, or Far West about their favorite baseball team, they would invariably talk about the St. Louis Cardinals. During this period St. Louis was the farthest west and south of any major league city, and automatically attracted the attention of baseball fans in those regions. But it was more than that. The Cardinals rose to prominence, captured the allegiances of those in the great heartland of America, and never released it. The quality of the team's play on the field and the dignity of the players both on and off the diamond sealed this dauntless love affair.

The attraction was almost magical. Journalist Warner Fusselle remembered nostalgically about how as a boy growing up in Lynchburg, Virginia, which had a low-level Cardinal farm team, he became a Cardinals fan. He went to see those young minor leaguers every chance he got, and followed their progress to the big leagues, but he also searched the airwaves on a 1946 RCA tabletop radio each night for the powerful KMOX station that broadcast the big league Cardinals games. Listening to Harry Caray, the voice of the Cardinals for more than twenty years beginning in the 1940s, Fusselle became obsessed with the Cards — the universal pet name for the team — and basked in their reflected glory.[25]

Until the middle of the 1920s *the* team to follow in the region had not been the Cardinals but the Browns. This only changed when Branch Rickey moved to the Cardinals and his "farm system" strategy began to produce winners. Supported enthusiastically by the Cardinals owner, St. Louis automobile dealer Sam Breadon, Rickey immediately implemented his farm system by purchasing controlling interests in five minor league teams. He expanded and by 1936 owned controlling interests in 28 minor league franchises scattered throughout the nation, a dozen more than any other major league team.[26]

The greatest Cardinal of them all, of course, was Stan "the Man" Musial, a sore-armed pitcher whose retreading into an outfielder proved perhaps the most fortunate transformation of any player since Babe Ruth moved from the pitcher's mound to right field for good in 1919. In a stunning 22 year career, the Man (and no other identification is necessary) wracked up a .331 career batting average and won the batting title seven times, hit 475 career home runs, hit safely 3,630 times, was named Most Valuable Player in the National League three times, enjoyed perennial all star game appearances, and upon retirement held 17 major league, 29 National League, and nine all-star game records. His career represented the pinnacle of all the great players produced by the Cardinals farm system. Musial's was also a career of great dignity and poetry both on and off the field, remaining an icon in St. Louis more than 35 years after his retirement.[27]

The Cardinals began their rise to glory in the mid-1920s. Early in the 1925 season, with the Cards in last place and Branch Rickey both general and field manager, Breadon reassigned Rickey full-time to the Cardinals front office in cozy Sportsman's Park (shared with the Browns), and replaced him on the bench with second baseman Rogers Hornsby.[28]

The switch to Hornsby worked. In 1926 they captured their first pennant by edging Cincinnati in the final week of the season. The season was made perfect by the Cards' first victory in the World Series, coming at the expense of Babe Ruth and the New York Yankees. St. Louisians were as proud as they could possibly be, and the Cardinals' dominance in the city for the allegiance of the fans could be traced to that great series in October 1926.[29] The Cardinals took the pennant a second time in 1928 but lost the World Series to the Yankees. They took the pennant again in 1930, losing the series to an exceptional Philadelphia Athletics team, 4 games to 2. Through 1930, therefore, the Cardinals had won three pennants in five years.[30]

But they were far from done. In 1931 the Cardinals put on the field what many consider to their best team ever. In that year the Cardinals won 101 games, leading all the way and finishing 13 games in front of their nearest challenger.[31] The 1931 World Series brought a rematch of the 1930 confrontation, but that year the Cardinals prevailed. Sparked by rookie Pepper Martin, the Cardinals hung tough and out-dueled Philadelphia in seven games to capture their second world championship.[32] After two lackluster years in 1932 and 1933, the 1934 Cardinals, dubbed the Gashouse Gang for their rowdy and daring play, took the world championship again.[33]

Through the rest of the 1930s the Cardinals were competitive, but not victors. In 1942 — Stan Musial's first full season — the Cardinals enjoyed their winningest season ever with 106 victories and took the World Series title once again. The Cardinals won three more pennants, and two World Series championships in the 1940s, taking the flags in 1943, 1944, and 1946, and triumphing in the World Series in 1944 and 1946.[34]

The Great Streetcar Series of 1944

But it was the 1944 World Series that captured the hearts of most Missourians. In that year both the Cardinals and the Browns took their respective league pennants and met in the World Series. The Cardinal win was expected by almost everyone, after winning 105 games in that year and running away with the pennant. No question, the Cards were the class of the National League. But the Browns surprised everyone by taking the American League pennant by one game over the Detroit Tigers by winning only 85 games. *Even the Browns* was the original title of William B. Mead's superb book on wartime baseball (*Baseball Goes to War*), and infers that the level of competition in the Major Leagues after America joined the fighting was suspect. This allowed "even the Browns" to win a pennant. The team had been so woeful since the late 1920s that many of the Browns' fans considered it a badge of honor — even a statement of machismo — to root for the hapless team. They took pride in the generally apt descriptor, "First in shoes, first in booze, and last in the American League." In reality, the Browns rebuilt into a decent team during this period, posting three winning seasons in the war years 1942-1945. They finished a distant third in the American League in 1942, but finally won the big one in 1944, capturing their only St. Louis pennant by edging the Detroit Tigers on the final day after trailing them through most of September.[35]

But the Browns survived that tough pennant race only to win the honor of serving as a sacrificial lamb for a truly outstanding Cardinal team. The Cards were so overwhelmingly favored in the World Series that it is doubtful that any serious people wagered against them. Cardinals shortstop Marty Marion, reflecting on the seemingly inevitable defeat of the Browns in the confrontation, opined, "If the Browns had beat us, that would have really been a disgrace."[36]

The 1944 version of the October classic represented the only World Series involving Missouri teams to take place in the same city. Common in New York, a streetcar series was unheard of elsewhere in the country. Only in 1906 when the Chicago Cubs and the Chicago White Sox played the World Series did another instance of a streetcar series take place. As such, this unusual occurrence captured the attention of the public. For Missourians, only the 1985 World Series between the cross-state Kansas City Royals and the St. Louis Cardinals equaled the 1944 contest for interest and drama.

The championship series indeed dripped with symmetry and irony. Both the Browns and the Cards shared Sportsman's Park in St. Louis, and the Browns were the owners with the Cardinals their tenants. Moreover, with the wartime shortage of housing, the two teams' managers, the Browns' Luke Sewell and the Cardinals' Billy Southworth, shared an apartment in the city during the year. This was convenient because when the Cards were in town, the Browns were on the road and vice versa. Finally, the Cardinals had long been considered the best of the National League. Its roster was filled with stars whose fingers were weighed down with championship rings. The Browns had long been the doormats of the American League. It was a World Series not to be missed. And the Browns, although ultimately proving anticlimactic for them as they lost to the Cardinals in six games, put on a good show.

Market Factors in St. Louis

Not until the 1960s did baseball executives begin to use terms like "small market" to describe their city. Even so, throughout the twentieth century "small market" has increasingly come to characterize St. Louis. In 1900 St. Louis was the fourth largest city in the United States, behind only New York, Chicago, and Philadelphia. Since then the city has experienced a gradual decline in population, and by definition also a gradual decline in market for its sports teams. In 1996 it ranked 47th in the United States.

POPULATION IN ST. LOUIS, 1900–1960

	1900	*1910*	*1920*	*1930*	*1940*	*1950*	*1960*
1	New York	NY	NY	NY	NY	NY	NY
2	Chicago	CHI	CHI	CHI	CHI	CHI	CHI
3	Philadelphia	PHI	PHI	PHI	PHI	PHI	LA
4	St. Louis	STL	DET	DET	DET	LA	PHI
5	Boston	BOS	CLE	LA	LA	DET	DET
6	Baltimore	CLE	STL	CLE	CLE	BAL	BAL

	1900	1910	1920	1930	1940	1950	1960
7	Pittsburgh	BAL	BOS	STL	BAL	CLE	HOU
8	Cleveland	PIT	BAL	BAL	STL	STL	CLE
9	Buffalo	DET	PIT	BOS	BOS	WAS	WAS
10	San Francisco	BUF	LA	PIT	PIT	BOS	STL

While Chicago retained its place in the forefront of the American cities, St. Louis declined so significantly that its cross-state rival, Kansas City, actually overtook it in population by the time of the 1990 census. Such non-major league cities as Nashville, Jacksonville, San Jose, and Columbus outranked it in population by 1980. A corresponding drop took place during the 1980s, to the extent that by 1990 St. Louis was ranked 35th, and the decline has not yet abated. By 1996 St. Louis fell to 47th compared to Kansas City's ranking of 33rd.

Compared to five other Midwestern cities — Cincinnati, Detroit, Indianapolis, Kansas City, and Milwaukee — St. Louis has also lost a great amount of ground as a major population center. Indianapolis, which has never been a major league baseball city, began ranking in the top 15 of U.S. cities by 1970 and by this measure should have received its own baseball franchise. From this chart, additionally, it looks as if both St. Louis and Cincinnati lost their capability to support major league franchises in the 1980s and that if decisions were made on that basis alone they should move elsewhere. Moreover, Milwaukee, which has always been considered a marginal major league city, should be able to support a franchise very well based on population statistics. Of course, these population statistics only speak to the city itself, and the St. Louis metropolitan area has a base that is large enough to sustain its activities, but nothing compared to what Chicago, New York, Los Angeles, and other major areas routinely demonstrate.

It seems that the Browns and the Cardinals were quite competitive through the middle 1920s insofar as their attendance was concerned. Neither team was stellar, but the Browns made a run at the pennant in 1922 and finished a close second. The Cardinals outdrew the Browns in home attendance — 25,784,213 to 15,377,027 — for the entire period that they shared the city of St. Louis between 1902 to 1953. For this 51-year period, the Cardinals averaged 505,573 per year to the Browns' 301,510 average per year. But until the Cardinals began to dominate the National League with their first World Championship in 1926, the two teams were essentially even in their ability to draw fans. The Browns actually outdrew the Cardinals — 8,353,058 to 7,073,290 — through the 1925 season, the Browns averaging 363,176 attendees to the Cardinals' 307,534 per year. For the

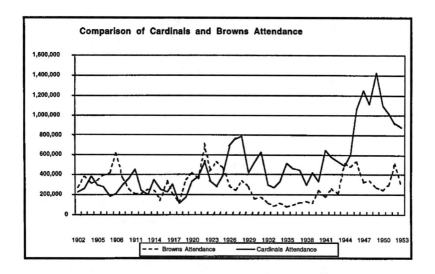

Comparison of Cardinals and Browns Attendance

period between 1926 and the last year the Browns played in St. Louis, 1953, the Cardinals averaged 692,989 spectators per year to the Browns' average draw of 260,147.

Of course, during the period 1926–1953, the Cardinals won nine pennants (with seven World Series championships), and that certainly made a difference. Also, the Cardinals finished second or third 12 additional times. The Cardinals were an exceptionally strong team that competed well every year. During the same period, the Browns won one pennant (1944) and finished second or third only three other times. In 1935, with a team that finished seventh in the league, thank goodness for the hapless Philadelphia Athletics, the Browns drew only 80,922 spectators.

Nothing points up the lack of paying customers that the Browns experienced better than a humorous story of Bill Veeck, who owned the Browns between 1951 and its move to Baltimore in 1953. When one of the Browns' faithful asked Veeck what time the game was that day, Veeck supposedly responded, "anytime you want, what time can you be there?" It was not quite that bad, but close. Using his now famous stunts, give-aways, and hucksterisms Veeck boosted Browns' attendance from 293,790 in 1951 to 518,796 in 1952. But it was a case of too little–too late, and for comparison the Cardinals drew over one million each of those years.[37]

There was a direct correlation between the attendance and the won/lost percentage for both teams. The better the team on the field, the greater the likelihood of drawing large spectators. Interestingly, in 1944, the year that the Cardinals and the Browns both won their league's pennants, the teams drew virtually the same numbers. But the Cardinals' attendance exploded in the postwar era while the Browns' turnstiles collapsed. Despite Veeck's efforts to boost Browns attendance, stunts such as the dwarf Eddie Gaedel batting and the desegregation of the Browns in 1951 while the Cardinals waited until the end of the 1950s, nothing seemed to work.

Conclusion

From these discussions, one can reach several reasonable conclusions about major league baseball in St. Louis. First, the Browns and the Cardinals shared a shrinking demographic throughout the first half of the twentieth century. Not only did the pie not expand as time passed, it actually got smaller. That meant that it was only a matter of time before one or the other of the two teams would have to depart the city. Because of demographic shifts since the 1960s one may legitimately speculate as to whether St. Louis remains a major league city as the twenty-first century dawns, since there are so many other larger population centers in the nation, many of them without major league representation.

Second, because of a stagnant population base, the two teams had to compete mightily for the limited dollars available for major league baseball in St. Louis. Competition took place on a broad front. Since baseball is essentially a part of the entertainment industry, delivering a good time to the spectators is critical to the success of a franchise. This can most effectively be accomplished through high quality play on the field. Without question the Cardinals ruled in this arena, at least after 1926, and they accordingly captured the majority of the baseball fans' loyalties in the city. In 1926, for instance, the Cardinals won the pennant and had an attendance of 506,000 for the season. The Browns' attendance was a woeful 81,000. To demonstrate this further, in 1935 the Browns averaged 1,051 per game. Until the Cardinals, buttressed by the brilliance of Branch Rickey's farm system, began to dominate the National League, the Browns competed very well for the baseball dollar in St. Louis.

Even without fielding a great team, attendance at games could be enhanced by offering other types of attractions. Bill Veeck was a master of this, as had been Chris Von der Ahe. Veeck's maxim that more people will pay to see a bad team play ball if other entertainment also takes place than will pay to see a poor team play ball is appropriate. And in 1952 he doubled Browns attendance by offering "bread and circuses" along with a woeful Browns game.

The Cardinals also froze the Browns out of the extended family of supporters in the Midwest and the South. Radio began to make an impact on the sport as early as 1920s, and the Cardinals were an early proponent of the new media's use to expand its market. The team found that its use of radio significantly expanded its fan base. Routinely broadcasting recreations of its games since the latter 1920s, in 1934 the Cardinals decided not to broadcast regular games that season. Despite an exciting pennant winning team, the Gashouse Gang led by Dizzy Dean, season attendance fell 283,000 below that of the last pennant winner, the 1931 team. Accordingly, the Cardinal front office believed it had to restore its regular season radio broadcasts.

By the time of the Cardinals dynasty of the 1940s the Cardinals boasted a regional network of 120 stations in nine states, anchored by the powerful KMOX station in St. Louis. From the Great Plains to the Deep South the St. Louis Cardinals became the team most of the heartland identified with, and they rewarded the franchise by making thousands of bus trips to St. Louis to see Cardinals games.[38] The voice of the Cardinals for most of those years was the irascible Harry Caray and millions tuned in every day to hear his stirring accounts of the boys in red. The Browns were late in adopting radio, and it never drew the listeners of the Cardinals.

One of the questions that must be asked about these two teams is if there is any evidence that certain groups followed one or the other of the teams? What was the ethnic, class, or other demographic loyalty for the St. Louis teams at various periods? From the very earliest time, both teams were largely Irish-American, and they were embraced by the large German/American constituency in the city. That close relationship remained throughout the Browns/Cardinals era. None of these teams, furthermore, gained much of a following from the African-American community, who reserved their loyalty for the Negro league teams.[39]

But there was more to this than ethnicity. The Cardinals became the embodiment of the American heartland in a way the Browns never did. They were hayseeds, just like most of the people who supported them. They represented rural America — simplicity, rusticity, small towns, Protestant beliefs, and hard-working commoners — and the fact that they won against the representatives of the big city, the New York Giants and Yankees, placed them in good stead with their fans.[40]

And their best players personified those perceived virtues. Dizzy Dean was a southern hick who beat the best anyone had to offer. Is it any wonder that once his playing days were over he could prosper as a broadcaster for the Cardinals cross-town rivals, selling homespun humor and hardcore American values? The greatest Cardinal, Stan Musial, demonstrated more than anyone those simple virtues. From the backhills of Pennsylvania's mining country, Musial strode across the National League as a giant for more than twenty years, but one who never forgot that hard work, good manners, and honorable actions brought him to greatness. His streak of 895 consecutive games played, which stood as a National League record until broken by Billy Williams of the Cubs in 1970, was one record that Musial especially prized for it demonstrated his commitment to the working class value of coming to work everyday.[41]

There is a Hollywood formula for any successful war movie, and from *The Sands of Iwo Jima* to *Saving Private Ryan* it has been played out in most of them. They all have as members of small combat units streetwise punks from Brooklyn or Newark and farmboys from the Midwest and southern country boys and city slickers from New York. The audiences identify with these characters depending on background and familiarity. Similar dichotomies are at play in major league baseball. While the Dodgers represented working class urbanites, and the Yankees reflected the glitter of the upper class in the big city, the Cardinals symbolized the Midwestern farming culture and the southern backcountry. To the extent that they were successful, and they were very successful during the second quarter of the twentieth century, the Cardinals served to heighten those regions' collective spirit.

Finally, the Cardinals were able to force the Browns out of St. Louis because of two horrendously bad decisions made by the Browns ownership. First, in 1917 Browns owner Philip C. Ball pushed Branch Rickey out of his organization. Rickey, who was on the way to building a winner and whose efforts bore fruit in the 1920s, went across town to the Cardinals. There he employed the same strategies that he had undertaken with the Browns and the result was Cardinal domination of the National League for the next generation. Had Ball left Rickey alone the Browns might have become the big winners in town.

Second, in 1920 the Cardinals wooden ballpark in St. Louis burned down. Branch Rickey persuaded Philip Ball to grant the Cardinals a long-term lease for the Browns state-of-the-art concrete and steel stadium, Sportsman's Park. Henceforth, the Cardinals shared the park with the Browns for longer than any other two teams, until 1953. Had the Browns owner said no, the Cardinals, who had no ready capital with which to build their own ballpark, would have been forced to seek a home elsewhere, perhaps somewhere other than in St. Louis. In an irony too great to ignore, the Browns owner sowed the seeds of his team's own demise in 1920, although it took decades for the team to reach its nadir.

In the end, St. Louis was not big enough for both teams, and perhaps it is no longer large enough for one. The Cardinals at present are seeking a new stadium and have vowed to achieve it either in St. Louis or elsewhere, perhaps even across the river in southern Illinois. Cardinals officials claim that a new stadium is critical to the team's balance sheet. The city's leaders, who saw the football Cardinals depart for Phoenix in the 1980s, are not about to allow the baseball team to fly to sunnier climes. But there is resistance among the small city population, and no resolution has been made as yet.

Notes

1. These include the Red Stockings (National Association, 1875); Brown Stockings (National Association, 1875, National League, 1876–1877); Maroons (Union Association, 1884, National League, 1885–1886); Cardinals (American Association, 1882–1891, National League 1892–present); Browns (American League, 1902–1953); Terriers (Federal League, 1914–1915); Giants (independent, 1910–1919, Negro National League, 1920–1921); Stars (Negro National League, 1922–1931, Negro American League, 1937, 1939, independent, 1940, Negro American League, 1941, Negro National League, 1943).

2. Cardinal Team histories abound. Among the recent best are, Bob Broeg, *Bob Broeg's Redbirds: A Century of Cardinals' Baseball* (Marceline, KS: Walsworth Pub. Co., 1992); Bob Broeg and Jerry Vickery, *St. Louis Cardinals Encyclopedia* (Chicago: NTC/Contemporary Publishing Group, 1998); Donald Honig, *The St. Louis Cardinals: An Illustrated History* (New York: Prentice Hall, 1991); Robert L. Tiemann, *Cardinal Classics* (St. Louis, MO: Baseball Histories, 1982).

3. Browns histories include, Bill Borst, *The Best of Seasons: The 1944 St. Louis Cardinals and St. Louis Browns* (Jefferson, NC: McFarland & Co., 1995); Bill Borst, *Still Last in the American League: The St. Louis Browns Revisited* (West Bloomfield, MI: Altwerger and Mandel Pub. Co., 1992); Roger A. Godin, *The 1922 St. Louis Browns: Best of the American League's Worst* (Jefferson, NC: McFarland & Co., 1991); William B. Mead, *Baseball Goes to War: Stars don Khaki, 4-Fs Vie for Pennant* (New York: Farragut Book Co., 1985, original title, *Even the Browns* [Chicago: Contemporary Books, 1978]); Carson Van Lindt, *One Championship Season: The Story of the 1944 St. Louis Browns* (New York: Marabou Publishing, 1994); Bill Veeck, with Ed Linn, *Veeck, as in Wreck* (New York: G.P. Putnam's Sons, 1962).

4. For a classic discussion of the rise of baseball in the nineteenth century see, Albert G. Spaulding, *America's National Game* (New York: American Sports Publishing Co., 1911, rep. ed., Lincoln: University of Nebraska Press, 1992). More recent interpretations may be found in Charles C. Alexander, *Our Game: An American Baseball History* (New York: Henry Holt, 1991); Warren Goldstein, *Playing for Keeps: A History of Early Baseball* (Ithaca, NY: Cornell University Press, 1989); Benjamin G. Rader, *Baseball: A History of America's Game* (Urbana: University of Illinois Press, 1992); Harold Seymour, *Baseball: The Early Years* (New York: Oxford University Press, 1960); David Quentin Voigt, *American Baseball*, Vol. 1 (Norman: University of Oklahoma Press, 1966).

5. Dean A. Sullivan, ed., *Early Innings: A Documentary History of Baseball, 1825–1908* (Lincoln: University of Nebraska Press, 1995), pp. 95–99.

6. Gregg Lee Carter, "Baseball in Saint Louis, 1867–1875: An Historical Case Study in Civic Pride," *Missouri Historical Society Bulletin* 31 (July 1975): 253–63;

Anthony B. Lampe, "The Background of Professional Baseball in St. Louis," *Missouri Historical Society Bulletin* 7 (October 1950): 6–34.

7. St. Louis *Republican*, May 7, 1875.

8. On this subject see, Dean A. Sullivan, "Faces in the Crowd: A Statistical Portrait of Baseball Spectators in Cincinnati, 1886–1888," *Journal of Space History* 17 (Winter 1990): 354–65; Stephen Freedman, "The Baseball Fad in Chicago, 1865–1870: An Exploration of the Role of Sport in the Nineteenth-Century City," *Journal of Space History* 5 (Summer 1978): 43–64; Anthony Oberschall, *Social Conflicts and Social Movements* (Englewood Cliffs, NJ: Prentice-Hall, 1973); William Gamson, *Power and Discontent* (Homewood, IL: Dorsey Press, 1968); S.N. Eisenstadt, ed., *Max Weber on Charisma and Institution Building: Selected Papers* (Chicago: University of Chicago Press, 1968), and Eric Hoffer, *The True Believer: Thoughts on the Nature of Mass Movements* (New York: Harper and Row, 1980).

9. Broeg, *Redbirds*, pp. 2–5; Koppett, *Koppett's Concise History of Major League Baseball*, pp. 37–66.

10. Chris Von der Ahe has received more than his share of historical treatment. In addition to discussions of his leadership in general histories of St. Louis baseball, specific studies of him include, Richard Egenriether, "Chris Von der Ahe: Baseball's Pioneering Huckster," *Baseball Research Journal* 18 (1989): 27–31; J. Thomas Hetrick, *Chris Von der Ahe and the St. Louis Browns* (Lanham, MD: Scarecrow Press, 1999); Jim Rygelski, "Baseball's 'Boss President': Chris Von der Ahe and the Nineteenth Century St. Louis Browns," *Gateway Heritage* 13 (Summer 1992): 42–53.

11. Peter Golenbock, *The Spirit of St. Louis: A History of the St. Louis Cardinals and Browns* (New York: Spike, 2000), pp. 12–19; David Nemec, *The Beer and Whisky League: The Illustrated History of the American Association — Baseball's Renegade Major League* (New York: Lyons and Burford, 1994), pp. 95–101.

12. Sullivan, ed., *Early Innings*, pp. 119–21.

13. Robert L. Tiemann, *Through the Years at Sportsman's Park*, commemorative booklet for April 27, 1991, dedication of plaque noting Herbert Hoover Club as site of Sportsman's Park, Missouri Historical Society, St. Louis; Dan Dickinson and Kieran Dickinson, *Major League Stadiums* (Jefferson, NC: McFarland, 1991), pp. 231–37.

14. Sullivan, ed., *Early Innings*, p. 139–40; Larry G. Bowman, "Christian Von der Ahe, the St. Louis Browns, and the World's Championship Playoffs, 1885–1888," *Missouri Historical Review* 91 (July 1997): 385–405; Jerry Lansche, *The Forgotten Championships: Postseason Baseball, 1882–1981* (Jefferson, NC: McFarland, 1989), pp. 9–20.

15. *Sporting News*, May 11, 1895, August 31, 1895, November 30, 1895, January 28, 1899, June 12, 1918.

16. On this team see, J. Thomas Hetrick, *MISFITS! The Cleveland Spiders in 1899* (Jefferson, NC: McFarland, 1991).

17. Koppett, *Koppett's Concise History of Major League Baseball*, pp. 77–78, 82–84; Glenn Porter, *The Rise of Big Business, 1860–1910* (Arlington Heights, IL: AHM Publishing Corp., 1973), pp. 42–71.

18. Sullivan, ed., *Early Innings*, 243–62; Eugene C. Murdock, *Ban Johnson: Czar of Baseball* (Westport, CT: Greenwood Press, 1982), pp. 43–55.

19. Interview with Bill Borst, March 30, 2000. On this subject see, Elliot Aronson and Judson Mills, "The Effect of Severity of Initiation on Liking for a Group," *Journal of Abnormal and Social Psychology* 59 (September 1959): 177–81; Harold B. Gerard and Grover C. Mathewson, "The Effects of Severity of Initiation on Liking for a Group: A Replication," *Journal of Experimental Social Psychology* 2 (1966): 278–87; Jacob E. Hautaluoma and Helene Spungin, "Effects of Initiation Severity and Interest on Group Attitudes," *Journal of Social Psychology* 93 (1974): 245–59.

20. Thorn and Palmer, with Gershman, *Total Baseball,* pp. 2068–69.

21. On Branch Rickey see, Gerald Holland, "Mr. Rickey and the Game," *Sports Illustrated* 38 (March 1955): 59–65; David Lipman, *Mr. Baseball: The Story of Branch Rickey* (New York: G.P. Putnam's Sons, 1966); Arthur Mann, *Branch Rickey: American in Action* (Boston: Houghton Mifflin, 1957); John J. Monteleone, ed., *Branch Rickey's Little Blue Book: Wit and Strategy from Baseball's Last Wise Man* (New York: Macmillan, 1995); Murray Polner, *Branch Rickey: A Biography* (New York: Antheneum, 1982).

22. White, *Creating the National Pastime,* pp. 285–92; Fred Leib, *The St. Louis Cardinals: The Story of a Great Baseball Team* (New York: G.P. Putnam's Sons, 1944), pp. 59–92; J. G. Taylor Spink, *Judge Landis and Twenty-Five Years of Baseball* (New York: Thomas Y. Crowell, 1947), pp. 226–40; Harold Seymour, *Baseball: The Golden Age* (New York: Oxford University Press, 1970), pp. 410–20; Donald Ray Anderson, "Branch Rickey and the St. Louis Cardinals System: The Growth of an Idea," Ph.D. diss., University of Wisconsin, 1975.

23. Borst, *Still Last in the American League,* pp. 31–40.

24. Roger A. Godin, *The 1922 St. Louis Browns: Best of the American League's Worst* (Jefferson, NC: McFarland, 1991).

25. Warner Fusselle, "Foreword," in David Craft and Tom Owens, *Redbirds Revisited: Great Memories and Stories from St. Louis Cardinals* (Chicago, IL: Bonus Books, 1990), pp. xi–xviii.

26. Koppett, *Koppett's Concise History of Major League Baseball,* pp. 175–77, 192, 205–206.

27. Stan Musial, *Stan Musial: The Man's Own Story,* as told to Bob Broeg (Garden City, NY: Doubleday and Co., 1964); Jerry Lansch, *Stan the Man Musial* (Dallas, TX: Taylor Pub. Co., 1994).

28. Charles C. Alexander, *Rogers Hornsby* (New York: Henry Holt, 1995).

29. Fred Lieb, *Baseball as I Have Known It* (New York: Coward, McCann, and Geohegan, 1977), pp. 185–90; Donald Honig, ed., *The October Heroes: Great World Series Games Remembered by the Men who Played Them* (New York: Simon and Schuster, 1979), pp. 98–102.

30. Broeg, *Redbirds,* pp. 14–43.

31. Golenbeck, *Spirit of St. Louis,* pp. 138–66.

32. David M. Jordan, *The Athletics of Philadelphia: Connie Mack's White Elephants, 1901–1954* (Jefferson, NC: McFarland, 1999), pp. 108–15; William C. Kashatus, *Connie Mack's '29 Triumph: The Rise and Fall of the Philadelphia Athletics Dynasty* (Jefferson, NC: McFarland, 1999), pp. 140–45, 152–57.

33. Bob Hood, *The Gashouse Gang* (New York: William Morrow and Co., 1975); J. Roy Stockton, *The Gashouse Gang and a Couple of Other Guys* (New York: A.S. Barnes, 1945).

34. James N. Giglio, "Prelude to Greatness: Stanley Musial and the Springfield Cardinals of 1941," *Missouri Historical Review* 90 (July 1996): 429–52; Anderson, "Branch Rickey and the St. Louis Cardinals System," p. 169; Robert W. Creamer, *Baseball in '41: A Celebration of the Best Baseball Seasons Ever — In the Year America Went to War* (New York: Viking, 1991); Broeg, *Redbirds,* pp. 64–78; Mead, *Baseball Goes to War,* pp. 41–50, 102–108, 120–24, 180–87, 222–23; J. Ronald Oakley, *Baseball's Last Golden Age, 1946–1960* (Jefferson, NC: McFarland, 1994), pp. 44–47; Richard Goldstein, *Spartan Seasons: How Baseball Survived the Second World War* (New York: Macmillan, 1980).

35. Mead, *Baseball Goes to War.*

36. Bill Borst, *The Best of Seasons: The 1944 St. Louis Cardinals and St. Louis Browns* (Jefferson, NC: McFarland & Co., 1995); Carson Van Lindt, *One Championship Season: The Story of the 1944 St. Louis Browns* (New York: Marabou Publishing, 1994).

37. Interview with Bill Borst, March 31, 2000, St. Louis, MO. Statistics compiled from Thorn and Palmer, with Gershman, *Total Baseball.*

38. Benjamin G. Rader, *Baseball: A History of America's Game* (Urbana: University of Illinois Press, 1992), p. 137.

39. Ibid., p. 214; Alexander, *Our Game,* p. 40.

40. This is a very difficult contention to prove, and I have no wish to overstate my case, but such sociological studies as Louis Wirth, "The Limits of Regionalism," in Merrill Jensen, ed., *Regionalism in America* (Madison: University of Wisconsin Press, 1951), pp. 381–393, support these contentions and in certain ways go much farther.

41. Thorn and Palmer, eds., *Total Baseball,* pp. 203–204; Musial, *Stan Musial.*

Baseball During World War II: An Exploration of the Issue

Gerald Bazer and Steven Culbertson

Overview

That major league baseball continued to be played during World War II is a well-known fact. Known also is the effect the War had on the quality of major league play. (After all, the St. Louis Browns — not the mighty Yankees — won the American League pennant in 1944.) This paper explores issues beyond the obvious disruptions in competitive balance.

This paper's purpose is to discuss the circumstances regarding the decision to continue baseball at all organized levels during World War II and the effects of doing so.

Scope

In accomplishing this paper's purpose, the following major themes and subtopics are included in this investigation:

• What factors (immediate and distant) motivated Franklin Delano Roosevelt's famous "green light letter" to Commissioner Kenesaw Mountain Landis? (What elements in FDR's background would lead an observer almost sixty years later to suggest that his decision could be viewed as a foregone conclusion?)

• How did a number of constituencies view the continuation of baseball, not only at the major league level, but also at the minor league and servicemen's games level? These groups include the following:

- Fans, the press, and prominent Americans, including elected officials
- Major league players who enlisted or were drafted
- Members of the armed forces in combat divisions
- Baseball officials
- America's allies
- What shared sacrifices would baseball and American society experience?

Sources and Methods

The authors of this paper have reviewed a considerable number of primary and secondary sources through material drawn from baseball books, newspapers and periodicals of the period, and the Internet. The notes provide information on each source. In drawing conclusions and citing statistics, more than one source, whenever possible, has been used for corroboration.

The Role of President Franklin Delano Roosevelt

I honestly feel that it would be best for the country to keep baseball going.
— Franklin Delano Roosevelt, January 15, 1942[1]

In the famous "green light letter," a one-page letter dated January 15, 1942, President Franklin Delano Roosevelt informed baseball Commissioner Kenesaw Mountain Landis, "I honestly feel that it would be best for the country to keep baseball going." [2] Roosevelt's reply was to an entreaty the previous day from Landis to Roosevelt.[3]

Thereby, major league baseball would continue to be played during the World War II years, 1942 through 1945. The authors of this paper contend, as stated above, that Roosevelt's decision could be viewed as a foregone conclusion. This can be seen through statements in the letter itself and through an examination of specific aspects of Roosevelt's background.

In the letter Roosevelt states the "recreational asset" of "5,000 or 6,000 players" to at least "20,000,000 of their fellow citizens." He states further that "Americans ought to have a chance for recreation and for taking their minds off their work even more than before." The letter further states that "night games be extended because it gives an opportunity to the day shift to see a game."[4]

The conclusion can be drawn from Roosevelt's words that the morale of the American people would be enhanced by continuing baseball as a recreational outlet. This was in keeping with Roosevelt's continual efforts throughout the War to keep morale high. Frequently, in speeches and in fireside chats, Roosevelt stressed the importance of morale, even during the darkest days of the War. His own physical stance, head held high, chin always upward, reflected his strong optimism that the American people and their allies would prevail. It was vital to Roosevelt that, despite the devastating War, "certain aspects of American life" would continue.[5]

Beyond morale, FDR, as a baseball fan, wished baseball to continue. To this day he holds the presidential record of having thrown out the first ball nine times — the first time in 1917 as Assistant Secretary of the Navy when President Woodrow Wilson, preoccupied with World War I, dispatched Roosevelt to the ballpark.[6]

Frequently, Roosevelt spoke of his affinity for the game or used baseball allusions to make a particular point. Among his comments were:

> If I didn't have to hobble up those steps in front of all those people, I'd be out at the ballpark every day.[7]

> I'm the kind of fan who wants to get plenty of action for my money. I get the biggest kick out of the biggest score — a game in which the hitters pole the ball into the far corners of the field, the outfielders scramble and men run the bases.[8]

> I have no expectation of making a hit every time I come to bat. What I seek is the highest possible batting average, not only for myself, but for my team.[9]

> You know how I really feel? I feel like a baseball team going into the ninth inning with only eight men left to play.[10]

We can trace Roosevelt's early involvement with baseball to his youth and years at Groton. There his enthusiasm appears to have exceeded his talent. In his second year he wrote his parents, "I have been playing baseball all day, and I am on a new team which is called the BBBB or Bum Base Ball Boys. It has no captain, but it is a republic and is made up of about the worst players."[11]

After his first game he wrote home: "The only ball I received, I nobly missed and it landed biff! on my stomach to the great annoyance of that intricate organ and to the great delight of all present."[12] More likely Roosevelt better served Groton baseball through four years as the varsity's manager, for which he earned a ribbon.[13]

After Groton and graduation from Harvard, it is reported by Geoffrey Ward and Ken Burns that Roosevelt as a young attorney almost lost his job by attending a weekly game at the Polo Grounds. They go on to state that, as President, Roosevelt "scanned the sports pages of at least half a dozen newspapers every morning."[14] Ward and Burns quote Roosevelt, after throwing out the first pitch for the 1941 season, that it was his "ninth year in the majors."[15]

That Franklin Roosevelt loved baseball can also be emphasized by how his love for the game actually ran contrary to the interests of the one person to whom FDR looked up to perhaps more than anyone — his cousin, President Theodore Roosevelt. It would be TR's career that FDR would echo as Assistant Secretary of the Navy, Governor of New York, and President of the United States.

However, as Teddy's irrepressible daughter, Alice Roosevelt Longworth, would state, "Father and all of us regarded baseball as a moddy-coddle game. Tennis, football, lacrosse, boxing, polo, yes; they are violent which appealed to us. Father wouldn't watch it [baseball], not even at Harvard."[16]

Thus, in 1942 baseball had a true fan in the White House. "It would help win the War," Roosevelt stated.[17] Roosevelt would state that about no other sport.[18]

The Views of Constituencies: The Fans, the Press, Prominent Americans

MAJOR LEAGUES

The decision to allow baseball to continue while twenty million American men and women served in the military or defense plants was bound to result in a host of views, some critical of the decision. What greatly helped to assuage criticisms was Roosevelt's view expressed in the "green light letter": "As to the players themselves I know you agree with me that individual players who are of active military or naval ages should go, without question, into the services. Even if the actual quality of the teams is lowered by the greater use of older players, this will not dampen the popularity of the sport."[19]

As will be seen below through a diversity of references, fans, the press, and prominent Americans did support major league baseball's continuation with Roosevelt's proviso.[20] It should not be overlooked, though, that there were continual criticisms, particularly as the War dragged on into 1945. These centered almost exclusively on players declared 4-F by their local draft boards yet possessed of good enough physical condition to play major league

Baseball, or on the chance that baseball might be declared an essential industry. Below we include some of this criticism and baseball's response.

As to support for continuation, we begin with Daniel Okrent's and Steve Wulf's *Baseball Anecdotes* in which they wrote, "Roosevelt's decision was widely supported; polls showed that substantial majorities believed that the war effort would be helped by the game's continuation."[21] The authors go on to quote prominent journalist, Quentin Reynolds, "Hitler has killed a great many things in the past few years. Do not let him kill baseball."[22]

Prominent Americans, including Congressmen and Senators, would agree with the fans. Wisconsin Congressman LaVern Dilweg stated, "What does baseball do for America? It provides an opportunity for thousands of war workers to relax in the fresh air and sunshine — and continue to enjoy something that has been a significant part of American life for almost 100 years."[23] Dilweg would go on to emphasize how important baseball was to those in combat who "hungrily await news of sports."[24]

Dilweg was joined in support by such legislators as James Wadsworth of New York, Samuel Weiss of Pennsylvania, Melvin Price of Illinois, Scott Lucas of Illinois, Millard Tydings of Maryland, and many others. Tydings spoke of how "we are all under tension we cannot appreciate and we must give our minds the occasional rest."[25] In the *Congressional Record*, Senator Lucas paid tribute to the role baseball had played for one of his constituents fighting in Sicily in 1943. The soldier's letter spoke with pleasure of the World Series broadcast which he and his buddies had heard via shortwave transmission.[26] Two years later, Representative Melvin Price offered yet another ringing endorsement of baseball:

> There has been much discussion in recent weeks concerning the duration future [sic] of the major sports, and in particular baseball. In my opinion baseball plays an important part in the war effort. It not only lifts morale on the home front, providing relaxation for workers in our war industries, but it lifts morale of our men in the armed forces in all parts of the world.[27]

Roosevelt's postmaster general, James Farley, spoke of the danger of curtailing baseball, "Interference with our sports might really retard our winning the War. This is no time for hysterics, for panicking our people to rule out our sports and our pastimes, which the great majority of Americans really and truly want."[28] FBI Director J. Edgar Hoover also stressed that baseball should continue.[29] Lieutenant General Brehon Somervell, Chief of the Service of Supply, issued an eloquent tribute to baseball in a 1944 address to the New York Chapter of the Baseball Writers Association:

I want to tell you how important a factor baseball is in the winning of the War. It has been said that the successes of the British army can be traced to the cricket fields of Eton, and I say the sandlots and big-league ballparks of America have contributed their share to our military success. Nearly seventy per cent of all major league players at the time of Pearl Harbor are wearing the uniform today and giving a splendid account of themselves.[30]

The Sporting News, picking up Roosevelt's emphasis on morale, intoned, "Both citizen and military morale must be maintained by all possible means and sports represents one of the most effective of all morale-building agencies."[31] The Chicago Sun called the "green light letter" "the most notable contribution to baseball in our time."[32]

Gallup polls in 1942 and 1943 asked the question: Should sports be continued or should we wait till after the War? The public responded 66 percent to 24 percent and 59 percent to 28 percent respectively to maintain sports.[33]

Attendance figures from the war years also help in concluding that the public wished baseball to continue.[34] In the last year of the War, 1945, total attendance reached 10, 951, 502, a major league record at the time and over 2,000,000 greater than in 1942.

Despite a lopsided 1944 National League pennant race, 178,000 more fans attended in 1944 than in 1943.[35] World Series figures also grew. While 236,000 saw the 1941 Series, 333,000 saw the 1945 Series.[36]

An additional indication of fan support was letters sent to sports departments of daily newspapers. A review of such letters in The New York Times for 1942, for example, reveals almost all letters in support, although it should be noted that letters were actually few. One could argue that if there had been an outcry against continuing baseball, it would have been reflected by numerous negative letters.[37]

In addition to the letters from the everyday fan, The New York Times was an outlet for letters from members of Congress. Several Senators and Representatives had letters published in 1942, including one from the House Minority Leader, Joseph Martin, who urged that a "full baseball program" be continued for the country's morale.[38]

Perhaps the best summary of this positive attitude is the advertisement in The Sporting News of July 29, 1943, featuring a perplexed war worker saying, "I gotta relax," as he considers attending a game. The war worker says, "All work and no play. If I could only … No … I couldn't do that. Time off now would just about wreck the new idea we're working on…." The ad replies: "Why don't you take in a ball game? Get out in the sun and let your skin soak up some Vitamin D. The ring of base hits will be music to your ears, balm to your mental muscles … Brother, Uncle Sam wants you to relax. And baseball lets you do it — completely — without losing one hour from your job."[39]

To be certain, as mentioned above, there were also criticisms of baseball's continuance as America's involvement in the War went into its third and fourth years. Much of this focused on players declared 4-F, or the possibility, quickly dispelled, that players would be declared to be in an essential industry thereby freed from the draft. Criticism occurred despite the fact that over 500 major leaguers, including some of the biggest stars (e.g., Ted Williams, Stan Musial, Hank Greenberg, Bob Feller, Joe DiMaggio) and 4000 minor leaguers, saw military action.

Exemplifying the criticism may be the May 18, 1942, *New York Times* letter from MBE of Flushing, Long Island, who complained about draft boards for changing Class 1-A players to a lower status: "Don't they [baseball officials and draft boards] realize that our country is at war for the preservation of our rights and freedom and that we need all the man power available both for active and non-combat service?"[40]

Baseball's response throughout the War, with minor exceptions, was to emphasize that no special favors were being requested. Early on, National League President Ford Frick stated, "Baseball is ready, yes eager to do its duty in national defense. We are not going to Washington with any appeal or even a request for information as to what the authorities intend to do about the players."[41] Later Frank Lane, White Sox general manager, stated, "We do not want to be exempt from the liabilities of common life in America."[42]

When Commissioner of Manpower Paul McNutt indicated that the "usefulness of sport is a separate question from the essentiality of individuals who play it,"[43] Branch Rickey replied that if players can do a better job than baseball "then we want to know the way they do it and we are anxious to do it."[44]

Director of War Mobilization and Reconstruction Jimmy Byrnes said, "It is difficult for the public to understand, and certainly it is difficult for me to understand how these men can be physically unfit for military service and yet be able to compete with the greater athletes of the nation in games demanding physical fitness."[45] However, a response was that the 4-F players were able to play only because of the extensive training room support that would not be available in the military.[46] Emphasized too was that players were found 4-F after all by army or navy doctors.[47] In fact, close to fifty 4-Fs were drafted late in the War only to see the need decrease as the War waned. Baseball also indicated that some 4-Fs were serving in defense industries. Additionally, Cardinals Manager Billy Southworth urged players to take War jobs during the winter.[48]

Baseball emphasized that who was drafted was a very local matter, centered on the local draft board, and as a result the available pool in a given locality would determine who might or might not be drafted, regardless of classification. As the War progressed, and needs grew, draft boards changed who might be draft-eligible based on tightening deferments regarding age, marital status, care of dependents, etc.

In his news conference of March 13, 1945, Roosevelt reiterated his stand that baseball would continue as long as "perfectly healthy people" were not being used in baseball instead of where they could be more useful in the War.[49] At the same time a National Service Act was proposed that all 4-Fs would be ordered to work in war plants. Also proposed was a federal review of local draft boards that had deferred players. Both proposals died prior to implementation.

Coming to the defense of the players and as they entered the service in growing numbers was J. Edgar Hoover who declared, "If any ballplayer or other athletes were attempting to dodge service, it would be our job to look into such cases. But our records show there are few, if any, such cases among the thousands of ballplayers."[50]

Appraising the positive and negative views of major league baseball's continuing, it is clear that the former by far surpassed the latter.

As our concentration to this point has been on the major leagues, we now turn to a briefer look at how our same constituencies viewed the continuance at other levels of ball.

MINOR LEAGUES

Clearly, minor league baseball suffered during the war years. This occurred, not because of the public's lack of support, but rather through several thousand ballplayers either enlisting or being drafted. The minor leaguers, younger and with fewer if any dependents, were more vulnerable to the draft than the major leaguers.

Statistics graphically illustrate how the War affected the minors, which had witnessed growing attendance in the 1930s. In 1940 there were forty-four leagues with 310 clubs averaging 48,700 fans. Total fans in 1940 numbered 15,100,000.[51]

By 1943 there were nine leagues with sixty-six clubs, with season attendance averaging 87,900 fans per club. Total fans in 1943 dropped to 5,800,000. With the War's end, 1945 saw a comeback with nineteen leagues, eighty-five clubs, an average club attendance of 125,400, and a total of 10,656,000 fans. (Two years later total attendance would jump to 40,505,210.)[52]

With leagues folding due to the War, Texas League President J. Alvin Gardner (whose own league had shut down) charged that only the protection of their investment motivated those who continued.[53]

A more optimistic view was expressed by American Association head, Colonel George Trautman, who projected that in 1943 that four clubs would make money; seven had a good chance; and only one club, already out of the race, could still make money by the sale of two or three of its players.[54]

One fan writing to the *New York Times* recommended an All-Star game between major and minor league players with the gate going for "deserving organizations." The editorial note following the letter stated, "The score for the major league side might be larger than the gate receipts."[55] This specific negative effect may be illustrative of the overall negative impact of the War on the minors.

Servicemen's Games

Ample evidence exists that all relevant constituencies supported servicemen's games and the formation of servicemen's leagues. And these games and leagues thrived throughout the war theatres.[56] Negative comments were reserved for major leaguers, especially the stars, now in service, who either states-side or overseas, played, coached, or managed rather than seeing combat.[57] Nonetheless, many saw the players' efforts as bolstering morale even when top service teams had past or future major leaguers at every position.[58]

Perhaps the best way to illustrate support is through the contribution that fans and major league teams made so that servicemen could play ball. On July 7, 1942, 62,094 fans paid close to $150,000 to attend a game in Cleveland between the American League All-Stars and a Service All-Stars team. One hundred thousand dollars of the total went to the Bat and Ball Fund (sports equipment for the military) with the rest going to Navy Relief. Fans had paid $2 per ticket, double the normal amount. One reporter said, "Finding 62,094 fans to buy them [tickets] says a lot about Cleveland, patriots, and Indians fans."[59]

Other examples include the $53,000 raised from the (pre-War) 1941 All-Star Game donated to the United Service Organization (USO). Additionally, foul balls into the stands at any game were routinely thrown back to be shipped to military camps. An extra $25,000 was authorized for equipment for Army and Navy sports programs coming from the 1942 All-Star Game.

Early on, team owners, not knowing whether baseball would be allowed to continue, pledged $125,000 for servicemen's sports equipment.

Equipment manufacturers joined the owners in helping by cutting the prices of their equipment.[60]

Beyond the above, by the time the War had ended, Major League Baseball had contributed $328,000 worth of athletic equipment from receipts of sixteen War relief All-Star games, each team hosting one game.

Women's League

While women had been playing baseball since the late 1800s, it was World War II that was the stimulant to the first and only women's major league, the All-American Girls Baseball League, formed in 1943. Several baseball owners, including Philip Wrigley, saw women's baseball as an attraction, given the diminished quality of wartime play in the major leagues.[61]

The All-American Girls Baseball League, with ten teams and 600 players, was only active in the Midwest with teams in Illinois, Indiana, Wisconsin, and Michigan. By 1954 the league had folded.

A small handful of women (e.g., Babe Didrikson) had played exhibitions against minor league and major league men. However, any thought that women might replace the major or minor leaguers in the service was quickly dispelled by Landis. Life in baseball is "too strenuous" for a woman.[62] As the men returned, women ballplayers, similar to women working in factories, were expected to return to their "wifely duties" at home.[63] A *Sporting News* July 2, 1952, headline said it all, "Women's Place is in Grandstand."[64]

Negro Leagues

World War II would not witness the emergence of Negro ballplayers in either the majors or minors — this despite the short supply of players, the recruitment of Cuban ballplayers, the quality and visibility of Negro league players, and the high levels of fan support for black baseball. Additionally, white and black ballplayers were playing against each other on military teams.

Baseball, like most of society, remained segregated. As segregation reigned in the military units, so did it reign with segregated military baseball teams. Two years before Jackie Robinson broke the color barrier, he was barred from playing for the all-white team at Fort Riley, Kansas.

The decision not to integrate baseball withstood even the success (financial as well as competitive) in exhibitions that black ballplayers had had against white teams. (For example, a May 24, 1942, game between the Kansas City Monarchs and a servicemen's team drew 29,775. By contrast, when the Tigers played the White Sox on the same day, only 19,198 fans turned out to Comiskey Park.)[65] And while some newspapers, especially the *Pittsburgh Courier-Journal*, launched major efforts toward integration, no change from the status quo would occur during the War. Arguments that blacks fighting in the War deserved the chance in Major League Baseball were not always convincing. According to one poll, six out of the ten white Americans "felt that Black Americans were satisfied with the way things were and received all the opportunities they deserved."[66] By 1943, *Newsweek* would observe, "Baseball's most interesting game this season has yet to see the combed grass of an infield. The opponents are baseball vs. racial discrimination."[67]

Disappointingly, these efforts at integration neither received assistance from President Roosevelt nor the baseball owners.[68] Roosevelt's Administration did little publicly to advocate racial reform during the War, not only in baseball, but for other aspects of society. Clark Griffith of the Senators was making money by renting his ballpark to a Negro team but, at the same time, was adamant against integrating baseball.[69] Nor could black athletes look to the Commissioner's office. Landis, who died in 1944, never used his office to argue with the owners for integrated teams.[70]

It would be the next Commissioner, Senator Happy Chandler, not Landis, who would oversee the integration of baseball. As he declared, "If they can fight and die on Okinawa, Guadalcanal, in the South Pacific, they can play baseball in America."[71]

Thus, while the Negro leagues were supported by our constituencies, the War would not see sufficient support for integrating baseball.

We now turn to exploring how our other constituencies — major league players who enlisted or were drafted, members of the Armed Forces in combat divisions, baseball officials, and America's Allies — reacted to baseball's continuation.

Major League Players, Enlistees or Draftees

While major league players were rightly concerned about what the War would do to their own careers, there is scant evidence that the players wished baseball to cease while the War continued. For most who served in the military, their duty time would come after a year or two of America's entering the War, thus allowing them more time in baseball.

There is more evidence that the players were concerned about their return to major league play upon military discharge. While they knew that the quality of play was weak during the war years, they still faced the understandable worry whether they would be able to once again compete. There also was the worry that they might have lost their prime years.[72] Bob Feller, however, stated, "Almost all of us were able to pick up our careers at our prewar levels of performance."[73]

Players along with our other constituencies felt that stopping baseball was giving in to the enemy. Continuing baseball would display that American society could continue despite the War, boost morale on the homefront and on the warfront, and be a factor in the eventual Allied victory.

Members of the Armed Forces in Combat Divisions

There are a variety of indicators that members of our Armed Forces wished baseball to continue. One of the most persuasive endorsements came in a 1943 survey conducted by the Athletic Round Table of Spokane, Washington. It found that ninety-three percent of 95,000 soldiers as well as ninety-nine percent of sailors surveyed supported baseball's continuation.[74]

That baseball was important to our servicemen can best be shown by the fact that when the Japanese found out how important baseball was, Japanese signal units tried to jam Armed Forces Radio Service broadcasts from home.

Further indicators include the equipment to the military teams made available from the receipts of specific baseball games; the use by the soldiers of baseball lingo and baseball facts when confronting suspected enemy infiltrators attempting to pass themselves off as Allies; the reminder of home that baseball served similar to the role played by touring USO celebrities[75]; the plethora of servicemen's teams across all theatres of war; the subscriptions available to *Baseball Digest* through contributions from fans at home who bought two subscriptions at reduced prices if one went to a serviceman[76]; and one bomber christened *Ott's Big Bat* and another *Winning Run*.[77]

Also indicative are the great interest in scores reported in *Stars and Stripes* and over the British Broadcasting Corporation (BBC)[78]; the picture from the *Guadalcanal Gazette* showing marines in the Solomon Islands studying their position on the map while also studying the baseball scores[79]; and the comment from a soldier wounded in 1944, "We're fighting for a lot of things in this war, and baseball is one of them."[80]

Beyond the above there was the request recalled by Landis from five soldiers that as soon as they got home, their main wish was for tickets to the next World Series[81]; and poignantly the question first asked of the Red Cross representative arranging prisoner exchanges, "Who won the World Series?"[82] And equally poignant, Joe Cronin on a Red Cross trip to Hawaii hearing a wounded soldier who could not sit up or hardly move, yell out, "Keep 'em playing."[83]

The importance of baseball can also be shown by the appearance of key military leaders at games, including General Dwight Eisenhower; pictures in the press of army and navy officers playing ball; and influential statements by officers on the value of baseball. One such statement was made by Admiral Ernest King, "Baseball has a rightful place in America at war. All work and no play seven days a week will soon take its toll on national morale."[84]

Baseball Officials

Not surprisingly, baseball officials were eager for ball to continue. It was, after all, major league baseball that had prompted FDR's letter. Throughout the War, officials through their comments, their fund-raising efforts for the troops, their statements that players should serve, their shared sacrifice with American society in general (see below), their honoring Medal of Honor winners at games and allowing servicemen in for free, their ordering the playing of the National Anthem prior to each game,[85] and in many other ways provided the view that baseball should continue.

A host of officials influenced both public and political perceptions of baseball: Commissioner Kenesaw Mountain Landis, National League President Ford Frick, Senators owner Clark Griffith, Reds General Manager Larry MacPhail, Yankees President Ed Barrow, Dodgers owner Branch Rickey, Commissioner Happy Chandler, and American League President Will Harridge.

America's Allies

This paper's authors cannot provide much positive evidence of support of America's Allies for baseball's continuance, neither is there any evidence to the contrary. The implication can be drawn that with the Allies so dependent on Americans, there would be no gain from disparaging a decision made by the President of the United States. Also, with so much to worry about, baseball's continuation would hardly top the list.

What is known is that the Canadians continued to play league hockey, the government quoted as saying, "In the interest of public morale the league should continue."[86] We also know of the attempt by a British crowd at London's Wembley Stadium to understand a service game between Americans and Canadians reported in the *New York Times*. One attendee was Mrs. Winston Churchill.[87] Bennett Cerf's *Saturday Review* column reported that "Sir Anthony Eden's gracious words of tribute add an unexpected dash of éclat to the Dodgers."[88] Already mentioned above was the BBC's decision to provide nightly five-minute summaries of that day's games.

We might rightly conclude that anything that would keep American spirits up would be favored by the Allies.

We turn now to this paper's concluding section: what shared sacrifices did baseball and American society as a whole experience?

That sacrifices by society were essential to winning World War II is well established. Below we provide examples of how baseball, too, made sacrifices. We recognize that some of these sacrifices were no doubt to stay in the public's good graces to keep the game going. However, many were made for the best of reasons — to help win the War.

Shared Sacrifices

There is no better place to begin than acknowledging again that among the twenty million Americans in the military or in defense plants were approximately 5,000 professional ballplayers. Like others in society these ballplayers would give up prime time from their careers; some, owing to the War, could never return to their careers.

Shared also was the rationing of key materials as part of the federal program to make essentials available for the military. Included were products like rubber and gasoline. The former would force baseball in 1943 to abandon rubber in its baseballs, switching to balata, a South American gum of the rubber family. The balata was reclaimed from golf ball covers (no military use). Unfortunately, the ball created a brief dead-ball era with batting statistics nose-diving.[89] Shortly thereafter, A.G. Spalding and Brothers, manufacturers of the balata ball, provided a livelier ball.[90]

The rationing of gasoline and wartime travel restrictions affected baseball in several ways: teams held spring training and exhibitions in northern cities despite less than ideal playing conditions[91]; players made do with shortages of cabs, hotels, meals on route, and no special train cars.[92] For the first time and only time in baseball history, an All-Star Game was canceled (1945) due to War-related transportation restrictions. This led to a series of individual games arranged between teams in the same city or nearby. Owing to travel problems no games were held involving Pittsburgh and Detroit.

Further, Will Harridge announced that each American League team would make three rather than four long trips, saving 40,000 miles of fuel. In the National League, Ford Frick followed Harridge's lead.[93]

As for individual players, the Office of Price Administration (OPA) declared that players were not essential users of gas and thereby would not receive a larger ration. However, club-owned buses would be eligible if they carried ten or more men.[94]

Shared sacrifices also centered on steel, aluminum, and copper, leading baseball fans to contribute used materials to scrap drives sponsored by individual clubs.[95] A September 1942 game between the Red Sox and Yankees witnessed more than 3,000 youngsters contributing nearly fifteen tons of scrap metal as their price of admission.[96] A Dodgers benefit game resulted in a huge pile of scrap outside the ball park when free admission was the reward.[97]

World War II also brought blackouts to America wherein all lights were shut off so as not to be used for potential air attacks by enemy planes.[98] Thus, President Roosevelt's desire that more night games be scheduled so that workers could attend led to such occurrences as mid-game blackouts.[99] At one game in Philadelphia's Shibe Park, the announcer spotting the glowing tips of several cigars and cigarettes announced, "You gentlemen who are lighting up cigars and cigarettes, if you are American, you won't do it."[100]

At a minor league game in Florida a pre-arranged blackout occurred in mid-pitch. John Kiernan in the *New York Times* wrote, "The catcher later claimed it was a perfect strike whereas the batter said it was a foot outside. The umpire said nothing. He went home to bed."[101]

Restrictions were also placed on how late a game could end, especially for games near the Atlantic coast where dim-out restrictions existed. Baseball was also asked to begin at the best time to reduce traffic congestion. The 1942 All-Star Game began at 5:30 PM in twilight.

Over fifty-seven thousand fans, the largest wartime crowd to see a game at the Polo Grounds, created a storm of protest when with the Giants behind in the ninth inning, but with two on and none out, the game was called at 9:10 PM owing to a military restriction. The irony was that it was an Army Emergency Relief Game with fans contributing $80,000 toward relief. After that, Giants President Horace Stoneham vowed no more twilight or night games because playing against the clock was too tough.[102]

Other sacrifices included players, umpires, and club presidents paying their own admission to the war relief games hosted by each team. In addition, in case of air raids, teams printed air raid directions on each seat, stressing that ball parks were the best bomb shelters. The Yankees Ed Barrow stated that 15,000 could be sheltered under the bleachers and 40,000 under the grandstand.[103] And to accommodate 4,000 soldiers on weekend leave from bases nearby to Charlotte, North Carolina, but without places to stay, Clark Griffith converted a minor league ball park to a camping ground.[104] These and other examples could be cited to illustrate shared sacrifices.

Conclusion

With President Franklin Delano Roosevelt's "green light letter," the history of baseball and World War II became intertwined. This paper has provided evidence on the inevitability of Roosevelt's decision, the views of several constituencies relative to baseball's continuing during World War II, and the sacrifices toward the war effort made by baseball and the greater society. Sadly, President Roosevelt did not live to see the victory he had so carefully engineered, nor did he achieve his wish expressed during a 1944 campaign stop at Ebbets Field to attend a Dodger's game in Brooklyn. Such are the bitter ironies of war.

Our paper, one could say, owes a great deal to that "green light letter." Being one of a kind, it is currently owned by the National Archives in Washington, D.C.

Notes

1. Roosevelt, Franklin D., *The Public Papers and Addresses of Franklin D. Roosevelt, Vol. 11* (New York: Random, 1950), 62.

2. Ward, Geoffrey C., and Ken Burns, *Baseball: An Illustrated History* (New York: Knopf, 1994), 276. Roosevelt's secretary, Dorothy Brady, remembered that prior to FDR's dictating the "green light letter," he replied "never" to her question as to whether he'd shut down baseball.

3. Landis, an ultra-conservative, actually despised Roosevelt's policies, especially the New Deal.

4. Roosevelt, 11: 62.

5. Turner, Frederick, *When the Boys Come Back* (New York: Holt, 1996), 15.

6. Harry S Truman with seven stands second in first ball throws. Fifteen presidents have thrown out the first ball on opening day, beginning with William Howard Taft in 1900.

7. *Baseball Almanac* <http://www.baseball-almanac.com>

8. *Baseball Almanac* <http://www.baseball-almanac.com>

9. *Baseball Almanac* <http://www.baseball-almanac.com>

10. *Baseball Almanac* <http://www.baseball-almanac.com>

11. Collier, Peter, and David Horowitz, *The Roosevelts: An American Saga* (New York: Simon, 1994), 105.

12. Collier and Horowitz 105.

13. Roosevelt didn't play varsity sports (e.g., football, baseball, boxing) because his physical stature as a youth — described as "too spindly" and "too delicate" — prevented his participation. Roosevelt was better suited to individual athletic endeavors such as horseback riding, swimming, and sailing. Roosevelt always feared that he would be remembered as "athletically rather too slight for success: no matter how hard he tried." Ward, Geoffrey C., *Beyond the Trumpet: Young Franklin D. Roosevelt* (New York: Book of the Month, 1997), 185–229.

14. Ward and Burns 267.

15. Ward and Burns 267.

16. Dickson, Paul, *Baseball's Greatest Quotations* (New York: Burlingame, 1991) 225.

17. Gilbert, Bill, *They Also Served: Baseball and the Home Front, 1941–1945* (New York: Crown, 1992), 4.

18. After Roosevelt's death on April 12, 1945, the Washington Senators opened the season wearing black armbands.

19. Roosevelt 11: 62.

20. Other levels of baseball are covered below.

21. Okrent, Daniel, and Steve Wulf, *Baseball Anecdotes* (New York: Oxford UP, 1989), 166.

22. Okrent and Wulf 166. Quoted also in *Cong. Rec.* 15 Nov. 1943: 9515.

23. Dickson 111.

24. Dickson 111.

25. Goldstein, Richard, *Spartan Seasons: How Baseball Survived the Second World War* (New York: Macmillan, 1980), 34.

26. *Cong. Rec.* 15 Nov. 1943: 9515.

27. *Cong. Rec.* 20 Feb. 1945: A734.

28. Goldstein 31.

29. Harrigan, Patrick J., *The Detroit Tigers: Club and Community, 1945–1955* (Toronto: U of Toronto P, 1997), 10.

30. "Baseball Gets Mandate from Army to Carry On," *Recreation* Aug. 1944: 274.

31. Goldstein 31.

32. *Baseball Almanac* <http://www.baseball-almanac.com>

33. Goldstein 33.

34. There was, though, a drop to 207,000 in 1944 from 277,000 in 1943.

35. Kurian, George Thomas, *Datapedia of the United States* (Lanham, MD: Berman, 1994), 150.

36. Kurian 150. The public's desire for baseball did not seem deterred by the lessened quality of play in the 1945 World Series or the age extremes among the players — from a forty-year-old Paul Waner to fifteen-year-old Joe Nuxhall.

37. All letters pertaining to baseball from 1942 in the *New York Times Index* were reviewed.

38. *New York Times* 9 Jan. 1942: 28.

39. Primary Sources — Baseball and World War II, advertisement published in *Sporting News* 29 July 1943. <http://www.baseballhalloffame.org>

40. *New York Times* 23 May 1942: 18.

41. Goldstein 4.

42. Dickson 236.

43. Gilbert 84.

44. Gilbert 84.

45. Gilbert 172.

46. Goldstein 199.

47. Goldstein 199.

48. Goldstein 59.

49. Goldstein 203. Also found in Roosevelt, Franklin D., *The Public Papers and Addresses of Franklin D. Roosevelt, Vol. 13* (New York: Harper, 1950), 592.

50. Gilbert 172.

51. Harrington 288.

52. Harrington 288. The shortage of players in 1943 forced the St. Louis Cardinals to advertise for players in *The Sporting News*.

53. Goldstein 58.

54. *New York Times* 5 Aug. 1942: 22.

55. *New York Times* 18 July 1942: 11.

56. Crissey, Harrington E., *Baseball and the Armed Services* 10–13. <http://www.totalbaseball.com>

57. Some players (e.g., Bob Feller and Hank Greenberg) saw action and also participated in service baseball.

58. Crissey 11.

59. Crissey 12.

60. Goldstein 17.

61. Gregorich, Barbara, *The Story of Women in Baseball* (New York: Harcourt, 1993), 84.

62. Gregorich 69.

63. Bloomfield, Gary L., "Big Leagues' Manpower Demands," *Veterans of Foreign Wars Magazine* Jan. 1993: 30.

64. Primary Sources — Baseball and World War II, article from *Sporting News* 2 July 1952. <http://www.baseballhalloffame.org>

65. "Negroes and Baseball," *Newsweek* 10 Aug. 1942: 58.

66. Wiggins, David K., "Wendell Smith, the *Pittsburgh Courier-Journal* and the Campaign to Include Blacks in Organized Baseball, 1933–1945," *Journal of Sport History* 10.2 (1983): 17.

67. "Negroes and Baseball" 58.

68. It would be Roosevelt's successor, Harry S Truman, who would order the integration of military units.

69. Wiggins 19.

70. Wiggins 23–24.

71. Bloomfield 30.

72. Statistics show that many of the stars — Ted Williams, Joe DiMaggio, Bob Feller, Stan Musial — picked up where they left off. Thirty players who fought in the War were later admitted to the Hall of Fame.

73. Gilbert, Bill, *Now Pitching: Bob Feller* (New York: Birch Lane, 1990), 121.

74. *Cong. Rec.* 30 Mar. 1943: A1538.

75. The list of touring celebrities sponsored by the USO is well known, beginning with such luminaries as Bob Hope and Glen Miller.

76. "A Real Mitt-full," advertisement, *Baseball Digest* Sept. 1943: n.p.

77. Goldstein 43.

78. *New York Times* 8 Aug. 1942: 2.

79. *New York Times* 25 Sept. 1942: n.p.

80. Goldstein 9.

81. Goldstein 40.

82. Goldstein 41-42.

83. Goldstein 41.

84. Dickson 222.

85. Before this time, the anthem was only played at special occasions including Opening Day and the World Series.

86. Bloomfield 31.

87. *New York Times* 4 Aug. 1942: 4.

88. Cerf, Bennett, "Trade Winds," *Saturday Review* 10 Apr. 1943: 28.

89. In the first seventy-two games of 1943, only five home runs were hit in the American League. In the National League, there were eleven shutouts in the first twenty-nine games. Six home runs were hit in the first day that the "revised" ball appeared. Okrent and Wulf 167.

90. "War Changes Baseball," *Science News Letter* 13 Feb. 1943: 110. See also "Big Leagues Get a War Baseball," *Popular Science* July 1943: 46–47.

91. Red Sox pitcher Mace Brown, for one, advised that throwing without a mound was not good for working on one's breaking pitches. Goldstein, Richard, "Life During Wartime," *Boston Magazine* Mar. 1999: 76.

92. Harrigan 10.

93. *New York Times* 8 Oct. 1942: 33.

94. *New York Times* 28 July 1942: 22.

95. Goldstein 87.

96. *New York Times* 28 Sept. 1942: 20. A single ton of high-grade scrap could serve as raw materials for two tons of new steel for a bomber, a tank, guns, and so on.

97. *New York Times* 22 Sept. 1942: 1+.

98. The Cubs had lights ready to be installed in 1941, but after Pearl Harbor they were donated to the War effort. Wrigley Field remained a daylight park for forty-seven more years. Additionally, announcers were told not to give the weather for fear enemy bomber pilots would use the information. Reportedly Dizzy Dean said at one game after a lengthy delay, "If you folks don't know what's holding up the game just stick your heads out the window." Okrent and Wulf 166. A good source for baseball and night games during the War is Pietrusza, David, *Lights On!* (Lanham, MD: Scarecrow, 1991).

99. The Polo Grounds' lights, it was claimed, could be put out in half a minute. New York Times 11 Apr. 1942: 17.

100. Okrent and Wulf 167.

101. Okrent and Wulf 167.

102. *New York Times* 4 August 1942: 22.

103. *New York Times* 11 April 1942: 17.

104. Goldstein 14.

Baseball in a Football Town: The Neighborhood Diamond, Heavy Industry, and High Attendance (1930–1949)

Peggy Beck

To the memory of my dad, Ralph Beck. Six days after we left Cooperstown and the 1998 Symposium, he died at the age of 77. We do build intergenerational relationships around baseball, and my work is living proof. This one is for him …

Introduction

The 1930s and 1940s were the most active, culturally interesting, and evocative decades for amateur baseball in Canton, Ohio. Known as "the cradle of pro football," Canton's interest in baseball long preceded football. Mary Cook deeded 16 acres of property to the City of Canton as early as 1891 for the express purpose of creating a community baseball field. A baseball field built by neighborhood residents already occupied the site — and the date of origin for that field has not been established.

Mankind has spent history trying to reconstruct origins — the origin of man, the origin of political and social organization, and the true origin of technology. Stories differ, and much of what we believe about origin is tinted by oral tradition or our own forgetting and remembering. Science tries to reconstruct origin by doing research, building conjecture and theory, and tearing it down again. As historians, we try to reconstruct as clearly and accurately as possible the struggles and successes that lead to the institutions we write about. The same goes for baseball, and local baseball is no exception.

If it can be said that art imitates life, then it can also be said that in Canton's case, grassroots community baseball imitates history. The numbers of players and teams, the numbers of fields and field permits, and the care and construction of those fields during the 1930s and 1940s indicates the interest and importance of the game. Canton's Class A League amateur baseball history parallels the nation's financial, industrial, and sociological history.

Amateur Class A league baseball in Canton during the 1930s and 1940s was very competitive, receiving the backing of heavy industry as sponsors for uniforms and bats, and land granters for baseball diamonds. The competition drew out the best in local neighborhoods, where fundraisers for the baseball team were common.

As the "national pastime" grew and changed in this middle-class working city, several cultural, political, and sociological developments occurred:

• Baseball diamonds blossomed on empty fields and in residential neighborhoods. Neighbors worked together to support "their" teams, holding fundraisers and attending games. Heavy industry (steel and the railroad) sponsored teams and donated land for playing fields, bringing interest and players to local baseball.

• Canton's amateur baseball enjoyed attendance rates like never before — or since. Average attendance at a Class A league game in the mid-1930s was close to 2,000 people. The more competitive games drew as many as 5,000 to 6,000 people.

• Clown baseball also played a part in this era — the Canton Clowns exemplified clown baseball all over northeastern Ohio.

• Class A league baseball during this era also received extraordinary community and media support, both contributing to the growth of the sport locally.

Through oral histories and newspaper accounts, this paper will trace the history of Class A League baseball in Canton during the 1930s and 1940s. Local amateur baseball provided recreational value, neighborhood togetherness, leisure activity, and structure to lives affected daily by the Depression and World War II. George Will says in his book *Bunts*: "Hemingway said the first requisite for a writer is an unhappy childhood. The world of letters will have to fend for itself, looking for no help from the boys who spend their summers on American Legion Field [or on the fields of Canton's Class A League]."[1]

Early History and Background on Canton's Class A League

In 1891, Mary Cook deeded property to the City of Canton that eventually became Cook Park, one of many baseball fields in the region. The Canton City Recreation Board (which oversees Class A league baseball) was not founded until 1927, although the Cook property was already an established baseball field when deeded in 1891.

The following is a quote from the City of Canton Recreation Department report in 1961. The report gives a brief history of Cook Park:

> This field has long been a baseball field, even before the organization of the Recreation Board in 1927. It was the home of the old Crystal Park Baseball Team [the Crystal Park Tigers]. In 1927 the field was starting to deteriorate so additional clay was placed on the infield. The old backstop of phone poles and chickenwire was changed to heavier wire by the Recreation Department in 1928. With the coming of the WPA and FERA in the middle 30's, this was made a project and the infields were graded and a new small overhanging backstop was placed on the field. There were also restraining lines for spectators placed along first and third baselines in 1949. Bleachers were placed along the first base line. These bleachers were purchased by the Citizens Committee.[2]

The Class A League in Canton, although amateur, has been well-organized, competitive, and almost semi-professional since the 1930s. Considered the highest level of adult amateur baseball (Stan Musial Division), much of this high level of competition is a result of the number of people involved, the number of games in the league and the quality of fields and sponsor support. An April 28, 2000, *Canton Repository* article started this way:

> The Walsh University baseball team took its lumps in the local Class A league last summer. "We played against minor leaguers and Division I guys and we were humbled," Head Coach Tim Mead said, "The Class A league helped prepare our kids to play at a higher level and win."[3]

Currently, Canton's Class A league plays under the auspices of the American Amateur Baseball Congress (the AABC). This organization provides a tournament structure and service assistance for amateur baseball in the United States. Canton's Class A league did not join the AABC until the late 1950s, so prior to that time it was the responsibility of the team manager to arrange any out-of-town games or tournament appearances.

The entry fee for teams entering the Class A league at that time was

$2,148.00.[4] The fees include liability and medical insurance for the players, as well as administrative costs, field maintenance, etc. The cost of league membership prevented some teams from joining the league even in the 1930s and 1940s. In an interview on October 21, 1998, Don Beck said "The northeast end of Canton was a hotbed of baseball in the Northeastern Ohio leagues, including teams from Crystal Park, Fairmount, etc. We [Fairmount Merchants] were an independent team because we couldn't afford the entry fee."[5]

Blooming Baseball Fields Neighbor with Heavy Industry

An August 10, 1931, entry in the Canton Recreation Board minutes reads as follows:

> There were a total of 105 league baseball games played during the month and 92 additional permits issued [to independent teams]. Total permits issued for all baseball games during the month —197.[6]

These numbers only reflect the games and practices held on city owned or city-run fields. The same notes list five baseball leagues in operation, and "various contracts for series have been drawn up between teams and the better class teams [Class A league teams] are now playing competitive series. Sunday baseball has been very active, although it is impossible to organize hardball teams into league. There are good attractions nearly every Saturday and Sunday afternoon at City and Cook fields."[7]

The Pennsylvania Railroaders: A Good Example

Although City and Cook were the baseball fields maintained by the City Recreation Department, others sprang up all over the area. Most of these fields were built on industry property and maintained by the teams. Pennsy Field (later called Fairmount Field), located on the northeast side of Canton, is a good example of this. Built next to the Pennsylvania Railroad YMCA, the field and the team playing on it were originally sponsored by the Pennsylvania Railroad. Since the field no longer exists, newspaper accounts, oral histories, and overhead photos from the Stark County Engineer's office are the only documentation of the field's existence.

The Pennsylvania Railroad owned a 100-acre railroad yard in Canton. The main building, built in 1918 as a steam locomotive backshop, also included a brass shop and a roundhouse. The ballfield was built on the northwest corner of the property.

Pennsy Field and the Pennsylvania Railroaders team exemplify the blend of heavy industry and the neighborhood closeness that pervaded this era of local baseball. At this point, history took a more personal turn for this author. Pennsy Field was built by my grandfather (Solomon Beck — a Pennsy Railroader) and my dad (Ralph Beck), along with other members of the Pennsylvania Railroad team. All of the members of the Pennsylvania Railroaders team came from the Fairmount neighborhood, and the railyard was located across the street from their neighborhood.

The first manager of the Pennsylvania Railroaders was Ed Pyle, a conductor for the Pennsylvania Railroad. Pyle managed the first 2 or 3 years the team existed, and lived at the YMCA. Because his job took him in and out of town, several people assisted with managerial and field duties. Most of the ballplayers and the residents of the surrounding neighborhoods worked for the Pennsylvania Railroad.[8] The area was ethnically diverse, and most residents were blue-collar workers on the railroad or other industrial locations like Timken, Diebold, or Macomber Steel.

Maintenance of the field included the use of two railroad ties bolted to an angle iron towed by a car for dragging the field. The infield was dirt, so it all had to be dragged. The team took pride in the ballfield, which included regulation size left and right field lines. The field was all open space, having no fences or anything to distinguish limits of the outfield except for where the grass was mowed. The team would report to the field on evenings when they didn't play and weed, level, and add sand to the playing field as well as mowing the grass. Don Beck, a batboy prior to becoming a pitcher with the team, said "we had one of the best ballfields around."[9]

The backstop at Pennsy Field was made of chickenwire attached to old telephone poles. Railroad ties formed the bleachers and the bench for the Pennsylvania Railroaders along the first base line, while a bench was provided for the other team on the third base side.

In order to raise money for the team, festivals were held on the grounds of the nearby Fairmount Church. The church, located on a boulevard, would seek and get permission to have the boulevard closed to traffic for the festivals. According to Mary Leggett, women in the neighborhood would contribute homemade canned goods and baked goods. Profits from the canned and baked goods made money for the ballclub.[10] Games of chance and cards at the festival helped also. No storage facility was available on the field property, so hard-earned bases, bats, balls, and other equipment was taken home after games and practices.

The team traveled extensively, including games in Butler and Kennywood Park, Pennsylvania, both trips made by train. In these games, the opponents were teams from the Penn-Ohio League.[11] Because independent teams scheduled their own games, the heaviness of the schedule, level of competition and transportation considerations always played a part in the success of the season. Most trips were made by car, with everyone meeting at the manager's home. Newspaper articles often listed addresses and phone numbers of managers as well as departure times and any players who should report.

World War II slowed down play in the Class A leagues, reducing the number of teams. During interviews, many players from the league will identify their time as "before the war" or "after the war," and many changed teams once they returned.

By 1942, the Pennsylvania Railroaders had become the Fairmount Merchants. The small shops and merchants of this close-knit area would each contribute $5 or $10 to assist the team, and managers often paid for whatever could not be raised at fundraisers or through sponsorships. Their contributions paid off, as this independent team won the Class A league championship in 1942.

The Timken Company and Its Role

Another example of heavy industry's support of Class A league amateur baseball is the Timken Company. H.H. Timken, the company's founder, contributed $200,000 to the City of Canton Parks Department following the passage of a recreation levy in 1926. The money created the Canton Recreation Board and allowed development of park areas, including Cook Park.

The following quote comes from the minutes of the Canton Recreation Board meeting on October 14, 1927:

> In organizing our baseball leagues, we found it advisable to charge a small entrance fee of $5 for league teams and $2 for each team in leagues within an organization, as the Timken and National Guard leagues. The reasons for charging this entrance fee was not for the use of the fields, so much as it was for organization of leagues, schedule making and controlling of same.[12]

In addition to the contribution of money, the Timken Company built the Timken Recreation Park on company land. Timken Recreation Park included four baseball fields, five softball fields, a track, horseshoe pits, and a fishing lake.

The Timken Company provided recognition to players and teams through awards banquets, prizes, and other events. For example, the awards banquet in 1949 drew the likes of Phil Rizzuto and George Stirnweiss of the New York Yankees, as well as Joe Gordon, Jim Hegan, and Bob

Lemon of the Cleveland Indians. At the same dinner, Mel Allen was master of ceremonies.[13]

Even though sponsorships of baseball by heavy industry were clearly very different from company to company, the heavy industries all were linked in one way or another. The Timken Roller Bearing Company Railway Division records in 1938 show that 412 Pennsylvania railroad cars and 92 locomotives ran on Timken roller bearings.[14] Most were serviced at the Pennsylvania Railroad facility in Canton.

Other companies that actively donated land for baseball fields in the late 1920s and early 1930s in Canton include Central Alloy Steel, Grasselli Chemical, Cook Realty, Dayton Malleable Iron, United Electric, Dueber-Hampden Watch, and United States Steel.

High Attendance

Canton Recreation Department Board minutes of June 29, 1928, state, "The month of June found baseball season at its highest point, there being 339 field permits, the majority for scheduled league games."[15] The number of permits issued helped the Recreation Board determine demand for fields and recreation facilities. The same report asserts that "if the present demand increases, it will be necessary to secure additional fields for the season of 1929." On October 9, 1930, the minutes indicate average attendance during the Championship series of the Class A league to be 4,000 people per game.[16]

Not until 1933 did any mention of attendance reappear in the Recreation Board minutes. The August 10, 1933, notes state that "during the past month there have been enormous crowds in attendance at all baseball games."[17] During May of 1933, the following notes were added to the Board Minutes:

> There has been a great deal of enthusiasm shown in baseball, especially by the spectators. Numerous games, especially Class A games, have brought from 5,000 to 6,000 in attendance, and 3,000 attendance would be an average for all Class A games.[18]

Interviews with former players back up the printed estimates. Former players report having seen people around the fences "two or three deep" all the way around the ballpark.

A *Canton Repository* article about the 1949 Class A league All-Star Game (n.d.) included a reference to the estimated crowd of 3,000 people. Published photos with the article show attendance at the game.[19]

Community Support

Class A league amateur baseball in Canton during the 1930s and 1940s enjoyed support from heavy industry and spectators alike. The league also received support from one other powerful source: local media.

Jim Muzzy, Sports Director at WHBC Radio in Canton, acted as head of the Community Recreation Committee, a group that raised money to pay for bleachers to be erected at city-owned ballfields. At the rededication of Cook Park after 100 years of existence, along with All-Star games and other official events, Muzzy acted as master of ceremonies. Along with these duties, his sports reports regularly included Class A league scores, notes of interest, and notification of deadlines for sign-ups and other important facts.

Even more important, the local newspapers provided extraordinary coverage and support for amateur baseball. Local Class A League baseball stories often included almost play by play accounts of important games, as well as box scores, player lineups, and pitching matchups.

Canton Recreation Board minutes for Thursday, July 8, 1948, included the following notes:

> In order to keep an accurate record of all league scores and standings and in order to have proper publicity in newspapers and on the radio concerning said leagues, all winning teams must turn in their scores in the Recreation Office immediately after the playing of a league game. Albert Rea is paid $2.50 a night and Jack Friedman $2.00 a night (These boys never work the same night together) to compile and keep all records and see that the publicity immediately gets to the newspapers and the radio stations....[20]

By the late 1940s, as illustrated above, the local Class A League knew just how important a role the media played in their success. The services discussed above were provided to registered league teams only, so the managers of independents still found it necessary to provide line scores, box scores, and descriptions of important plays to the media.

The Canton Clowns: An Outgrowth of Canton's Class A League

The Canton Clowns played exhibition games in towns all over northeastern Ohio. Most opponents never knew that the team also played together in Canton's Class A League — one of the most competitive leagues in the nation. It did not take them too long to find out.

"Barnstorming" exhibition games from the end of the Class A League season in August until the first snowfall, the Canton Clowns played at their own Loop Field on Fridays or Saturdays and traveled to play away games on Sundays. With stops in Salinesville, Beach City, Robertsville, Newcomerstown, Painesville, West Lafayette, Zanesville, and Dover, most "seasons" included at least 15 games.

Accompanied by three professional clowns (Bud Byer, Rich Pettay, and Mitch Page) and a host of hometown fans, Canton would bring laughter and smiles to crowds of 2,000 to 5,000 anywhere they went.

The team first assembled in the mid-1930s. Sponsorship was an impossibility, because the Depression eliminated any disposable income and, in many cases, any income at all. The laughter and smiles created by the troupe were much needed — life was not easy and entertainment dollars just weren't available. When World War II began in 1941, most of the Canton Clowns became G.I.s and the group disbanded.

When the war ended, the team reassembled and played in Canton's Class A League as the "B & B Clowns." The group's first exhibition game in 1946 drew 3,000 people to Canton's Cook Park. Although the exhibition season was not sponsored, at most games they "passed the hat" to defray the costs of travel, food, equipment, and uniforms for the ballplayers. Several of the exhibition games, called "guarantee games," would guarantee the Canton Clowns at least a certain amount of money for playing. The biggest guarantee game for the Clowns was Lake Placentia, where the entire team would make $35.00 and be able to enjoy the park after the game. Usually, the paid attendance at Placentia averaged around 2,000 people.

Even history did not ignore the Canton Clowns. They played in several historic games, including the first night game ever played in Painesville, Ohio, and the first game to be played on the Timken Park Fields in Canton.

Although they were the best known and their games were the best attended, the Canton Clowns did not have a monopoly on the clown player idea. The Bulldog Clowns, a much older group of ballplayers from the Canton area, also participated in clown baseball.

Even though three professional clowns formed the heart of the Canton Clowns on-the-field act, all of the players eventually got involved somehow. During one road game, the Clowns forgot their bats, so someone gave them an old wagon tongue. True to their nature, the Clowns wore out the wagon tongue, got another bat, and even won the game.

As with most clown acts, props play a part in entertaining the fans. Some of the Clowns' most treasured tricks included a bat loaded with a spring that wobbled when players went to bat and a "pail of water" filled with paper thrown on unsuspecting Clowns manager Charlie Babcock. Babcock would later go on to become the Mayor of Canton.

It was not just the props or the professional clowns encouraging the laughter — sometimes it was the field and sometimes it was the fans. During a late fall stop in Salinesville, the snow began to fall. Snow was not the only thing that fell that day — one of the outfielders also disappeared as he fell in a hole created by old mine shafts. At one game in Goat Hill Field, a Clowns player got caught between all the bases and still scored. Following the play, a woman walked out of the crowd, handed the player a dollar, and told him "it was for the show he put on."

Bud Byers always was a fan favorite. When he got a hit, he ran around the bases — backwards. After several minutes of yelling at Byers to "go back," one of his teammates would take out a gun and shoot him. Once he fell down, the Clowns called for a stretcher and went out after him. The stretcher was useless, so Byers would fall off. As Byers whistled for them to come back and pick him up, any teammates on base would have a chance to score.

The business side of the Canton Clowns included a summer of booking exhibition games for the fall. Not having a baseball field was not a problem — they once made $15 playing on a football field in Dover. A booking manager would take care of lining up the exhibition season. In order to draw a crowd, the Clowns would be covered in the local newspaper, the *Canton Repository*. Word of mouth also helped bring out the fans. For away games, once they played one game at a site, they would become perennial favorites. Time limitations sometimes hampered the players — most were factory workers so games were scheduled on weekends.

The Canton Clowns accomplished a lot in their exhibition seasons. They were already good ballplayers in a very competitive league. They got the chance, as amateurs, to see people stand around the fences 4 or 5 deep to watch them perform. They brought happiness and laughter to a lot of people. And celebrity never went to their heads. They all had to go back to work on Monday.[21]

Conclusion

The 1930s and 1940s provided some of the most interesting baseball anywhere in a town known principally for its contributions to football. In a small, heavily industrial town that founded companies such as Hoover, Timken, and Diebold, the very fabric of community included hard labor, and neighborhoods joined in support of their local baseball teams. Regardless of the ravages created by World War II and the Depression, people stuck together and assisted one another. The ballfield became not only recreation, but an opportunity for fans and supporters to lock the world away for just a while and enjoy life.

Notes

1. George F Will, *Bunts* (New York: Scribner, 1998), p. 81.
2. Canton Recreation Board, *History of Canton Recreation Board Properties* (Canton, OH: Canton Recreation Board, 1961).
3. *Canton Repository*, 28 April 2000, C-1.
4. Tim Trbovich, interview by author, Canton, Ohio, 2 June 2000.
5. Don Beck, interview by author, Canton, Ohio, 21 October 1998.
6. Canton Recreation Board. Board Minutes. 10 August 1931.
7. Ibid.
8. Don Beck, interview by author, Canton, Ohio, 21 October 1998.
9. Ibid.
10. Mary Leggett, interview by author, Canton, Ohio, 21 October 1998.
11. Don Beck, interview by author, Canton, Ohio, 21 October 1998.
12. Canton Recreation Board. Board Minutes. 14 October 1927.
13. Timken Trading Post. Company Newspaper. July 1949.
14. Timken Company Railway Division. Report. 15 December 1938.
15. Canton Recreation Board. Board Minutes. 29 June 1928.
16. Canton Recreation Board. Board Minutes. 9 October 1930.
17. Canton Recreation Board. Board Minutes. 10 August 1933.
18. Canton Recreation Board. Board Minutes. May 1933.
19. *Canton Repository*, n.d., n.p.
20. Canton Recreation Board. Board Minutes. 8 July 1948.
21. Pete Trbovich, interview by author, Canton, Ohio, January 1999.

The Game in Sepiatone and Soft Focus: Nostalgia and American Baseball in Historical Context

Thomas L. Altherr

Among the more common of baseball clichés are the phrases, "We just have to play one game at a time" and "Wait 'til next year!" The first suggests a focus on the present and the second a look towards the future. Yet many Americans view their baseball through the rosy-colored lenses of nostalgia, a near-wallowing in several overly idealized and even commoditized versions of the history of the game. Why and whence this wave of nostalgia? What functions does it fulfill? Does it energize or enervate fans in their attempts to understand or appreciate the current renditions of the sport? Is it a process of self-delusion and commercialized manipulation, or, as one scholar maintained, a crucial psychological mechanism of identity formation in a time of crisis? Nick Trujillo is surely right that functionalist social scientists "assert that baseball teaches us not about the virtues of an idealized past but about the values of a real present," but their analyses may fail to gauge the grip nostalgia has on supporters of the sport.[1] To paraphrase Richard Louv from his book *America II*, we are awash in baseball nostalgia.[2]

Before any attempt to grapple with these questions, a look at the dimensions of this baseball nostalgia wave may be in order. Baseball movies have featured giant dollops of prettified scenes of nostalgic interpretation. At the start of *Bull Durham* (1988), a montage of black and white photographs of baseball scenes and players greeted the viewers; at the end, after Costner and Sarandon close out the plot with a wistful porch swing conversation (in which

Sarandon's very strong feminist character melted as she offered to become a traditional wife or girlfriend tagging along with Costner to his prospective managerial job), the camera panned over Annie's baseball shrine replete with all sorts of baseball artifacts surrounding a photograph of the great, late Yankees catcher Thurman Munson. In *A League of their Own* (1992), former All-American Girls Professional Baseball League players gathered at Cooperstown to celebrate the opening of an exhibit at the Hall of Fame. Memories misted their eyes continually; at the end, with Madonna's song about a former playground as the vocal backdrop, the women played a game at Doubleday Field. *Bingo Long Traveling All-Stars and Motor Kings* (1976) took some of the sting out of the realities of Negro League or black barnstorming baseball with some comic scenes of grandstanding, exploding baseballs, and dancing pageantry. When *The Natural* (1984) wasn't filming the game with a certain interesting grittiness, the director washed the scenes with enormous amounts of soft yellow lighting, soft-focus lens work, and slow-motion action scenes. Although set in the late Depression years, the film conveyed a beguiling attractiveness for the times, and in a nod to nostalgia's constant connection with pastoralism, the manager, Pop Fisher, repeatedly lamented that he should have remained a farmer.[3] Even *Eight Men Out* (1988), a film about one of baseball's low points, the 1919 Black Sox scandal, relied on some stereotypical imagery of the late 1910s and early 1920s to color in around the plot. And then there was *Field of Dreams*, which among other themes, was one long-running exercise in nostalgia: unrelentless pastoralism, resurrected old-time players, therapeutic (and miraculous) restoration of a father-son rupture, closure of the 1919 Black Sox scandal and the pre-Jackie Robinson exclusion of African-American players, and the creation of a Mecca for millions of baseball pilgrims. (Match *Field of Dreams* against another Iowa-based film, *A Thousand Acres* from 1997.) Many other baseball movies could supply additional examples. Even films that haven't been mainly about baseball have included heart-tugging scenes of baseball. One baseball scholar, for example, remains mired in his adulation of a scene from *The Pope of Greenwich Village* (1984), in which Mickey Rourke played stickball.

Television shows and made-for-television videos have likewise contributed to the baseball nostalgia boom. Although shows exclusively about baseball have not flourished on network television, numerous baseball references pop up in the programming. The long-re-running sitcom *Cheers* drew off of Sam Malone's connections to the mystique as a former Red Sox reliever. Detectives or other characters wore baseball logo caps and T-shirts. Ken Burns' massive PBS epic, *Baseball*, despite its less-than-successful attempt at factuality, gave the public a large dose of nostalgia, even for those less-than-glorious chapters of baseball history. The two-part

HBO special, *When It Was a Game* (1994), trafficked heavily in nostalgia.[4] Even the sports networks have frequently supplemented their broadcasts with soft-tone photomontage remembrances of former players and baseball figures, broadcast booth interviews with the same, the constant patter of baseball stories from the announcers, and other obeisances to baseball's glorified past. One memorable example that comes to mind is the photomontage of Houston Astros pitcher J.R. Richard during the 1981 All-Star Game, right after he had a brush with death from a possible stroke. Having settled the grueling fifty-day strike of that summer, the players returned, starting with making up the All-Star Game; the network sweetened the return with a saccharine look at Richard's career with Alan Parsons Project's haunting song "Time" on the soundtrack.

Baseball stadiums likewise have fueled the nostalgia craze. In 1992, the Baltimore Orioles moved into their new stadium, Oriole Park at Camden Yards. This has touched off a trend that has spawned new ball parks in Arlington, Texas, Cleveland, Denver, Atlanta, Houston, Detroit, San Francisco and in the near future in Cincinnati, Boston, and Pittsburgh, and maybe elsewhere. But these parks are new only in certain senses. Invariably their architecture has tried to combine modern features with "retro" infrastructure and images. Rebelling against the rather sterile qualities of multi-event stadiums constructed in the late 1970s, these new parks ruthlessly try to incorporate the old look and feel. Brickwork, antique columns, old-style grillwork, paint schemes, Art Deco paintings and logos, mandatory grass infields and outfields, quirky outfield shapes and distances, billboards and advertising, hand-operated scoreboards all jostle with electronic scoreboards and messageboards, mascots, luxury boxes, glassed-in restaurants, gourmet (or at least something beyond "traditional") ball park food and beverages, wider concourses, modern restroom facilities, an increased number of concession stands, television monitors, video games, child care areas, and other newer amenities. The new ball parks have not been without their critics who have complained about some of the architecture and poor seating as well a bunch of die-hard fans who argue that nothing new can replace an old stadium. One element is very clear, however: all the new ball parks have sought to capitalize on nostalgia, provide the late twentieth, early twenty-first century fan with a sensation that even with skyrocketing salaries, labor wars, city deterioration and gentrification, and other changes, baseball can transcend the temporal and restore the (mis)perceived tranquilities of the past. As Daniel H. Rosenszweig wrote in his dissertation on the new ball parks, "[T]he retro stadium movement of the 1990s is but one feature of a late-millennial culture desperately searching the past for a tonic to a sense of belatedness. Like bell-bottom jeans, or re-emergent swing dance societies, wrap[-]around porches on suburban homes and a host of popular movies like *Back to the Future* and *Pleasantville*, retro ballparks at once commemorate, commodify and fetishize cultural norms from earlier in the final century of the millennium."[5] Ironically Rosenszweig found the experience at the new Camden Yards diluted. Fans in the cheap seats were "so eerily well-behaved." "I found myself terrifically nostalgic," he declared, "for the excessive, the inappropriate, the picaresque — the vernacular behavior and comportment of the rowdies blissfully exiled together in the cheap seats at the old park [Memorial Stadium]. I longed for foul[-]mouthed commentary about the umpire's decisions or for someone to *accidentally* spill beer on the patrons in the corporate luxury boxes just below."[6]

Vintage baseball and over-40 baseball leagues also have depended on and activated baseball nostalgia. For various reasons, a small but growing group of re-enactors have tried to re-create "authentic" presentations of 1850s, 1860s, 1870s, and occasionally later styles of baseball, as well as preliminary versions such as town ball. (Apparently stool ball, trap ball, rounders, and other very early baseball-type games have yet to attract re-enactor teams.) The results have been curious. Some organizations insist on as scrupulous a re-enactment as they can manage, getting almost fundamentalist about the rules. Others have mixed together a mash of rules and uniforms and equipment to re-create a "period." Ironically, within organizations there have been disputes over which rules to follow, thus paralleling and re-enacting the very reasons why nineteenth-century players revised the rules! The few women's vintage baseball teams that have emerged have had similar problems, debating, for example, bloomer outfits versus long skirts and hats. But whatever the uncertainties of presentation, vintage baseball has resulted from and played to nostalgia. Even the word "vintage" is loaded with all sorts of nostalgic associations. Some players play vintage game because of disgust with modern baseball, lack of physical talents necessary to play the modern renditions, and general affinity for a particular period of the past that happens to coincide with a specific era of baseball history.[7]

With the recent upsurge of over-30, over-40, over-50, and Senior League baseball opportunities, a different aspect of nostalgia is at work. Aging players don't wish to bring back an antique version like vintage baseball, sandlot baseball, or Little League. The emphasis here is on playing the modern game on as well-groomed fields as are financially feasible, with relatively up-to-date equipment, bigger gloves, aluminum bats, hockey-style catchers masks, and the like. Ironically, however, for nearly each if not every player the impetus has been to recapture skills, feelings, and memories of playing baseball at various points in one's personal past. Some players may see it as a form of physical exercise, an indulgence in machoism, a denial of aging (or self-delusion about one's body), but lurking around the edges of such sentiments is that old bogeyman of nostalgia. Players who should have hung up their spikes permanently some time ago propel themselves onto the field for one more fling in what they hope will be a series of many more flings and swings. As anthropologist Bradd Shore remarked in 1990:

> For many Americans baseball encapsulates their own biographies through a seamless chain of teams that propels youth into age and projects age back to reclaim its lost vitality. From Little League to Babe Ruth League, high school, college, the Minors and the Majors, baseball is an idiom by which the dream of the endless summer is tied up with an individual life history. This may be why it is with a swing of the bat that most old-timers seem to think they can recapture youth. As the San Francisco columnist Herb Caen mused: "Whereas we cannot imagine ourselves executing a two-handed slam-dunk or a 50-yard field goal, we are still certain we have one base hit left in us."[8]

Few of the players vocalize their attachment to their baseball past. Indeed there's almost a resolute code of silence about how or where one used to play the game. But nostalgia lingers in unspoken sentences.

Similarly, there has been a sense, perhaps wishful thinking in some cases, that baseball has served to smooth over generational differences and tensions. Poet Donald Hall touched on this theme repeatedly in his collection of essays, *Fathers Playing Catch with Sons*, especially in this passage: "Baseball connects American males with each other, not only through bleacher friendships and neighbor loyalties, not only through barroom fights but, most importantly, through generations. When you are small, you may not discuss politics or union dues or profit margins with your father's cigar-smoking friends when your father has gone out for a six-pack, but you may discuss baseball."[9] Similarly Bob Krizek wrote of his father and baseball: "I never truly grieved for my father when he died.... I never really took the time to say good-bye to my dad or allow myself the warmth and contentment of recalling the good times we had spent together watching baseball. In fact baseball at Comiskey was the backdrop for the most genuine interactions I had with my dad. He was removed from the pressures of work, and we were clear of the relational tensions of home. At Comiskey, our tenuous relationship was at ease."[10] From *The Natural* to *Field of Dreams* to *The Sandlot*, baseball films have re-enforced this therapeutic connection, as the game of catch helps the males of different generations transcend their differences.

Visual phenomena supply more evidence of the pervasiveness of this nostalgia. Two famous American illustrators, Norman Rockwell and Charles Schultz, come to mind. In the past couple of years there has been a "Rockwell Revival," inexplicable or understandable depending on one's art history perspectives.[11] Although Rockwell himself was not much of a baseball player (golf seems to have been his sport) or a ranting fan, for that matter, he painted several memorable baseball paintings, mostly as covers for *The Saturday Evening Post*. In one of his very first covers, Rockwell portrayed a boy pushing a baby carriage, while two baseball-uniformed boys sneered at him. Even that early Rockwell understood the hierarchies of boyhood, how integral baseball was to puerile prestige levels. As art historian Ben Sonder remarked, "Rockwell's deep interest in the mythology of boyhood seemed two-edged. On the one hand, boyhood served him as a source of nostalgia, a lighthearted way of examining social behavior, and an invocation of innocence.... On the other hand, boyhood for Rockwell is also a time of competition and new challenges, peppered with moments of embarrassment or humiliation."[12] Another early illustration involved an older, portly grandfatherly male taking a turn at bat while the impish catcher signaled for an outside pitch to fool the old gent. In 1939, commemorating baseball's supposed centenary, the painter drew a striking cover, in which a pitcher dressed in an 1860s or so era baseball uniform wound up to deliver a pitch while an enthusiastic umpire looked through the pitcher's raised leg towards the batter. Another cover encapsulated some of the conflict of post–World War II residential development: a construction engineer with a bulldozer behind him confronted three sandlot boys pleading to have him spare their home plate and, by extension, baseball field. A 1958 cover offered the viewer a peek through a knothole at a pitcher in the distance warming up, which by 1958 was definitely a reference to the bygone days when urchins could glimpse the game through the wooden fence. Another earlier drawing showed four sandlot kids performing the time-honored ritual of throwing the bat. One charming cover from Rockwell's mature period, displayed the sandlot kid getting fitted for glasses in the optometrist's office. The boy, who is holding a Brooklyn Dodgers cap and his glove, was clearly chagrined at having to submit to his physical imperfections, which would subject him to ridicule on the boyhood fields of baseball. In one of Rockwell's occasional multiple scene covers, one delineating a "day in the life of an American boy," the obligatory visual references to baseball demonstrated how matter-of-factly the game integrated into the quotidian horizons of the American boy.

But Rockwell is better known for a few other baseball canvases. In the 1960s, when Rockwell broke away from *The Saturday Evening Post*, which clamped down on his subject matter, especially concerning the Civil Rights movement, he painted a stunning scene of an African-American family moving into a new neighborhood, which was probably all-white. Two groups of kids, black and white, stood eyeing each other near the end of the moving van. In each group one of the males was holding a baseball glove, and one of the white kids was wearing a baseball uniform. So powerful was the appeal of baseball, Rockwell seemed to be suggesting, that it could smooth racial integration, bridge those barriers. After all, if kids are all playing baseball, how different can people be? In another *Post* cover, Rockwell chronicled the arrival of the rookie in the clubhouse, in this case the Red Sox (with a player in the background looking uncannily like Carl Yastrzemski, even though this cover preceded Yaz's rookie year by several years). The cover captured the rookie's brimming optimism and the mandatory suspiciousness of the grizzled veterans quite effectively. A similar situation informed another cover, in which Chicago Cubs players and coaches slouched on the dugout bench while the bat boy stared in shock at the action on the field and the hometown crowd jeered the hapless Cubs. And last but not least, Rockwell will always be associated with the classic "Bottom of the Sixth" cover from 1947. Three umpires test the rain while the Brooklyn coach taunted a Pirates coach that the rain would ensure a Brooklyn victory. Probably few baseball images have been so recognizable and conveyed so much information about an era, right down to the number of umpires, their uniforms and equipment, the scoreboard and the game situation. The cover immediately conjured up for the viewer a time when baseball was simpler, when umpires were respected, and the prospect of rain ruled the day.[13]

This past February the beloved cartoonist Charles Schulz, creator of the "Peanuts" comic strip, died. Over his nearly fifty years of drawing "Peanuts," Schulz chose baseball as the subject for about ten percent of his cartoons, a significant percentage given all the possible topics for such cartoons. Recently the Hall of Fame in Cooperstown enshrined Schulz and his lovable characters. Over and over Schulz featured the hapless Charlie Brown on the mound, Lucy as probably the worst right-fielder in the world, Snoopy at shortstop, and assorted other "Peanuts" characters at other positions. Never once does this ragtag team win a game, or even come close. Futility reigns. But surprisingly this endearing cartoon has also stimulated baseball nostalgia. On a simple level, the cartoons have been appealing because "Peanuts" has been around so long, has accompanied three generations or so as they grew up. Yet at other levels, the comic strip has triggered yearning for the bittersweet experiences of a Charlie Brown. The situations in "Peanuts" baseball cartoons were hardly simplistic; Schulz repeatedly drew on irony. Usually irony and self-reflection undercut the more basic forms of nostalgia. In this case, it is that sense of futility and irony that inspire the nostalgia. Charlie Brown elicits much empathy because many baseball nostalgicists have come to realize that such losses characterized their past play. But "Peanuts" softens and mediates the pain of those failures and embarrassments. No matter how much defeat stung in younger days, Charlie Brown's Sisyphean efforts to win a game, to hang in there against overwhelming odds, ennoble those defeats. It would be a mistake to see baseball nostalgia as always celebrating previous success and statistics. "Peanuts" has caused Americans to yearn, albeit ironically, for the glorious and not-so-glorious failures.

Poets, too, have employed or indulged in baseball nostalgia. One example will suffice here. In Kentucky poet Joe Bolton's "The Green Diamonds of Summer," in a collection appropriately titled *The Last Nostalgia*, he evoked a wonderfully bittersweet memory of childhood baseball. He led off with a trenchant quote from Lewis H. Lapham: "On the other side of the left-field wall the agents of death and time go about the dismal work of the world's corruption.... But inside the park the world is as it was at the beginning. The grass is as green as it was in everybody's lost childhood; nobody grows old, and if only the game could last another three innings, or maybe forever, nobody would ever die." Then Bolton described himself, through a persona known as Lonnie, throwing plastic baseballs against a fence where he had clothespinned a welcome mat to serve as a strike zone. He noted his motivation: "I could tell you it's something more sublime/Than the remembered heroes/Or the imagined strikeouts and home runs/Or even some undying boyhood dream/That keeps me at it far into the first warm afternoons/Of the year, into the twilight,..." In the second stanza, he recalled how he would make his friend Dale pitch to him even when darkness made the ball almost unseeable. Bolton declared, "It was like Zen, the ball gone invisible/In the dark —/Only the sweet buzz of leather and seams on air/To tell me where it was./I'd hit it, too, more often than not,..." In the fifth stanza, the poet reminisced about how they constructed baseball fields, how he outgrew the size of those parks, how his friend Dale warned him against throwing out his arm, which he did in a high school playoff game when he gave up a game-winning home run. Then in the last part of the poem, Bolton recounted how his baseball career disintegrated in college, how in adulthood he became reduced to chain-smoking and beer-drinking through *Monday Night Baseball*, and how he and Dale tried one more time to recapture their baseball days, pitching plastic balls to each other. The poem closed with some haunting ambiguities: "In my dream of endless extra innings,/The long drive/That could be the last out failing at the track/Or the winning homer/Disappearing beautifully over the left-field wall/Never quite falls,/But rather hangs suspended in the dusk/Above the field...."[14]

Memory, even false memory, is thus crucial to nostalgia. Extremely powerful in its nostalgic content has been the baseball memorabilia craze. During the past several years at least three conversations have provoked, for me, some thought about the meaning of baseball memorabilia. A couple of summers, while in Vermont, I caught a pre-release screening of a film based on Howard Frank Mosher's novel, *A Stranger in the Kingdom*.

Although the movie unfortunately neglected much of the novel's delicious banter about the Boston Red Sox, the adolescent protagonist wore a Red Sox cap, ostensibly an early 1950s model in keeping with the time setting of the story. Yet the fact he had a cap hit my historicity button. Would a boy, in the 1950s in one of the more backwater sections of New England, have had a spanking new cap, resembling in every detail the ones the Fenway favorites wore? Maybe yes, but today, thanks to the adventurous marketing of logos by Major League Baseball under Peter Ueberroth's commissionership in the 1980s, you can't swing the proverbial dead cat on my campus without hitting a baseball jacket, cap, or other piece of paraphernalia. Has the change been so pervasive in these thirty or forty years?

Second, about a week after Charlie Metro gave a guest talk in my baseball history class, a student came up to me with a September, 1945, issue of *Baseball* magazine, in which he had spotted a photograph of Metro sliding into home plate. When I asked him where he found the magazine, he responded that his grandfather had a whole run of them from that time period. Amazing, I thought. What spurs someone to keep a whole collection of what essentially was ephemera at that time all these years? With all due respect to the archivist of *The Sporting News*, these days I keep my *TSN*s about six months and then they enter the recycling program, except for a few choice articles and reviews that I have saved.

Third, recently one of my baseball history students and I were discussing his wish to join our local Frank Haraway SABR chapter. As we were closing the conversation, he mentioned that he was related to the Hall of Famer "Rabbit" Maranville on his mother's side. That disclosure launched another avenue of talk. I asked him if his family had any surviving papers, letters, and the like from the famous shortstop. The student said he didn't think anything remained except a box of old clothes and an old glove. Assuming that the leather was Maranville's, I said, "Hold onto that glove!" He said that it was just a beat up old glove, but he guessed they'd hang onto it.

Later in the day I ruminated on the dimensions of the discussion. Why had I, as a baseball historian, asked only about written sources? Why didn't I inquire about photographs and paraphernalia? Did my younger student understand what I meant by written sources, or had his focus already moved on to the visual, the tactile, the artifacts, a perspective so much more comfortable to his generation? But it also struck me as odd that in these days of the fast buck, the mega-merger, and other examples of the mercenary tone of the times, that Maranville's glove, instead of being cashed in for funds was still cached in a box of old clothes. Why had not Barry Halper and the other supercollectors tracked down the glove? Not to mention the old clothes, any of which might have been parts of a uniform the Rabbit wore in 1914 while inspiring the greatest single-season team comeback in baseball history? The old philosophical conundrum of the tree falling alone in the forest popped up. Is that glove, are those old clothes, memorabilia if they are stashed away in a closet, in a box, at the back of a garage?

These interchanges forced me to ponder the matter of memorabilia. What constitutes memorabilia? Who decides what is valuable and what is dross? What explains the enormous explosion of memorabilia in the last ten or fifteen years? Who buys this stuff? Why do men (and some women) who grumble and flinch at paying for necessities happily fork out gobs of dough for cards, autographs, signed photographs, uniforms? Have baseball historians examined this topic seriously enough or are we still entrenched in the written word? What effect does baseball memorabilia have on our memory of the game and its history? Is the baseball memorabilia phenomenon the coming index of the baseball past? Or is it just an indiscriminate hodgepodge, the Smithsonian-Institution-as-Nation's-Attic syndrome run wild? Is the industry still in "its infancy," as Barry Halper claimed in *Total Baseball* in 1993, that "the lure of baseball and its collectibles is a constant?"[15] If this is the infancy, what will the memorabilia market look like twenty, thirty years from now?

What is memorabilia? Does a Barry Halper rule of sorts apply? If Barry, or other large-scale collectors like Marshall Fogel, collected it, it's memorabilia; if not, it's trash? If a baseball player signs a ball or a uniform, is it automatically memorabilia, even if he's a scrubeenie? My vintage baseball colleagues were astonished a couple of years ago when a horde of kids and even older adolescents besieged them for autographs, even though none of them are ever likely to be famous athletes. Is a ball hit into the stands during a game more important than one hit there in batting practice? Does rarity of the item always produce memorabilia status, or does there have to be a critical mass, a minimum number of them in circulation to stimulate the market? Does memorabilia exist for the personal memory or the collective memory or both equally? Will there be a winnowing of the melange? Will some items persist as memorabilia while others figuratively fade away? Time and chance, fire and flood will take their toll of certain items, and kids will hit or throw a Babe Ruth autographed ball into the next yard where dwells the monster dog, as in the movie *The Sandlot*, but will selective erosion of memory disqualify some items as memorabilia?

What would explain the suddenness of the memorabilia phenomenon? No longer satisfied with a run of cards and maybe a pennant or two on the wall, many kids and not-so-kids today surround themselves with an abundance of memorabilia, even to the extreme in which one Denver fan has converted his whole basement to a baseball field, the floor painted green, the lines painted in white, the fences simulated, and the rooms crowded with an astounding private collection of memorabilia. Admittedly people in previous cultures have saved the holy items in sacred shrines. Museums abound with them. In Catholicism, for example, there may be only one Shroud of Turin, but there are, as the joke runs among lapsed Catholics, enough pieces of the True Cross to construct Notre Dame Cathedral. Have we hit the same level of saturation with memorabilia? Will the market burst of its own exuberance or become the new standard of taste? Will the sports logo in general, baseball ones as one major subspecies, become the new casual dress item *de rigueur*? Will sports bar bouncers throw out the unfortunate who tries to enter without wearing an approved MLB article of clothing? If everyone has a Mickey Mantle-signed baseball, authentic or replica, will that diminish the meaning of it or establish it as the badge of identity, the certificate of membership in the mass culture of America?

Preliminary evidence indicates that the major group of consumers of memorabilia is not the throng of kids buying the various series of baseball cards in their wax packs, but males in their thirties and forties. As Bill Gallo, a writer for the local Denver alternative weekly, *Westword*, noted, "The prime targets for athletic signature are not gullible teenagers. They are star-struck American men."[16] Other than perhaps the obvious reason that these males may have accumulated enough disposable income to afford the flashier items of memorabilia, are there other forces afoot? Does the modern game disappoint and launch these males on journeys into the dangerous territory of nostalgia? Is it safer to cling to an unchanging object or artifact than grapple with the fluidity of rosters, flukishness of the Florida Marlins, and the crushing effects of the Strike of 1994? Has the present become so hollow and unsatisfactory that these males lunge willy-nilly after a time when supposedly the game was purer, when players played for fun and pride rather than filthy lucre? Is the memorabilia explosion symptomatic of a gigantic mid-life crisis creeping across Baby Boomerdom and its successor generation? Are baseball memorabilia items the new trophies of maledom, the black rhinos and rogue elephants the Strenuous Lifers would have bagged in Africa in the past? Or are these males petty princes and pharaohs assembling their entourage items for entombment? Why, as mentioned above, have several of our recent powerful baseball movies been exercises in pure memorabilia? What was *Field of Dreams* if not the wildest extension of memorabilia yet: by building your own field you could bring back the actual ball players (and an estranged father to boot!)?

Any morbidity references aside, perhaps the motivations have been healthier, more expressive of humanity than expected. In her text to the wonderful photographs in *Baseball Archaeology*, Gwen Aldridge suggested the following about baseball objects:

> An object used by a famous person or in a famous deed takes on a life
> of its own. It has a power to intrigue that far outweighs portraits or
> autographs or autobiographies. Perhaps because artifacts have a
> unique way of reflecting the essentials of that person or that moment,
> they are physical, and they survive and hold time. The way they are
> put together, the care that was or wasn't taken to make them, the mate-
> rials used, all tell us something.

With them, we touch another time. We understand at a very human level
how it was.[17] And maybe former Hall of Fame librarian Tom Heitz came close
to the primary reason when he conjectured to Charles Fruehling Springwood,
for his provocative book *Cooperstown to Dyersville*, that moderns were con-
forming to an ancient pattern known to anthropologists, wherein people
appropriate material items from the rich and powerful and famous to "gain
access" to their "special aura" and even "own" the player, that the object or
artifact is a metonym of the complete player.[18] Indeed, some people
wouldn't wash for weeks the shoulder that Babe Ruth had touched.

This returns us to the subject of memory. After all the word "memorabilia" comes from the same root as does the word "memory." What effects
do memorabilia have on historical interpretations, personal and collective,
of the game? Historians, of course, are very interested in memory, how it
works, what its means, how it is manipulable. Some forms or memory,
called archival memory, are so indelible that individuals repeat their
descriptions of an event or person verbatim fifty years later. Other types of
memory are fleeting or subject to embellishment or vulnerable to subtraction. Does a complete set of scorecards from a game in every major league
and minor league stadium in one summer reinforce archival memory or
allow the holder of the cards to let memory go fuzzy because one can always
consult the cards? Does a certain autographed pennant trigger a veritable
flood of memories, à la Proust, or keep alive a very focused fragment of
time? Again, do the artifacts pitch the owners and viewers into the land of
nostalgia, where one can dismiss the actual past while simultaneously constructing a glorified version? Or perhaps even worse, are baseball memorabilia, in some cases, disconnected from their actual baseball roots? A case
in point: several years ago, a middle-school teacher I knew told me of a
twelve-year old in her class who had a very sizable baseball card collection,
which she had allowed him to bring in for show-and-tell. One Monday
morning, knowing there had been a major card show in Denver that weekend, she asked the boy if he had gone. He misunderstood her and said that
he had gone and done quite well; then he corrected himself to tell her that
he had flown to California for a show and made nearly $10,000 instead! Pre-
suming he was telling the truth, I wondered, first, just what a twelve-year
boy understood about $10,000, but second and more importantly, I worried

whether or not the boy had any historical understanding of the players whose cards he trafficked in, or were they so many pork bellies and wheat futures to a child who had lost his childhood long ago. Will memorabilia ironically deprive us of any accurate memory of the game?

There may be no substantive answers to many of the questions above. Even when I turned to examine my own situation, I found little more than befuddlement. Aside from a couple of baseball cards and a few ticket stubs, a bat my brother lathed out of ash from his Ohio woodland, a Bob Feller autographed ball whose chief significance is that it's from my grandfather who was a diehard Tribe fan, and a replica 1911 Philadelphia Athletics cap, which was a Christmas present, I have to admit that I have hardly any memorabilia. When I was a kid, I collected baseball cards passionately for a while. In 1958 I had garnered all of the Topps baseball cards, except one, Harry Bright of the Pirates. I bought pack after pack of Topps cards vainly searching for a Harry Bright. My "best friend," Dave, had *three* Harry Brights, but wouldn't trade or give me one. I suffered all summer. But it didn't matter, because eventually my mother pitched them all away sometime in my high school or college days. These days, much to the amazement of my students, I don't collect any baseball memorabilia. I have plenty of books on baseball and copies of the famous movies, but little of what my colleagues and teammates would call memorabilia.

But why still all this nostalgia? Was Nicholas Davidoff right when he asserted in a 1992 *New Republic* piece, "Indeed, America is so swamped in baseball nostalgia that the game threatens to be obscured by a cloud of kitsch?" For Davidoff the nostalgia about the national pastime was a "response, no doubt, to our increasingly fractured and fracturing society" and has been serving as a "social balm" that has been ironically embalmed itself. The danger, Davidoff warned, was that nostalgia "undermines the authentic appreciation of the game," a process which television had already damaged for decades.[19] Davidoff's concerns echoed those of other culture critics who wrote about nostalgia. In a 1984 essay in *Harper's*, historian Christopher Lasch wrote of nostalgia in general:

> Nostalgia ... seeks not so much to preserve the past or to understand the ways in which it unavoidably influences our lives as to idealize lost innocence. Nor does it unambiguously assert the superiority of bygone days. It contains an admixture of self-congratulation. By exaggerating the naive simplicity of earlier times, it implicitly celebrates the maturity and worldly wisdom from which we look back on them. Not only does nostalgia misrepresent the past but — what is not so obvious — it diminishes the past.[20]

Yet other analysts have seen a slightly more positive explanation for nostalgia. In his book, *Yearning for Yesterday*, sociologist Fred Davis described different levels of nostalgia, depending on self-introspection, and argued that nostalgia has served as a mechanism of "identity repair," a concept to which Davidoff alluded. In a time of rapid change and societal dislocations, people would retreat into nostalgia as a refuge in which to reintegrate identity. Thus, although Davis certainly admitted that nostalgia often contained false interpretations of the past, it would seem that baseball nostalgicists would be undergoing an important psychological process while confronting change both within and outside of the baseball orbit. According to Davis, "Nostalgia reenchants, if only for a while until the inexorable processes of historical change exhaust that past which offered momentary shelter from a worrisome but finally inexorable future."[21]

Baseball nostalgicists play the angles both ways. One theme has emphasized the continuities of baseball. According to this position, baseball has been a bedrock of unchangability in a fluid world. In *Field of Dreams*, James Earl Jones' character makes a stirring speech that baseball has been the one constant as America has steamrolled along over generation after generation. The sentiment is definitely seductive, and has a certain grain of truth, but essentially it is false. Baseball *has* changed, sometimes quite a bit. The rules have seemed relatively unchanged since the 1860s, but the key word there is relatively. Rules were in constant fluctuation during the latter decades of the nineteenth century. Even after the settling in of the National and American Leagues, rules occasionally changed. Then came 1969 with the lowering of the pitcher's mound and shrinking of the strike zone, and in 1973, the designated hitter. Even had the rules stayed the same, players in the various decades have played the game differently in terms of emphasis on speed and stolen bases, pitching, the home run, and overall strategies. Uniforms and equipment have caused change. Larger gloves allow better fielding and subtraction of offense. The resiliency and bouncability of the ball reeks havoc with attempts to level out statistics over eras. The composition of the player force has always produced changes on the field. Whether it was the shiftings of various Euroamerican ethnic groups before 1947, or the increase in players of color since that date, and the more recent expansion of Latino and Asian numbers, the style and quality of baseball changed as did the makeup of the audiences (although not to the same proportions as on the field). Yet to many baseball nostalgicists, the game has gone blithely along isolated from outside (or even internal) forces.

But other baseball nostalgicists not only admit and describe the changes, but lever them to buttress their arguments that the game in the past was so much better than the current product. These memoirists, of the when-I-was-a-kid-I-walked-to-school-ten-miles-through-eight-feet-of-snow-uphill-both-ways school, rarely tire of conjuring up a Golden

Past. This position, too, collapses under examination. In a recent piece in *The New Yorker*, James Surowiecki discussed the discrepancies:

> When was the Golden Age of baseball? It's a phrase that conjures sepia-toned photographs and heavy flannel uniforms, not polyester-clad players skidding their way across Astroturf. But when music and fashion were at their worst, baseball was at its best. The fifteen years after free agency was introduced, in 1976, were the most competitive in the game's history: between 1978 and 1987, ten different teams won the World Series. In the second half of the eighties, the game's revenues nearly doubled, and even small-market teams were successful on the field and at the box office.

Surowiecki went on to lament the more recent effect correlation of massive spending and championships.[22] Fans complain mightily that modern commercialism has ruined the game, corrupted its pristine past. As David McGimpsey asserted, "What baseball has created out of its own nostalgia is a division where the good game's purists are in opposition to those who will allow baseball television-era glitz like the NFL."[23] The confusion is inherent in the word "game." Baseball nostalgicists assume there was a period in baseball history, even in the professional period, when baseball players played for pride, fun, competition, exercise, ego stroking, fame, almost anything except for money, when owners owned franchises for reasons of boosterism, civic virtue, public service, noblesse oblige, almost anything except financial profit, when spectators could attend games cheaply, identify with the players who never or rarely switched teams, count on teams staying in their city decade after decade. Even the most cursory skimming of Robert Burk's book, *Never Just a Game*, should dispel that illusion quickly. As he demonstrated, there was hardly any time where players, owners, and fans cooperated smoothly in an economic partnership to put on the game.[24]

African-American baseball before the advent of Jackie Robinson presents a sticky situation for nostalgicists. The establishment of the Negro League Hall of Fame in Kansas City has fueled some nostalgia about the Negro Leagues. Despite taking a hard look at the vicissitudes of Negro League ball, Ken Burns' *Baseball* probably engendered as much nostalgia for those tough times. The many celebrations of Robinson's achievements in the fiftieth-anniversary year in 1997 similarly fostered some waves of fond memories for the late 1940s and 1950s, the Brooklyn Dodgers (as if they needed any further nostalgicization!), and the (mis)perceived simpler ambiance of those momentous days. But these warm-hearted remembrances may paper over the pain of the enforced segregation. As David McGimpsey noted, "While African American reflections on the game are not entirely free of the usual idyllic riffs on youth, greenness, and fathers bonding with sons, indulging in nostalgia often courts a history that finds vicious and systematic racism as easily as it finds mythic moments of innocence." Indeed, suggested McGimpsey, this bittersweet qualities of nostalgia may lie behind the reluctance of recent generations of African-American youth to bond with the game as strongly as they attach themselves to basketball and football.[25]

Baseball nostalgia can take collective and individual forms. Fans recall games and players and moments that they shared collectively with a crowd, a family, a group of friends, or a team, and remember those baseball images in the context of the group. Regarding these baseball experiences, the baseball nostalgicist did not experience them alone. He or she submerged him- or herself into the collective experience and earn the right to collective memory, which like other interpretations of the past, is subject to erosion and embellishment. Baseball nostalgia can also be intensely private, concentrating on particular memories or points in time, some extremely specific to an individual. Such nostalgia may find resonance among other baseball nostalgicists who have their own particular memories. Some of this personal nostalgia may be inarticulate, inchoate, diffuse, inexpressible, but nevertheless powerful and on occasion empowering. Baseball museums, most notably the Cooperstown Baseball Hall of Fame, and "sacred sites" such as the *Field of Dreams* movie location in Dyersville, Iowa, play off both the collective and individuals forms of nostalgia, as Charles Springwood discovered in his analysis.[26] Perhaps this is predictable. As historian Steven Pope wrote, "Sports halls of fame reside at the intersection of history and nostalgia."[27] But Springwood detected some categorical changes at work:

> In recent years, the museum has more fully embraced the discourse(s) of nostalgia in promoting itself, even adopting some of the affective epistemologies of the Field of Dreams [the Dyersville location] by promising to serve up emotions and dreams and to replenish relationships and family bonds. For many people today, the Hall of Fame experience is largely an affective rather than a cognitive one. That is, many dance through the museum and the village in an emotional way, consuming Cooperstown as a spatial symbol of baseball and American history, writ large. Moreover, the Cooperstown site elides a distinction between history and nostalgia in conflating education, affective imagery, spectacle, and a "time-capsule" historical narrative. The Hall of Fame actively encourages visitors to explore and reflect on their own personal and emotional attachments to the events of baseball's past being represented there.[28]

But should we really worry about the nostalgicization of baseball? Is it temporary, and in the end harmless? Shouldn't we remind ourselves that Americans have applied nostalgia to the game repeatedly, even from the earliest days of professionalism? As historian Warren Jay Goldstein reminded us in *Playing for Keeps*, baseball has had both a linear, chronological and emotional cyclical history, and players and fans as early as 1868 were lamenting that the game had deteriorated from what it had been in the 1850s.[29] Perhaps Bradd Shore's comments summed up the matter:

> Why all the fuss? Baseball is, after all, just a game, a diversion from life's serious business. Maybe. But a more considered view suggests that while it is incontestably a game, our national pastime is also something more. Baseball symbolizes for many Americans a nostalgia for childhood and summer and a lost agrarian age; it engages our passions, shapes our weekends and helps lubricate our casual social relationships; it transcends the control of the clock over our harried lives; and understood as a kind of ritual drama, baseball takes us beyond the uncertainty of play in motion to the enduring forms that make it a cultural institution.[30]

And Roger Kahn's pronouncement assuredly should enter our considerations: "No existential proclamation, or any tortured neo-Freudianism, nor any outburst of popular sociology, not even, or least of all, my own, explains baseball's lovelock on the American heart. You learn to let some mysteries alone, and when you do, you find they sing themselves."[31]

One last thought about baseball and nostalgia. Originally the word "nostalgia" referred to a condition of homesickness. A Swiss doctor, Johannes Hofer, drafted the term to refer to a type of extensive homesickness among Swiss mercenaries fighting in foreign lands.[32] Connecting this up to the dramatic importance that home, especially as represented by home plate (or originally home base), has had in baseball, it might be fair to say that the psychological drive to return home is inherent in the game, that perhaps a certain amount of nostalgia, at least in its original connotation, is unavoidable.

Notes

1. Nick Trujillo, "Interpreting (the Work and the Talk of) Baseball: Perspectives on Ballpark Culture," *Western Journal of Communication*, v. 56, n. 3 (Fall 1992), 351.

2. Richard Louv, *America II* (New York: Jeremy P. Tarcher, 1983), 6.

3. See David McGimpsey's discussion of these pastoral linkages in his *Imagining Baseball: America's Pastime and Popular Culture* (Bloomington, Indiana: Indiana University Press, 2000), 61–88.

4. See Roger C. Aden, "Nostalgic Communication as Temporal Escape: *When It Was a Game*'s Re-construction of a Baseball/Work Community," *Western Journal of Communication*, v. 59, n. 1 (Winter 1995), 20–38. For an adulatory review, see Steve Wulf, "Home (Plate) Movies," *Sports Illustrated*, July 1, 1991, 50–51.

5. See Daniel H. Rosenszweig, "Retro Accents and Carnival Pleasures: the Cultural Role of the Ballpark in Renewing the American City," unpublished Ph.D. dissertation, University of Virginia, 1999, 21.

6. *Ibid.*, 16. Rosenszweig's italics.

7. Doug Stewart, "The Old Ball Game," *Smithsonian* (October 1998), 98–104.

8. Bradd Shore, "Loading the Bases: How Our Tribe Projects Its Own Image into the National Pastime," *The Sciences*, v. 30., n. 3 (May/June 1990), 13.

9. Donald Hall, "Baseball and the Meaning of Life," in *Fathers Playing Catch with Sons: Essays on Sport (Mostly Baseball)* (New York: Dell Publishers, Laurel paperbound edition, 1985), 49–50.

10. Bob Krizek, quoted in Krizek and Nick Trujillo, "Emotionality in the Stands and in the Field: Expressing Self through Baseball," *Journal of Sport and Social Issues*, v. 18, n. 4 (November 1994), 317–318. See also McGimpsey, *Imagining Baseball*, 129–157 for an expanded treatment of this theme.

11. See Maureen Hart Hennessey and Anne Knutson, *Norman Rockwell: Pictures for the American People* (New York: Harry N. Abrams, 1999); Ben Sonder, *The Legacy of Norman Rockwell* (New York: Todtri, 1997); and Herbert J. Gans, "Can Rockwell Survive Cultural Elevation?" *The Chronicle of Higher Education*, April 21, 2000, B8–B9.

12. Sonder, *The Legacy of Norman Rockwell*, 28.

13. Rockwell had one other baseball-oriented illustration, a bizarre one quite out of character and even his artistic style, in which an outfielder made an over-the-shoulder catch of a young boy, also dressed in a baseball uniform, while a policeman looked on in dismay.

14. Joe Bolton, "The Green Diamonds of Summer," in Bolton, *The Last Nostalgia: Poems 1982–1990*, Donald Justice, ed. (Fayetteville, Arkansas: The University of Arkansas Press, 1999), 79–84.

15. Barry Halper with Bill Madden, "Baseball Collecting," in John Thorn and Pete Palmer, eds., *Total Baseball, Third Edition* (New York: HarperCollins, 1993), 600.

16. Bill Gallo, "Warning Signs," *Westword*, February 26–March 4, 1998, 43.

17. Gwen Aldridge and Bret Wills, *Baseball Archaeology: Artifacts from the Great American Pastime* (San Francisco: Chronicle Books, 1993), 9.

18. Charles Fruehling Springwood, *Cooperstown to Dyersville: A Geography of Baseball Nostalgia* (Boulder, Colorado: Westview Press, 1996), 95.

19. Nicholas Davidoff, "Field of Kitsch," *The New Republic*, August 17 and 24, 1992, 22–24.

20. Christopher Lasch, "The Politics of Nostalgia: Losing History in the Mists of Ideology," *Harper's*, November, 1984, 68–69.

21. Fred Davis, *Yearning for Yesterday: A Sociology of Nostalgia* (New York: The Free Press, 1979), 16–26, 31–50, and 116.

22. James Surowiecki, "How to Bust the Baseball Trust," *The New Yorker*, May 15, 2000, 43. See also Chapter One, "Passion for the Past," in Richard Skolnik, *Baseball and the Pursuit of Innocence* (College Station, Texas: Texas A & M Press, 1994).

23. McGimpsey, *Imagining Baseball*, 33.

24. Robert F. Burk, *Never Just a Game: Players, Owners, & American Baseball to 1920* (Chapel Hill, North Carolina: University of North Carolina Press, 1994).

25. McGimpsey, *Imagining Baseball*, 106–107.

26. Springwood, *Cooperstown to Dyersville, passim*.

27. S[teven]W. Pope, "Sports Films and Hall of Fame Museums: An Editorial Introduction," *Journal of Sport History*, v. 23, n. 3 (Fall 1996), 310.

28. Springwood, *Cooperstown to Dyersville*, 147. See also Eldon E. Snyder, "Sociology of Nostalgia: Sport Halls of Fame and Museums in America," *Sociology of Sport Journal*, v. 8 (1991), 228–238.

29. Warren Jay Goldstein, *Playing for Keeps: A History of Early Baseball* (Ithaca, New York: Cornell University Press, 1989), 1–2. See also David Lamoreux, "Baseball in the Late Nineteenth Century: The Source of Its Appeal," *Journal of Popular Culture*, v. 11 (1977), 597–613.

30. Shore, "Loading the Bases," 12.

31. Roger Kahn, *A Season in the Sun* (New York: Harper and Row, 1977), 8.

32. Davis, *Yearning for Yesterday*, 1. See also Ralph Harper, *Nostalgia: An Existential Exploration of Longing and Fulfillment in the Modern Age* (Cleveland: Western Reserve University, 1966), 26–29.

Part 3

THE BUSINESS OF BASEBALL

of the National League.

split-second decisions, the
managers, the difference in
, and the need for umpires to
es and for the game can cause
It in inappropriate behavior on
es.
ere employed either by the Amer-
NL). When unacceptable behavior
es' presidents or the Commissioner
appropriate discipline. How these
ed the labor relations climate between
ent. Umpires expect league officials to
ut discipline which reflects the serious-
players or managers. Luciano identified
ue officials handled discipline issues as an
anger into working harder for the union.[8]

ajor League Umpires

umpires began organizing secretly in 1963 and
of National Baseball Umpires — Independent.
ginated the idea of unionizing, urged others to fol-
hey kick us around like a rubber ball because they
ay with it." Al Barlick, Shag Crawford, Jocko Con-
ill Jackowski, Stan Landes, Mel Steiner, and Eddie
y union activists. The new union invited the Ameri-
s to join. However, they chose not to join, probably
a negative reaction from Joe Cronin, president of the
.[9]
pires presented their demands to Warren Giles, president
League. Shag Crawford stated that there was some resent-
t of the owners, and that the umpires were aware that orga-
cost them their jobs. He believed however, that the league
mp all twenty-four of us at the same time" unless it really
et nasty." He further explained, "There were some really great
s with outstanding reputations involved, so I think they didn't have
of a choice but to sit down and talk to us."[10]
When the umpires told the National League that they had unionized,

Major League Umpires and Collective Bargaining

Karen Shallcross Koziara

Baseball labor relations have exposed fans to fierce disagreements, including bitter strikes and lockouts and a canceled World Series. In 1999 a new collective bargaining issue rocked major league baseball. The Major League Umpires Association (MLUA), looking ahead to negotiations and a possible lockout in 2000, voted to use mass resignations as a tactic to pressure baseball management to negotiate. The consequences of that action included the termination of 22 umpires, the union president's removal from office, the decertification of MLUA, and certification of a new union, the World Umpires Association. This paper analyzes the background and implications of these events.

The Labor Market

Almost all professional umpires begin their careers at an accredited umpire school. An aspiring umpire learns the school's system and culture, including how to wear equipment, how to make calls, and how to make decisions quickly in stressful conditions. Durwood Merrill, a recently retired major league umpire, described umpire school as a cross between going to Marine boot camp and mucking horse stalls. The schools focus on exposing students to the reality of professional umpiring. For example, the instructors work to determine whether their students can handle stress. Merrill explained that after a close call, "You turn around and one of the instructors, pretending to be a manager, is yelling and spitting in your face … You've got to react quickly. You can't back down or stutter. You've got to defend your call and stand your ground." He stated that often instructors are more concerned with whether students have the "guts" to back up a call than whether the call was correct. It was also at umpire school where he learned the odds of becoming a professional umpire. About one percent get to the majors.[1]

The next step in becoming a professional umpire is attending a try-out camp. Major League Baseball and the Professional Baseball Umpire Corporation jointly employ minor league umpires. The Corporation indicates how many umpires it needs for the year, and the schools send approximately twice that number to tryout camps. The Corporation's evaluators select umpires for the minor leagues at the camps. On average, about fifteen minor league umpires retire annually, and there are a few promotions to the majors. There are generally fewer than 20 openings for new umpires annually.[2]

Employment conditions for minor league umpires vary according to the level of the league. The starting salary for Class AAA umpires is about $3,400 a month, and in the lowest ranked league, the Rookie League, umpires earn about $1,800 a month. Class AAA umpires may fly between cities or travel in league vans, with the umpires doing the driving. In Class A umpires use their own vehicles and are reimbursed for gas.[3]

The late Ron Luciano, a former umpire and president of the Major League Umpires Association, described minor league life as, "Long automobile rides between small towns to work games under lighting too dim to brighten a porch, dressing in closets, sleeping in hotel rooms so small that you eat in the room and gain weight you can't get off, and surviving on cold hot dogs and warm soda."[4] The work is intense because every call is important to the players and managers desperately trying to make the majors.

The Major Leagues

For the professional umpires who make it to the major leagues, some working conditions improve dramatically. The starting salary was $75,000 a year in 1999, air travel is common, and the ballparks are significantly better than in the minors. However, some working conditions remain difficult.

First, the work itself is stressful. Umpires must make calls quickly and accurately, and aggravated players and fuming fans frequently and publicly question their judgment. Umpiring at home plate is particularly

league officials at first did not take them seriously. Two owners, Walter O'Malley of Los Angeles and John Galbreath of Pittsburgh, surprised at the umpires' low salaries, supported the umpires. At the time the starting salary was $7,500, the average salary was about $13,000, and the pension, which was deducted from the umpires' salaries, was $150 per year for every year of service. The union negotiated its first contract in 1964. Wages and the pension program were major bargaining topics. Over the next ten years there were substantial gains in pensions and benefits, and the starting salary rose to $12,500.[11]

The AL umpires were aware of the gains made by the NL umpires, and they began discussing unionization in 1965. These talks were communicated to Cal Hubbard, the AL's supervisor of umpires who reported directly to President Cronin. The umpires did not establish a formal union at that point. In August the umpires appointed a committee of five senior umpires to meet with Cronin to discuss a list of 19 items, including salaries, pensions, other employee benefits, and expenses. The committee met with Cronin and presented him with the list and parts of the minutes from the umpires' original meeting. These minutes indicated that the umpires were not attempting to form a union, but merely attempting to get better working conditions. The minutes noted that the NL umpires already had won all the items requested by the AL umpires.[12]

At a January, 1966, meeting with all the AL umpires, Cronin said that he had acted positively on many of the 19 items. However, he believed salaries should continue as private matters between each umpire and himself. In a similar January 1967 meeting the umpires again asked to discuss salaries and pensions. Cronin became angry with the umpires, and again made it clear that he was not interested in discussing salaries.[13]

The AL umpires became increasingly interested in unionization in 1968. Alexander Salerno and William T. Valentine, Jr., were particularly active organizers. They talked to other umpires about organizing, and in July sought labor relations advice from an attorney. On September 12 Salerno met with the union representing the NL umpires. The union agreed to accept the AL umpires as members if they all agreed to join. On September 13 Salerno sent letters to the AL umpires for them to sign in order to join the union. On September 16, with two weeks of the season remaining, Cronin called Salerno and Valentine, telling them that they were "not competent or good umpires" and that he was not renewing their contracts for 1969. They received pay for the balance of the season and 30 days severance pay. They never again worked as professional umpires.[14]

The American League's actions in response to umpire unionization led to two National Labor Relations Act (NLRA) cases. The National Labor

Relations Board (NLRB) decision in the first of these cases has had a major impact on both umpire and player labor relations. It set the precedent that the NLRA covered collective bargaining in baseball. The second case followed that precedent.

The Role of the National Labor Relations Act

In the United States, the National Labor Relations Act regulates most private sector collective bargaining. The NLRA encourages collective bargaining by providing protections for workers interested in unionization and for the collective bargaining process. Section 7, the heart of the NLRA, guarantees employees the right to form a union and engage in collective bargaining. The National Labor Relations Board, the agency responsible for administering the NLRA, has two primary functions. One is to determine when unfair labor practices as outlined in the NLRA have been committed. Unfair labor practices are actions that undermine collective bargaining, such as employers threatening employees and discriminating against union activists.

The other major NLRB function is to decide representation questions, or whether a particular group of workers wants a union to represent them. The NLRB allows employers to directly recognize a union when the employer and union agree that a majority of the employees want representation. This process is called direct recognition.

More commonly employers do not voluntarily recognize unions. In these instances the NLRA provides for secret ballot elections to determine whether or not employees want union representation. If a majority of the employees vote for unionization, the NLRA requires that the employer bargain with the union.

The National League's decision to bargain with the umpires' union was direct recognition. Because the National League voluntarily recognized and negotiated with the union, it did not request an election. Because the NLRB was not involved, the legal question of whether the NLRA covered major league baseball was not addressed.

The NLRA's jurisdiction was a potential issue because for most of the 20th Century major league baseball was exempt from federal antitrust legislation. This exemption began with the *Federal Baseball* (1922) decision.[15] In *Federal Baseball* the Supreme Court ruled that baseball was not "commerce" and was only incidentally involved in interstate commerce. This reasoning appeared to preclude baseball employees from NLRA protections because its jurisdiction is limited to organizations in interstate commerce.

The decision that the NLRA covers major league baseball resulted from a representation question. After the termination of Salerno and Valentine, the NL umpires' union, renamed the Major League Umpires Association, Inc. (MLUA), petitioned the NLRB for an election to determine whether the AL umpires wanted union representation. AL management opposed the petition. Its position partially rested on major league baseball's longstanding judicial exemption from antitrust law. In cases following *Federal Baseball*, the court continued baseball's exemption from antitrust law in the belief that it was the responsibility of Congress to legislate any changes in the exemption.

In its 1969 decision the NLRB's most important arguments focused on whether the antitrust precedents exempted major league baseball from NLRA regulation. The Board decided that the antitrust exemption did not preclude NLRA coverage. It explained that neither the Congressional deliberations over the NLRA nor the language of the NLRA showed any intent to exempt baseball from coverage. If Congress chose, it could have included baseball among the NLRA's other exemptions. In an almost prophetic statement the Board stated, "There is persuasive reason to believe that future labor disputes — should they arise in this industry — will be national in scope, radiating their impact far beyond individual State boundaries." The NLRB explained that although Congress had not passed legislation to revoke baseball's antitrust exemption, there was no indication that it sanctioned a government wide policy of "non-involvement" in all baseball matters. To the contrary, Congress enacted the NLRA specifically to provide employees in almost every industry the right to organize and bargain collectively.[16]

With this decision the NLRB established the precedent that the Sherman Act did not remove major league baseball from NLRA coverage. The immediate impact of the case was to provide the AL umpires with protected bargaining rights. The broader impact was the provision of NLRA protections for all Major League Baseball employees, including players, groundskeepers, and others.

AL management also argued that NLRB involvement was not needed because the Commissioner's office provided an internal self-regulatory mechanism. The NLRB found that the commissioner, chosen and paid by the owners, was not an appropriate neutral. The league also contended that umpires were supervisors, and ineligible for NLRA protections. The NLRB ruled that the umpires do not have the authority to "hire, fire, transfer, discharge, recall, promote, assign or reward." The umpires' responsibility is to make sure games are played in conformance with the rules. An umpire does not, "tell a player how to bat, how to field, to work hard or exert more effort, nor can he tell a manager which players to play or where to play them."[17]

In 1971 the NLRB decided a second case involving umpires and Major League Baseball. This case focused on whether Cronin engaged in an unfair labor practice when he terminated umpires Salerno and Valentine in 1968. The union alleged that the American League discriminated against Salerno and Valentine in order to discourage union activity, an NLRA violation. The NLRB General Counsel stated that the reason given by the AL for the terminations was a pretext for the real reason, which was the umpires' organizing activity. He also pointed out that terminating umpires during the season was unprecedented, and occurred without warning. Further, although no direct proof existed that Cronin knew about the umpires' union involvement, there was substantial circumstantial evidence that he was aware of and opposed to unionization.[18]

The NLRB's decision in this case focused on the lack of direct evidence that Cronin knew of the union activity of Salerno and Valentine. The AL officials involved testified that they did not know the two umpires were active in organizing a union until after their termination. The case was dismissed.

The decisions in these cases may seem contradictory. The decision in the election request case strongly supported the right of baseball's employees to engage in collective bargaining. The unfair labor practice decision, in contrast, was much less protective of the umpires' organizing rights. The difference in the decisions in these cases most likely reflects the political nature of appointments to the NLRB. The NLRB has five members, with appointments spread over five years. Normally the President of the United States appoints one NLRB member each year. In 1969, for the first decision, although Richard Nixon was president, a majority of the NLRB members were Democratic appointments. In 1971, a majority of the members were Republican appointments.

Early Labor Relations Experience

Given the outcome of the Salerno-Valentine case, it is not surprising that the early collective bargaining relationship between the umpires and baseball management was relatively nonconfrontational. Merrill described the umpires, particularly those from the AL, as "scared to death of the Baseball Lords." He explained, "We didn't have a strong union, and we got kicked around like a bunch of yard dogs.... The bosses knew that our union would split like a piece of dry wood if they threatened to send guys back to the minor leagues.... We needed a bully to run the union."[19]

Perhaps due to the lack of solidarity described by Merrill, from 1963 until 1978 negotiations were generally peaceful, and there was only one strike. That strike, which had a contract as its objective, occurred on the first day of the 1970 playoffs. The union struck in both Pittsburgh, Pennsylvania, and Bloomington, Minnesota. The leagues used replacements to umpire the first playoff game in each league, a tactic they were to use frequently in the future. A settlement occurred just before the second game was to begin. Shag Crawford, a union officer, explained, "We didn't want to strike, but it was one of those situations where we had no alternative because the leagues tried to back us against the wall. We knew there was risk ... there were a lot of guys in the minor leagues just itching to go up to the majors.... Besides, we were only asking for what was right." [20] Gorman's description is similar. He said, "We didn't want to strike and hurt the good name of baseball, but we were forced into it.... We were fighting for a contract."[21]

In 1978 the MLPA, looking for stronger representation, hired Richie Phillips, whose experience included representing the National Basketball Association's referees. With his arrival, the relationship between the umpires and baseball management changed rapidly. Luciano, who became MLPA president in 1979, said of Phillips, "After Phillips took over the joking stopped. He immediately made it clear that we were willing to do whatever was necessary to gain benefits we felt we deserved."[22] In a similar vein, Merrill described the owners and baseball bosses as getting "Pepto-Bismol stomachs when they see Richie swaggering into a bargaining room." He stated, "Some people think he is a loose cannon but, by gosh, that's what umpires needed back in 1979 when our collective backbone didn't amount to a couple of herniated disks."[23]

One of Phillips's first public strategies was to orchestrate a one-day strike in 1978. A new contract had been agreed to in 1977, but several clauses remained to be negotiated. The union made a number of unsuccessful attempts to meet with the Commissioner's office to negotiate these clauses. The strike's objective was to get resolution of these issues. A federal judge enjoined the strike, in which replacements were again used, because it violated the contract's no-strike clause.[24] However, that strike was a harbinger of things to come, including a bitter strike in 1979, replacement umpires, lockouts, and strike threats with contracts in effect. The following is an overview of the relationship between Major League Baseball and the umpires from 1979 through early 2000.

Labor Relations Following 1978

The changed nature of the collective bargaining relationship between the umpires and baseball was made clear by a seven-week strike in 1979. At the time the leagues had individual contracts with the umpires. To simplify negotiations, each umpire designated Phillips as his personal attorney, so theoretically Phillips represented individual umpires rather than a union. Prior to spring training, the league offices sent umpires individual contracts along with a letter warning that no umpire would be allowed to attend spring training without a signed contract. In an effort to negotiate better wages and benefits, the umpires, after much soul searching and with cajoling from Phillips, did not sign the letters or attend spring training. During spring training the leagues sent the umpires letters indicating their readiness to hire replacements. The umpires did not report and the strike began. Luciano, MLUA's president, described Phillips as "masterful" in orchestrating the strike. He explained, "He told us what to say, when to say it, who to say it to, and how to say it. Other than that we were on our own. But he was best at meetings.... If I hadn't been out already, I would have gone on strike right then and there."[25]

The season began with replacement umpires. From the standpoint of the leagues, replacement umpires were preferable to the economic costs of canceling games. This strategy made sense for several reasons. Although umpires are necessary to baseball, they are relatively few-in-number and not well known individually to fans. They are easier to replace, particularly for short periods, than players.

Using striker replacements typically increases strike bitterness, and the bitterness often lingers to affect the bargaining relationship after the strike ends. Strikers see replacements as undercutting their bargaining power, and taking their jobs and incomes for an unpredictable period of time, and perhaps permanently. In many instances the use of replacements increases strike length by enabling employers to avoid some income losses. Luciano felt this was the case in the 1979 strike. He explained, "There is a strong feeling that the strike lasted seven weeks because these men worked, so, since the end of the strike, very few umpires have talked to them off the field."[26]

Tensions between MLUA and the leagues were somewhat reduced in the 1980s. Perhaps the costs of the 1979 strike taught the parties lessons that they did not wish to repeat. Another possible factor was increased sensitivity to umpires' concerns from the Commissioner's office. Some observers felt that the Commissioners during that period influenced the labor relations climate. Author John Feinstein, for example, felt that Peter

Ueberroth, Bart Giamatti, and particularly Fay Vincent, were viewed as pro-umpire.[27]

Nonetheless, the 1984 contract negotiations involved a seven-game strike during the playoffs. The issues were wages, benefits, and job security. As in 1979, the leagues used replacement umpires. The union's timing of the strike was designed to increase bargaining power by forcing the use of replacements for critical games.

The union threatened to use this strategy again to disrupt the 1985 playoffs in a dispute over compensation for playoff games. In 1985 the playoff schedule expanded from five to seven games. The existing contract based compensation on a five game playoff schedule. Because a contract was in effect, the union could not legally strike. Arbitration, rather than through a work stoppage, resolved the dispute. The arbitrator, former President Richard M. Nixon, ruled that the umpires' playoff pay should increase 40 percent. He recommended that the leagues recognize the umpires' unique relationship to baseball. He wrote, "Umpires should not be treated as employees but as judges who are independent of both players and owners and whose primary responsibility is to maintain the integrity of the game.... They should be generously compensated, having in mind their indispensable contribution to the integrity of the game"[28]

A work stoppage was avoided in the 1987 negotiations, although the new contract was not signed until 11 A.M. on Opening Day. In 1991 a new four-year contract was negotiated with only a brief work stoppage. When the umpires refused to work the last two days of spring training, replacements were used for these games. Due to time constraints and logistical difficulties, only one union crew was umpired on Opening Day.[29]

The 1995 negotiations were difficult. The dispute between the Major League Baseball Player Association and the owners that began in 1994, resulting in cancellation of the World Series, remained unsettled in early 1995. The leagues locked out both the players and the umpires during spring training. The players' lockout was enjoined, and they returned to a short spring training and the start of the 1995 season. The leagues continued the umpire lockout, employing replacement umpires. Baseball management appeared ready for a long lockout, but two forces intervened and led to a settlement. First, managers and players were increasingly agitated about the quality of umpiring by replacements. Secondly, the Ontario Labor Board ruled that umpire replacements could not be used in Toronto.[30]

The 1990s saw increasing usage of lockouts as an employer strategy in many industries. Lockouts enable employers to time work stoppages in order to increase their bargaining power. Lockouts are particularly potent weapons when combined with replacement workers. This allows the employer both to time the work stoppage to its advantage and to continue operations and generate income. Locked out employees have little power to place economic pressure on the employer.

The use of replacement workers during a strike often negatively affects the subsequent relationship between the union and the employer. The impact of using replacement workers during a lockout is likely to have an even more detrimental impact on the parties' relationship. This tactic signals the employer's intention to use a no-holds-barred approach to negotiations. Even when, as with the 1995 lockout, external pressures force the employer to forgo the lockout, its adversarial implications were clearly communicated to the union and its members.

Given the use of a lockout and replacements, it is not surprising that the new contract did not end hostilities between MLUA and league officials. One example of the adversarial nature of their relationship involved a 1996 conflict over Fox and ESPN broadcast policies. The umpires objected to the networks using overhead cameras to "second guess" ball and strike calls, as well as to the "overly critical" comments of some announcers. In protest the umpires refused to enforce the two minute, 23 second commercial break between innings. This resulted in a shorter break period, with viewers missing pitches, and the networks shortening commercials and losing money as a result. Network officials were furious, and took the issue to the league offices. In response, the league officials filed a grievance against the umpires. Phillips contended that the union's contract did not require the umpires to monitor the time elapsed between innings. The impartial arbitrator, however, ruled that it was an established past practice and found for the American and National Leagues.[31]

Past practice is a common concept in labor arbitration. The relationship between the parties is made up of more than what is written in the contract. Customary practices that are consistently used take on legitimacy as part of the relationship. In this instance, umpires historically had monitored the time between innings, and thus it became an established past practice.

Later in 1996 another situation exacerbated tensions between Major League Baseball and the umpires. Baltimore Oriole Roberto Alomar spat on American League umpire John Hirschbeck several days prior to the end of the regular season. The American League president disciplined Alomar by suspending him for five regular season games. The umpires were outraged because of the briefness of the suspension and its timing, which allowed Alomar to participate in the playoffs. The umpires, believing that baseball had violated their contract by failing to adequately protect them, voted to strike unless Alomar was suspended during the playoffs. The strike was enjoined because the umpires' contract had a no-strike clause. The injunction prevented a strike, but did not resolve underlying conflicts between the umpires and the league presidents. In fact, Phillips encouraged the umpires to disobey the injunction, but they chose to work.[32]

In response to the controversy generated by the Alomar incident, Acting Commissioner Bud Selig arranged a meeting to discuss discipline issues early in 1997. Representatives from the umpires' union, the players' union, the presidents of both leagues, and other management officials attended. Selig described the meeting as a full discussion with the views of all the parties heard. Although the participants agreed to have a study group examine baseball discipline, little concrete change occurred.[33] Given that the discipline procedures for both players and umpires are governed by their respective collective bargaining contracts, it is not surprising that the meeting resulted in few changes in discipline policies and umpires' attitudes.

At the meeting Richie Phillips made clear that the umpires' source of unhappiness was the league presidents and their policies, not the players. In his view the underlying issue was whether league officials would give umpires the support needed to maintain discipline. However, some players saw tensions growing due to umpires being increasingly combative and aggressive.[34]

The acrimony between the umpires and baseball management continued. In October 1997, Phillips sent a letter to league officials that announced the union was directing umpires to eject players who argued close plays. The letter accused the league presidents of refusing to deter player misconduct, and complained that National League President Coleman had fined umpires after superimposing his judgment on their decisions.[35] Baseball management responded with a stern warning that umpires would face legal action if they tried to impose a code-of-conduct that differed from standard practice.[36]

Recent Events

The tensions between the leagues and the umpires continued through 1999. The contract ran until 2000, and there were indications that negotiations would be difficult, and have an emphasis on noneconomic issues. The Commissioner's office wanted more control over umpires and the quality of umpiring. Its goal was to manage umpires directly, rather than through the league presidents. In order to encourage consistency, Commissioner Selig wanted to mix umpires from the National and American Leagues on crews and to institute an evaluation system.

The potential increase in management control had little appeal to the union. It saw these measures as the beginning of management efforts to undermine the union. Phillips said that league officials informed him privately of plans to terminate 20 low-rated umpires, and job security was an issue.[37] Management's "deteriorating respect" and the lack of a code of conduct promised by baseball management after the Alomar spitting incident were also concerns. The Commissioner's efforts to influence the strike zone, including asking home teams to monitor balls and strikes, was another issue.[38] These issues promised to be contentious. As the end of the contract neared, the union grew concerned about the possibility of another spring lockout and reviewed its strategy options. Striking during post season games was precluded by previous judicial decisions outlawing strikes while a contract was in effect.

The union voted to use mass resignation as a tactic on July 14, 1999, with the resignations effective as of September 2. This tactic's objective was to apply bargaining pressure while avoiding a lockout and circumventing the contract's no strike clause. The union planned to set up a corporation to provide the umpires for baseball management.[39]

The mass resignation strategy was legal, but risky. First, for any hope of success, the umpires had to be committed to remaining united. Unity was a challenge in this stressful situation because umpires, like people in most organizations, have differing tolerances for risk and ambiguity. Even if they had remained united, the strategy might have failed. Its success depended on the Commissioner's willingness to contract with the union for umpires rather than hire them directly. This did not interest baseball management given its objective of centralizing control over umpires.

Some umpires rethought the wisdom of resignation, and 23 of the 68 umpires who had resigned rescinded their resignations on July 23. On July 27 the remaining 45 umpires rescinded their resignations, but were informed by Commissioner Selig that some of them would lose their jobs because 25 replacements had been hired. On July 28 the Commissioner's office informed 22 of the umpires that their resignations were accepted and they could not work past August 2. The fate of these 22 umpires depends on the outcome of an arbitration case heard in May, June and July 2000, and the 2000 contract negotiations.

MULA was decertified as the umpires' bargaining representative late in 1999, and its contract with the National and American Leagues ended December 31, 1999. The owners voted in January 2000 to eliminate league offices and presidents. This consolidated umpire supervision in the Commissioner's office. In February 2000 the NLRB certified the results of an election in which the umpires chose the World Umpires Association (WUA) as their bargaining representative.[40]

The WUA and the Commissioner's office entered into an interim agreement in March 2000. The agreement provided for merger of the umpires from the American and National Leagues into one unit, retroactive wages upon settlement of a final contract, and no strikes or lockouts until June 2000.[41] The parties did not agree to a final contract before the interim contract expired.

When negotiations began in 2000, WUA president John Hirschbeck hoped for a less confrontational relationship with baseball management.[42] July 2000 found the parties stymied over several noneconomic issues, and a new tone characterized their public statements. Baseball management wanted to restrict the right of umpires to speak with media representatives, and to continue the right to discipline umpires without being subject to arbitration. The right to discipline would facilitate management's efforts to implement increased consistency in calling balls and strikes. The union demands included discipline only for "just cause" and with the right to appeal to an arbitrator (a common standard in most contracts, but not for major league referees and umpires). The WUA wanted umpires to be able to make calls as they see them and to express their views in public. Another union demand was a remedy for the terminated 22 umpires.[43]

These issues are all related to baseball management's efforts to centralize control over umpiring. Sandy Alderson, executive vice president for baseball operations, made clear management's intent to take a hard line on the "control" issues. He described baseball management as resolved in 1999, and no less resolved in 2000. In the event of a strike, baseball management had a list of amateur, mostly college, replacements.[44]

Amateurs would be used because the WUA formed an alliance with the Association of Minor League Umpires, which is in the process of organizing minor league umpires. The WUA is also trying to heal its divisions with the umpires who supported the MLUA. For example, WUA leaders invited Jerry Crawford, former president of MLUA, to join them at the bargaining table.[45]

Lessons Learned

The first lesson is that an adversarial labor relations strategy, whether in baseball or in other industries, is a management choice. Much of the media attention to the 1999 events in the relationship between Major League Baseball and the umpires centered on Richie Phillips' leadership style and tactics. However, to focus on Phillips' role ignores the long and contentious history Major League Baseball has had with both players and umpires. Although the National League voluntarily recognized the umpires' union, the American League failed to follow suit. That decision was the first of many strategic choices destined to foster a combative relationship. These choices began with the terminations of Salerno and Valentine, and continued through strikes, lockouts and replacement umpires, up to the events of 1999. At many points major league baseball opted for a strategy likely to increase mistrust and confrontation.

In many ways, the umpires' choice of Phillips as their representative was a reaction to the strategies chosen by management. In turn, the choice of Phillips meant that confrontation was countered with more confrontation and escalating tensions, not cooperation. This reflects the tendency for coercive tactics, rather than conciliatory strategies, to increase an opponent's resolve, thereby escalating conflict.[46]

Confrontation is a risky strategy, and its outcomes are unpredictable. The history of baseball labor relations provides many illustrations of these unpredictable outcomes, including the canceled 1994 World Series. Certainly the umpires' resignation tactic produced an outcome that they had not anticipated. That outcome makes it appear that baseball management bested the umpires' union with the use of confrontation. Unfortunately we do not know how baseball labor relations, and even the game of baseball today, might be different if management had worked to develop collaborative relationships with its unions.

Notes

1. Durwood Merrill and James Dent, *You're Out and You're Ugly Too!* (New York: St. Martin's Press, 1998), 27.
2. Steve Strunsky, "One Eye on the Ball, the Other on the Majors," *The New York Times*, 22 August 1999, Sec. 4, p.1.
3. Ibid.
4. Ron Luciano and David Fisher, *Strike Two* (New York: Bantam Books, 1984), 33-35.
5. Merrill, *You're Out!* 77.
6. John Feinstein, *Play Ball* (New York: Villard Books, 1993), 193-194.
7. Tom Gorman and Jerome Hotzman, *Three and Two!* (New York: Charles Scribner's Sons, 1979), 1-2.
8. Ron Luciano and David Fisher, *The Umpire Strikes Back* (New York: Bantam Books, 1982), 123-124.
9. Gorman, *Three and Two!* 198-199.
10. Larry R. Gerlach, *The Men in Blue* (Lincoln, Nebraska: The University of Nebraska Press, 1980), 211.
11. Gorman, *Three and Two!* 200.

12. The American League of Professional Baseball Clubs and The Major League Umpires Association, Inc., 189 NLRB 85 (1971), 543.

13. Ibid., 544.

14. Ibid., 542.

15. Federal Baseball Clubs, Inc. v. National League of Professional Baseball Clubs, 295 U.S. 200 (1922).

16. The American League of Professional Baseball Clubs and Association of National Baseball League Umpires, 180 NLRB 30 (1969).

17. Ibid., 192-193.

18. The American League of Professional Baseball Clubs (1971).

19. Merrill, *You're Out!* 220-221.

20. Gerlach, *Men in Blue* 211-212.

21. Gorman, *Three and Two!* 200-201.

22. Luciano, *Umpire Strikes Back*, 232.

23. Merrill, *You're Out!* 220-221.

24. Luciano, *Umpire Strikes Back*, 232-233.

25. Ibid., 233-234.

26. Ibid., 238.

27. John Feinstein, *Play Ball*, 196.

28. Cerisse Anderson, *United Press International Sports News,* 28 Oct. 1985, BC Cycle.

29. Robert McG. Thomas, Jr., "Umpires Get 4-Year Pact and All Are to Return Today," *The New York Times*, 9 April 1991, Sec. B, 11.

30. Murray Chass, "Umpires Will Return Tomorrow," *The New York Times,* 2 May 1995, Sec. B, 11.

31. Bob Raissman, "Arbiter Ruling Balks at Umps," *New York Daily News*, 7 December 1997, 84.

32. Merrill, *You're Out!* 232.

33. Peter Schmuck, "Players, Umpires to Form Disciplinary Study Group; No Sweeping Changes Made for Unruly Behavior," *The Baltimore Sun,* 5 February 1977, Sec. D, 2.

34. Murray Chass, "Umpires Pitching for Peaceful Coexistence," *The New York Times,* 4 February 1997, Sec. B, 9.

35. John Rawlings, "Lousy Timing," *The Sporting News*, 6 October 1997, 34.

36. Peter Schmuck, "This Stance Should Get the Heave-Ho," *The Sporting News,* 13 October 1997, 34.

37. James C. McKinley, Jr., "Man Who United Umpires Now Divides Their Strength," *The New York Times*, 5 August 1999, Sec. A, 1.

38. Ibid., 1.

39. Andy McCue, "Andy McCue Column," *The Press-Enterprise*, 29 July 1999, 1.

40. Ronald Blum, "Baseball and Umpires Reach Interim Agreement," *The Associated Press State Local Wire*, 21 March 2000.

41. Ibid.

42. Murray Chass, "Baseball Roundup," *The New York Times*, 29 February 2000, Sec. D, 6.

43. Blum, "Interim Agreement."

44. Hal Bodley, "Owners Still Playing Hardball with the Umpires," *USA Today,* 23 June 2000, Sec. C, 12.

45. Ronald Blum, "In Possible Step Toward Peace, Old Union President Joins Talks," *The Associated Press*, 29 June 2000, DC Cycle.

46. Leigh Thompson, *Making the Team,* (Upper Saddle River, NJ: Prentice Hall, 2000), 149.

Customer Discrimination in Memorabilia: New Evidence for Major League Baseball

Rhonda Sharpe and Sumner J. La Croix[1]

Economic studies of racial discrimination have proliferated over the last 20 years, and North American Major League Baseball (MLB), due to its long history of racial discrimination by owners, players, and fans, has been the subject of numerous such studies. This chapter contributes to the literature on customer discrimination by using a detailed data set to analyze discrimination by MLB fans in the market for four types of baseball memorabilia: autographed baseballs, autographed photos, game jerseys, and gloves. We examine the prices of these baseball memorabilia to determine whether baseball fans prefer the memorabilia of white players to black or Latin players, all else equal. Because detailed statistics are maintained on the productivity of individual baseball players, we are able to control relatively precisely for the effect of player productivity on the prices of memorabilia. This enables us to isolate the effect of race on customer choices more effectively than most other studies of customer discrimination.

Racial Discrimination in Baseball: A Quick Review of the Literature

Discrimination studies examining MLB are typically distinguished from other studies of labor markets by their use of far more extensive controls for individual performance. In general, these studies have found extensive evidence of employer and customer racial discrimination against minority players in MLB.[2] Studies of customer racial discrimination in baseball can be separated into four types: (1) studies of variation in the willingness of baseball fans to pay to attend an MLB game as the ethnic composition of the team and certain key positions changes; (2) studies of discrimination in player salaries; (3) studies of variation in the prices paid by baseball fans for the baseball cards of individual MLB players; and (4) studies of fan voting to select the starting players for the National and American Leagues in MLB's annual All-Star Game. We review the last two types of studies below, as they have the most relevance to this article.

Nardinelli and Simon tested for discrimination by MLB fans by examining a market for a product related to MLB: baseball cards depicting MLB players and listing annual measures of their performance.[3] Their regression analysis showed that the prices paid by fans for baseball cards reflected the performance records of the players depicted as well as other player characteristics. In particular, they found discrimination against Latin hitters and black pitchers. Estimated coefficients on dummy variables for Latin pitchers and black hitters, while negative, were statistically insignificant at the 5 percent level.

Andersen and La Croix also examined the market for baseball cards.[4] They used the same statistical methods as Nardinelli and Simon, but used aggregate player productivity variables to allow player productivity to interact with the two race variables. They found a complex set of results. For the 1960-61 sample of hitters, card collectors did not discriminate against blacks or Latinos; for the 1960–61 sample of pitchers, card collectors discriminated against average and below-average black pitchers but paid a premium for superstar black pitchers. For the 1977 sample of hitters, a black player's card registered a lower price at all productivity levels and increased less with additional productivity than did a white player's card price. And for the 1977 pitchers sample, they found that a black player's card price increased less with additional productivity than a white player's card price; thus, card collectors discriminated against above-average black pitchers while paying a premium for average and below-average black pitchers.

Gabriel, Johnson, and Stanton and McGarrity, Palmer, and Poitras have criticized the Andersen and La Croix and the Nardinelli and Simon studies for analyzing card prices from a data set of heterogeneous cards; for using inefficient statistical techniques; and for not incorporating relevant variables into their statistical analyses.[5] Their econometric studies of the baseball card market found little evidence of racial discrimination by baseball fans in their purchases of baseball cards. The contrasting results may be due to their use of more recent card prices (1995 prices) than those employed in earlier studies (mid-1980s prices), as racial discrimination has lessened over the last 30 years in most walks of life.

Hanssen and Andersen investigate more systematically the possibility that racial discrimination by baseball fans has been declining over the last 30 years.[6] They examine patterns of voting for MLB's National League and American League All Star teams, searching for substantial evidence of fan racial discrimination. They begin by examining whether there was racial discrimination in the League's selection of players for the All-Star ballot. If this were the case, then MLB fans would be voting from a ballot containing a racially biased sample of players. Finding no evidence of discrimination in selecting players for the ballot, they then examined fan voting. Their central finding is that the preferences of fan voters have changed dramatically over time: Substantial racial discrimination in fan voting during the early 1970s had totally disappeared by 1979. Remarkably, Hanssen and Andersen "find that in 1996 the best black players were *more* likely to be among the top vote getters for a given level of performance. These results support the conclusion that public attitudes towards African Americans have improved substantially" over the last two decades.[7] Hanssen and Andersen's findings are important for our investigation of prices paid for baseball memorabilia, as we analyze prices paid by baseball fans from late 1995 to April 1996.

The Market for Baseball Memorabilia

The market for baseball memorabilia has exploded since the 1970s. Autographed memorabilia has become widely available in general purpose and specialized hobby shops in most cities, and has been regularly sold (and autographed by former and current players as you watch) on cable TV's home shopping channels since the mid-1980s. The revolution in the baseball memorabilia market arrived in 1998 with the rapid ascendancy of Internet auctions of memorabilia owned by average baseball fans. During Spring 2000, over 100,000 items of baseball memorabilia were listed daily on eBay, the on-line auction house. Many other web sites, including Beckett.com and MrBaseball.com, regularly list and auction a wide variety of items, including autographed photos, gloves, game jerseys, bats, and balls.

Memorabilia associated with unique, well-known milestones in baseball history have been auctioned by established auction houses such as Christie's and Sotheby's, as well as by new-comers like Creative Properties

Management Group. Prices received at auction have notably increased during the 1990s. In 1992 the actor Charlie Sheen paid $93,000 for the ball that Red Sox first baseman Bill Buckner saw squirt between his legs in the 1986 World Series. A Honus Wagner baseball card was sold in September 1996 by Christie's for $640,500. These prices pale before the $3.005 million paid on January 12, 1999, by comic-book publisher Todd McFarlane for Mark McGwire's 70th home run ball. Minutes after the McGwire ball sold, Sammy Sosa's 66th home run ball sold for $150,000.[8]

Prices of more generic baseball memorabilia are not nearly so stratospheric, yet are high enough to discourage less wealthy collectors. For example, the 1996 price of a Barry Bonds jersey worn in a 1994 San Francisco Giants home game was $2,195.[9] A near-mint condition glove used by Gil Hodges of the Brooklyn Dodgers sold for $85 in 1996. A Louisville Slugger bat used by George Foster in games during 1977–1979 sold for $125 in 1996.

Is the market for baseball memorabilia a competitive, national market? While there is no central organized market for baseball memorabilia, prices in memorabilia shops, on-line and on-site auctions, and informal transactions are linked by on-line sites and print publications that regularly report transaction prices. These price-reporting mechanisms tend to narrow the price bounds within which transactions occur and ensure that the market is a national market. Given the widespread, decentralized ownership of baseball memorabilia, it seems unlikely that any one participant has the ability to exercise significant market power.

Examination of the prices of autographed jerseys, balls, photographs, and gloves revealed that they are typically much higher than prices of the baseball cards for the same players. We conjecture that the higher prices generally would have the effect of pushing younger, less wealthy baseball fans out of the resale market. This means that memorabilia prices are more likely to reflect the ethnic and racial preferences of higher-income, older (>21 years old) baseball fans. Thus, a potential advantage of our study over earlier studies of customer discrimination in the MLB card market is that it focuses on racial preferences of a single group — older male baseball fans — rather than mixing the potentially quite different preferences of older and younger fans.

Our Methodology

We use state-of-the-art statistical techniques to determine whether MLB fans discriminate against black and Latin players in the market for baseball memorabilia. Since the market for baseball cards has already been extensively studied, we focus on other memorabilia, in particular autographed baseballs, gloves, player jerseys, and photos. As we discussed above, there is a large national resale market for this merchandise, and several catalogs report recent transaction prices in major cities with relatively large markets for this merchandise.

To estimate whether there is racial/ethnic discrimination in the market for baseball memorabilia, we first merged three databases: (1) memorabilia pricing and supply information, (2) player performance and characteristics data, and (3) racial and ethnic identity information. Memorabilia pricing information was taken from the widely available *Complete Guide to Baseball Memorabilia.*[10] The *Guide* provides pricing information on everything from autographed pictures to collectible figurines, and for some items provides rough information on their supply. We utilized the *Guide's* price quotes for autographed photos and baseballs as well as jerseys and gloves. *BaseBall DataBase 5.1* contains virtually complete career performance statistics, place and date of birth, as well as rookie and retirement years for all players from 1875 to 1998.[11] Our data set only includes players who were inactive after the 1994 season to eliminate the effect of buyers speculating on an active player's future performance. We classify players into racial and ethnic categories by two methods: place of birth and visual inspection of baseball cards. All players in the league prior to Jackie Robinson integrating baseball in 1947 or born in the United States and not classified as black are classified as white. A player is considered Latin if he is born in a Latin American or Spanish-speaking country. A player is classified as Caribbean, Asian, or European if he is born in a country with the same geographic descriptor.[12] Players are classified as black if they were born in the USA and visual inspection of Topps baseball cards published in *The Complete Picture Collection: A 40 Year History 1951–1990* indicates the player to be black.[13] Players not found in the *Collection* were identified from team photos, baseball cards, and publicity pictures.[14]

Our empirical analysis of memorabilia prices proceeds in two stages. In the first stage, we analyze whether the *Guide's* sample of player memorabilia was randomly drawn from the overall population of baseball players. This would seem to be unlikely, as its author would surely have included players with higher productivity, as these players are more well known to collectors and their memorabilia is more likely to be highly valued. We would also like to know whether the *Guide's* author selected memorabilia on the basis of player race or other player characteristics. Our first-stage analysis proceeds by running a probit regression to determine whether white players were more likely to be listed in the *Guide* than black or Latin players, holding other characteristics and productivity constant. The probit equation is specified as

$$(1)\ B_i = \gamma X_i + \alpha Y_i + \gamma D_i + v_i$$

where B_i is 0 if a player's memorabilia is not listed in the *Guide* and 1 if it is listed, X_i are player productivity measures, Y_i are player characteristics, D_i are dummy variables for ethnicity/race, and v_i is an error term.[15] Using the results from the estimated probit equation, we calculate a new variable (the inverse Mill's ratio) that allows us to correct for sample selection bias in the next stage of the empirical analysis stemming from the author's selection of player memorabilia for the *Guide*.

In the second stage of the empirical analysis, we investigate whether the *Guide's* prices for each type of baseball memorabilia incorporate price premia or discounts for Latin and black players. We run an ordinary least squares regression

$$(2)\ \text{Log } P_i = \beta X_i + \alpha Y_i + \gamma D_i + \mu S_i + \delta \lambda_i + \varepsilon_i$$

of the log of memorabilia price (Log P_i) on player productivity measures (X_i), player characteristics (Y_i), dummy variables for race (D_i), dummy variables for the supply and condition of the memorabilia item (S_i), the inverse Mills ratio (λ_i), and ε_i is an error term. If the estimated coefficients on the race dummy variables are negative and statistically significant, then we will infer that customers are discriminating in this particular memorabilia market with respect to player race.

Summary Statistics

Table 1 presents simple averages of several components of career productivity for all fielders and designated hitters who played in at least one MLB game between 1875 and 1994 *and* who were inactive after the 1994 season. The average productivity measures are decomposed into white, Latin, and black categories.[16] To provide appropriate comparisons to black and Latin players who were barred from MLB until 1947, productivity statistics for white players are reported for the 1947–1994 period as well as the 1875–1994 period. Table 1 reports disaggregated measures of productivity, such as home runs, bases-on-balls, and stolen bases as well as two indexes of productivity constructed from the raw measures. Batting average, career hits divided by career at bats, is a widely reported and highly flawed index of player productivity.[17] Offense average overcomes these difficulties by incorporating all major measures of hitter productivity into the index as well as weighting each base hit by the number of bases reached.[18]

All measures of average career productivity in Table 1 register one dominant pattern: Average career productivity measures for black players exceed those for Latin players which exceed those for white players. For example, the average black hitter hit 118 doubles, the average Latin hitter 91, and the average white hitter 47. Part of the reason for this overwhelming career dominance is that black and Latin hitters have much longer average careers than white hitters: 9.64 seasons for black hitters, 8.92 seasons for Latin hitters, and 5.64 seasons for white hitters. If we transform career productivity statistics to per-season statistics (not reported), the original ranking of productivity remains, but the productivity gap between black, Latin, and white hitters is somewhat smaller on a per season basis. For example, an average black hitter hit an average of 9.6 doubles per season, an average Latin hitter 7.7, and an average white hitter 5.07.

Table 2 presents simple averages of several components of career productivity for all players listed in Table 1 who also have autographed balls, photos, gloves, and jerseys listed in the *Guide*. Four major patterns stand out in Table 2. First, white hitters listed in the *Guide* tend to be from a much earlier era than black or Latin hitters. Even when we restrict ourselves to the post-1946 sample of white hitters, we find that white hitters listed in the *Guide* are still from an earlier era than black or Latin hitters.[19] Black hitters selected for the *Guide* tend to have the vintage of a typical black hitter in the overall sample, while Latin hitters tend to come from an earlier era than the average Latin hitter in the overall sample. Second, the vast ethnic disparities in average hitter longevity are eliminated in the memorabilia sample, with ethnic rankings actually inverting. Black hitters listed in the *Guide* play an average of 14.38 seasons, white hitters 14.49 seasons, and Latin hitters 14.96 seasons.[20] Third, the ranking of productivity by ethnic groups observed in the overall sample is, with a few exceptions, also observed in the memorabilia sample. The exceptions are Latin productivity exceeds black productivity in singles and triples, and white productivity exceeds Latin productivity in bases on balls, home runs, and runs batted in. In general, career productivity gaps between the three ethnic groups are smaller in the memorabilia sample than in the overall sample. Finally, hitters who later become managers of MLB teams compose a much bigger proportion of the *Guide's* hitters than the overall hitter sample.

Table 3 presents category breakdowns — gloves, balls, pictures, and jerseys — for selected measures of average productivity and memorabilia prices by race. The most striking feature of Table 3 is the difference in average prices across memorabilia categories and racial and ethnic groups. Players with "excellent-grade" gloves tend to be of an earlier vintage than players from other memorabilia categories, while white players with jerseys tend to be more productive than white players with other types of memorabilia.

Regression Results

The first stage of our empirical analysis investigates the criteria used by the compilers of the *Guide* in the selection of MLB player memorabilia. As discussed in Section III above, we specify a probit regression using measures of player productivity, player characteristics, and player race as explanatory variables. Our regression analysis uses two different specifications of hitter productivity. Our first specification, taken from Nardinelli and Simon, incorporates six measures of productivity: hits, doubles, triples, home runs, walks, and stolen bases.[21] The advantage of allowing each component of hitter productivity to enter the regression separately is that it allows the data to "talk" without imposing a weighting scheme on it. Our second specification, taken from Andersen and La Croix, uses a well-known index of player productivity, offensive average (OA).[22] One advantages of using OA is that it allows us to add interaction variables (Latin-OA and black-OA) between player productivity and ethnicity to the regression, thereby enabling us to determine whether ethnic bias in selection of players for the *Guide* is related to player productivity. A second advantage of using OA is that we can include OA^2 in the regression, allowing us to determine whether there is a quadratic relationship between productivity and inclusion in the *Guide*. A disadvantage of using OA is that the weights used to aggregate the various measures of productivity may not reflect fan valuation of each productivity measure, e.g., fans may value a triple more or less than three times the value of a single.

Probit regression results are reported in Table 4.1 for each memorabilia category using disaggregated measures of player productivity. Of the eight estimated coefficients for player productivity that are statistically significant, only the doubles coefficient in the baseball regression was negative. All estimated coefficients for home runs are positive and statistically significant at the 5 percent level. Twenty-one of 24 estimated coefficients on player characteristics were statistically significant: MLB manager after retirement, year retire as a player, career at bats, World Series games, league championship games, and Hall of Fame status.[23] Finally, the Latin dummy variable was not statistically significant in any of the regressions. The black dummy variable was positive and statistically significant in the baseball and photo regressions, positive and not statistically significant in the jersey regression, and negative and statistically significant in the gloves regression.[24] The mix of positive/negative estimated coefficients could be due to a number of phenomena. Bias on the part of the Guide's editor is one possibility; another is supply of memorabilia across ethnic groups, a factor we do not control for in these regressions.

Table 4.2 reports probit regression results using the OA index of player productivity. The estimated coefficients on OA and OA^2 are, respectively, positive and negative, but only statistically significant at the 5 percent level in the gloves regression. The lack of importance of player productivity for inclusion in the Guide is surprising, but other player characteristics are more prominent. Most estimated coefficients on player characteristics had the expected signs, were statistically significant and were broadly consistent with those reported for the disaggregated specifications.

For autographed baseballs and photos we find that the estimated coefficients on the black-OA variables are positive and statistically significant while the estimated coefficients on the black dummy variables change to become negative and statistically significant. Latin variables are not statistically significant in any regressions except the glove regression, where the Latin dummy is negative, the Latin-OA variable is positive, and both estimates are statistically significant at the five percent level. How do we interpret the negative estimated coefficients on the racial/ethnic dummies and the positive estimated coefficients on the OA-interaction variables?[25] In general, this tells us that racial/ethnic bias with respect to selection to the *Guide* falls as the player's productivity increases. We find that the positive effect from the black-OA variable outweighs the negative effect from the black dummy variable in the baseball and photo regressions for average and above-average black players. This is also true for the glove regression with respect to Latin players. The glove regression indicates a bias against black players except black super stars in that the positive effect of the black-OA variable only off sets the negative effect of the black dummy variable for OA values above .61.[26]

The second-stage regressions for each memorabilia category considers whether the same or an augmented set of variables can explain prices paid by fans for memorabilia. For autographed baseballs and pictures, the explanatory variables are identical to those in the first-step probit equation. For autographed gloves, we also have crude measures of the supply of each player's gloves: common, rare, very rare, and unknown.[27] For jerseys we have additional data on the characteristics of the jersey, such as whether it is signed by the player, is in good condition, and/or bears the player's name. Results from these regressions are reported in Tables 5.1 and 5.2. Table 5.1 regressions use the disaggregated measures of player productivity with Latin and black dummy variables, while Table 5.2 regressions use OA as an index of player productivity and include Latin and black dummy variables as well as variables interacting productivity-and race (Latin-OA and black-OA).

We identify several important patterns in the second-stage regressions results. First, the influence of player productivity on memorabilia prices depends on the specification of player productivity. In the regressions with disaggregated productivity (Table 5.1), we obtain positive estimates for 22 of 24 estimated coefficients, but only 5 of the 22 positive coefficients are statistically significant at the five percent level. In the photo regression, all estimated coefficients on productivity are positive, but only the estimated coefficients on home runs and stolen bases are statistically significant. In the jerseys and gloves regressions, only estimated coefficients on home runs are statistically significant, and in the baseball regression only the estimated coefficient on doubles is statistically significant. It appears that fans are fixated on a player's home run performance and place little value on most other measures of productivity.

Replacing these disaggregated measures of productivity with OA and OA^2 produces very different results (Table 5.2), as productivity now becomes an important predictor of price. In all regressions, OA is negative and statistically significant at least at the ten percent level, while OA^2 is positive and statistically significant at the five percent level. This means that the premium fans pay for memorabilia of highly productive players increases with player productivity.

A second pattern is that estimated coefficients on Year Retire are large, negative, and statistically significant in all regression specifications in Table 5.1 and 5.2.[28] Note the striking contrast with our earlier probit results: players from older cohorts are less likely to be included in the *Guide* but consumers place higher values on the memorabilia of players in the *Guide* from older cohorts. A possible explanation for this result may be grounded in our earlier speculation that most purchasers of relatively expensive baseball memorabilia are older (>21) and wealthier men. These consumers could be purchasing the memorabilia of the heroes of their youth, players who retired 10–25 years earlier.

We pay special attention to the gloves regression, as its specification is superior to our other memorabilia regressions. The sample of gloves is relatively homogeneous — all were graded "excellent" — and the regression includes crude controls for glove scarcity (unknown, very rare, rare, and common). The dummy variables measuring degrees of scarcity have positive estimated coefficients, are correctly ranked in size (with dummy variables indicating greater scarcity having larger estimated coefficients), and are all statistically significant at the 5 percent level. Estimated coefficients on player productivity and characteristics were, however, very similar to the ones obtained in the jersey, ball and photo regressions lacking supply controls.

And finally, our central result: We find little evidence for the proposition that MLB fans bid up or down memorabilia prices on the basis of a player's race. In all regression specifications in Tables 5.1 and 5.2, neither the Latin dummy, black dummy, black-OA, nor the Latin-OA variables are ever statistically significant at even the 10 percent level.

Conclusion

Our central conclusion is that we find little evidence of discrimination against black and Latin players in the prices paid for baseball memorabilia. We find some evidence of a preference for selecting baseballs and photos of black players for the *Guide*, and more complicated racial/ethnic preferences when selecting gloves of black and Latin players.[29]

One reason for our finding of no racial/ethnic discrimination in memorabilia prices may be that we have chosen to analyze a relatively recent sample of prices from 1995–1996. By contrast, Anderson and Hanssen examined a series of cross-sectional samples for All-Star Game voting and found a high level of racial discrimination in the 1960s and 1970s that declined in the 1980s and disappeared in the 1990s.[30] A similar pattern of declining or vanishing discrimination has been observed in the baseball card studies (see Section II), with discrimination in the 1960s and 1980s vanishing in the 1990s.

How reliable are our regressions estimates? Our main concern is with the supply of memorabilia, which clearly varies across players and cohorts. Some retired players seem to spend all their retirement days signing baseballs, photos, and jerseys, while others seek more privacy, die at an early age, or have little demand for their items. The differential supplies of memorabilia introduce more noise into our analysis, with the result that the coefficients in our reduced form regressions are estimated with less precision and have higher standard errors. This means that we are more likely to reject the hypothesis of racial discrimination. However, the differential supplies of memorabilia should not bias the coefficient on the race variables unless the differential supplies are correlated with the race/ethnicity variables. Whether such a correlation exists is unclear. On the one hand,

black players have a lower opportunity cost of producing additional autographed memorabilia due to lower market wages for black males than
white males. The increased supply of black memorabilia would lead to
lower prices for black memorabilia and a tendency to find racial discrimination in memorabilia prices. On the other hand, a premium on white
players' memorabilia could provide white players with incentives to produce more memorabilia. Since the increased supply would reduce prices
of white players' memorabilia, this would reduce the tendency to find racial
discrimination in memorabilia prices.

TABLE 1: AVERAGE CAREER PRODUCTIVITY STATISTICS AND PLAYER CHARACTERISTICS

Variable	Black Players	Latin Players	White Players	All Players	Post–1946 White Players
Career Totals for Average Player					
Hits	730	587	296	327	294
Singles	517	441	220	241	211
Doubles	118	91	47	52	48
Triples	23	17	13	13	8
Home Runs	72	38	16	20	28
Total Bases	1109	825	419	466	440
Runs	370	269	148	163	140
Runs Batted In	332	230	129	142	136
Walks	264	165	103	114	118
Stolen Bases	91	69	45	48	44
Batting Average	0.244	0.235	0.218	0.220	0.214
Offensive Average	0.442	0.392	0.361	0.366	0.377
Player Position					
Catcher	4.04%	8.45%	17.76%	16.79%	17.92%
First Baseman	3.36%	4.93%	8.62%	8.24%	8.75%
Second Baseman	4.71%	5.63%	8.42%	8.15%	7.18%
Third Baseman	2.02%	3.52%	7.50%	7.11%	5.60%
Short Stop	2.91%	11.97%	8.46%	8.20%	6.76%
Multiple Positions	40.58%	42.96%	17.96%	19.74%	26.53%
Characteristics of Average Player					
Seasons	9.7	8.9	5.6	6.0	6.1
Rookie Year	1970	1974	1928	1931	1968
Year Retire	1979	1982	1933	1936	1973
Career Games	847	693	336	373	390
Career At Bats	2726	2201	1107	1222	1151
Manager	2.47%	2.11%	6.00%	5.72%	4.54%
World Series Games	3.1	1.9	1.1	1.2	1.6
League Championship Games	3.1	1.6	0.3	0.5	1.2
Observations	446	142	7067	7655	2160

Note: All data come from Kenneth Matinale, BaseBall DataBase, Version 5.1, 1999.

TABLE 2: SUMMARY STATISTICS FOR PLAYER WITH MEMORABILIA

Variable	Black Players	Latin Players	White Players	All Players	Post–1946 White Players
Career Totals for Average Player					
Hits	1556	1610	1417	1452	1232
Singles	1077	1186	1004	1025	860
Doubles	259	250	239	243	202
Triples	47	49	57	55	33
Home Runs+A27	174	123	119	129	137
Total Bases	2430	2328	2129	2195	1913
Runs	794	757	730	743	610
Runs Batted In	751	668	688	699	606
Walks	557	452	548	545	505
Stolen Bases	163	149	141	145	134
Batting Average	0.268	0.272	0.268	0.268	0.255
Offensive Average	0.498	0.464	0.477	0.481	0.467
Player Position					
Catcher	3.3%	0.0%	11.4%	9.4%	11.3%
First Baseman	4.1%	0.0%	10.0%	8.5%	7.5%
Second Baseman	3.3%	7.4%	4.5%	4.4%	4.2%
Third Baseman	0.8%	0.0%	5.1%	4.1%	5.4%
Short Stop	2.5%	14.8%	5.1%	5.0%	4.6%
Multiple Positions	53.3%	44.4%	39.8%	42.6%	50.2%
Characteristics of Average Player					
Rookie Year	1967	1962	1942	1948	1961
Year Retire	1981	1976	1955	1961	1974
Career Games	1613	1625	1445	1485	1386
Career At Bats	5632	5663	5000	5148	4607
Seasons	14.4	15.3	14.4	14.9	14.7
Manager	7.4%	3.7%	24.5%	20.3%	15.9%
World Series Games	8.3	6.2	8.4	8.3	7.5
League Championship Games	7.4	4.1	2.0	3.1	5.0
Observations	122	27	490	639	239

Notes: All data on players are from Kenneth Matinale BaseBall DataBase. The manager variable is taken from the Baseball Encyclopedia (1999). Players with memorabilia are those in Larsen's Complete Guide with gloves, jerseys, autographed photos, and autographed baseballs.

TABLE 3: SELECTED SUMMARY STATISTICS FOR HITTERS WITH GLOVES, BASEBALLS, PHOTOGRAPHS, AND JERSEYS LISTED IN THE COMPLETE GUIDE TO BASEBALL MEMORABILIA

| | Player Ethnicity | | |
	Black	Latin	White
		Gloves	
Price of Excellent Glove	$70.97	$55.00	$116.89
Offensive Average	0.511	0.471	0.472
Seasons	15.08	15.24	13.52
Year Retire	1971	1971	1953
Observations	36	17	314
		Photographs and Baseballs	
Price of Photograph	$99.22	$41.11	$354.87
Price of Baseball	$70.80	$200.59	$989.20
Offensive Average	0.502	0.469	0.493
Seasons	15.09	16.41	17.2
Year Retire	1982	1976	1958
Observations	86	17	220
		Jerseys	
Price of Jersey	$2,976.36	$1,095.00	$10,863.66
Offensive Average	0.512	0.52	0.516
Seasons	16	19	24.9
Year Retire	1984	1985	1975
Observations	22	1	41

All data on players are from Kenneth Matinale, BaseBall DataBase (1999). Memorabilia price data are from Larsen (1997).

TABLE 4.1: FIRST STAGE REGRESSION RESULTS

Dependent Variable	Player in Guide with Autographed Baseball Yes=1, No=0	Player in Guide with Jersey Yes=1, No=0	Player in Guide with Glove Yes=1, No=0	Player in Guide with Autographed Photo Yes=1, No=0
Black	0.26*	0.01	-0.19	0.27*
	(0.11)	(.18)	(.13)	(.11)
Latin	0.02	—	0.22	0.02
	(0.19)	—	(0.17)	(.19)
Hits	0.0007	.0017**	0.0004	0.0008
	(0.0006)	(.0009)	(0.0005)	(.0006)
Doubles	-0.0052*	0.0003	-0.0037	-.0052
	(0.0014)	(.0021)	(.0013)	(.0015)
Triples	-0.0030	.0072**	0.0024	-0.0020
	(0.0025)	(.0044)	(.002)	(.0025)
Home Runs	0.0035*	0.003*	0.0017*	0.0036*
	(0.0007)	(.001)	(.0007)	(.0008)

Dependent Variable	Player in Guide with Autographed Baseball Yes=1, No=0	Player in Guide with Jersey Yes=1, No=0	Player in Guide with Glove Yes=1, No=0	Player in Guide with Autographed Photo Yes=1, No=0
Walks	0.0001	-0.0002	0.0007*	-0.0002
	(0.0003)	(0004)	(.0003)	(.0003)
Stolen Bases	0.0003	0.0005	-0.0036*	0.0004
	(0.0006)	(.0008)	(.0006)	(.0006)
At Bats	.0025**	-0.0003	0.0003*	0.0002*
	(0.0001)	(.0002)	(.0001)	(.0001)
Manager	0.42*	0.63*	0.36*	0.43*
	(0.12)	(.21)	(.10)	(.12)
Year Retire	27.44*	32.75*	12.58*	27.91*
	(4.26)	(10.35)	(2.74)	(4.31)
Hall of Fame	2.32*	.47**	-0.85*	2.31*
	(0.20)	(.29)	(.18)	(.21)
World Series	.02*	0.00	0.05	.021*
	(.0055)	(.0087)	(.005)	(.006)
League Championship	.02*	.049*	-0.08*	.024*
	(.001)	(.013)	(.01)	(.010)
Constant	-210.66*	-251.50*	-97.75*	-214.23
	(32.27)	(78.54)	(20.73)	(32.66)
Observations	7655	7655	7655	7655

Notes: * indicates statistical significance at the 5 percent level and ** at the 10 percent level.

TABLE 4.2: FIRST STAGE PROBIT REGRESSIONS WITH OFFENSIVE AVERAGE

Dependent Variable	Player in Guide with Autographed Baseball Yes=1, No=0	Player in Guide with Jersey Yes=1, No=0	Player in Guide with Glove Yes=1, No=0	Player in Guide with Autographed Photo Yes=1, No=0
Black	−1.57*	0.15	−1.94*	−1.56*
	(.73)	(1.24)	(.93)	(.74)
Latin	−1.96	—	−3.51*	−1.79
	(1.40)	—	(1.58)	(1.4)
Offensive Average	0.83	4.83	6.7*	0.84
	(.78)	(3.43)	(2.08)	(.78)
Offensive Average2	−0.23	−2.04	−4.94*	−0.23
	(0.45)	(2.64)	(2.08)	(.46)
Black*OA	3.88*	−0.29	3.18**	3.93*
	(1.53)	(2.5)	(1.87)	(1.54)
Latin*OA	4.53	—	8.17*	4.12
	(3.12)	—	(3.50)	(3.13)
At Bats	.0002*	0.0002*	.0002*	0.0002*
	(.00000)	(.0000)	(.0000)	(.0000)
Manager	0.36*	0.54*	.32	0.387*
	(.12)	(.21)	(.1)	(.12)
Year Retire	35.03*	545.99*	20.12*	34.22*
	(3.95)	(9.94)	(2.54)	(3.92)
Hall of Fame	2.10*	0.698*	−.83*	2.25*

Dependent Variable	Player in Guide with Autographed Baseball Yes=1, No=0	Player in Guide with Jersey Yes=1, No=0	Player in Guide with Glove Yes=1, No=0	Player in Guide with Autographed Photo Yes=1, No=0
	(.167)	(0.245)	(.15)	(.18)
World Series	.022*	0.001	.052*	.0252*
	(.005)	(.008)	(.005)	(.005)
League Championship	.016**	.041*	.075*	.0175*
	(.009)	(.012)	(.009)	(.009)
Constant	−268.49*	−353.77*	−156.66*	−262.30*
	(29.99)	(75.58)	(19.24)	(29.73)
Observations	7653	7653	7653	7653

Notes: * indicates statistical significance at the 5 percent level and ** at the 10 percent level.

TABLE 5.1: SECOND STAGE OLS REGRESSIONS
WITH DISAGGREGATED PRODUCTIVITY

Dependent Variable	Log Price of Autographed Ball	Log Price of Player Jersey	Log Price of Glove in Excellent Condition	Log Price of Autographed Photo
Black	−0.14	−0.18	−0.05	−0.01
	(0.15)	(.21)	(0.09)	(.13)
Latin	0.14	—	−0.17	0.01
	(0.25)	—	(.12)	(.23)
Hits	0.0006	.0022*	0.0001	0.0009
	(0.0006)	(.0009)	(.0003)	(.0005)
Doubles	0.0032*	−0.0031	0.0013	0.0014
	(0.0014)	(.0024)	(.0008)	(.0013)
Triples	0.0030	0.0011	0.0014	0.0032
	(0.0024)	(.0054)	(.0013)	(.0022)
Home Runs	0.0005	.43*	0.0009*	.0013*
	(0.0007)	(.0011)	(.0003)	(.0006)
Walks	0.0000	0.0004	0.0001	0.0001
	(0.0003)	(.0002)	(.0001)	(.0003)
Stolen Bases	0.0011	−0.0006	0.0007	.0001
	(0.0005)	(.0011)	(.0004)	(.0005)
At Bats	−0.0005*	.0005*	−0.0001	−0.0005*
	(0.0001)	(.0002)	(.0001)	(.0001)
Manager	−0.2261	0.38	−0.03	−0.06
	(0.1450)	(.28)	(.06)	(.13)
Year Retire	−117.37*	−82.12*	−48.33*	−97.56*
	(8.1)	(17.00)	(3.65)	(7.51)
Hall of Fame	0.12	.91*	0.12	−0.02
	(0.21)	(.3)	(.11)	(.19)
Name	—	0.15	—	—
	—	(.18)	—	—
Signed	—	−.18	—	—
	—	(.23)	—	—
Condition	—	0.02	—	—
	—	(.26)	—	—
Rare	—	—	.20*	—
	—	—	(.06)	—

Dependent Variable	Log Price of Autographed Ball	Log Price of Player Jersey	Log Price of Glove in Excellent Condition	Log Price of Autographed Photo
Very Rare	—	—	.51*	—
	—	—	(.07)	—
Unknown	—	—	0.69*	—
	—	—	(.07)	—
World Series	–.009**	.03*	.0085*	–0.0045
	(.005)	(.01)	(.0029)	(.0047)
League Championship	0.0101	0.02	–.0025	.0144**
	(.0092)	(.01)	(.007)	(.0084)
Inverse Mills Ratio	–0.8301*	0.5557*	–0.0118	–0.6421*
	(.091)	(.292)	(.079)	(.1049)
Constant	895.60*	627.68*	369.99*	755.52*
	(61.12)	(129.46)	(27.69)	(56.94)
Observations	322	64	367	323

TABLE 5.2: SECOND STAGE OLS REGRESSIONS WITH OFFENSIVE AVERAGE

Dependent Variable	Log Price of Autographed Ball	Log Price of Player Jersey	Log Price of Glove in Excellent Condition	Log Price of Autographed Photo
Black	1.72**	–0.26	0.55	1.46
	(1.02)	(1.54)	(.69)	(0.94)
Latin	–0.52	—	–0.52	–0.71
	(2.05)	—	(1.05)	(1.88)
At Bats	–0.0001*	0.0010	0.0001*	–.0001*
	(.00)	(.0001)	(.00)	(.00)
Offensive Average	–15.38*	–28.56*	–4.02**	–16.50*
	(–2.34)	(12.32)	(2.20)	(2.16)
Offensive Average2	18.80*	36.22*	5.44*	20.74*
	(2.76)	(11.77)	(2.36)	(2.55)
Black*OA	–3.81**	0.20	0.93	–3.03
	(2.06)	(2.97)	(1.35)	(1.90)
Latin*OA	1.28	—	0.79	1.43
	(4.37)	—	(2.22)	(4.00)
Manager	0.16	0.15	0.04	0.02
	(.15)	(.32)	(.06)	(.13)
Year Retire	–118.03*	–77.93*	–52.23*	–97.02*
	(7.15)	(20.27)	(3.27)	(6.47)
Hall of Fame	0.24	1.01*	0.15	0.02
	(.20)	(.30)	(.10)	(.18)
Name	—	0.07	—	—
	—	(.18)	—	—
Signed	—	–0.12	—	—
	—	(.24)	—	—
Condition	—	–0.03	—	—
	—	(.26)	—	—
Rare	—	—	0.17*	—
	—	—	(.06)	—

Dependent Variable	Log Price of Autographed Ball	Log Price of Player Jersey	Log Price of Glove in Excellent Condition	Log Price of Autographed Photo
Very Rare	—	—	0.52*	—
	—	—	(.07)	—
Unknown	—	—	0.69*	—
	—	—	(.07)	—
World Series	−.015*	.035*	.007*	−.01*
	(.005)	(.010)	(.003)	(.005)
League Championship	0.00	0.01	.0027	0.01
	(.01)	(.01)	(.01)	(.01)
Inverse Mills Ratio	−0.97*	0.47	−0.06	−0.87
	(.08)	(.35)	(.08)	(.08)
Constant	903.77*	601.45*	400.35*	743.85*
	(54.08)	(155.60)	(24.93)	(48.95)
Observations	322	64	367	323

Notes

1. Rhonda Sharpe is Carolina Minority Post Doctoral Fellow at the University of North Carolina at Chapel Hill, Economics Department CB 3305, Chapel Hill, NC 27599. E-mail: sharper@unc.edu. Sumner J. La Croix is Professor, Department of Economics, 2424 Maile Way, University of Hawaii, Honolulu, Hawaii 96822. E-mail: lacroix@hawaii.edu. We thank Barnard College for its financial support; Sonya Dewan, Trinidad Avcedo, Megan Hageberger, Rachael Allen, Marisol Bae and Martha Townley for research assistance; and Lalith Munasinghe for helpful discussions.

2. See Lawrence M. Kahn, "Discrimination in Professional Sports: A Survey of the Literature," 44 *Industrial and Labor Relations Review* 395–418 (1991).

3. Clark Nardinelli and Curtis Simon, "Customer Racial Discrimination in the Market for Memorabilia: The Case of Baseball," 105 *Quarterly Journal of Economics* 575–595 (1990).

4. Torben Andersen and Sumner J. La Croix, "Customer Racial Discrimination in Major League Baseball," 29 *Economic Inquiry* 665–677 (1991).

5. Paul E. Gabriel, Curtis Johnson, and Timothy J. Stanton, "An Examination of Customer Racial Discrimination in the Market for Baseball Memorabilia," 68 *Journal of Business* 215–230 (1995); Joseph McGarrity, Harvey D. Palmer, and Marc Poitras, "Consumer Racial Discrimination: A Reassessment of the Market for Baseball Cards," 20 *Journal of Labor Research* 247–58 (1999).

6. F. Andrew Hanssen and Torben Andersen, "Has Discrimination Lessened Over Time? A Test Using Baseball's All-Star Vote," 37 *Economic Inquiry* 326–352 (1999).

7. See Hanssen and Andersen, *supra* note 6, esp. at 351–52.

8. The memorabilia market is not just limited to baseball equipment but has expanded to personal effects. Ty Cobb's dentures sold for $7,500 at Sotheby's, the wooden leg of former Chicago White Sox owner Bill Veeck sold for $10,000 at a Chicago auction, and a lock of Mickey Mantle's hair was offered at a 1997 auction. The contract between the Boston Red Sox and the New York Yankees to sell Babe Ruth to the Yankees sold for $189,500 in September 1999.

9. Larson, Mark K., *The Complete Guide to Baseball Memorabilia*. esp. 100 (1996).

10. Larson, *supra* note 9.

11. Kenneth Matinale, *BaseBall DataBase* (1999).

12. Caribbean is defined as born in a non-Spanish-speaking country located in the Caribbean Ocean.

13. Frank Slocum, *The Complete Picture Collection: A 40 Year History 1951–1990* (1990). Race and ethnicity are mutually exclusive in the paper, i.e., a player is not classified as race–Hispanic.

14. This identification was done by M. Kristian Connolly, photo intern at the National Baseball Hall of Fame Library.

15. See William H. Greene, *Econometric Analysis*, 2nd ed., esp. Ch. 21 636–42 (1993) for a more elaborate discussion of the foundations of the probit model.

16. Summary statistics for the 3 Asian, 28 Caribbean, and 9 European players are not reported in Tables 1–3, and we do not use these observations in our regression analysis.

17. Its failure to capture the power of a player's hits means that it systematically biases the productivity of power hitters downwards compared to singles hitters.

18. See Jay M. Bennett and John A. Flueck, "An Evaluation of Major League Baseball Offense Performance Models," *The American Statistician* 76–82 (1983), for a complete evaluation of various measures of hitter productivity. Offense Average =(total bases gained on base hits + walks + stolen bases)/(at bats + walks).

19. Part of the reason for this is that there were relatively few black and Latin hitters in MLB from 1947 to 1970. Thus, it's not surprising that most of the star players from that era were white.

20. A smaller, but still substantial, longevity disparity remains if we compare games played across racial groups rather than seasons.

21. Nardinelli & Simon, *supra* note 3.

22. Andersen & La Croix, *supra* note 4.

23. The Hall of Fame variable is negative and not statistically significant in the glove regression.

24. Results are similar when position dummy variables (catcher, first, second, third, short, multiple, with outfield the omitted category) are included in the regressions. In the jersey regression with position variables, the black dummy variable was positive but statistically insignificant.

25. Consider the following mathematical example: at what OA value would the positive effect of the black–OA coefficient equal the negative effect of the black dummy variable coefficient? To answer this question we solve: $OA*3.61 = 1.44$, where 3.61 is the black–OA coefficient and 1.44 is the black dummy variable coefficient. An OA value of .39889 would cause the equality to be true. Since this is less than the average OA value for black players (see Table 1), we conclude that the positive effects of the black–OA variable offset the negative effects of the black dummy variable for average or above average black players.

26. The mean OA value for black players is .442. Frank Robinson, Willie Mays, Hank Aaron, and Matt Alexander are the only black players with OA values above .61.

27. We ran regressions on three grades of gloves: very good, excellent, and mint. Results were broadly similar across regressions.

28. Because Year Retire is a large number relative to the other player productivity statistics, a logarithmic transformation of Year Retire generates a number whose value is more in line with the other player productivity statistics.

29. We are unable to discern if the preferences for inclusion in the *Guide* are those of the compilers or the consumers for baseball memorabilia.

30. Hanssen & Andersen, *supra* note 6.

Despoiling the Sleeve: The Threat of Corporate Advertising Upon the Integrity of the Major League Uniform

Ken Moon

On March 29 and 30, 2000, major league baseball set one precedent and, possibly, a second. The certain precedent was that major league baseball played its first regular season games outside of North America.[1] The possible second precedent involved advertising and where it appeared. Among the seven sponsors participating in baseball's opening of the 2000 season in Japan, AIU Insurance advertised via a patch on the uniform sleeve of both the New York Mets and the Chicago Cubs.[2] This particular instance of sleeve advertising has a possible precedent since big league baseball may have had, prior to World War I, one other instance of sleeve patch advertising.

This pilot project in sleeve advertising came a year after Major League Baseball first considered sleeve advertising as a means of generating more revenue.[3] Specifics of the plan were that the patches would be one to one and a half inches square in shape and that no alcohol, tobacco, or media companies could purchase advertising space.[4] In addition, individual teams could sell patches to local advertisers, and if enough teams utilized such advertising, baseball officialdom would consider revenue sharing among all of the clubs.[5]

Despite patch advertising appearing in the Japanese series, sources at

the Commissioner's office claim their representatives are not currently acting on the proposal.[6] What that means is unclear, and, perhaps, purposely
so given the proposal's limited practice.

What is clear about sleeve patch advertising is that it was met with a
mixed response. Baseball executives resigned themselves to the business
reality of baseball. Tim Brosnan, baseball's senior vice president for domestic and international properties, sees the dollars and cents angle:

> We're serious about bringing more marketing partners into baseball....
> The truth is, this is a business, the sports and entertainment business.
> We do recognize that our most important constituency is our fans. But
> by the same token, like any business, we have to find ways to offset
> costs.[7]

Dodger President Bob Graziano liked the specific idea, "[M]y sense is that
[the patches] can be done tastefully...."[8] Green Party presidential candidate Ralph Nader echoed the sentiments of many fans when he
implored baseball to reject the idea because of its naked commercialism:
"We urge Major League Baseball not to emulate NASCAR. Don't turn
baseball players into walking billboards.... If you let commerce interfere
too overtly with baseball, fans will angrily drift away from the sport."[9]
Perhaps the best reflection of baseball's mixed perspective to sleeve patch
advertising comes from a comment by Anaheim Angel right fielder Tim
Salmon:

> If you can generate revenues and bring more equality [among the
> teams], it would be worth exploring.... You don't want it [sleeve patch
> advertising] to be like Little League, where you're playing for Tony's
> Tortillas or something. I don't want to look like those Indy-car racers
> with all those patches. You want it to be a baseball uniform, not a
> walking billboard.[10]

Obviously, with such ambivalent assessments, Major League Baseball
is approaching this idea strategically. Marketing arrangements, or potential violations to them, may be one possible reason why baseball is pro-
ceeding cautiously with patch advertising in the states and Canada: New
Era, Majestic, Rawlings, or Russell, all marketing partners with Major
League Baseball,[11] may object to having their product used as a billboard
for advertising patches that are larger than their logos.

But why are writers, some owners and players, and a majority of fans
more upset with this form of advertising than with advertising approaches
already being practiced, such as advertising around stadium seats, billboards hanging from stadium facades, and the revolving signs behind home
plate — all necessary to generate even more money so owners can pay the

ever-escalating salaries of players? A possible answer could be that Major League Baseball is now considering using the uniform itself since, in a given televised game, the uniform is shot from many angles — particularly the jersey and cap. From a marketing standpoint alone, uniform advertising makes perfect sense.

In fact, it is not as if the uniform does not have some form of advertising placed on it already. Baseball's current marketing arrangement with corporate partners — Majestic, maker of jackets, practice jerseys, shirts and shorts for all thirty teams and game jerseys for seven teams; Rawlings, maker of game jerseys for eight teams; and Russell, maker of game jerseys for fifteen teams — allows them the choice of placing their logo on uniforms, which they do. [12] New Era, maker of the cap for all thirty teams, does not place its logo on the cap.[13] In addition to league arrangements, each team sets up arrangements with equipment manufacturers, many with logos appearing, and each player makes his own shoe deal, with logos there as well.[14] The point is that even before patch advertising during the Japanese series, trademark logo advertising had been in practice for quite some time. And such advertising does not openly upset most writers and fans. The common thinking would be this: If Rawlings makes the jersey, then the company has the right to place its logo on the jersey. And the logo is usually small enough that it is discreet.

Yet logos are not patches, so fans, sports writers, and some people in baseball still object to patch advertising on the sleeve. Perhaps their objections stem from their perception of the uniform historically. When fans reminisce about baseball, they commonly think back to the Golden Age of baseball from the twenties to the late fifties. That spans the years from when Babe Ruth began slugging home runs as a New York Yankee to the departure of the Brooklyn Dodgers and New York Giants to the West Coast. Older baseball fans especially picture the look of the flannel whites and grays the sixteen teams of that era wore. Besides the lettering on the cap, the lettering and team logo on the front of the jersey, the number on the back, and color piping along the jersey collar and down the pants, there were no advertising patches, logos, or players' names besmirching the uniform's design. That is the romantically classic tableau purists envision when they think of traditional baseball. And, though there is truth in that vision, there is also some illusion.

During the Golden Age, in fact, several teams in particular took liberties with their uniform designs, some not lasting more than one or several years, but nevertheless taking liberties. The Dodgers were quite the innovators during the late thirties and mid-forties. For instance, they adopted a kelly green look for the 1937 season,[15] and then adopted a "satin

... rich pale blue" scheme for the 1944 season.[16] In 1939 they tried zipper fronts,[17] which the Chicago Cubs first tried in 1937 and which many other clubs tried for two decades.[18] The Detroit Tigers and Boston Braves placed profiles of their respective mascots, feline and Native American, on the back of their jerseys shortly before numbers gained common usage.[19] In the early 1940s, the Cubs adopted the "sleeveless vest" look.[20] A year before and during the Dodgers' kelly green look, the Cincinnati Reds adopted a solid red trouser look for occasional home games — which stood out from all the other teams that year.[21] In addition, many team uniforms had the team logo or initial either on the breast or the sleeve.[22] These harmless mutations took place long before the double-knit, multi-color onslaught of the 1970s and 1980s.

Prior to the twenties, ironically, some baseball uniforms were more varied, at least by today's standards, than were uniforms of the Golden Age. In fact, during the nineteenth century, experimentation and showmanship marked uniform design. The first team to sport an official club uniform was the 1849 New York Knickerbockers whose outfit consisted of "blue woolen pantaloons, a white flannel shirt and a straw hat"; the straw hat was replaced in 1855 by a mohair cap.[23] By the late nineteenth century, many teams featured solid colored uniforms (such as a white uniform with block lettering, a belt, and stockings as an offset, and vice-versa).[24] The jersey was a pullover shirt that either buttoned or laced from the chest to the throat and featured a fold-down collar, possibly a pocket, and full cuffs on the sleeves. Some jerseys had lettering and some did not. There were several cap styles, ranging from the "pillbox" shape (such as the Pirates wore in the late seventies and early eighties) to several styles with a "rounded close-fitting crown" and "the button tilted more toward the front."[25] The pants were the knicker and knee-high stocking look.[26] A heavy one-piece, "over-the-knee" style wool stocking was common nineteenth century sock wear. In fact, this was the distinguishing feature of the uniform for such clubs as Cincinnati, Boston, and Chicago. [27] Indeed, Chicago's National League team was originally known as the "White Stockings."[28]

Some of this variety in uniform styling could be credited to the showmanship of such mavericks of the time as Harry Wright and Albert Goodwill Spalding. In 1869, Wright, manager of the Cincinnati Red Stockings, the first recognized all-professional team in baseball, designed his team's uniform for both competitive and commercial advantage. He dressed his players in knickers so they could run faster, and red stockings provided distinctiveness.[29] In 1871 Wright would take the same uniform concept to Boston and create the Boston Red Stockings.[30]

After Spalding had muscled an exclusive deal with the National League in the late 1870s to use only a Spalding-manufactured baseball,[31] he ventured a step further by convincing the National League owners to adopt a short-lived fashion experiment in which all teams wore multi-colored uniforms — with each position on the field being distinguished with a different colored cap and silk jersey ensemble.[32] Reaction to Spalding's uniform concept then was similar to reactions to sleeve patch advertising now. A Chicago sports writer wrote that the Chicago players looked like a "Dutch bed of tulips."[33] Boston outfielder "Orator" Jim O'Rourke[34] bemoaned the look: "It is an insult to all of us to make a professional baseball player dress like a clown. If we are unfortunate enough to play near a lunatic asylum, we are likely to wind up inside looking out."[35] Such negative comments have resounded over the years about team uniform designs that were bold or even iconoclastic by baseball standards, such as John McGraw's Oriole and Giant teams of the early twentieth century[36] and Major League Baseball's 1999 experiment with "Turn Ahead and Clock" uniforms.

On a more conservative note concerning jersey fashion, the 1882 Cincinnati Reds placed numbers on the jersey for the first time. Unfortunately, the experiment failed because the numbers were difficult for fans to see.[37] In 1888 New York Giants pitcher Tim Keefe designed and sold an all-black uniform with white lettering, referred to as "funeral" uniforms, and a year later the Baltimore Oriole club would play in similarly designed uniforms.[38]

Essentially, uniform design trends were being experimented with throughout the late nineteenth century. This is not to say that there are not recognized traditions about the baseball uniform. First and foremost, all baseball fans accept that a uniform has always consisted of — from head to foot — a cap, a jersey, pants, socks, and shoes. For a century, tradition has produced jerseys and caps that have lettering and insignias.[39] Socks are still a distinguished feature of the uniform (although that tradition has been altered over the last decade). In addition, teams today still wear distinct versions of their uniform for home and road games, a practice dating back to the early part of the century.[40] Beyond these, a static tradition about the major league uniform is difficult to establish since the entire uniform has been constantly evolving. Examining the evolution of each article of uniform clothing demonstrates this phenomenon.

Perhaps the least evolving part of the uniform has been the cleats. They were always black leather with the potentially lethal metal spikes on the sole. One small style change would be the slight drop of the shoe's ankle height in 1910.[41] No other changes would take place until Charlie Finley's Kansas City Athletics trod out on to the playing field in white cleats in 1966.[42] In 1973 the Cardinals, Phillies, and Red Sox would further add to the color revolution by wearing red shoes.[43] Contemporary players' shoes match their endorsement deals and their team's uniform color scheme.

Until the 1990s, the way players wore pants or trousers changed very little. One big difference between the pants of modern baseball and the pants of pre-1900 uniforms, beyond their materials, was the quilted padding sewn in for sliding protection.[44] Belt tunnels placed on trousers after the turn of the century are still common on uniforms today.[45] The basic idea Harry Wright had of dressing his 1869 Red Stockings in knickers for ease of movement and flashy style did not change in professional baseball for nearly 120 years. Players did not wear their pant cuff much lower than the low calf in order to display the stirrup and white under socks. In the last ten years, many players have adopted the trend of completely covering the sock with the pant cuff, which often does not include a stirrup sock, only a solid colored sock. The one novel exception to the entire uniform pant style was Chicago White Sox owner Bill Veeck's 1976 Bermuda shorts-wearing club[46] — if only for one regular season game.[47]

As referred to already, socks evolved from heavy wool stockings in the nineteenth century, to some candy stripping in the twenties and thirties, to high-stretched stirrups in the seventies and eighties,[48] to no sock showing at all during the nineties. Interestingly, socks have gone from being a distinguishing feature in the nineteenth century to a somewhat inconsistent feature by the year 2000.

Unlike today, teams were wearing as many as five different styles of cap during the early part of the twentieth century.[49] By today's standards some of those cap styles would resemble a short-visored umpires cap — the crown tight-fitting and the visor flatter and wider. Even during the first decade of the century, a number of teams sported wide, horizontal stripes around the crown of the cap[50] — better known as the "pillbox," "cake box," or Chicago-style cap, which the Pirates popularized in the 1970s and 1980s.[51] Several teams at the turn of the century that wore the tight-fitting crown cap placed lettering on the crown of the cap.[52] In fact the 1901 Detroit Tigers sported a "red silhouette tiger" on their black cap.[53] The point is that insignia and lettering were used by a number of teams at the turn of the century.[54] By the middle of the twentieth century, all teams had either insignia or lettering on their caps.

The jersey has gone through the most notable metamorphosis. At the turn of the century jerseys were pullovers, buttoned or laced from the breast to the collar, and/or had fold-down collars, with some having button sleeves and pockets on the breast. The pocket had disappeared by 1908[55] and the fold-down collar by 1913.[56] John McGraw innovated the collarless look in 1906,[57] but versions of the cadet collar would remain into the early twenties[58] and versions of a flared extension to the collar would remain into the late 1930s.[59] The lace up jersey would be gone by 1910,[60] and the pullover button up would disappear by the late 1930s.[61] The most constant fashion statement would first appear permanently in 1915 when the Yankees dawned pinstripes[62]; although the 1907 Cubs wore a pin striping scheme in the World Series as did the Boston Nationals for their 1907 road uniforms.[63] In fact a number of teams adopted a pinstripe design for brief periods between 1907 and 1915.[64]

In the late 1920s and early 1930s, teams added numbers to the back of uniforms. After the Indians' failed 1916 experiment of placing numbers on the sleeves, the Yankees in 1929 were the first to do so permanently.[65]

Perhaps two of the most novel trends in jersey design happened in the late 1930s and early 1940s. The first took place in 1937 when the Cubs introduced zippers to their jerseys.[66] This trend would be copied by seven other clubs for varying intervals into the early 1960s,[67] then resurrected by the Astros in the early 1970s[68] and subsequently adopted by the Phillies during the 1970s and 1980s.[69] The second trend began when the Cubs, from 1940-1942, adopted the sleeveless jersey.[70] The Pirates, Reds, Athletics, and Indians would later adopt the sleeveless jersey design during the 1950s and 1960s.[71] In the 2000 season, the Reds, Marlins, Angels, Blue Jays, and White Sox wore sleeveless versions of the jersey.

Even after the zipper and sleeves were tinkered with, the threads themselves changed in the 1960s from cotton with wool to an Orlon blend with wool.[72] But if that were not enough, the Pirates completely busted the thread mold by introducing double knit fabrics in 1970[73]—ironically the pullover was back again. White Sox owner Bill Veeck, long before the Bermuda shorts stunt, first introduced names to the back of his team's jerseys in 1960,[74] but the practice would not become common for many teams until the 1970s. The Pirates were not alone in introducing the retrospective look with the "pillbox" style cap in 1976, the National League's centennial and the nation's bicentennial; the Phillies, Mets, Reds, and Cardinals also used variations on this style cap in 1976.[75] During America's bicentennial year, the White Sox brought back the fold-down collar and retained it through the 1981 season.[76] As the 1970s and the 1980s progressed, teams changed designs, sometimes going back to old looks. And during the "Turn Ahead the Clock" series in 1999, teams tried to anticipate the appearance of twenty-first century uniforms.[77]

The traditions associated with major league baseball uniforms have evolved due to fashion trends, technological advances in clothing materials, as well as league, owner, and player whims. Yet given all that, why do many still believe in some unfettered mythical quality about the uniform that makes it sacrosanct — especially from corporate advertising?

The answer may be two fold. The first answer can be traced back to 1939 when both the National Baseball Hall of Fame was inaugurated[78] and the Yankees retired Lou Gehrig's number.[79] The second answer can be found in the tradition of how the jersey sleeve has been used.

When the Yankees retired Gehrig's number four in 1939, an important transformation took place with the uniform jersey: it became a symbol of a player's greatness and a means by which to immortalize him. Keep in mind that the Yankees became the first team to introduce numbers on the backs of players' jerseys ten years earlier and less than a decade before all teams would adopt the use of numbers,[80] so it was only appropriate that the Yankees be the first team to retire a player's number. Given that Gehrig was probably more beloved at the time than Ruth among Yankee as well as all baseball fans, due largely to his tragic illness, the grandeur of the gesture was all the more significant.

The uniform number was also often the only means by which fans could identify a player.[81] Names, as stated, did not become common until the seventies. And many players, such as Ty Cobb, Honus Wagner, and Christy Mathewson who played before 1932, when numbers fell into common usage, did not have a number[82] — although the Pirates did retire Wagner as number 33 in 1956.[83] That is not to say that baseball has not enshrined early century players' entire uniforms. They have. But when numbers finally became tradition, players' identities became synonymous with the numbers they wore. Hence, the number and jersey have become symbolically important in a way that the rest of the uniform has not.

The retiring of numbers has usually been reserved for only great players and/or managers: a little over a hundred players'/managers' numbers have been retired since 1939.[84] So how have players who had only average careers but who became endeared to their team's fans or who died tragically during their careers been recognized?

The tradition of uniform sleeve use over the century renders it a unique symbol. The uniform sleeve has been used in three ways. Its first use has been to display teams' and the league's logos or monograms, teams' lettering, or players' numbers. The first team to use the sleeve for display was the 1906 St. Louis Browns when they placed the "St-L" monogram on the sleeve.[85] In 1908 the famous "NY" monogram first appeared on the Giants' sleeves.[86] The monogram-lettering trend peaked in the early century in 1909 when nine of the sixteen major league teams displayed their insignia on the sleeve.[87] From 1963 to 1965, the Kansas City Athletics resurrected the failed experiments of both the 1882 Reds and the 1916 Indians[88] when they placed numbers on the sleeves of the green sweatshirts worn under their sleeveless jerseys.[89] In 1969 players wore a patch with the major league logo on their uniform sleeve to celebrate the centennial of the professional game. And the 2000 Phillies wore numbers on their sleeves.[90] Thus, throughout the century teams have periodically worn lettering or logos on the sleeve.

The second use of the uniform sleeve has been for commemoration. Throughout the century baseball has commemorated anniversaries and events important to America, baseball, and individual teams.[91]

The third and perhaps most significant use of the uniform sleeve has been in eulogizing deceased players, managers, owners, and other team and league personnel. The specific eulogies made by teams are too numerous to list. Over the last century, there have been approximately forty-five cases of players or managers dying while still active.[92] In the cases of players, some were not eulogized — at least not on the sleeve — while others received the eulogy for only part of a season.[93] There are, however, several aspects about sleeve eulogizing which are important to discuss.

The most common way teams have performed a eulogy is either through the display of a black band or a patch on the left sleeve.[94] Second, when the first confirmed sleeve eulogy took place is difficult to establish. There certainly have been cases of tragic deaths that have prompted teams to make eulogies. For instance, 1903 marked two tragedies. In January Detroit pitcher Win Mercer committed suicide, and during mid-season Washington outfielder Ed Delahanty mysteriously fell from a train en route from Detroit to New York.[95] Another tragic death took place during spring training 1907 when Boston Red Sox player/manager Chick Stahl committed suicide.[96] On August 2, 1940, Cincinnati catcher Willard Hershberger also committed suicide.[97] And on June 27, 1955, Boston Red Sox player Harry Agganis died.[98]

There have been two notable deaths which did result in eulogies. Cleveland shortstop Ray Chapman remains the only player to have died from an injury that directly resulted from a game. On August 16, 1920, Chapman was hit in the head by Yankee pitcher Carl Mays and died the next day.[99] As a result, the Indians wore arm bands in his memory for the remainder of the season[100] and on to their first World Series title.[101] It is important to note this eulogy because it came nineteen years before Gehrig's number was retired. Although eulogies like this have not been as consistent or as recognized as the retirement of numbers, a tradition was established, one that was understood by the baseball fraternity.

The second notable death occurred on New Year's Eve 1972 when

Pittsburgh Pirate right fielder Roberto Clemente died in a plane crash while on a humanitarian mission for the earthquake victims of Managua, Nicaragua. For the entire 1973 season, the Pirates wore a white and black patch that displayed his number 21.[102]

More recently, the 1993 Cleveland Indians eulogized relief pitchers Tim Crews and Steve Olin after their deaths in a spring training boating accident.[103] On a patch shaped like a baseball, the players' numbers — Olin's 31 and Crews' 52 — were placed on the top and bottom of the ball.[104] And the Cubs eulogized popular announcer Harry Caray after his death in February 1998 with a caricature-designed patch.[105] The tradition of the arm band and patch eulogy designates the sleeve of the uniform as a place of reverence transcending baseball itself. In this manner, baseball honors its own.

Given that distinction, one has to wonder whether baseball's consideration of overt advertising on the sleeve would sully the sleeve's symbolic meaning. Certainly baseball's experiment of opening the season in Tokyo makes it appear that jersey manufacturers would allow such billboarding on their products given the right marketing arrangements. Perhaps, at this juncture, the terse speculation at the beginning of the paper that patch advertising may have precedence merits attention.

During the existence of the Federal League in 1914–1915, there was a team in Brooklyn, New York. It just happened that the owner of the team also owned the company that made Tip-Top Bread — in fact the team was known as the "Tip-Tops."[106] And on the sleeve of the team's uniform appeared a patch with the words "Tip-Top."[107]

Whether that should be considered outright advertising might be answered by a more recent, and humorous, example. In 1976 new Atlanta Braves owner Ted Turner was advised to put his players' names on the backs of their jerseys. On the offbeat suggestion of newly acquired pitcher Andy Messersmith, each player placed a nickname instead of his real name of his uniform. Messersmith, for kicks and out of respect to Turner, placed "Channel" above his number 17, which just happened to be the channel of Turner's television station in Atlanta. Then National League President Chub Feeney objected — but not on bad taste alone. He made Messersmith remove "Channel" from his uniform because he appeared to be billboarding for Turner, which, at that time, Major League Baseball regarded as a violation of the uniform code.[108]

So for years baseball has had a code prohibiting players and managers from placing any unauthorized markings or patches on the uniform.[109] Over the past several years, though, some players, and even teams, have chalked or marked on their caps the numbers of players who suffered season-ending injuries as an expression of solidarity. However, such displays of honor were done without formal approval. Now those expressions, unlike the Messersmith stunt, did not seem to bother the baseball bureaucracy — that is until 2000. In the millennium season, Major League Baseball, with consent of the players' union, made the decision to crack down on all non-approved marking on the uniform.[110]

It certainly seems that baseball desires some type of "uniformity." Ironically, the Japanese experiment suggests that the major leagues may not be "uniform" much longer toward the tradition of keeping blatant advertising off the uniform.

Rest assured, the one tradition baseball will not break is the one Harry Wright recognized, after his once invincible Cincinnati Red Stockings suffered their first defeat in 1870, causing attendance to plummet and investors to dry up.[111] Commenting on his abandonment of Cincinnati for Boston, along with that of several of his best players, Wright said,

> Baseball is business now, and I am trying to arrange our games to make them successful and make them pay, irrespective of my feelings, and to the best of my ability.[112]

Notes

1. Guy Curtright, "Baseball and Eggs Season Begins Wednesday at 5 — A.M.! Cubs, Mets Meet in Historic Opener in Tokyo," *Atlanta Journal*, 28 March 2000, A1.
2. "Opening Series 2000-Sponsorship," Office of the Commissioner, Major League Baseball, fax to the author, 16 June 2000.
3. Danny Woodward, "Baseball Is One Sport That Should Keep It Clean," *Arlington Morning News*, 2 April 1999, 2B.
4. Woodward, 2B.
5. Ross Newhan, "Ads Idea May Be a Little Patchy; Baseball: Revenue Plan Would Have Players Wearing Small Advertisements on Sleeves," *Los Angeles Times*, home edition, 1 April 1999, D1.
6. Office of the Commissioner, Major League Baseball, telephone interview by author, 25 April 2000; and Office of the Commissioner, Major League Baseball, telephone interview by author, 14 June 2000.
7. Tony Jackson, "Home-Field Ad-Vantage? Has Baseball Sold Out to Shameless Commercialism or Will Additional Revenue Ultimately Save the Game?" *Denver Rocky Mountain News*, 5 May 1999, 9C.
8. Newhan, D1.
9. Ralph Nader, "Bad Sign for Baseball: Walking Billboards," editorial, *Denver Rocky Mountain News*, 5 May 1999, 9C.
10. Newhan, D1.
11. Partners, Office of the Commissioner, Major League Baseball, fax to author, 19 April 2000.
12. Partners.

13. Office, interview April 25 2000.

14. Office, interview April 25 2000.

15. Marc Okkonen, *Baseball Uniforms of the 20th Century* (New York: Sterling, 1991), 163.

16. Okkonen, *Baseball*, 49, 177.

17. Ibid., 49.

18. Ibid., 2, 23, 212.

19. Ibid., 4.

20. Ibid., 23.

21. Ibid., 7, 32, 161.

22. Ibid., 4.

23. David Nemec, *Great Baseball, Feats, Facts, and Firsts*, revised ed. (New York: Signet, 1999), 4.

24. Nemec, *Great*, 11; and Okkonen, *Baseball*, 1.

25. Okkonen, *Baseball*, 2.

26. Geoffrey C. Ward and Ken Burns, *Baseball: An Illustrated History* (New York: Knopf, 1994), "Inning 1."

27. Okkonen, *Baseball*, 3.

28. Nemec, *Great*, 65.

29. Ward and Burns, 20.

30. Ibid., 23.

31. Ibid., 27.

32. Ibid., 27-28.

33. Ibid., 27.

34. *The Baseball Encyclopedia: The Complete and Definitive Record of Major League Baseball*, 10th ed. (New York: Macmillan, 1996), 1439.

35. Ward and Burns, 28.

36. Okkonen, *Baseball*, 6.

37. Jim Capel, "Why Major Leaguers Favor Certain Uniform Numbers," *Baseball Digest*, October 1990, 60.

38. Nemec, *Great*, 11.

39. Okkonen, *Baseball*, 89-91.

40. Nemec, *Great*, 61; and Okkonen, *Baseball*, 1.

41. Okkonen, *Baseball*, 2.

42. Ibid., 220.

43. Ibid., 234-235.

44. Ibid., 3.

45. Ibid., 3.

46. Ibid., 30.

47. Public Relations Department, Chicago White Sox, telephone interview by author, 14 June 2000.

48. Okkonen, *Baseball*, 3.

49. Ibid., 2.

50. Ibid., 9, 15.

51. Ibid., 2.

52. Ibid., 31, 35, 36, 39.

53. Ibid., 39.

54. Ibid., 89-90.

55. Ibid., 104-105.

56. Ibid., 114-115.

57. Ibid., 2.

58. Ibid., 130.

59. Ibid., 164.

60. Ibid., 108.

61. Ibid., 166.

62. Okkonen, *Baseball*, 118; and "This Day in Baseball History — February 27," Nationalpastime [web site], accessed 10 January 2000.

63. Okkonen, *Baseball*, 1, 103.

64. Ibid., 103-119.

65. Capel, 60.

66. Okkonen, *Baseball*, 23, 163.

67. Ibid., 23, 212.

68. Ibid., 43.

69. Ibid., 235, 267.

70. Ibid., 223, 173.

71. Ibid., 33, 59.

72. Ibid., 1.

73. Ibid., 68.

74. Nemec, *Great*, 185; and Okkonen, *Baseball*, 5.

75. Okkonen, *Baseball*, 241.

76. Ibid., 30.

77. "Century 21 Real Estate Corporation Announces Two-Year Sponsorship with Major League Baseball®," *PR Newswire*, 9 February 1999.

78. Okkonen, *Baseball*, 5.

79. "Retired Numbers," information and presentation by Christian Ruzich, 1998, accessed 10 January 2000, 5.

80. Capel, 60; and Okkonen, *Baseball*, 5.

81. Ward and Burns, 256.

82. Capel, 60; and Okkonen, *Baseball*, 5.

83. "Retired Numbers," 6.

84. Ibid., 6.

85. Okkonen, *Baseball*, 5, 100.

86. Ibid., 105.

87. Ibid., 106-107.

88. Capel, 60.

89. Okkonen, *Baseball*, 59, 218.

90. Ibid., 5.

91. Ibid., 5.

92. David S. Neft and Richard M Cohen, *The Sports Encyclopedia: Baseball*, 6th ed. (New York: St. Martin's/Marek, 1985).

93. Marc Okkonen, telephone interview by author, 2 May 2000.

94. Okkonen, *Baseball*, 5; and Okkonen, interview 2 May 2000.

95. Neft and Cohen, 20.

96. Ibid., 36.

97. Ibid., 204.

98. Ibid., 326.

99. Neft and Cohen, 124; and Ward and Burns, 153.

100. David Nemec and others, *20th Century Baseball Chronicle: Year-By-Year History of Major League Baseball* (Lincolnwood, Ill.: Publications International, 1999), 90; and Okkonen, *Baseball*, 36.

101. Morris Eckhouse, *Day by Day in Cleveland Indians History* (New York: Leisure, 1983), 342; and Nemec and others, 88.

102. Bruce Markusen, *Roberto Clemente: The Great One* (Champaign, Ill.: Sports Publishing, 1998), 343; and Okkonen, *Baseball*, 235.

103. Nemec and others, 591; and Bart Swain, Media Relations, Cleveland Indians, telephone interview by author, 30 May 2000.

104. Swain.

105. Nemec and others, 627.

106. Marc Okkonen, *The Federal League of 1914-1915: Baseball's Third Major League* (Pittsburgh: SABR, 1989), 19.

107. Okkonen, *Federal*, 30.

108. R. Fimrite, "Bigwig Flips His Wig in Wigwam," *Sports Illustrated*, 19 July 1976, 26.

109. Office, interview, 14 June 2000.

110. Office Interview, 14 June 2000.

111. Ward and Burns, 21, 23.

112. Ibid., 23.

Part 4

RACE, GENDER, AND
ETHNICITY IN THE
NATIONAL PASTIME

Houston's Latin Star Cesar Cedeno and Death in the Dominican Republic: The Troubled Legacy of Race Relations in the Lone Star State

Ron Briley

During the 1999 baseball season, businessman and owner of the Houston Astros Drayton McLane was involved in a controversy with the Texas Hispanic community. According to Marco Comancho, general manager of KTMD Television and a subsidiary of the Telemundo Group, and Rod Rodriguez, the station's sales manager, McLane made disparaging and belittling comments regarding Mexicans and Mexican-Americans shortly before a dinner honoring the businessman with the Houston Advertising Federation's Trailblazer Award for service to the community. An outraged McLane vehemently denied having uttered any remarks which might be construed as racist.

Following an investigation of the incident, Telemundo's chief executive, Roland Hernandez, apologized to McLane, stating that he found no evidence of racially-biased comments being made by the baseball owner. In a prepared statement, a relieved McLane insisted, "Having spent a lifetime honoring the values of integrity and honesty, this episode has been unsettling. Despite a rush to judgment by some, this action by Telemundo, hopefully, will help to speed the healing process."[1]

But if McLane devoted his life to the values of integrity, honesty, and community service, why were so many in the Hispanic community so quick to question the baseball executive's motives? The answer to this question may lie in the troubling history of race relations in the Lone Star State of Texas, where, in the words of Carey McWilliams, "Anglos have always been 'gringos' to the Hispanos while Hispanos have been 'greasers' to the Anglos." In *Occupied America: A History of Chicanos*, Rodolfo Acuna asserts that racial animosities in Texas are a result of Anglo economic domination of the Mexican community enforced by official state violence, such as that perpetuated by the Texas Rangers, an organization so much admired by the dean of Texas historians, Walter Prescott Webb. Chicano activists, such as José Angel Gutierrez, argue that education in Texas is presented from an Anglo perspective, ignoring the fact that "the land of the West and Southwest, beginning with Texas, was stolen from Mexicans." While less confrontational and more scholarly in its approach, David Montejano's study of Anglos and Mexicans in Texas, which received the 1988 Frederick Jackson Turner Award from the American Historical Association, maintains that the history of Texas has been Anglo economic control perpetuated by cultural, political, and social Jim Crow legislation, whose hegemony has been challenged by the Chicano civil rights movement.[2]

It is within this historical context that the alleged racist remarks of Astros owner McLane must be placed. While the Houston organization has produced talented Latin players, such as José Cruz and Joaquin Andujar, it should be noted that Astros management, unlike the Los Angeles Dodgers with the marketing and pitching success of Fernando Valenzuela, has tended to maintain an Anglo identity; building the team around such stars as Nolan Ryan, Jeff Bagwell, and Craig Biggio. While it is impossible to deny the athletic achievement of these ball players, the failure to develop and especially market more Latin star players flies in the face of Southwestern demographics. From a 1980 base of 8.7 million people, the Mexican-origin population of the United States grew by 4.7 million to a 1990 total of 13.4 million; a 54 percent intercensual increase. And the Mexican-origin people constitute approximately two-thirds of Latins, who, in turn, comprise over 8 percent of the United States population. Nearly 75 percent of all Mexican-origin persons live in California and Texas, both of whom have populations in excess of 25 percent Mexican roots.[3]

Yet, the major league baseball establishment in Houston has historically failed to capitalize on these demographics by consistently developing and marketing Latin talent. While perhaps operating on an unconscious level, this policy, nevertheless, may be reflective of the city's conservative to reactionary political traditions. According to Don E. Carlton, the Houston establishment's fears of growing diversity in the city produced a right-wing backlash which labeled efforts at city planning and zoning as communist plots. City biographer George Fuermann argues that Houston has been dominated by merchants and businessmen, whose goals have been material, rather than altruistic, humanitarian, or community-oriented. In fact, Houston's greatest claim to fame, embodied in the hyperbole of the Astrodome as the ninth wonder of the world, may be as the most air-conditioned city in the world. According to city historian David G. McComb, "There is nothing closer to hell in modern American than to be caught after a rain in a Houston traffic jam in an unair-conditioned car. It is possible, at that moment, to appreciate the plight of a steamed clam, and the situation does nothing to improve human temperament." The Houston way of coping with this environment has been to build huge structures of steel and concrete, while paying little attention to zoning and creation of open space.[4]

But while progressive in providing air-conditioned structures, Houston tends to maintain a more reactionary political framework. Francisco A. Rosales and Barry J. Kaplan maintain nineteenth-century values have retained a stronghold in Houston, arguing, "Individualism, opportunity, capitalism, and limited government, virtual dogma in American government before the 1929 crash, have remained sacred in Houston."[5] Thus, when major league baseball came to Houston in 1962, the city's baseball fathers elected to fashion the team's identity and logo with the Colt .45; the gun that tamed the West and, by implication, the Mexican and Native American populations, making way for the progress of Anglo civilization.[6] While the smoking Colt .45 logo embraced the symbolic values of nineteenth-century Texas, the Houston franchise's handling of its first Latin star, Cuban-born Roman Mejias, demonstrated a lack of sensitivity and appreciation for the potential of its Spanish-speaking community. Drafted out of the Pittsburgh Pirates organization, Mejias would lead the fledgling Houston team in home runs and runs batted in, while hitting for a .286 average. Following his banner year in Houston, Mejias was traded to the Boston Red Sox for singles-hitting Pete Runnels, an Anglo who hailed from nearby Pasadena, Texas. The story of Roman Mejias suggests that Houston management failed to market and develop Mejias as a star, establishing a club tradition of extolling Anglo players, while eschewing the potential of its Latin community and falling into the pattern of racial segregation which has characterized the troubled history of race relations in the Lone Star state.[7]

However, at the peak of the Chicano civil rights movement of the 1960s and early 1970s, Houston management, while continuing to ignore

Mexican talent, made a concentrated effort to develop Cesar Cedeno, whom baseball scouts lauded as possessing exceptional athletic qualities. Cedeno was born February 25, 1951, in Santo Domingo, Dominican Republic, to a family of modest means. Cesar's father Diogene worked in a nail factory, but he aspired to be a small businessman, purchasing a family grocery store. According to biographical portraits of Cedeno placed in sporting publications after the Dominican cracked the major leagues, Diogene perceived of baseball as a meaningless pursuit and wanted his son available to help with family chores and delivering groceries. However, Cesar's passion for baseball was abetted by his mother who purchased him a glove and shoes without the knowledge of the family patriarch. Despite the ambitions of the elder Cedeno, the family continued to struggle economically, and Cesar, one of four children, dropped out of school in grade eight, working as a laborer in the nail factory which employed his father.[8]

Contrary to the wishes of Diogene, Cesar continued playing baseball in Santo Domingo, where the sixteen-year-old boy was discovered by Houston scouts in the fall of 1967. Astro representatives Pat Gillich and Tony Pacheco were combing the Dominican Republic searching for prospects, and they stumbled upon Cedeno while looking at another young player. According to Gillich, "We saw him throw and then we saw him go up and get a hit and go up and get another hit. We decided we wanted to look at him. After the game, we arranged for him to go with us and some more players to San Pedro, about sixty miles away, for a workout."[9] The reason for moving the try out to San Pedro was to escape the notice of other scouts, as under organized baseball's rules the Caribbean was open territory to which the sport's draft laws were inapplicable. In addition, with a growing cadre of major league Latin stars, such as Orlando Cepeda, Roberto Clemente, Rico Carty, Juan Marichal, and the Alou brothers, the Houston organization was finally becoming aware of the talent pool available in Latin America.

Gillich and Pacheco were even more impressed after observing Cedeno in San Pedro, and the Houston agents moved quickly to sign the young Dominican who had also been scouted by the St. Louis Cardinals. However, there was a stumbling block in the person of Diogene Cedeno, whose signature on a contract was necessary for his underage son. The elder Cedeno reportedly wanted his son to either work in Santo Domingo or return to school, but not to pursue something as frivolous as baseball. Gillich initially offered the Cedeno family a contract for $1,200; however, when Gillich learned that a Cardinal representative was on his way to the Cedeno home, the Houston scout, on his own initiative, upped the ante to $3,000. To the economically-strapped Cedeno household, this amount of money was persuasive, and the elder Cedeno, despite misgivings, gave his assent to his son pursuing a baseball career in the United States. Allegedly, as Gillich and Pacheco were departing the Cedeno residence, a Cardinal scout was just getting out of his car. An elated Gillich waved the Cedeno contract, exclaiming, "You're a few minutes too late."[10]

Houston club officials had little reason to question the judgment of their talent agents, for Cedeno quickly established himself as a first-rate prospect. In 1968, at age seventeen, he hit .374 in thirty-six games for Covington, Kentucky, of the Appalachian League and .256 for Cocoa of the Florida State League. The following season, Cedeno continued to impress, hitting .274 with a league-leading thirty-two doubles for the Newport News of the Carolina League. The teen prospect was working his way through the Houston organization, while coping with the challenges of learning English and racial relations in the American South.[11] He also maintained an affinity for ham, eggs, and chicken; a literal representation of what Sam Regalado termed the special hunger of Latin American ball players. According to Regalado, competition on America's baseball diamonds carried crucial social and economic implications for Latin players:

> Baseball was a path out of poverty, it helped to bring distinction to their homelands; it was a means to ease the pain and suffering of kinfolk and compatriots; and it provided a sliver of hope to many younger Latins who might otherwise have envisioned a dim future. Their determination to succeed in the ace of an unwelcoming culture reveals the human spirit of Latin players. For they, unlike so many other newcomers, faced these barriers alone, without the aid of support groups. And it was this willingness to break through cultural roadblocks that made their hunger special.[12]

Although he possessed a special hunger and was making steady progress with his mastery of the English language and baseball fundamentals, the Houston organization challenged the sport's conventional wisdom by promoting the nineteen-year-old Cedeno to their AAA affiliate in Oklahoma City for the 1970 season. Apparently, one of the reasons for the assignment was the fact that Oklahoma City 89ers' manager Hub Kittle spoke Spanish and possessed an established reputation "for keeping the Latin players loose and happy." The Houston baseball establishment, which had essentially ignored the cultural and racial barriers confronting the organization's first Latin star Roman Mejias, was making an effort to support the assimilation of its Latin players. However, Cedeno's predominantly Anglo teammates insisted upon referring to the Dominican as "Sandy." Nomenclature aside, Cedeno devoured AAA pitching, hitting safely in all but three of Oklahoma City's first thirty-four games. Manager

Kittle refused to tinker with Cedeno's aggressive batting style, observing, "I tell him to go up there and take his cuts. Believe me, if anybody gets this kid messed up, I'll shoot the guy."[13] Ironically, Kittle's comment foreshadowed a 1973 Dominican shooting which would cast a cloud over Cedeno's career and life.

However, in 1970 Cedeno was the toast of the baseball world. After terrorizing AAA pitching (In fifty-four games for Oklahoma City, Cedeno hit .373, with 14 home runs and 61 runs driven in.), the nineteen-year-old teenager was promoted to the major leagues in July, playing in ninety games for the Astros, while hitting for an average of .310 with 7 home runs, 42 runs batted in, and seventeen stolen bases; coupled with outstanding defensive play in center field. This phenomenal performance by one so young immediately established Cedeno with a "can't miss" reputation. Astro manger Harry Walker, who was an excellent hitter during his National League career, described Cedeno as a natural, insisting, "He's cat-quick in the outfield, he can throw with the best of them and he can hit. Barring injury, he'll be one helluva ball player by the time he's 22 years old." Praise for Cedeno's performance was also forthcoming from the Pittsburgh Pirates Roberto Clemente, who proclaimed, "He's one of the best young players I have ever seen. He has great control of his movements in the outfield." When asked if he expected to live up to such accolades, Cedeno reportedly grinned sheepishly and replied, "I guess so."[14]

Nevertheless, the young Houston player suffered through a sophomore slump during the 1971 baseball campaign, in which Cedeno hit for a .264 average with 10 home runs, 81 runs batted in, and 20 stolen bases. The over-swinging twenty year old continued to excel in the field, and reporter John Wilson, representing the views of the Houston organization and many baseball talent scouts, concluded, "He still is a young player with the seeming natural ability to do it all, and do it big."[15]

Cedeno more than met the expectations of the Houston baseball establishment with banner seasons in 1972 and 1973; hitting for a .320 average in both campaigns, coupled with power and speed figures of 22 and 25 home runs, 82 and 70 runs batted in, and 55 and 56 stolen bases. The center fielder's defensive contributions were recognized with consecutive golden glove awards. The young Dominican was the shining star of the baseball universe, with pundits as well as players suggesting that Cedeno was as talented as the superstars Willie Mays, Hank Aaron, and Roberto Clemente. Baltimore Orioles scouting chief Jim Russo described the Houston athlete as "the best young player in baseball." Meanwhile, Harry Walker, who had also managed Clemente in Pittsburgh, favorably compared Cedeno with the Puerto Rican icon, asserting, "Clemente and

Cedeno are the two most exciting players in baseball today. Whether they're catching the ball or throwing it or running the bases or batting, they do it all-out and with a flair. When they're involved, you're always on edge expecting something to happen. They make things happen." Of course, the emphasis upon the similarities between Clemente and Cedeno was partially based upon stereotypes of Latin American ball players as emotional and flamboyant individuals who embraced a flashy or "hot dog" style over that of more disciplined and serious Anglo athletes.

On the other hand, Clemente was uncomfortable with both the stereotypes and comparisons. Acknowledging that Cedeno possessed more talent than anyone entering the league during his time, the Pittsburgh outfielder, nevertheless, believed it was unfair to label Cedeno as another Clemente. The Puerto Rican athlete concluded, "I don't think it is fair to him. When I came up, I did not like to be compared with other players." Cedeno concurred, adding, "I don't want to be the second Clemente, I would rather be the first Cedeno."[16]

Yet, Cedeno's reservations did little to silence his boosters. Cincinnati Reds manager Sparky Anderson labeled the Houston center fielder as the best young player in the game; while Atlanta Braves slugger Hank Aaron observed, "He's the youngster with the greatest ability to hit this league since me." However, perhaps the most dramatic pronouncement regarding Cedeno's unlimited potential came from baseball legend Leo Durocher, who replaced Walker as Houston's manager late in the 1972 season. Durocher, who had managed Willie Mays early in his brilliant career and claimed to be a father figure for the Giants center fielder, maintained that Cedeno was a better player than Mays at a similar stage in his career.[17]

Such hoopla obviously placed tremendous pressure upon the Houston star, but during the 1972 and 1973 baseball seasons Cedeno responded superbly at the bat and in the field. But off the playing field, there were signs that Houston management had little prepared their young Latin star for the price of fame. More might be needed than a Spanish-speaking manager at the AAA level. Rumors of heavy drinking followed Cedeno, and his private life was tumultuous. In 1970, Cedeno married a Puerto Rican woman with whom he fathered a child. Following a divorce, he was married again, this time to a twenty-year-old Houston woman. Nevertheless, Cedeno was still perceived by the sporting press as a man who had it all. In a 1973 profile entitled "Rendering Unto Cesar," Arthur Daley of *The New York Times* concluded, "On what meat doth this, our Cesar, feed? Apparently he also feeds on luck. He's got everything else. This has to give him an unbeatable combination."[18]

However, Cedeno's luck was about to desert him. During the winter of 1973, he was playing baseball in his native Dominican Republic. In the early morning hours of December 11, Cedeno, who had apparently been drinking, checked into a Santo Domingo hotel. He was accompanied by nineteen-year-old Altagracia de la Cruz, the mother of a three-year-old daughter and an acquaintance of Cedeno, for found in the hotel room was a photograph of the ball player and de la Cruz in an embrace. After arriving at the hotel, Cedeno ordered beers from room service, and there were reports of an argument and loud noises coming from the hotel room. Shortly thereafter, a shot was heard, and Cedeno phoned a hotel employee to report that de la Cruz was dead. The athlete then fled the scene in his sports car, reportedly finding sanctuary with his wife Cora in their Dominican home. The next day, Cedeno, accompanied by his wife, turned himself into authorities, almost eleven hours after the shooting. Although Cedeno claimed the death of de la Cruz was accidental, the ball player was initially held on charges of voluntary manslaughter, which under Dominican law called for prison sentences ranging from three to ten years upon conviction. The severe charges levied against Cedeno made him ineligible for bail, and he spent the Christmas holidays in jail. However, according to newspaper accounts, Cedeno was being held in "preventive custody" in Santo Domingo's most modern jail with a room of his own. An anonymous prison source was quoted in an Associated Press account as saying, "The Cedeno case is a special one. He is no common prisoner."[19]

Nor was Cedeno a common prisoner for Houston Astros management, who saw the future of their franchise and a valuable investment about to be extinguished by gunfire in a Santo Domingo hotel. The Houston baseball establishment had refused to intervene when their first Latin star Roman Mejias's family was unable to get out of Cuba in the early 1960s. However, within months of his trade to the Red Sox, Boston management was able to arrange a reunion between Mejias and his family.[20] In Cedeno's case, within days of the shooting, a delegation of Houston officials were dispatched to the Caribbean island. The Astro representatives included General Manager Spec Richardson, Assistant General Manager John Mullen, minor league operations chief Pat Gillet, and Dominican scout Epifanio Guerrero. After visiting with the incarcerated Cedeno, the delegation expressed confidence that the shooting was accidental and the Houston star would be acquitted of all charges, free to assume his position in center field at the Astrodome, which team hype had begun referring to as Cesar's Palace.

In public statements to the press, Mullen and Richardson described de la Cruz's death as a tragedy and demonstrated paternalistic attitudes regarding Cedeno, and by inference, Latin culture. Mullen stated, "Cesar was very quiet and subdued…. You know Cesar. He's usually so effervescent, so outgoing. Now he has very little to say and is obviously feeling very downcast." General Manager Richardson echoed the sentiments of Mullen, concluding, "I came down here to cheer up Cedeno and give him confidence and find out for myself what state the boy is in. He's very concerned about what happened and a little frightened." Concerned about the future of their franchise player, Houston executives failed to express much concern or sympathy for de la Cruz and her family.[21]

Meanwhile, back in the United States, teammates and baseball officials weighed in with support for Cedeno. Jim Wynn, who had yielded his center field job to Cedeno and was traded to the Los Angeles Dodgers only days before the shooting, said that he was not surprised to learn that Cedeno was carrying a pistol in a Latin American nation. Wynn asserted, "I played one year over there, and I think it is a fairly common thing. I know a lot of people do it. They have so much trouble down there and a lot of it has to do with changes in government." While Wynn's comments revealed common assumptions and misconceptions regarding Latin America, Houston third baseman Doug Rader insisted that Cedeno was innocent until proven guilty. Rader argued, "Just because he's a ball player doesn't mean he is guilty. If he was Joe Blow he'd get the benefit of the doubt. Why shouldn't he [Cedeno] get the same benefit? Sometimes when something sensational happens to someone in the public eye, people automatically feel he's guilty. I say Cesar Cedeno is a human being. More than that, he's a good person. Like anyone else, he should get the benefit of the doubt until proven guilty."[22]

Tal Smith, Executive Vice-President of the New York Yankees, and who as a Houston executive had approved the contract bringing Cedeno to the United States, told *The New York Times* that he was stunned regarding Cedeno's involvement with the death of de la Cruz. Smith observed that in the United States it was all too common to take a young man from another culture and "give him all the adulation and expect him to handle it. I know guys that can't. But Cesar could." Cedeno's character was also vouched for by the Dominican Ambassador to the United States, Federico Antun, who also happened to be president of the team for which Cedeno played before inking his contract with the Astros. Antun characterized Cedeno as "a very nice boy; he never used bad words." However, he acknowledged that exposure to American culture, fame, and money might have changed the Dominican athlete. The Ambassador asserted, "Cesar was the best player my country gave you, better than Rico Carty. He didn't smoke or drink, but I knew he liked the girls. They said he was drunk when he went to the motel with the girl that night. Maybe he was. Maybe he changed. But when I knew him, he didn't drink."[23]

While there is little evidence that the Astros prepared Cedeno to deal with his new found fame and fortune, which the team had hyped in order to sell tickets, the club certainly rushed to his defense after the Dominican shooting and arrest. In late December, Cedeno's attorney Quirico Elpidio Perez, who had been retained by Houston management, was successful in getting the charges against the ball player reduced to involuntary manslaughter, allowing Cedeno to leave jail after posting a ten thousand dollar bond. In mid-January, District Attorney Frank Diaz appealed to Judge Porfirio Natera to dismiss all charges against Cedeno, citing a police report which indicated that paraffin tests proved de la Cruz had fired Cedeno's weapon in her right hand. The paraffin test apparently corroborated Cedeno's testimony that the young woman had grabbed the loaded revolver, and he had tried to take it away from her. In the ensuing struggle, a shot was fired and de la Cruz was dead. After taking the prosecutor's motion into account, Natera, nevertheless, found Cedeno guilty of involuntary homicide. However, the judge assessed Cedeno only a one hundred dollar fine and determined that the ball player would receive no period of incarceration. Cedeno and his wife Cora, who appeared at all court proceedings by her husband's side, made immediate plans to return to the United States.[24]

Felicia de la Cruz, an aunt of the young woman killed in Cedeno's hotel room, termed the verdict "an injustice." Family members filed a civil suit on behalf of de la Cruz's three-year-old daughter, whose father was not acknowledged to be Cedeno. Meanwhile, the ball player was free to leave the Dominican Republic. Ostensibly, the law suits initiated by the de la Cruz family were settled out of court, amid accusations, although never documented, that the Houston franchise had arranged a financial settlement with the family as well as Dominican legal officials.[25] While the Houston organization had generally ignored both the athletic talent and marketability of its first Latin athlete, Mejias, the ball club certainly invested time, effort, and money in the case of Cedeno. However, management involvement on behalf of the ball player in the death of de la Cruz provides little indication that the Houston baseball establishment was appreciative of Latin American culture and sensibilities. Instead, the action of the Astros in the Cedeno-de la Cruz affair appeared to coincide more with American military interventions in Central America and the Caribbean to protect business investments.

While Houston officials breathed a sigh of relief upon the release of their superstar, other observers were less comfortable with the deliberations of the Dominican justice system. Columnist Dick Young believed the Houston club was overly focused on how the promising career of its center fielder might by impaired by the events of December, 1973, in a Dominican hotel room. Young pointed out, "Maybe Altagracia de la Cruz, 19, did not have a promising career, but whatever it was, it is ended." In another column, Young speculated, "In America, a man would be innocent by reason of accidental death. If guilty, you get a prison sentence; if innocent, you get off, but how does anyone put a $100 price tag on a human life?"[26]

Cedeno recognized that many baseball fans and players shared Young's questions about what had transpired in the Dominican Republic. To those who maintained that the tragedy of de la Cruz had been obscured by concerns over Cedeno's baseball career, the athlete replied, "I feel very sorry because that happened ... that she got herself killed. I will say it this way: God and me know that I didn't do it. She killed herself. I tried to take the gun away from her. I knew it was dangerous. I told her not to get it ... because it was loaded. What else could I do?" As for hecklers, Cedeno insisted, "Some players on other teams will try to take my concentration away, but it's not going to work. I won't pay any attention to those players. I'll just put on my uniform and play my game." The Houston athlete maintained that he had learned from the Dominican tragedy, which would make him a better person. He also expressed his appreciation for his wife who had supported him throughout the ordeal. But the bottom line for Cedeno was apparently neither de la Cruz nor his domestic and personal life. When asked why he had not immediately turned himself into the police, Cedeno explained, "I was scared. I saw my baseball career was in danger."[27]

While the intervention of Houston officials had succeeded in saving the athlete to play another day, Cedeno's 1974 performance failed to match the expectations established by the 1972 and 1973 seasons. Nursing a knee injury, and bothered more by the de la Cruz affair than he was publicly admitting, Cedeno slumped to a .269 batting average, although he still managed 26 home runs, 102 runs batted in, and 57 stolen bases.

And Cedeno was reentering a baseball world in which ball park violence, reflecting the larger culture, reached a crescendo in 1974. As the nation reeled from the disillusionment of military defeat in Vietnam and political corruption at the highest levels with the Watergate scandal, opening day for the Chicago White Sox was marred by heavy drinking and fighting fans, as well as seven streakers, both male and female, who pranced through the outfield grass clad only in baseball caps. A ten cent beer night promotion in Cleveland resulted in a riot and forfeiture by the Indians to the visiting Texas Rangers. And on May 12, 1974, Houston Astros outfielder Bob Watson crashed into the left field wall at Cincinnati's Riverfront Stadium.

With his sunglasses shattered and his face bloodied, Watson was afraid any movement might endanger his eyesight. Meanwhile, some spectators in the bleachers began pouring beer over the prone and bleeding figure of Watson. Teammates such as Cedeno engaged in a shouting match with unruly fans, while Watson was carried from the field. While deploring the behavior of those individuals who harassed the injured Watson, the ever-caustic Dick Young reminded his readers that the Astros' Cedeno might want to be careful about calling others hoodlums.[28]

In 1975, Cedeno raised his batting mark to .288, but his power figures declined with only 13 home runs and 63 runs driven in. The center fielder was also gaining a reputation as a malcontent, which Cedeno blamed upon the publication of Leo Durocher's autobiography *Nice Guys Finish Last*. In this book, Durocher maintained that while the Houston player possessed as much talent as anyone in the game, Cedeno often did not give 100 percent. Cedeno objected to such accusations, asserting that he always gave his best, but that he would not play injured for anybody as that would endanger his career (Interestingly enough, this was almost the same reasoning used by Cedeno to defend his actions in the de la Cruz shooting.). Cedeno also complained about being labeled by the media as immature for emotional outbursts such as throwing a batting helmet. A frustrated Cedeno insisted that he was tired of being compared with such veteran ball players as Mays and Aaron. Cedeno pointed out that he was still only twenty-five years of age, and he assumed that the great Mays must have done his share of equipment tossing during his earlier years.[29]

Frustration on the part of Cedeno led to rumors that the Dominican would be dealt to the New York Yankees. However, Houston management was not prepared to turn its back on Cedeno as it had done with Mejias following the 1962 season. Bill Virdon, who assumed the managerial reins in Houston late in the 1975 season, made it clear that he wanted Cedeno to remain an Astro, calling the Dominican the "number one player in the National League." Houston executives agreed with Virdon's evaluation, and, in an effort to forestall Cedeno from declaring free agency, provided the Houston outfielder with a ten year, three and one-half million dollar contract, making him the highest paid player in the game.[30]

However, the return on Houston's investment was mixed. While Cedeno continued to be a fine player, he never again amassed the .320 batting averages of 1972 and 1973. In fact, only in the 1980 season would Cedeno ever again cross the .300 batting average plateau, and Houston, although it came close in 1980, would never win a National League pennant during his tenure. Cedeno missed more than half of the 1978 campaign due to a seventeen stitch wound inflicted when he smashed his fist into a Plexiglas dugout roof after failing to drive a run in from second base, followed by a knee ligament injury suffered when he slid into second base in Chicago. Cedeno's increasing vulnerability to injury and failure to attain the elite status predicted by pundits led many baseball people to wonder what had happened to Cesar Cedeno. For example, Joe Morgan, who played with Cedeno in Houston before gaining Hall of Fame credentials as the second baseman for Cincinnati's Big Red Machine, asserted, "I don't think Cedeno's been as good a player as I thought he would be." Such great expectations might be blamed upon Houston officials' use of public relations in likening the Dominican to Mays, Aaron, and Clemente.

Since Cedeno would only hit .300 once in his career after the de la Cruz shooting, the baseball press began to wonder whether that traumatic event might have taken away from him that slight edge that a truly great athlete must have. Teammates and Houston management asserted that they never discussed the shooting and that it had no effect on the Houston star. Cedeno was also in a state of denial. In response to the allegation that he was never the same after that December, 1973, evening in Santo Domingo, Cedeno maintained, "Like I say, I don't want to talk about it. I feel satisfied, and as long as I feel satisfied I can live with myself. The incident means nothing, nothing at all. I'm a better ball player than I was then."[31]

The Houston ball player's batting statistics failed to support such an assertion, and the de la Cruz shooting continued to haunt Cedeno. In 1981, Cedeno suffered through another sub par campaign, batting only .271 and missing over half the season due to a broken ankle sustained during the 1980 play-off series with the Philadelphia Phillies. Late in the season, Cedeno was fined $5,000 by the National League, but not suspended, for climbing a fence and entering the fourth row of box seats in Atlanta Stadium, confronting three hecklers who were taunting Cedeno and his wife. National League President Chub Feeney condemned Cedeno's actions, but he observed that there were mitigating circumstances. According to witnesses, three male spectators were continuously shouting "killer, killer, killer," in the direction of Cedeno and his wife Cora, who accompanied her husband to Atlanta. In explaining his actions, Cedeno proclaimed, "I'm not going to say what he called me, but it has to do with something that happened a long time ago, something I will have to live with the rest of my life. I don't like people calling me something I'm not ... If I had been here alone, I probably would not have reacted that way. But my wife has been subjected to the same language and treatment. She was near tears. I don't think any man would want to have his wife hear people call him that."[32]

Houston management defended Cedeno for his actions in Atlanta, refusing to impose any additional fines upon the player. However, Houston's patience had worn thin with its increasingly temperamental and oft-injured Latin star. Before the 1982 season Cedeno was traded to the Cincinnati Reds for Ray Knight. Cedeno was unhappy during his tenure with the Reds. After starting in center field during 1982, Cedeno became a platoon player his last years in Cincinnati, while gaining a reputation as a malcontent. For example, after a 1983 game in Chicago, Cedeno was incensed when he was denied a first class seat on the team's return flight to Cincinnati. There were only nine seats available in first class, and they were all assigned to players in the starting line-up. Cedeno demanded a seat in first class, tore up his coach ticket, and stormed out of the terminal, refusing to accompany the team on the flight. The Reds responded with an undisclosed fine, and manager Russ Nixon, alluding to Cedeno's reputation as a malingerer who would not play in pain, remarked, "There were only nine seats in first class, and if he feels that he has to have priority over people who beat their brains out for nine innings, that's his problem."[33]

Late in the 1985 season, the disgruntled Cedeno was dispatched by the Reds to the Cardinals for the stretch drive. Cedeno, insisting that leaving the Reds was like "getting out of jail" (And apparently Cedeno was not being ironic about his past.), played an instrumental role in the Cardinals winning the National League pennant, although St. Louis was defeated by the Kansas City Royals in the World Series.[34] Cedeno finished out his major league career by playing briefly with the Los Angeles Dodgers during the 1986 season. Leaving the game at the relatively early age of thirty-five, Cedeno amassed impressive major statistics; playing in over two thousand games, with a lifetime batting average of .285, 199 home runs, 976 runs driven in, and 550 stolen bases.[35] The Dominican enjoyed a successful major league career, most of it employed with the Houston franchise, but he failed to achieve the Hall of Fame numbers associated with Mays, Aaron, and Clemente. Injuries and, perhaps of utmost importance, the death of Alagracia de la Cruz had prevented Cedeno from attaining the status of greatness predicted by so many observers of baseball talent.

On the other hand, Houston management, perhaps learning a lesson from how the club had handled Roman Mejias, attempted to break the cycle of troubled race relations in Texas between Anglo and Latin by marketing and building the team around a Latin star in the person of Cedeno. While the Houston baseball establishment lavished money and publicity (Although the club's public relations machine may have been responsible for raising unrealistic expectations for Cedeno.) upon Cedeno, the athlete's involvement in the death of de la Cruz offers scant evidence that the Houston franchise had prepared their young player to deal with the pressures of fame and fortune. Also, in its intervention with the criminal justice system of the Dominican Republic and apparent disregard for a dead Latina woman, Houston officials demonstrated little respect for Latin culture and institutions in their efforts to preserve the team's economic investment in a valuable commodity, Cesar Cedeno.

However, Houston's endeavors to build a pennant-winning franchise around Cedeno failed. Although the Astros have signed popular and successful Latin players, such as José Cruz, Joaquin Andujar, and José Lima, the club has not tied its identity to a Latin player since Cedeno. Instead, the Houston baseball establishment has done little to alleviate the legacy of racial distrust between Anglo and Latin; organizing and marketing the team around such Anglo stars as Ryan, Biggio, and Bagwell, who despite their achievements have never been able to lead the Houston franchise to a National League pennant.[36] The Houston Astros, based upon their experience with Cedeno, seem to have, apparently on an unconscious level, bought into the racial stereotype that Latin ball players, albeit talented, are overly emotional, temperamental, and unreliable, lacking the leadership, work ethic, and marketing characteristics around which one should organize a team. It is within this historical context that the rush to judgment by many in the Hispanic community regarding allegations of racism against Astros owner Drayton McLane must be understood.

Notes

1. For an account of the controversy between Drayton McLane and representatives from KTMD-TV, see: *The New York Times*, July 13, 1999.

2. For race relations in Texas between Mexican-Americans and Anglos, see: Carey McWilliams, updated by Matt S. Meier, *North from Mexico: The Spanish-Speaking People of the United States* (New York: Praeger, 1990), p. 112; Rodolfo Acuna, *Occupied America: A History of Chicanos* (New York: HarperCollins, 1988), p. 40–41; José Angel Gutierrez, *The Making of a Chicano Militant: Lessons from Cristal* (Madison: The University of Wisconsin Press, 1998), p. 16–17; Armando Navarro, *The Cristal Experiment: A Chicano Struggle for Community Control* (Madison: The University of Wisconsin Press, 1998); and David Montejano, *Anglos and Mexicans in the Making of Texas, 1836–1986* (Austin: The University of Texas Press, 1987).

3. Susan Gonzalez Baker, "Demographic Trends in the Chicano/a Population: Policy Implications for the Twenty-First Century," in David R. Maciel and Isidro D. Ortiz, *Chicanos/Chicanas at the Crossroads: Social, Economic, and Political Change* (Tucson: University of Arizona Press, 1996), p. 6–23.

4. For the history of Houston, see: Don E. Carlton, *Red Scare: Right-wing Hysteria, Fifties Fanaticism, and Their Legacy in Texas* (Austin: Texas Monthly Press, 1985);

George Fuermann, *Houston: The Once and Future City* (Garden City, N.Y.: Doubleday, 1971); and David G. McComb, *Houston: A History* (Austin: University of Texas Press), p. 192.

5. Francisco A. Rosales and Barry J. Kaplan, eds., *Houston: A Twentieth Century Urban Frontier* (Port Washington, N.Y.: Associated Faculty Press, 1983), p. 3.

6. For the efforts to bring major league baseball to Houston, see: Clark Nealon, Robert Nottebart, Stanley Siegel, and James Tinsley, "The Campaign for Major League Baseball in Houston," *The Houston Review*, 7 (1985), p. 3–46; Ron Briley, "The Houston Colt .45s: The Other Expansion Team of 1962," *East Texas Historical Journal*, 27 (1994), p. 59–74; and Robert Reed, *A Six-Gun Salute: An Illustrated History of the Houston Colt .45s* (Houston: Lone Star Books, 1999). For the New Western history, see: Patricia Nelson Limerick, *The Legacy of Conquest: The Unbroken Past of the American West* (New York: Norton, 1987), and Richard White, *"It's Your Misfortune and None of My Own": A New History of the American West* (Norman: University of Oklahoma Press, 1991).

7. For biographical sketches of Roman Mejias, see: Larry Moffi and Jonathan Kronstadt, *Crossing the Line: Black Major Leaguers, 1947–1959* (Jefferson, North Carolina: McFarland Publishers, 1994), p. 138–139; and Roman Mejias File, Baseball Hall of Fame Museum and Library, Cooperstown, New York.

8. For background information on Cesar Cedeno, see: John Wilson, "Cesar Cedeno … The Next Superstar?" *The Sporting News*, August 19, 1972; David Pietrusza, Matthew Silverman, and Michael Gershman, *Baseball: The Biographical Encyclopedia* (New York: Total/Sports Illustrated, 2000), p. 186–187; and Charles Morey, "Cesar Cedeno — The Next Willie Mays," *Pro Sports* (May, 1973), p. 34–37 and 62–63, clipping from Cesar Cedeno File, Baseball Hall of Fame Museum and Library.

9. Morey, "Cesar Cedeno — The Next Willie Mays," p. 62–63.

10. *Ibid*. For background information on baseball in the Dominican Republic, see: Alan M. Klein, *Sugarball: The American Game and the Dominican Dream* (New Haven, Connecticut: Yale University Press, 1991); and Rob Ruck, *The Tropic of Baseball: Baseball in the Dominican Republic* (Westport, Connecticut: Meckler, 1991).

11. Bob Dellinger, "Astros Hail 89ers' Cesar as Minors' Top Prospect," *The Sporting News*, June 6, 1970; and Bob Moskowitz, "Teen-Ager Cedeno a Terror at Bat," *The Sporting News*, n.d., clipping from Cesar Cedeno File, Baseball Hall of Fame Museum and Library.

12. Samuel O. Regalado, *Viva Baseball: Latin Major Leaguers and Their Special Hunger* (Urbana: University of Illinois Press, 1998), p. xiv. For issues of segregation in minor league baseball, see: Bruce Adelson, *Brushing Back Jim Crow: The Integration of Minor-League Baseball in the American South* (Charlottesville: University of Virginia Press, 1999).

13. Dellinger, "Astros Hail 89ers' Cesar as Minors' Top Prospect."

14. "Great Cesar — And Only 19!" Binghamton, New York *Press*, July 27, 1970, clipping from Cesar Cedeno File, Baseball Hall of Fame Museum and Library.

15. John Wilson, "Astros' Super Baby Goes Hungry at Plate," *The Sporting News*, May 29, 1971.

16. For the comparisons of Cedeno and Clemente, see: Wilson, "Cesar Cedeno … The Next Super Star?" For the racial stereotyping of Latin American ball players, see: Regalado, *Viva Baseball*; and Peter C. Bjarkman, *Baseball with a Latin Beat: A History of the Latin American Game* (Jefferson, North Carolina: McFarland Publishers, 1994).

17. Morey, "Cesar Cedeno — The Next Willie Mays," p. 37; and Leo Durocher and Ed Linn, *Nice Guys Finish Last* (New York: Simon & Schuster, 1975).

18. Arthur Daley, "Rendering Unto Cesar," *The New York Times*, July 15, 1973. For a survey of Cedeno's marital history, see: Gerald Eskenazi, "Astros' Outfielder, 22, Is Called Proud and Dedicated Player," *The New York Times*, December 13, 1973.

19. For coverage of Altagracia de la Cruz's death, see: "Cedeno Questioned, Stays in Jail in Fatal Shooting," *The New York Times*, December 13, 1973; and "Cedeno Slated to Stay in Jail During Holidays," *New York Daily News*, December 19, 1973, clipping from Cesar Cedeno file, Baseball Hall of Fame Museum and Library.

20. Hy Hurwitz, "Red Sox Worked to Rescue Mejias' Family From Cuba," *The Sporting News*, March 30, 1963, clipping from Roman Mejias File, Baseball Hall of Fame Museum and Library.

21. Joe Heiling, "Cedeno Tragedy Tosses a Cloud over Astros," *The Sporting News*, December 29, 1973.

22. *Ibid.*; and Milton Richman, "Cedeno Never Liked Publicity," *The New York Times*, December 13, 1973, clipping from Cesar Cedeno File, Baseball Hall of Fame Museum and Library.

23. Eskenazi, "Astros' Outfielder, 22, Is Called Proud and Dedicated Player."

24. "Prosecutor Calls for Cedeno's Full Acquittal," *The New York Times*, January 15, 1974; and "Cedeno Guilty," *The New York Times*, January 16, 1974, clippings from Cesar Cedeno File, Baseball Hall of Fame Museum and Library.

25. "Cedeno Found Guilty," *New York Daily News*, January 16, 1974, clipping from Cesar Cedeno File, Baseball Hall of Fame Museum and Library. For allegations that Houston management influenced the court settlement in the Dominican Republic, see: Abby Mendelson, "Whatever Happened to Cesar Cedeno?" *Baseball Quarterly* (Winter, 1978), p. 47–57, clipping from Cesar Cedeno File, Baseball Hall of Fame Museum and Library.

26. Dick Young, "Cesar Cedeno Goes on Trial," *New York Daily News*, January 14, 1974; and Dick Young, "Cheap Price for Justice," *The Sporting News*, February 2, 1974, clippings from Cesar Cedeno File, Baseball Hall of Fame Museum and Library.

27. Joe Heiling, "Cesar Set for Brickbats: 'I May Be Better Player,'" *The Sporting News*, February 9, 1974; and "Cedeno Expects Reaction by Fans, Players," *The New York Times*, January 23, 1974, clipping from Cesar Cedeno File, Baseball Hall of Fame Museum and Library.

28. For a discussion of baseball violence in 1974, see: Ron Briley, "As American as Cherry Pie: Baseball and Reflections of Violence in the 1960s and 1970s," p. 115–134, Peter M. Rutkoff and Alvin Hall, eds., *The Cooperstown Symposium on Baseball and American Culture, 1999* (Jefferson, North Carolina: McFarland Publishers, 2000).

29. Harry Shattuck, "Questions Arise Over That Which Is Cesar's," *The Sporting News*, June 21, 1975; and Durocher, *Nice Guys Finish Last*.

30. Harry Shattuck, "No Swap Sign on Cedeno, Says Skipper Virdon," *The Sporting News*, October 18, 1975; and Harry Shattuck, "New Cedeno Sheds His Loner Image," *The Sporting News*, May 15, 1976.

31. Mendelson, "Whatever Happened to Cesar Cedeno?" p. 45–57.

32. "Cedeno Is Fined: Goes After Fan," *The Sporting News*, September 26, 1981, clipping from Cesar Cedeno File, Baseball Hall of Fame Museum and Library.

33. "No First-Class Plane Seat, No Cesar Cedeno," *Albany Times Union*, March 24, 1983, clipping from Cesar Cedeno File, Baseball Hall of Fame Museum and Library.

34. Rick Hummel, "Cedeno's Baseball Life Takes on New Meaning," *St. Louis Post-Dispatch*, n.d.; and Jared Hoffman, "What a Move: When the Cardinals Acquired Aging Cesar Cedeno for '85 Stretch Run, They Found the Ultimate Difference Maker," *The Sporting News*, n.d., clippings from Cesar Cedeno File, Baseball Hall of Fame Museum and Library.

35. All baseball statistics used in the preparation of this paper are from John Thorn and Pete Palmer, eds., *Total Baseball: The Ultimate Encyclopedia of Baseball* (New York: HarperPerennial, 1993).

36. The Texas Rangers, who relocated to Arlington from Washington following the 1971 baseball season, while failing to win an American League pennant, have been much more successful in marketing and attracting such premiere Latin players as Juan Gonzalez, Ivan "Pudge" Rodriguez, and Rafael Palmeiro. This contrasting approach to Latin ball players by the two major league entries from Texas is a topic which merits additional study and analysis.

Comparative Ethnicity: Joe DiMaggio and Hank Greenberg

William Simons

Introduction

A comparison of Joe DiMaggio and Hank Greenberg as ethnic standard bearers illustrates their significance for baseball, their respective ancestral groups, and American culture.[1] Although a considerable literature examines the ethnicity of both icons separately, there is little in the way of sustained, systematic comparison aside from a chapter, "Ethnicity and Baseball: Hank Greenberg and Joe DiMaggio," in G. Edward White's *Creating the National Pastime: Baseball Transforms Itself: 1903–1953.* Although White's 1996 study makes a significant contribution, it offers more parallel than comparative treatment of DiMaggio and Greenberg.[2] Moreover, much new material about both Greenberg and DiMaggio has appeared since the publication of *Creating the National Pastime,* allowing for a fuller discussion of the topic. Apart from copious tributes by sportswriters, DiMaggio's March 8, 1999, death inspired a plethora of serious commentary from intellectual and cultural authorities. Likewise, the January 12, 2000, New York City debut of the documentary film *The Life and Times of Hank Greenberg* and the analysis it generated from diverse sources, including *The New Yorker* and National Public Radio, offered fresh insight about the Detroit slugger as an ethnic standard bearer.[3] DiMaggio's importance for Italian-Americans had its counterpart in Greenberg's significance for Jewish-Americans.

Joe DiMaggio, a center fielder, was arguably the greatest all-around player in baseball history. A gifted five-tool player, DiMaggio hit for average, slugged home runs, ran the bases flawlessly, made impossible catches look routine, and threw superbly. "If you said to God, 'Create someone who was what a baseball player should be,' God would have created Joe DiMaggio," mused ex-Dodger manager Tommy Lasorda.[4] In addition, the Yankee Clipper was the most significant Italian-American athlete of all time. A number of Italian Americans triumphed in the boxing ring, but pugilism lacked baseball's aura. From "Poosh 'em Up Tony" Lazzeri to Mike Piazza, many Italians have excelled on the diamond, but clearly none rivaled Joe DiMaggio. The fact that DiMaggio was baseball's best player when it was the undisputed national pastime elevated his place in the national culture. So too did his good fortune in playing for the Yankees, sports most storied franchise, during the team's most successful era in New York, the city that dominated the nation's media. A *New York Times* editorial asserted, "The combination of proficiency and exquisite grace which Joe DiMaggio brought to the art of playing center field was something no baseball average can measure and that must be seen to be believed."[5] For many, the mere mention of Joe DiMaggio's name conjures up a series of indelible tableaux. His place in American culture far transcends baseball. For Italian Americans, however, DiMaggio possesses special meaning.

Just as DiMaggio was the premier Italian-American athlete, Hank Greenberg was the most significant athlete in Jewish-American history. Hank Greenberg, a first-baseman-outfielder, ranks with the most powerful sluggers who ever played the game. Swimmer Mark Spitz, boxer Benny Leonard, and basketball star Dolph Schayes may have been as good or better athletes than Greenberg, but their sports did not have the status of the national pastime. A generation later, Sandy Koufax achieved at least as much in baseball, but Koufax played at a time when American Jews, feeling more at home with both their Jewish and American identities, did not respond to an ethnic standard bearer with the same intensity.

Neither Greenberg nor DiMaggio was the first of his ethnic group to reach the major leagues, but just as DiMaggio was the first great Italian ballplayer, Greenberg was baseball's first Jewish superstar. Like DiMaggio, Greenberg was a big, right-handed batter. They both wore the number 5 on their uniforms. DiMaggio spent his entire major league career (1936–1942, 1946–1951) with the New York Yankees. Aside from a final season with the Pittsburgh Pirates, Greenberg's major league career (1930, 1933–1941, 1945–1947) was spent with the Detroit Tigers. They were both on major league rosters for all or part of 13 seasons and retired from active play at age 36. The career statistics of both Greenberg and DiMaggio were circumscribed by injury and military service.[6] Despite four and one-half years lost to military service, Greenberg won four home run and four RBI titles. DiMaggio lost three seasons to military service but still accumulated two batting, two RBI, and two home run titles. Greenberg was the first Jewish-American to receive a Most Valuable Player award, and DiMaggio was the first Italian-American to receive that designation. Twice Greenberg received the American League's Most Valuable Player accolade compared to DiMaggio's three selections. Both were the first of their respective ethnicity named to the Baseball Hall of Fame.

DiMaggio was clearly a better all-around player than Greenberg. While flat feet hampered Greenberg's running, the Yankee Clipper was never thrown out going from first to third. DiMaggio's running, throwing, and fielding surpassed that of Greenberg. But Greenberg hit with more power although it need be acknowledged that Joltin' Joe's power hitting was penalized by the then vast 457 feet distance from home plate to the wall in his left-center field power alley at Yankee Stadium. Still, DiMaggio never hit more than 46 home runs in a season. In contrast, no right-handed batter exceeded Greenberg's 1938 season total of 58 home runs until 1998. Only four players have higher lifetime slugging percentages than Greenberg's .605; DiMaggio is sixth on the list with a mark of .579. In the category of RBI's per game, DiMaggio is fourth on the all-time career list with a figure of .89. Nonetheless, Greenberg averaged .92 RBI's per game, a mark that Lou Gehrig and Sam Thompson matched but no one has exceeded. DiMaggio's career batting average (.325), however, is higher than Greenberg's (.313). Greenberg drew more walks (852 in 1394 games) than DiMaggio (790 in 1736 games). Like most sluggers, Greenberg struck out with some regularity while DiMaggio had only 8 more career strikeouts (369) than home runs (361). By way of comparison, Greenberg had more than twice as many career strikeouts (844) as home runs (331). DiMaggio had more career home runs than Greenberg because he had many more at bats (6821) than the Tiger slugger (5195). While Greenberg led the Tigers to 4 pennants and 2 World Series championships, this pales before the 10 pennants and 9 World Series championships of DiMaggio's invincible Yankees. But the significance of these two great players clearly transcends their enormous athletic accomplishments. Both Greenberg and DiMaggio were the most popularly celebrated members of their respective ethnic groups during the 1930s.

Beyond their ethnic significance and athletic eminence, DiMaggio and Greenberg shared other attributes. They were both big, good looking men. Separated in age by only 3 years, Greenberg was born in 1911 and DiMaggio in 1914. Greenberg was baseball's highest paid player; DiMaggio later enjoyed that designation. And both considerably augmented their wealth after their playing days were over. Joe DiMaggio dressed well, as did Hank Greenberg. Actress wives, divorce, two marriages, brothers who played professional baseball, salary disputes, injuries, dramatic comebacks, wartime military service, formal ties to baseball following their retirement from active play, Ivy League sons, apotheosis in song and art, long lives, and death from cancer punctuate the biographies of both men. It is as ethnic standard bearers during a crucial era, however, that Greenberg and DiMaggio share their most important similarity.

Ubiquitous Ethnicity

From the inception of their craft during the late nineteenth century, sportswriters frequently commented on the ethnic antecedents of athletes. This practice accelerated during the 1920s, peaked during the 1930s, and declined precipitously after World War II. Journalists of the 1930s described outfielder Morrie Arnovich of the Philadelphia Phillies, for example, as a "Jewish athlete," "the chunky Hebrew lad," and "the little Hebrew."[7] The Cleveland *Press*, oblivious that Jews attend synagogues, not churches, and celebrate the Sabbath on Saturday, called Milt Galatzer "a bird who has a right to wear a hat in church on Sunday."[8] Rudy York, offered one pundit, "is called Chief because he is part Cherokee."[9] A *Sporting News* article identified fifteen players from fifteen different ethnic backgrounds, ranging from Canadian George Selkirk to Italian Joe DiMaggio.[10] A myriad of evidence, including such press excerpts as "the fiery Frenchman," "the even-tempered Bohemian," "McCarthy ... the Buffalo Irishman," "Urbanski ... hard-working, likable Polish recruit," and "Lou Novikoff ... the mad Russian," illustrates the pervasiveness of ethnicity in baseball literature during the Great Depression.[11]

The press portrayed players with ethnic antecedents as symbols of the assimilation process at work. Ethnic standard bearers, as depicted by sportswriters, generated pride in ancestral heritage even as they facilitated the Americanization of their partisans by participation in the baseball melting pot. Pundits welcomed the employment of ethnicity to spur baseball attendance and profits. *The Sporting News*, for example, endorsed the Cincinnati Reds' exploitation of Alex Kampouris, "the only Greek in the big show," as a useful device for luring other Greeks to the game:

> ...for the last three seasons, a delegation of swarthy citizens would march to the home plate....
>
> The swarthy citizens always are Greeks. And when the Greeks come bearing gifts where the Reds are playing, it is Alex Kampouris, dashing second baseman of Cincinnati's team, who gets them.[12]

Reflecting the demographics of major league cities, Italian and Jewish ballplayers of the 1930s generated more ethnic commentary than did peers from other groups. Moreover, given their baseball prowess, the ethnicity of DiMaggio and Greenberg attracted more attention than that of their Italian and Jewish contemporaries in the national pastime. The peak baseball years of Joltin' Joe and Hammerin' Hank coincided with a general intensification of ethnic awareness in America that brought Jews and Italians, in particular, into sharp focus.

Depression-era sportswriters frequently noted Greenberg's ethnic identity even in accounts of mundane incidents. Numerous ethnic sobriquets attached to Greenberg, including "Hebrew star," "the Tigers' great Jewish first baseman," "the Jewish slugger," and even "a conscientious orthodox Jew."[13] At times the press demonstrated imagination in its allusions to Greenberg's ethnicity as with *The Sporting News'* explanation that he "does everything in orthodox fashion."[14] And a New York *Evening Journal* article repeatedly referred to Greenberg as "Henry David," "David's" connotation being more obvious than "Benjamin," Greenberg's actual middle name.[15]

Likewise, a number of articles, particularly early in his career, emphasized DiMaggio's Italian background by calling him "Giuseppe."[16] During the 1930s, references to DiMaggio's ethnicity were ubiquitous. A New York *World-Telegram* article stated that DiMaggio hailed "from the spaghetti society."[17] *Life* magazine described him as "the young Italian" and an "Italian youth."[18] Even the sedate *New York Times* described DiMaggio as "the Coast Italian."[19] Joe DiMaggio and Hank Greenberg were not simply great ballplayers: they were ethnic standard bearers.

Natural Versus Self-Made Ballplayers

In commenting on the physical and intellectual attributes of DiMaggio and Greenberg, Depression-era commentators reinforced prevailing stereotypes about Italians and Jews. Journalists credited the Italian DiMaggio's success to physical rather than cognitive attributes. Conversely, pundits portrayed the Jewish Greenberg as nimble of mind but not of body.

Sportswriters depicted Greenberg as the quintessence of traditional Jewish respect for learning, which America transformed into a passion for secular knowledge. Commentators lingered over his cerebral qualities. Some of the depictions of Greenberg's intellect conjure up a Talmudic scholar more readily than an athlete: "put more thought ... into his work than any other player"; "has demonstrated ... intelligence and imagination";

"the most energetic ... researcher"; "he studies the best methods and practices as earnestly as a young physician"; "has the persistence of a reporter when it comes to rounding up information"; "smart and knows how to express himself"; "shrewd guy"; and "his anxiety to learn."[20] A contemporary observed, "Greenberg doesn't play baseball, he works at baseball."[21] Newspaper photographs of the articulate Greenberg, who had attended New York University for a year, often displayed a neat, immaculate gentleman, dressed in tie and jacket with a newspaper in hand and resembling a young professional or businessman more than he did a baseball player.

In contrast, the 1930s press depicted the Italian DiMaggio as a comic book reader of modest intelligence. By denying that DiMaggio possessed high intelligence, journalists endorsed a prevailing bias against Italian-Americans. Noel Busch's 1939 *Life* profile on DiMaggio emphasized that DiMaggio was not cerebral: "It cannot be said ... that he has ever worried his employer by an unbecoming interest in literature or the arts, nor does he wear himself down by unreasonable asceticism."[22] A photograph accompanying the *Life* profile on DiMaggio showed him in conversation with the great black boxer Joe Louis. Merging stereotypes about blacks and Italian-Americans, the caption beneath the photograph reads, "Like Heavyweight champion Louis, DiMaggio is lazy, shy and inarticulate."[23]

Many journalists viewed DiMaggio as an exceptionally gifted natural athlete who did not need to train very hard. Busch's *Life* profile, however, went further, linking DiMaggio to the bias common in the 1930s that Italians were indolent. According to the *Life* feature, DiMaggio's "inertia caused him to give up school after one year in high school."[24] "Joe DiMaggio's rise in baseball," wrote Busch, "is a testimonial to the value of general shiftlessness."[25] According to the article, "In laziness, DiMaggio is still a paragon." "On winter mornings," claimed Busch, DiMaggio "gets up at about eleven."[26]

Busch associated DiMaggio's baseball success with ethnic canards: "Italians, bad at war, are well suited for milder competitions, and the number of top-notch Italian prize fighters, golfers and baseball players is out of all proportion to the population."[27] By denying that DiMaggio possessed either high intelligence or a strong work ethic, *Life* endorsed prevalent ethnic stereotypes. As portrayed by Busch, DiMaggio was not a self-made athlete; the Yankee star was instead depicted as a natural ballplayer. "DiMaggio's reflexes," according to the *Life* article, "are so fast that even a curve which breaks perfectly may not be effective."[28] Busch wrote that the "lazy" Italian outfielder possessed a "mysterious quality called baseball instinct. In this respect Joe DiMaggio is without peer."[29]

DiMaggio was a natural ballplayer. Creating the illusion of slow motion through his balletic movements, DiMaggio made the difficult look easy. It was said that DiMaggio made few theatrical plays in the field; his mastery and self-control were such that he had no need for dramatics.

Media imagery and his athletic grace obscured DiMaggio's hard work. As a baseball player, DiMaggio pushed himself relentlessly. Joltin' Joe suffered from ulcers and insomnia. Asked why he always drove himself so hard, DiMaggio responded, "Because there might be somebody out there who's never seen me play before."[30] A meritocracy, sport produces an elite of talent. Remarkable ability and maximum effort brought DiMaggio to the top of his profession. He became, in David Halberstam's apt phrase, "the preeminent *athlete*" of his generation.[31] DiMaggio's pursuit of excellence extended beyond his baseball craft.

DiMaggio reinvented himself. Extensive dental surgery enhanced DiMaggio's appearance. He learned to dress well, making Taub's list of ten best-dressed men in 1939. He confronted his shyness and insecurities by attending the Dale Carnegie Institute. DiMaggio, the son of Italian immigrants, and Greenberg, the son of Jewish immigrants, transformed themselves.

In contrast to journalistic imagery of DiMaggio's natural brilliance, Greenberg, as depicted by sportswriters, was ungainly. Hammerin' Hank's strength, power, and large size were frequently noted, but so too was the perception that he was not a natural athlete. Jews were viewed as the people of the book, not of the bat. Journalists repeatedly cast the Detroit slugger as a self-made ballplayer. Numerous articles portrayed the Tiger mainstay as "clumsy," "naturally slow," "awkward," "[possessing] little natural ability," "handicapped by his flat feet," and "[having] trouble coordinating his ... body."[32] Aviva Kempner's documentary film *The Life and Times of Hank Greenberg* states that the Jewish star often looked lumbering on the field as a montage visually illustrates his less than fluid movements.[33] Baltimore *Sun* pundit Chris Kaltenbach wrote that Greenberg "ran with all the grace of a train wreck and, on a swinging strike, looked about as bad as a ballplayer could look."[34]

Despite his lack of physical grace, Greenberg, in mid-career, for the good of the team, moved from first base, whose defensive demands he had mastered through endless practice, to the outfield. This allowed the Tigers to place hard hitting Rudy York on first base, the position that would place the fewest demands on York's deficient fielding. Diligence transformed Greenberg into a competent outfielder. Hard work compensated for physical awkwardness sufficiently for Greenberg to become the first to win Most Valuable Player awards at two different positions.

As a self-made athlete, Greenberg, unlike the naturally talented

DiMaggio of mythology, worked obsessively to master his craft. With near unanimity, scribers cast Greenberg as a Jewish Horatio Alger hero who "overcame ... (his) glaring weaknesses" by "hard work and determination."[35] A *Saturday Evening Post* article, entitled "Hank Made Greenberg," contended, "Greenberg is purely a self-made star.... His enormous capacity for work staggers everyone.... He has spent so much time in Tiger Stadium that the groundskeeper once suspected he had set up light housekeeping there to save rent."[36] The Detroit *Evening Times* glowingly reported that "Greenberg is a good first baseman because he works at the job.... He works at it 24 hours a day...."[37] Arriving at the ballpark early for extra batting practice, Greenberg frequently paid ushers, peanut vendors, and older boys to shag balls for him.

Americanization

The United States is a nation of nations. Balancing ethnic/racial affiliations with a larger American identity poses a dilemma. Although Joe DiMaggio and Hank Greenberg were standard bearers for their respective ethnic groups, they were also symbols of a more generic process of Americanization.

During the 1930s baseball's ethnic composition changed substantially, and this highly visible transformation attracted extensive contemporary comment. The Irish, German, and Scandinavian presence in the national pastime receded somewhat. A 1934 article in *Baseball Magazine* noted that "in recent years there had been a grand invasion of other nationalities," prominently featuring players with southern and eastern European antecedents.[38] Americans of Italian and, to a lesser degree, Jewish descent, sons of immigrants who left Europe between 1880 and the outbreak of World War I, contributed significantly to the ethnic recasting of baseball during the 1930s. As with their counterparts from other ethnic groups, Italian and Jewish major leaguers confronted the universal dilemma of the second generation, resolving the conflict between the "Old World" values of their immigrant parents and those of the larger society, embodied in the national pastime.

Beyond the shared "marginal man" phenomena, however, Italian and Jewish major leaguers of the 1930s faced additional anxieties not encountered by other athletes. By decade's end, Benito Mussolini, Italy's Fascist dictator, was on a collision course with the United States, raising questions about the loyalty of Italian-Americans. Furthermore, domestic stereotypes about Italian-Americans often centered on images of clownish, highly emotional simpletons and violent gangsters.

As for Jewish-Americans, the economic abrasions of the Great Depression frequently cast them in the familiar role of scapegoat for hard times, and Jewish concerns with persecuted European brethren complicated relations with gentiles in the isolationist America of the 1930s. Thus, given the ambiance of the 1930s, the second generation's struggle to resolve the tension between ethnic and host society expectations assumed a special dimension for Italian and Jewish athletes.

A number of Italian-Americans preceded Joe DiMaggio in the big leagues. Nor was DiMaggio the first Italian-American star. That distinction would belong to "Poosh 'Em Up Tony" Lazzeri, the Yankees' hard hitting second baseman and future Hall of Famer, who made his major league debut in 1926. But DiMaggio was baseball's first Italian-American superstar.

Although, for a time, many ethnic partisans hailed him as a superstar, Andy Cohen, a Jewish infielder, had a less substantial major league career than Tony Lazzeri. There are parallels between Cohen and Lazzeri, however. Prior to DiMaggio, Lazzeri provided a preliminary sketch of the Italian baseball hero, and prior to Greenberg, Cohen provided a preliminary sketch of the Jewish baseball hero. During the 1920s, both Cohen and Lazzeri were second baseman for fabled New York franchises.

In 1928 and 1929, New York Giants second baseman Andy Cohen elicited more enthusiasm from his co-religionists than had any previous Jewish baseball player. *The Jewish Daily Forward* started to print Giant box scores on the front page. A cartoon showed a Jewish mother imploring her son to eat his chicken soup with the assurance that the mixture was responsible for Andy Cohen's success. Polo Ground vendors sold ice cream Cohens, and some Jewish fans, new to baseball, asked for seats right behind second base close to Andy. One Cohen partisan advocated changing the name of the bluff above the Polo Grounds from Coogan's to Cohen's. Alas, Cohen's appeal exceeded his abilities, and in 1930 he was sent down to the minor leagues.[39] During the 1930s, however, the ethnicity of Hank Greenberg and Joe DiMaggio would receive even more attention than that of Lazzeri and Cohen in the 1920s.

It is instructive to examine the May 1, 1939, *Life* cover story on "Joe DiMaggio" by Noel Busch. At the time, *Life* was America's most widely read magazine, and Busch's eight page article gave significant attention to DiMaggio's Italian background. The *Life* article teemed with ethnic references. DiMaggio's father, wrote Busch, "was a poor Italian crab fisherman," and the senior DiMaggio was "an expert at the Italian bowling game of *bocci*."[40] Joe himself was referred to as "Giuseppe Paolo DiMaggio." And Busch reinforced the association of Italian culture with food. In 1936, claimed the *Life* feature, DiMaggio's mother "rode to the World Series in a drawing room on a streamlined train carrying an armful of Italian sausage for Joe."[41] At Joe DiMaggio's Grotto, the restaurant owned by the Yankee outfielder, Busch asserted that the "specialty of the house is *cioppino*, for which an alarming recipe is attached to menu."[42] The writer further associated DiMaggio's ethnicity with food by commenting, "At home, Joe DiMaggio passes most of his days at the Grotto or in the DiMaggio kitchen."[43]

Busch emphasized that DiMaggio was a standard bearer for other Italian-Americans: "When in 1936 Joe DiMaggio gave unmistakable signs of being the greatest Italian star in the history of baseball, the effect upon New York's Italian population was amazing. Subway guards as far away as Coney Island were accosted by recent immigrants who wanted to know 'Which way da Yankee Stadium?'"[44] The *Life* article suggested that the Horatio Alger experience was open to Italian immigrants by commenting on "Joe DiMaggio's sudden transformation from a penniless newsboy to a national celebrity."[45] Despite his employment of patronizing stereotypes, Busch implied, albeit in paternalistic fashion, that DiMaggio provided fellow ethnics with a model of Americanization: "Although he learned Italian first, Joe, now 24, speaks English without an accent and is otherwise well adapted to most U.S. mores. Instead of olive oil or smelly grease, he keeps his hair slick with water. He never reeks of garlic and prefers chicken chow mein to spaghetti."[46]

In identifying the ethnicity of DiMaggio, reporters were not treating him differently than players from other ethnic groups. A myriad of evidence, including such articles as *Baseball Magazine's* "An Italian Baseball Guide," demonstrates the ubiquity of ethnic references in journalism of the 1930s.[47] Sports pundits incessantly cast the national pastime as assimilation's melting pot, promoting the Americanization of the game's diverse participants.[48]

Sportswriters of the Depression decade depicted DiMaggio and other ethnics as emblematic of the assimilation process. Although scribes thus viewed ethnic standard bearers, such as DiMaggio, as transitional figures, leading their co-ethnics to the figurative melting pot, writers enthusiastically approved of depicting DiMaggio and others as ethnic standard bearers to attract fans and increase baseball's profits.

For many years, DiMaggio, with his reserved and dignified demeanor, largely alone provided a counterbalance to the stereotype of the Italian-American as clown. Chico Marx (who ironically was Jewish), Jimmy Durante, Lou Costello, and other entertainers rendered the emotional, not too bright *paesan* a staple of American popular culture. And two of

DiMaggio's Italian-American teammates, Phil Rizzuto and Yogi Berra, despite their immense athletic talents, catered to that image, perhaps making fun of themselves before others did. Even Fiorello La Guardia, New York City's great mayor, reinforced perceptions about Italian emotionality. Banker Amadeo Peter Giannini and scientist Enrico Fermi were not emblematic of the popular culture. Only in the past generation did other Italian-Americans, including Lee Iacocca, A. Bartlett Giamatti, Mario Cuomo, and Rudolph Giuliani, with DiMaggio's emotional gravity garner extensive public visibility.

Likewise, DiMaggio, by his integrity, demonstrated that not all Italian-Americans were criminally inclined. During DiMaggio's era, Italian gangsters figured prominently in the American imagination. Al Capone and Lucky Luciano were household names. And most gangster movies of the period depicted organized crime as an Italian-American enterprise. Even non-Italian actors, such as Jewish film stars Edward G. Robinson and Paul Muni, portrayed Italian gangsters. It was rumored that boxer Primo Carnera, singer Frank Sinatra, and nearly every other celebrity of Italian background were mob connected. Not Joe DiMaggio. He was incorruptible. According to the New York *Daily News* organized crime boss Albert Anastasia "wanted idol of millions Joe DiMaggio to lend his name to a mob-backed hotel. But the Yankee Clipper wouldn't bite."[49] And in *Me and DiMaggio: A Baseball Fan Goes in Search of His Gods*, cultural authority Christopher Lehmann-Haupt ultimately discounts DiMaggio's involvement in the business of an underworld gambler.[50] Despite the recent muckraking of Richard Ben Cramer, Joe DiMaggio epitomized integrity at a time when the Italian-American gangster loomed large in the popular culture.[51] Author Gay Talese wrote of DiMaggio's significance for Italian Americans: "They had somebody who was making headlines who wasn't shooting somebody in dark alleys."[52]

As scholar Richard Gambino noted in *Blood of My Blood*, his informal history of Italian-American life, popular stereotypes of Italian-Americans distort reality. The buffoon and the gangster were the two most prevalent images of the Italian in American popular culture, but most Italians valued a very different ideal of masculinity. As their maxim "revenge is best cold" suggests, Italian immigrants believed that a real man kept his emotions under check. Italian immigrants felt that action taken without reflection would bring disaster. It was better to let emotion cool before preceding. The ideal man of Italian culture husbanded his resources for the appropriate occasion. Part of the appeal of "Deadpan Joe" to fellow Italian-Americans was that his controlled style of play and contained demeanor reflected their ethnic values. Likewise, according to Gambino,

Italian culture upheld an ideal of masculinity that included an erect body, an impassive face, silence until addressed, courteous but brief responses to inquiries, and a wariness of the outside world.[53] Italian-Americans saw those qualities in their standard bearer DiMaggio.

To Italian Americans, Joe DiMaggio was a colossus. Sportswriter Jerry Izenberg wrote in the Staten Island *Advance,* "Italian-Americans ... would tell you DiMaggio was the ultimate rebuttal to names like *dago* and *wop.* They would tell you that his spectacular debut just nine years after the executions of Sacco and Vanzetti was for many of them the first emotional dividend of their American dreams."[54] They flocked to Yankee Stadium. Immigrants who spoke little English and knew less of baseball came to cheer their Joe, covertly carrying Italian flags and banners into Yankee Stadium. Early in DiMaggio's career, according to *Time,* "most of his fan mail ...[came] from Italian well wishers."[55] Italian-Americans delighted in cheering one of their own. In 1941 residents of the Little Italy in Utica, New York, set up loudspeakers on the streets to better follow DiMaggio's 56 game hitting streak. Former New York Governor Mario Cuomo, an Italian-American, said of DiMaggio, "His life demonstrated to all the strivers and seekers — like me — that America would make a place for true excellence whatever its color or accent or origin."[56] Sportswriter Mike Lupica wrote of Italian-Americans, "There was only one ballplayer for them, an Italian-American ballplayer of such talent and fierce pride that it made them fiercely proud."[57]

There are several similarities in the media treatment accorded the ethnicity of Joe DiMaggio and Hank Greenberg during the Depression decade. The press trumpeted the athletic accomplishments of DiMaggio and Greenberg, deeming them the preeminent ballplayers of their respective ethnic groups. References to their ethnicity were ubiquitous. Both were depicted as ethnic standard bearers whose success would hasten the assimilation of their respective ancestral groups. During their early years in baseball, both experienced colorful journalistic references to their cultural antecedents. Paralleling *Life* magazine's emphasis on the centrality of Italian food to the DiMaggio family, *Baseball Magazine* suggested that an individual might favorably impress the Greenberg family by gorging "himself on *gefilte fish* and herring."[58]

And there were differences between the media treatment accorded the ethnic backgrounds of Greenberg and DiMaggio. With repeated assertions that "Hank was born with a silver spoon in his mouth," the press of the Depression decade exaggerated the economic situation of Greenberg's parents, thus paralleling prevailing, and erroneous, stereotypes about Jewish wealth.[59] Although Hank's father, a Rumanian immigrant, did own a cloth shrinking plant, the Greenbergs were not wealthy. In contrast, journalists emphasized the humble circumstances of DiMaggio's Italian immigrant parents.

Media portrayals of Greenberg as a Jewish standard bearer burgeoned during September 1934 owing to controversy over whether the Detroit slugger should play on the Jewish High Holidays. Although rookie Greenberg's decision not to play on the 1933 High Holidays attracted little attention, the improved play of the twenty-three-year-old Greenberg and of his team during the 1934 season created new pressures. Not since 1909 had the Tigers won the American League pennant, and the Bengals' 1934 surge, which culminated in a first place finish, created a "frenzied public."[60] Apart from loyalty to the Tigers, social bonds between residents of Detroit, a "tough town" hard hit by the Depression, were "frail."[61]

Historian Ralph Jones asserts that "Detroit's ... susceptibility to economic, ethnic, racial, and territorial outbursts is impressive and persistent."[62] Also, Greenberg's High Holiday dilemma hardly occurred during a golden age in Detroit's ethnic dynamic. Greenberg's Detroit had a propensity for lifting bigots, such as Henry Ford and Father Charles Coughlin, to the status of folk hero. Neither the city of Detroit, which had a Jewish population of only 5 percent, nor Greenberg's Tiger teammates, over 80 percent of whom hailed from parochial areas of the South and Southwest, entered September of 1934 with much understanding of the reasons for observing the Jewish High Holidays.[63] According to the press, however, Tiger players and fans clearly understood the importance of Greenberg to their feverish dreams of a pennant.

Publications varied markedly in the extent of coverage they granted Greenberg's High Holiday conflict. Most journalistic depictions of the episode, however, shared a core of common assumptions. Some minor differences in nuance did occur. Nevertheless, a widespread consensus of interpretation dominated press portrayals of Greenberg's behavior during the 1934 High Holidays.

When Greenberg casually mentioned he might not play in the September 10th home game against the Boston Red Sox since the contest fell on Rosh Hashanah, the Jewish New Year, the media promptly recited Greenberg's secular responsibilities. Although the Tigers led the second place New York Yankees by four games on the eve of the Jewish New Year, the press still referred to a "neck-and-neck pennant race."[64]

Given the tight pennant race, journalists stressed Greenberg's obligation to the city of Detroit. People wrote letters to Detroit newspapers pointing out that "whereas Rosh Hashanah came every year, Detroit had not won a pennant since 1909." [65] In addition, sportswriters emphasized

Greenberg's special "duties toward his teammates."[66] The New York *Evening Journal* stated that Greenberg's Rosh Hashanah absence from the line-up would constitute a massive "loss to his companions."[67] Moreover, every member of the Tiger infield had thus far played "every inning of every game," a record that Greenberg's observance of the Jewish New Year would snap.[68] Finally, and least important of the secular responsibilities cited by the press, Greenberg, on the eve of Rosh Hashanah, needed "only 11 more [doubles] to equal the American League record of 67."[69]

During September 1934 the media also gave prominent attention to Greenberg's religious responsibilities although journalists ultimately found them less imperative than his secular obligations. The Anglo-Jewish press and several general circulation journals described the nature of the Jewish New Year as Rosh Hashanah approached. The Detroit *Evening Times*, for example, stated: "Essentially, Rosh Hashanah is not a joyful but a thoughtful day. Unlike the celebrations of the New Year among other nations the New Year of the Jew is devoted to supplications and to the searching of one's self."[70] Some newspapers, including the Detroit *Free Press*, noted that Orthodox Jews, such as Greenberg, "did not work ... [or] play" on Rosh Hashanah.[71] Nevertheless, references to the Jewish temple or synagogue as a "church" in a number of papers, suggest a muted understanding of the High Holidays by the media.[72] Furthermore, whereas the press related Greenberg's secular responsibilities to loyalty to community and teammates, it tended to depict religious obligations as largely a matter of individual conscience or preference.

Several newspapers reported and analyzed the formal statement of Dr. Leo M. Franklin, chief rabbi of Detroit, concerning Greenberg's problem. Rabbi Franklin's comments, issued just prior to the Rosh Hashanah game, appeared in a number of journals:

> In the Jewish faith there is no power granted to the rabbi to give dispensation to anyone for doing anything which reads contrary to his own conscientious convictions — indeed we insist upon the doctrine of personal responsibility.
>
> In such a case as this, Mr. Greenberg, who is a conscientious Jew, must decide for himself whether he ought to play or not.
>
> From the standpoint of Orthodox Judaism the fact that ballplaying is his means of livelihood would argue against his participation in the Monday game. On the other hand, it might be argued quite consistently, that his taking part in the game would mean something not only to himself but to his fellow players, and in fact at this time, to the community of Detroit.[73]

Despite the ambiguous tenor of Dr. Franklin's remarks, writers, while conceding the impossibility of dispensation, eagerly noted that the rabbi's comments constituted no fiat against Greenberg's participation in the Rosh Hashanah game. *The Sporting News*, for example, interpreted Rabbi Franklin's proclamation to mean "that the question lay strictly between Greenberg and his conscience and that the church had no right to ... criticize him if he played."[74] Thus the terse headline of a Detroit *Evening Times* story on Dr. Franklin's statement read "Greenberg Decision Own."[75]

Some journals also reported and examined another Detroit rabbi's position on Greenberg's conflict, that of Joseph Thumim. Rabbi Thumim's declaration, which was even more enigmatic than that of Dr. Franklin, implied that "Greenberg ... can play ball today" subject to "three stipulations ... no tickets could be bought by the Orthodox on the day of the match; that there should be no smoking; and that the refreshments distributed should be kosher."[76] Oblivious to the three restrictions Rabbi Thumim cited, a Detroit *News* article, entitled "Talmud Clears Greenberg for Holiday Play," proclaimed, "Henry Greenberg need have no pangs of conscience because he plays baseball during the Jewish holidays...."[77] The Detroit *Jewish Chronicle*, the only Anglo-Jewish newspaper then published in Michigan, agreed with the *News'* interpretation of Rabbi Thumim's statement.[78]

In the end, Greenberg, after much soul searching, decided to play on Rosh Hashanah. The Tigers triumphed 2 to 1 over the Boston Red Sox in the crucial Rosh Hashanah game, extending their American League lead to four and one-half games. Moreover, emphasized the press, Greenberg "almost single-handed[ly] won ... the ball game with two home runs."[79] The Detroit *Free Press* exclaimed, "Greenberg ... had enjoyed the best day of his career.... Ruth at his best never hit a baseball to more effect or ever won a ball game more dramatically."[80] Given the heroic victory of Greenberg's Tigers, some sportswriters interpreted the triumph as heavenly approval of his Rosh Hashanah activities. According to *The Sporting News*, for example, Greenberg concluded, "Some divine influence must have caught hold of me that day."[81]

The post-game trivialization of Rosh Hashanah markedly differed from the tone of respect accorded this solemn holiday in pre-game commentary. The Detroit *Free Press* saluted Greenberg's hitting with the refrain, "A Happy New Year for Everybody."[82] A woman reporter for the Detroit *News* coquettishly wished "every day were Rosh Hashanah, [so] our [baseball] worries would be over" as Detroit fans, "grinning broadly," yelled "Happy New Year."[83] "Iffy the Dopester," august commentator for the Detroit *Free Press*, magnanimously declared, "I'm here to testify to the world as a baseball expert that the two hits he [Greenberg] made in the ball game were strictly kosher."[84] Stuart Bell of the Cleveland *Press* demonstrated a dubious sensitivity: "Only one fellow blew the shofar yesterday so you could hear it. He was Hank Greenberg. He blew the shofar twice, and the ears of the Boston Red Sox are still ringing. Blast No. 1 from his shofar was a homer.... Blast No. 2 from Hank's shofar was a home run ... will you please take me home shofar?"[85] Amid the post-game euphoria the press depicted the solemn Rosh Hashanah as a near twin of the larger society's first of January.

Although Greenberg still faced a conflict over whether to play on Yom Kippur, this episode generated much less media attention than his New Year's ordeal as the Tigers had the pennant "in the bag" by Yom Kippur. When Greenberg chose not to play on Yom Kippur, the folk poet Edgar Guest wrote, "But he's true to his religion — and I honor him for that!"[86]

Both the Anglo-Jewish and general circulation press perceived a lesson for Greenberg's co-religionists in the slugger's September 1934 behavior, the appropriateness of an ethnic standard bearer, and by implication his followers, giving priority to the demands of the secular community over those of the ethnic group. Pundits claimed even "the most orthodox Jews" "respected" Greenberg for subordinating his religious preferences "for the good of the whole" on Rosh Hashanah.[87] According to the media, "the public judges people by the idols they produce," and the Jews ought then to take pride in Greenberg, "a credit to ... Jewry."[88] "The Jewish people are to be congratulated," editorialized the Detroit *Jewish Chronicle*, "that Greenberg is such a splendid type of their people. He is in a position to do untold good in breaking down the mean and vicious prejudices against an ancient and honorable people."[89] For the most part, the press portrayed Jewish standard bearer Greenberg as a symbol of assimilation, leading the way toward the melting pot. Greenberg's baseball heroics, suggested most 1930s commentators, facilitated the Americanization of his fellow Jews. *Baseball Magazine*, for example, cast Greenberg as a latter-day Moses:

> ...He had led his ancestral race into a new promised land, the field of major league baseball, a field where they have been comparative strangers.
>
> Since America is the melting pot of all nations, it is quite fitting and appropriate that baseball should be represented by players of all racial strands and stocks.[90]

Both Greenberg and DiMaggio were portrayed by journalists as symbols of the rewards that athletic excellence could bring the sons of immigrants in baseball's melting pot. Greenberg and DiMaggio provided counterbalances to negative stereotypes about their respective ethnic groups. During the Great Depression, DiMaggio gave Italian-Americans a hero to blunt stereotypes concerning Italian buffoons, gangsters, and

Fascists. Likewise, Greenberg provided Jewish-Americans of the 1930s with a standard bearer to offset popular portrayals of Jews as weaklings, victims, and greedy shylocks. Greenberg was an especially potent symbol to second-generation Jewish Americans, the children of East European immigrants. They wanted acceptance, and Greenberg became their role model. Like DiMaggio, Greenberg was the first of this ethnic group to become a hero to all Americans. Unlike the Jewish boxing champions of the era, Greenberg did not carry the legacy of the ghetto with him. In an era when second-generation Jewish Americans sought to distance themselves from the world of their parents and to make the American Dream a reality, Greenberg, like DiMaggio, offered an example of success that generally elicited approval, rather than resentment, from those beyond the ethnic group.

Notes

1. Portions of this study are adapted from William Simons, "The Athlete as Jewish Standard Bearer: Media Images of Hank Greenberg," *Jewish Social Studies* 44, no. 2 (1982), 95–112; William Simons, "*The* Jewish American Sports Hero," in *Sports and the American Jew*, ed. Steven A. Riess (Syracuse: Syracuse University Press, 1998), 185–207; and William Simons, "Joe DiMaggio and the American Ideal," in *Joltin' Joe DiMaggio*, ed. Richard Gilliam (New York: Carroll & Graf, 1999), 14–52.

2. G. Edward White, *Creating the National Pastime: Baseball Transforms Itself, 1903–1953* (Princeton: Princeton University Press, 1996), 245–274.

3. *The Life and Times of Hank Greenberg*, written, produced, and directed by Aviva Kempner, 95 minutes, Presented by The Ciesla Foundation, Distributed by Cowboy Booking International, 1999.

4. "DiMaggio Dies at home at 84," Binghamton *Press & Sun-Bulletin*, 9 March 1999, 7D.

5. Quoted in Joseph Durso, "Joe DiMaggio, Yankee Clipper Dies at 84," *The New York Times*, 9 March 1999, D4.

6. Statistical data derived from Jim Thorn, et al., *Total Baseball*, 6th ed. (New York: Total Sports, 1999).

7. Chick Feldman, "Arnovich Started Out to Be Shortstop," *The Sporting News*, 1 July 1937, 3; and George Kirksey, "The Trading Mart," *Baseball Magazine*, August 1940, 408.

8. Stuart Bell, "Rookie Stops Indians: Greenberg Slams Pair," *The Cleveland Press*, 11 September 1934, 18.

9. "Thumb-Nail Sketches of Cards and Tigers," *The Sporting News*, 4 October 1934, 3.

10. "League of All Nations! No, It's the Majors, America's Melting Pot," *The Sporting News*, 25 March 1937, 1.

11. Samuel Merin, "An Italian Baseball Guide," *Baseball Magazine*, March 1934, 464; Ed McAuley, "Boudreau and Mack, 'Mike and Ike' of Indian Infield," *The Sporting News*, 30 May 1940, 3; "Russian Attack on Tokyo Due," *The Sporting News*, 19 July 1945, 6; John J. Ward, "Urbanski of the Braves," *Baseball Magazine*, June 1935, 368; and "McCarthy Picks Tigers," Detroit *Free Press*, 21 September 1934, 20.

12. Tom Swope, "Alex Kampouris, Majors' Only Greek," *The Sporting News*, 26 August 1937, 3.

13. Franklin Lewis, "Tiger Park Still Hard on Slugger," Cleveland *Press*, 22 September 1934, 7; "Rick Ferrell's 2-Bagger ... Ends Battle," Boston *Globe*, 12 September 1934, 20; "Greenberg Proves His Loyalty to Tigers and Faith in Religion," New York *World-Telegram*, 11 September 1934, 32; and "Tigers Defeat Red Sox," New York *Herald Tribune*, 11 September 1934, 20.

14. "Thumbnail Sketches of Cards and Tigers," *The Sporting News*, 4 October 1934, 3.

15. "Greenberg Will Not See Action with the Tigers Today," New York *Evening Journal*, 19 September 1934, 25.

16. Quoted in White, 269.

17. Ibid.

18. Noel F. Busch, "Joe DiMaggio," *Life*, 1 May 1939, 63.

19. White, 269.

20. "September's Brightest Star: Hank Greenberg," *The Sporting News*, 3 October 1934, 4; Sam Murphy, "Tigers Needed Heavy Hitting of Greenberg," New York *Sun*, 19 September 1934, 33; Arthur Anderson, "The Bronx Bomber," *Baseball Magazine*, September 1938, 451; Charles Wood, "Hammering Hank," *Baseball Magazine*, March 1941, 437; and Sam Otis, "Hank Seeks Advice and Rises Fast," Cleveland *Plain Dealer*, 22 September 1934, 9.

21. Quoted in Ira Berkow, "Greenberg: A Kind of Beacon," *The New York Times*, 7 September 1986, S3.

22. Busch, 69.

23. Busch, 68.

24. Busch, 66.

25. Busch, 66.

26. Busch, 69.

27. Busch, 64.

28. Busch, 67.

29. Busch, 64.

30. David Halberstam, *Summer of '49* (New York: William Morrow and Company, 1989), 48.

31. Halberstam, 260.

32. Quoted in Simons, "The Athlete as Jewish Standard Bearer," 98.

33. *The Life and Times of Hank Greenberg*.

34. Chris Kaltenbach, "Documenting Greenberg's Athletic, Spiritual Sides," Baltimore *Sun*, 17 March 2000.

35. Bernard Postal, Jesse Silver, and Ray Silver, *Encyclopedia of Jews in Sports* (New York: Bloch Publishing Company, 1965), 61.

36. Stanley Frank, "Hank Made Hank," *Saturday Evening Post*, 15 March 1941, 35.

37. Bud Shaver, "Foxx Helps Tutor Hank," Detroit *Evening Times*, 10 September 1934, 18.

38. Ferdinand C. Lane, "Baseball's New Sensation, Hank Greenberg," *Baseball Magazine*, October 1935, 483.

39. William Simons, "Andy Cohen: Second Baseman as Ethnic Hero," *The National Pastime: A Review of Baseball History*, 1990, 83–87.

40. Busch, 64.

41. Busch, 67.

42. Busch, 63.

43. Busch, 69.

44. Busch, 67–68.

45. Busch, 67.

46. Busch, 69.

47. Samuel Merin, "An Italian Baseball Guide," *Baseball Magazine*, March 1934, 464.

48. "League of All Nations! No, It's the Majors, America's Melting Pot," 1.

49. George Rush and Joanna Molloy, "DiMag Walked on Mobster's Pitch," New York *Daily News*, 14 March 1999, 14.

50. Christopher Lehmann-Haupt, *Me and DiMaggio: A Baseball Fan Goes in Search of His Gods* (New York: Simon and Schuster, 1986), 282–289.

51. *The American Experience, Joe DiMaggio: The Hero's Life*, co-written and narrated by Richard Ben Cramer, PBS, 2000.

52. Quoted in Simons, "Joe DiMaggio and the American Ideal," 39.

53. Richard Gambino, *Blood of My Blood: The Dilemma of the Italian-American* (Garden City, New York: Anchor Press/Doubleday, 1974), 128–159.

54. Jerry Izenberg, "A Monument for a N.Y. Icon," Staten Island *Advance*, 26 April 1999, C3.

55. Quoted in White, 269.

56. "We Love You, We'll Miss You," New York *Daily News*, 9 March 1999, wrap 4.

57. Mike Lupica, "DiMaggio: Golden Standard," New York *Daily News*, 9 March 1999, wrap 10.

58. Charles P. Wood, "Hammering Hank," *Baseball Magazine*, March 1941, 473.

59. John G. Spink, "Three and One," *The Sporting News*, 7 November 1940, 4.

60. "Career as Business Tycoon Opens for Greenberg," *The Sporting News*, 28 February 1946, 7.

61. Constance McLaughlin Green, *American Cities in the Growth of the Nation* (New York, 1957), 214.

62. Ralph Janis, "Flirtation and Flight: Alternatives to Ethnic Confrontation in White Anglo-American Protestant Detroit, 1880–1940," *The Journal of Ethnic Studies*, 6, no. 2 (1978), 1.

63. "Thumbnail Sketches of Cards and Tigers," 3.

64. Stuart Bell, "Flag Race Still Hot," Cleveland *Press*, 14 September 1934, 36.

65. Quoted in Simons, "The Athlete as Jewish Standard Bearer," 99.

66. Frank, 45.

67. "Greenberg Will Not See Action with Tigers Today," 25.

68. Harry G. Salsinger, "Playing for Community," Detroit *News*, 11 September 1934, 21.

69. "Mack and Mickey Friends But...," Detroit *Free Press*, 8 September 1934, 12.

70. Wendell Parker, "Jewish Holy Days Begin," Detroit *Evening Times*, 8 September 1934, 10.

71. Charles Ward, "Greenberg's Two Home Runs Give Tigers 2 to 1 Victory," Detroit *Free Press*, 11 September 1934, 19.

72. "Greenberg Goes to Church, Then Wins for Tigers," Chicago *Daily Tribune*, 11 September 1934, 21.

73. Salsinger, 21.

74. Sam Greene, "Greenberg's Punch Gains Clean-up Job," *The Sporting News*, 20 September 1934, 1.

75. "Greenberg Decision Own," Detroit *Evening Times*, 10 September 1934, Sports Section, 1.

76. "Talmud Clears Greenberg for Holiday Play," Detroit *News*, 11 September 1934, 1–2.

77. Ibid.

78. Yaaleh Veyoveh, "Hank's Rosh Hashanah," Detroit *Jewish Chronicle*, 14 September 1934, 6.

79. Quoted in Simons, "*The* Jewish American Sports Hero," 197.

80. Jack Carveth, "Henry Prayed and Swung His Way to Baseball Glory," Detroit *Free Press*, 11 September 1934, 19.

81. Dick Farrington, "Greenberg, Young Tiger Star," *The Sporting News*, 4 October 1934, 3.

82. "A Happy New Year for Everybody," Detroit *Free Press*, 11 September 1934, 19.

83 George Stark, "She Learns About Homers First Time at Ball Game," Detroit *News*, 11 September 1934, 23.

84. Iffy the Dopester, "Hank's Homers Strictly Kosher," Detroit *Free Press*, 11 September 1934, 19.

85. Stuart Bell, "Greenberg Slams Pair," Cleveland *Press*, 11 September 1934, 18.

86. Edgar Guest, "Speaking of Greenberg," Detroit *Free Press*, 4 October 1934, 6.

87. "Greenberg Will Not See Action with Tigers Today," 25.

88. Harold Ribalow, *The Jew in American Sports*, rev. 2nd ed. (New York: Bloch Publishing Company, 1948), 46.

89. Malcolm W. Bingay, "Will Break Down Vicious Prejudices," Detroit *Jewish Chronicle*, 21 September 1934, 1.

90. Bill Bryson, "League of Nations," *Baseball Magazine*, July 1938, 365.

Baseball in the Ocean State: Rhode Island Black Baseball, 1886–1948

Lawrence D. Hogan and Jeffrey L. Statts

People ask me what I do in winter when there's no baseball. I'll tell you what I do. I stare out the window and wait for spring.
— Rogers Hornsby, St. Louis, National League

Rogers Hornsby, National Baseball Hall of Fame Member, appears in a box score for a game at Freebody Park in Newport, Rhode Island, Sunday afternoon, July 29, 1919, St. Louis, National League vs. the Newport Trojans.

We loved the game. There was nothing like baseball in those days.
— William "Ready" Cash, Philadelphia Stars, Negro National League

Bill Cash, a Negro League All Star catcher, appears in box scores for games at Cardines Field, Newport, Rhode Island, for July 20, 1947, and July 21, 1948, Philadelphia Stars, Negro National League vs. Newport Sunset League All Stars, and the Newport Hoboes.[1]

Introduction

The black baseball bookshelf has been filled across the last decade or more with a host of works that make this subject area one of the most written about topics of perhaps the most written about sport in America. At a recent Cooperstown Baseball Symposium, one of the best authors of several of the best books and articles about that subject, Jules Tygiel, remarked that the film and video documentary record of this long neglected area of our national pastime is as full as the written record. That documentary record, Tygiel noted, now stands as a model pointing us toward what we could and should be profitably doing in so many other areas of American baseball history.

It is interesting to note that with all the research, interviewing, documentary production and writing about this recently discovered subject, the best telling of the story was the first. Robert Peterson's sports classic, *Only the Ball Was White*, was published in 1970, long before the multitude of recent work was even thinkable. Peterson's book remains unsurpassed for its telling of the story of Negro professional baseball.[2]

A perennial question of every author of every significant book is how did you become interested in your subject. Bob Peterson's answer to that question takes us back to his childhood memories of a boyhood in a small Pennsylvania town where twice a summer the special baseball event was the coming to town of Negro League teams barnstorming outside their regular league schedule. It was the excitement and specialness of their coming that author Peterson remembers as the seed of a lasting fascination that never went away through all his adult years as baseball fan and writer. That fascination came to fruition in the researching and writing of his classic study.

I was asked several years ago by a fellow researcher and writer in this now much documented field of Negro League history what I thought were the areas where significant work could still be done. My reply to that question was an echo of the answer Bob Peterson gives to where his interest in Negro professional baseball began. It is time I said to go to the local level. We need to go to the many small American towns where from the 1890s through the 1940s the great national Negro professional teams came to play their "only the ball was white" version of our national pastime, and find out from those who experienced their coming what that story was all about.[3]

Talk to folks on the local level, I said then. Go to the fans that turned out in large numbers to see their locals go up against some of the best players ever to play the game. Plumb the memories of those who played against the legendary Joshes and Satchels of Negro League lore. See those legends as they played away from the spotlight of the big cities where their Grays and Monarch teams frequently held forth in major league ballparks. Move from the accounts in great national black weeklies like the *Courier*, *Afro American*, and *Defender* to headlines and stories that appear in local papers all across the America where these awesome Black teams brought their special brand of baseball. See what that local story is all about, and then we will know the history of Negro professional baseball in all its richness and fullness.

This past December when my nationally traveling exhibit on the history of Black baseball went on display at the Scholar Athlete Hall of Fame of the Institute for International Sports on the University of Rhode Island Campus in Kingston, I had an opportunity to do what I had preached. As has been the case wherever our *Before You Can Say Jackie Robinson* exhibit has gone, I began to research into the history of Negro teams playing in the locality of the exhibit site. I have done this kind of research in Florida, Texas, Connecticut, and other areas where my exhibit has been displayed. Generally these are places which no Negro Major League team called home. But as is the case just about anywhere in this country where baseball has been played, those great Negro teams with colorful names like Monarchs and Grays, Black Yankees and Bacharach Giants, came to play in these places summer after summer through the 1910s, 20s, 30s and 40s — and in many cases in earlier decades as well.[4]

Each place where I have done this kind of research I have been rewarded with wonderful stories about baseball and life. But Rhode Island turned out to be a special situation. This is so because the Ocean State, while having an extensive record of Black baseball, also has a baseball history in its resort city of Newport that is arguably unique to the history of American baseball.

History of Rhode Island Blackball

Our starting place in this presentation is not with Rhode Island uniqueness, but with a sketch of the presence of Blackball as it appears in the Ocean State across the traditional period for the Negro version of our national game, namely from the 1880s through the 1940s. This sketch, while uniquely Rhode Island in its particulars, is similar to the general picture that emerges elsewhere when we seek out the history of Negro professional baseball.

As far as we are presently able to determine, the Ocean State Blackball story begins almost precisely in the middle of the decade where most historians date the beginnings of Negro professional baseball. That beginning is usually marked with the establishment of the now famous Original Cuban Giants in the summer of 1885 at a Babylon, Long Island, hotel. Rhode Island's beginning followed by only a year. On September 10, 1886, we have a report in the Burrillville Gazette of the Providence Colored Grays traveling by train with "their own colored umpire whose decisions were quick and impartial and gave entire satisfaction." What that umpire could not do that day was give the Grays the satisfaction of a victory against the Pascoags. Two other games for that year involving the Colored Grays have been found, with the colored club losing a close contest in August by a score of 17–15 to the Olneyville Temperance Cadets, while coming out on the short end of a lopsided 20–5 defeat to the Pawtuckets on September 21.[5]

We can speculate that the Colored Grays name comes from the more famous Providence Grays, a founding member of the Negro National league, and in 1884 winner of the first World Series involving a New York team. But as is frequently the case in the beginnings of research of this sort, we know nothing more about this club than what we read in these sketchy newspaper accounts. Nor at the moment can we relate the Colored Grays to the Black community of Providence. We should not be surprised that such a team exists in a decade where the color line of exclusion and separation was going up all across an America caught up in the thralls of the beginnings of a love affair with Jim Crow segregation. If one force for the origins of Negro teams of this sort came from the negatives of the Jim Crow world of that time in our nation's history, a second and more positive originating force came from Black communities seeking their own identity in institutions that were their own to create and enjoy. But the specifics of those two creating forces, or any others that might have been at work in the origins story of this Colored Grays team remain to be unearthed.

One other Blackball report from the 1880s surfaces — and that too seems to fit the pattern we see elsewhere in the origins of Negro professional baseball. That pattern is connected to where Blacks during the era of segregation could and could not be employed. The "could not" was always considerably larger that the "could," with the latter usually including jobs as waiters and bus boys at resort hotels. Thus we have the Original Cuban Giants of 1885 in their first season playing out of a resort in Babylon, Long Island; numerous Black teams such as the Shelbourns connected to resort hotels in Atlantic City around the turn of the century; and clubs like the famous Poincianas and Breakers teams based at leading hotels in Florida at the end of the 19th and through the first two decades of the 20th century. So too in the Ocean State we have a report in June of 1888 of the Rhode Island Club meeting the colored waiters of the Narragansett Hotel at a baseball match at the Messer Street grounds. Unlike their earlier Babylon, Long Island, counterparts who won most of their games handily, these Rhode Island colored waiters suffered an ignominious defeat. "For five innings" the newspaper account tells us, "the waiters hunted leather" and then left the field on the deficit end of a 22–8 score.[6]

The period from 1900 to 1920 marks the first great national era of Negro professional baseball, with strong independent teams with roots in their local communities springing up to play outstanding baseball. With these teams begins the tradition of barnstorming throughout their geographical regions and beyond that would be so much a mark of Negro baseball clubs throughout their existence. These were the years of the founding in the Midwest of the legendary Chicago American Giants of Rube Foster; in the West of the Monarchs of Kansas City; and in the East of the famed Bacharach Giants of Atlantic City. One of the most feared of these independent teams, the Lincoln Giants of New York, boasted such future Hall of Famers as Smokey Joe Williams and one of the consensus greats of all time, John Henry "Pop" Lloyd.

From preliminary research it appears that several of these Negro independent teams made appearances in Newport playing at Wellington Park against the first great professional club in the city, the famous Trojans. Several inducements were present to bring the Black independents as well as White major league teams to Newport. At the time Newport clubs were the only baseball teams in the United States playing Sunday ball in their own park. One report notes that "because of a presence of a connection to New York City from Boston via the trains and the Fall River Line steamboats, Major League and Negro League teams would use the layover on travel days (which for Negro teams might well include Sundays) to get a game in at Wellington Park, or later, after Wellington's demolition in 1920, at Freebody Park. The famous Negro team, the New York Black Giants, played at Wellington." So did the Boston Braves of 1914 and 1919; the Cardinals from St. Louis; and the Pirates from Pittsburgh. Wellington's sister stadium, Freebody Park, hosted the Babe Ruth led Boston Red Sox in 1919. In a history of Newport baseball that appears in a 1946 centennial issue of that city's *Daily News*, it is noted that "other incidents which will flit across the minds of fans in thinking of Wellington Park will be the remarkable throw of a ball over the grandstand from center field by one of the Cuban Giants."[7]

Rhode Island Negro professional baseball history finds its zenith in the two decades when on the national level Negro League baseball reached its apogee. The high points came briefly in the Depression America of 1930 with the establishment of a team run from Providence by a Black entrepreneur whose untimely demise at the hands of gunmen brought to an end his dream of Negro baseball greatness; and then in the period immediately after World War II with barnstorming Negro National League teams playing at a baseball site that is arguably one of our national game's truly special places.

With America's decline in 1929 into depression, Negro League baseball fell on hard times. The league structure that had come into being in 1920 with Rube Foster's founding of the Negro National League, which had expanded in 1922 with the establishment of the Eastern Colored League, and had culminated in 1924 with the first Negro League World Series, disappeared after 1929. Several Negro professional teams, suffering the financial ravages which beset businesses all across the nation, went under in the face of dwindling revenues.

This declining baseball situation prompted a woeful account from Rollo Wilson, writing in the Pittsburgh *Courier* on March 1, 1930, about prospects for the upcoming baseball season. In a story on the recent dissolution of the Negro American league, Wilson quoted at length from a letter he had received from the great veteran Negro League shortstop and now manager of the Lincoln Giants, John Henry "Pop" Lloyd. The legendary "Pop" expressed regret at the passing of the loop, and commented on the problems players now faced. "This will throw the players back about ten years. Little did some of them think when they were cursing the league and calling it a handicap to them that the league was then getting ready to be counted out. But some of these same players will wish before the season is out that they had the league to fall back on. Some of them will have to show their skills in lines other than baseball and will be lost to the game forever. There is nothing for the young players to shoot at now, and whatever thought the young man had about entering baseball is gone for some time to come. And ball players who in the past have demanded — and received — big salaries will now listen to what the owners have to say on that subject."

One man's decline is another man's opportunity. By 1930 Arthur "Daddy" Black, retired United States Navy veteran, Negro entrepreneur, and Colored Elks grand poo bah in Providence, Rhode Island, had established himself as a man to be reckoned with. Black built up a substantial nest egg through the operation with two white confederates of what the Providence *Journal* called "the Nigger Pool," a policy numbers operation that made him a rich man. His riches provided the financial means to indulge his passion for baseball. He would see in the situation Pop Lloyd touches on an opportunity to secure for his home city and area Negro baseball players of considerable talent.[8]

Out of these circumstances was born in 1930 what on the face of its roster appears to be the best Negro professional team in the history of New England. Black's Providence Colored Giants seem for the most part to have played their home games out of Boston. A report describing this team in a story written on the occasion of Black's murder in September 1932 notes that "two years ago he organized the Providence Colored Giants, a professional team having its home grounds in Boston. At the same time he was one of the chief figures in the Boston Twilight League, a fast circuit. In baseball circles, Black always was known as a free spender. He bought a large bus for his team and always was prompt in payments to his players."[9]

Based on the great names from national Negro League baseball that appear on Black's inaugural 1930 roster, his team must have fared quite well. A strong candidate today for induction into the Baseball Hall of Fame, Oliver "Ghost" Marcell, held down the hot corner at third base. Outstanding right-hander Jess Hubbard anchored a powerful mound corps. The veteran of many a Negro major league tilt, Luther Farrell, gave these Providence Giants a considerable presence in the outfield.[10]

A projected search through Boston papers will hopefully fill out a record for this team that will confirm what appears to be from the talent on its roster the high point, albeit transitory, of New England Negro professional baseball. The short-lived aspect of the history of these Providence Giants blares forth in the fall of 1932 in Providence *Journal* headlines recounting the murder of owner Black by five Providence Negroes. It would turn out that the perpetrators were bent on robbery, and not, as the *Journal* first suspected "a desire to wipe Black out of the lottery racket by out-of-town lottery runners seeking to muscle in on Black's rich territory."

With the demise of the baseball venture of Daddy Black's Providence Giants, our Rhode Island focus shifts to what was always a mainstay of Negro baseball. Throughout the 1930s one finds national barnstorming teams seeking a profitable payday here, there and wherever, turning up as stellar attractions on playing fields across the Ocean State. In the spring of 1930 an undefeated Malden team boasted the likes of Andy Mullaney of the Lynn, New England, club, Jim Fitzgerald leading hitter and collegiate home run slugger from Tufts College, and Bill Marshall of the Lynn club, recognized as the best big league prospect in Greater Boston. The Malden club took on as the second part of a Sunday double header at Kinsey Park the winner of the first game between Dan Whitehead's Cleveland Colored Giants and the Philadelphia Colored Giants. In Woonsocket in the midst of the Great Depression, the Pullman Porters from Boston, with the "world's Greatest Woman Pitcher, Harriet Smith," squared off regularly at St. Ann's park against top local talent or fine touring teams such as the Pittsburgh Hoboes.[11]

America's Oldest Baseball Site

By the end of the decade, the reestablished Negro Major Leagues were supplying opponents like the Philadelphia Stars and New York Black Yankees to several baseball sites across the Ocean State. The most notable of those locales, upon close investigation, turns out to be one of the most notable baseball places in the history of our national game.

A headline from the Newport *News* of June 19, 1940, announcing a "Night Game Program for Cardines Tonight" is a good way to get us to that site. The story that follows the headline notes at the outset that "another cluster of lights has been added to the already brilliant system at Cardines Field for the game tonight between the New England Colored Giants and the Sunset Stars." To go with the game was an evening of festivities that included a parade from Washington Square to the field led by the Elks Junior Marching Band from Boston. The band, made up of junior musicians from 8 to 16 years of age, was scheduled to give a concert at the field, and a foot race would be staged between local and visiting speedsters.

The Newport Sunset All Stars, opponent of the New England Colored Giants that June night, as well as the site of that evening's contest, involve us with a record that arguably is Rhode Island's most substantial claim to a special place in baseball history. The Sunset League Stars of June 19, 1940, could date the origins of their league far enough back across the decades to lay a strong claim to be representing the oldest continuous amateur baseball league in the country. In 1908 a group of men working at the Old Colony Steamship Company repair shop obtained permission from the New York, New Haven and Hartford Railroad Company to use a field at the present site of Cardines Stadium for the playing of baseball games. That field was in poor and dangerous condition. There were no public or private funds available to cover the expense of putting the grounds into shape for playing games on what then and is now referred to by residents of Newport as the Basin. A group of boilermakers from the Old Colony took the situation in hand and worked a few hours each evening, and in a short time the field was in playing condition.[12]

It was this Old Colony group that bought about the organization of the Newport City Baseball League. All games were played at the Basin, with the first game of the six-team league taking place on May 25, 1908. The Torpedo Station Clerks won the first championship.

One report has the league folding at the end of the year because the railroad that owned the land objected to the number of broken windows caused by errant fly balls. Whatever the problem with broken windows, this City League seems to have continued for several years after its founding. In 1909 and 1910 the Old Colony team won the championship. In 1913 Harry Cook, who at that time was Newport's supervisor of recreation, established the City Government leagues. The two leagues, a senior and junior circuit, played their games at Basin Field and at Vernion Field. They remained in existence until 1919.[13]

In 1914 Newport's Recreation Commission was given permission to use the Basin for play by small children. In 1918 the railroad consented to allow Army and Navy and other teams to play baseball on the field again. In 1919 when the city agreed to carry a $100 insurance policy against broken windows, new league games started. The games in this new league began at 5:30 and ended at sunset whether the game had been completed or not. Hence was born "The Sunset League." It claims today to be the oldest continually operating amateur baseball league in the United States.

With William Kelly as the Sunset League's first President, the inaugural game was played at the Basin, then a sandlot, on August 4 with the Orioles, behind the two hit pitching of George Tubley, defeating the Tigers 8–2. Other teams in the league that first season were the Richmonds, Cleanups, Ironsides, and Braves.

The Newport *Daily News* noted proudly in a 1946 story that the August 4, 1919, game marked the start of "a program which down through the years was to present a parade of over 2,000 games witnessed by upwards of 2,000,000 fans. Since then through the efforts of the Recreation Commission and its chairman, William A. Martin, the Basin has been developed into one of the best fields to be found in a city the size of Newport in this section of the country. Over 60 different teams and hundreds of players representing fraternal bodies and other organizations, business establishments, army and navy posts, and even ships of the fleet have helped in developing the league."

Older by a considerable margin than the Sunset League itself is the Basin field where the league staged its games. A small urban gem of a baseball park today fronts along a section of America's Cup Avenue appropriately renamed Billy Bull Way in a recent commemorative ceremony to honor a founding father of the Sunset League. This baseball place takes its name, Bernardo Cardines Memorial Field, from Newport's first casualty of World War I. As is the case with much of the area where it resides, the field was at one time part of Narragansett Bay. From the founding of Newport through the 1800s the area to the north and east of the ever-lengthening Long Wharf was the part of the Bay known as the "Cove." It was eventually connected to "the Point" area by the extension of Washington Street. The area to the east of it was gradually filled to its present day condition, completely filling what was once water.

On the present site of Cardines Field, there was from 1870 to 1890 a horseshoe shaped "basin" with a stonewall and cap built around it to receive water from several springs on adjoining land. There was a small brick pump house with a little boiler and steam pump, which was used to supply water to the steamers of the Old Colony Steamship Company. About 1891 the basin was filled in and the pump house dismantled.

Up to 1900 the area still continued to be swampy. It was not an uncommon sight to see the field covered with water deep enough for people to peddle around in household washtubs. It was because of these facts that the field became known as the Basin. By the Spanish-American War of 1898, the area was usable for embarkation of troops of the Newport Artillery Company for service in that conflict. The 1907 Atlas shows the street edges clearly defined with West Marlborough Street and what would later become known as Corridon Street.

From 1900 to 1908 installation of nearby sewers drained off much of the water, which used to accumulate there, so it was possible to use the open field for running and jumping events on the Fourth of July, for an occasional carnival, and for games and play by children. Some youngsters can be seen playing baseball in an early photograph.

As we have seen, in 1908 Basin Field became the site of Newport City League games, and after 1919 the home field for the City League's famous successor, Sunset League. From 1925 to 1936 the city leased the field for $1.00 per year from the railroad. No permanent structure could be put up until the city bought the property in 1936. Until that time wooden bleachers were erected on the first and third base sides and a backstop was put up.

In the mid-1930s WPA and State projects made possible the reconstruction of the entire field. Stone and concrete bleachers with facilities under it along the third base line, and a stone wall all around the east and south sides with concrete sidewalks outside were built around 1936. After the hurricane of 1938, the wooden curved grandstand that is the park's identifying outside feature was constructed.

The work on this grandstand structure revealed a stone rubble foundation wall, wood piers made of logs in some locations, and evidence of an earlier stair up from West Marlborough Street. These logs and stairs may be the remains of the backstop built in 1908 or some other date earlier than the 1939 date given to this building. Also in 1939 the wooden first base bleachers were remodeled adding locker rooms and dugouts, but the interior finishing of the locker rooms was never completed.

Additional land was acquired in January 1939 to the east to extend right field. In 1940 new wooden roofed bleachers were extended down the right field line, and rented lights appeared to be replaced by permanent light stanchions in 1942. The last structure, a 20 bay wooden third base bleacher, was completed in 1944. This point marks the zenith of construction. Cardines now totaled 17,813 gross feet of structures while seating about 2,570 people. The northern nine bays (54 feet) were demolished in the 1980s to make room for the present bullpens.

Like Fenway in Boston, Wrigley in Chicago, and the now demolished Ebbets Field in Brooklyn, Bernardo Cardines Stadium is famous among ballpark connoisseurs for its intimate setting as judged by the closeness of spectators to the field. It is interesting to note the return of the concept of intimacy and fan contact to the field of play in the model ballpark design of the 1990s with the retro parks in Camden Yards in Baltimore and Jacobs Field in Cleveland. Arguably, Newport has an original!

Newporters can boast that since the field that would become Cardines witnessed its first organized baseball game on May 25, 1908, they can claim their little gem to be a playing field older than the current Major League elder, Boston's Fenway Park of 1912. There are other non major-league fields that claim older beginnings than Fenway. Rickwood Field in Birmingham, Alabama, with a 1910 construction date has staked out a claim to being the oldest stadium. St. Cloud Commons in Huntington, West Virginia, posits a birth date in that same year of 1910. Damaschke Field in Oneonta, New York, takes its claim four years further back to 1906. A field in Ontario, Canada, claims a heritage going back to 1900. Warren Ballpark in Bisbee, Arizona, seems to date to 1909. These are the oldest fields that The Society for American Baseball Research's Ballparks Committee has been able to identify as yet.

The present day Cardines Field clearly has a record of baseball structures being built that date back to the turn of the century. It is a site on which baseball has been played since between 1893 and 1898. What all this means is that at this point Cardines Field can make clear claim as a site on which baseball has been present in some form since the mid to late 1890s, and is among the oldest, if not in fact the oldest, baseball field still in use in North America. This history, and the people who have played there, make it a place of national historic significance.

Floodlight Blackball at Cardines

What gives it special significance for students of Blackball is that the roster of those who played there is marked with names that resonate in the annals of Negro professional baseball. Gordon Ross recalls that as a youngster in the late 1930s, just coming into the Sunset League in which he would star after World War II, he saw the great Josh Gibson holding forth behind home plate with a skill that was awesome. Josh was an anchor on the great Homestead Grays teams that would dominate Negro Major League play in the late 30s and early 40s. In 1950 a young woman, Katie Grovell, a favorite of Sunset League players as a bat girl and mascot for several teams, earned a permanent baseball memory for all seasons when she warmed up Satchel Paige on the sidelines of an exhibition game at Cardines. But it would be in between Josh and Satch in the three years following World War II when a Black Major League presence became a regular occurrence at one of America's oldest baseball sites.[14]

"Floodlight Baseball" reads the advertisement in the Newport *News* of August 21, 1946, urging fans to come out to Cardines Field at 8:30 p.m. on Wednesday night. For a general admission price of 50 cents, with "Children 18 Cents as Usual" they could enjoy a baseball contest between the New York Black Yankees of the Negro National league, and the local favorites, the Sunset Stars, with Sam Nahem pitching. Wednesday night Floodlight Baseball was a Newport summer fixture by 1946 continuing a tradition that had started in 1940 when rented floodlights made possible night play at Cardines, with permanent light stanchions going up in 1942.

The excitement of that August 21, 1946, baseball moment comes across in the opening paragraphs of the account of the game carried by the *Newport News*.

> Even three hits by Jack "Pepper" Martin, and a four hit 1-strike out performance by Sam Nahem, failed to hurtle the fighting Sunset Stars to victory over the New York Black Yankees of the Negro National League before a record Cardines crowd Wednesday.
>
> Shut out 1–0 until the seventh, the Yankees launched a brief but effective rally, scoring twice to win 2–1 in the season's fastest and best played game. The tilt required only one hour and 25 minutes and only one error was committed.
>
> Nahem, who was certain he would beat the Yankees, showed that his confidence was well founded by muffling the dangerous New York batting alignment. A gathering of 2,729 paid fans saw the Yankee's win on superb defensive playing. Fully 3,200 counting the free section behind the left field screen must have viewed the proceedings. Many persons were unable to gain admittance to the field.

The floodlights at Cardines were turned on for many other Wednesday evenings as well as an occasional Sunday during that 1946 season. Five of those games involved Negro professional teams. The Boston Colored Giants, "New England's Fastest Negro Team," came into Cardines on Gay Nineties Festival Sunday sporting a battery of 51-year-old long time Negro submarine baller Will Jackman pitching to 53-year-old Burlin White, one of the best catchers in Negro ranks for over 30 years. The Boston club won that Gay Nineties Night contest 4–2, and in two other well-attended games bested the locals by score of 7–0 and 3–2.[15]

In that later game, Sam Nahem, an ex major-leaguer and in today's terms, a "gun for hire," was imported from New York to pitch as he often was for important Floodlight games. Nahem was a stand out for the Anti-Aircraft Redlegs in the 1943 Sunset League season. A former National League hurler, he had a skein of 32 consecutive scoreless innings in that 1943 season while fashioning an earned run mark of 0.85 for all time Sunset League records. The 3-2 loss to the Boston team was a thrill paced 12-inning tilt in which Nahem set a Cardines field record when he fanned 22 Colored Giants.

September 5 saw the Cincinnati Crescents, with future major league star Luke Easter, losing to the locals by a 1-0 score. The high point of the Negro part of the Cardines season came on September 11 with Nahem scattering five hits and driving in the winning run in a 1-0 revenge victory over the Black Yankees.[16]

That the elite stars of the Sunset League of 1946 could play competitive baseball against top Negro League talent should come as no surprise to baseball historians. As was the case with so many returning veterans of the 1946 season, typical Sunset All Stars like Gordon Ross, Ed Pado, and Bernie Kane were matured physically and mentally by their experiences of World War II. Age-wise they were at the peak of their ability. Across the two seasons of 1946 and 1947 Gordon Ross would set Sunset League records with 30 wins and earned run averages of 2.02 and 2.81. Ross considers Ed Pado to have been the best player in the league — and clearly of major league ability. Bernie Kane was a consistent .300 hitter and, like his counterparts, learned his baseball from sound teachers of the game such as the redoubtable Billy Bull, manager of the league champion Bull Memorial team. In that 1946 season the Sunsetters would win the amateur championship of Rhode Island against top competition from across the state. Like all good and able competitors they would welcome the challenge the Negro teams represented, and rise to the occasion. And in Sam Nahem, their Wednesday night import from New York, they had a starting pitcher of major league caliber.[17]

The year 1947 would see pitcher Ross again leading Bull Memorial to the league championship. That season also witnessed a continuation of the highly successful Wednesday Floodlight Baseball with Jimmy Foxx and his All Stars, along with several top notch Negro League teams appearing at Cardines during a July that might well have been dubbed Negro League Baseball Month. On Wednesday, July 31, the Philadelphia Stars, featuring top Negro League talent in players such as Gene Benson, Mahlon Duckett, Bill Cash, Stanley Glenn, and Wilmer Harris, left Newport with a 10-3 drubbing of the locals in their pockets. The previous week had seen the Baltimore Elite

Giants, with future major league great Junior Gilliam at second, and 1950s ace Joe Black pitching, defeat the local Stars by a lopsided 14–2 count.[18]

The Sunsetters had fared better on July 17 behind another import, Brendan Reilly, a young Harvard twirler, who pitched a fancy four hitter to spark a 2–1 win over the Boston Colored Giants. The Sunset Stars also acquitted themselves well on July 2, losing to a New York Black Yankees squad by a 10–8 count.[19]

Among the highlights of the 1948 season was a return appearance by the Philadelphia Stars, and a June 17th contest featuring the 1947 Negro League champion New York Cubans. While the game with the Cubans was reported to have been witnessed by 1,600 fans, an ominous note about the now clouded future of Floodlight Baseball appeared in the Newport *News* article reporting the Philadelphia Negro League's squad late July 14–5 trouncing of the Newport Hoboes. The *News* noted the less than 1000 fans who attended, and reported that the Sunset League had taken another financial jolt to the tune of $180. "Although the Board of Recreation still considers baseball the major activity at Cardines Field, a novelty at least for Newport will be presented August 13 when women wrestlers will appear in the feature event of a mat show."[20]

In historical terms, what does all this post–World War II Cardines Floodlight Blackball mean? Put into the larger national political and social context of those years, the games at Cardines involving Negro touring teams mark the poignant ending to the positive side of the era when America separated her Black populations from her White. The Newport *News* that reported these games so joyfully also followed on its sports pages the entry of Jackie Robinson, Larry Doby, and Dan Bankhead into the majors. Their arrival in the big leagues, for all its obvious positive connotations, would spell the demise of the glory years of Negro professional baseball. Rhode Island, and especially Newport, first at Wellington and Freebody Parks, and then at historic Cardines Field, had showcased across the full length of our nation's segregation era the best part of the baseball side of Jim Crow America. That part had Blacks doing for themselves in positive and constructive ways what the larger society told them they were not suppose to do — and occupying places that were by custom in many areas of the country, and by law in others, not theirs to occupy.

The historian, Clement Price, puts the meaning of the Cardines Black baseball scene into historical context. "Negro baseball would come to represent," Dr. Price notes, "what in many ways was best in the separate world of Black America. It was a business, it was a ceremony, it was a means by which Blacks in the late 19th and early 20th centuries would become a modern people."

Beyond the identity building for Blacks themselves was a powerful, sometimes subtle and sometimes blunt challenge to America's world of segregation that was continuously present in the kind of public achievement and public presence found in Black baseball. Again listen to Dr. Price: "We talk a lot about the civil rights movement. Where it began? Who starts it? It may be that the civil rights movement had many beginnings. Some of those beginnings are found on buses, and at lunch counters, and on dusky roads in the South. And also on the playing fields of Negro baseball. It seems to me these guys must have known they were involved in the most American of all pursuits — competition. But they weren't recognized, they weren't lionized in the larger American society. They were only recognized and appreciated, if you will, by their own people. So I think they must have looked to a day when perhaps on their own terms they would be recognized as great athletes — as great American athletes. It seems to me that those sentiments, that vision is one of the beginnings, one of the seeds of the modern civil rights movement."[21]

These are telling and thoughtful words that give us context to judge and better understand the meaning of what we are looking at. They miss the mark in only one particular — the purely baseball meaning of Negro professional baseball. That meaning for the history of Cardines is relatively easy to calculate. Across the first three post–World War II years Bernardo Cardines Stadium hosted 12 Wednesday night games that brought to Newport some of the best talent in Negro professional ranks. These games were attended by a generation of fans numbering in the tens of thousands who presumably loved the game of baseball, and had to love the quality of the play they witnessed in the intimate confines of Newport's urban gem of a ballpark. Clearly present during those years at what is possibly America' oldest continuously used organized baseball site were great Black players and great Black teams representing a legacy now in its waning years that stretched back to the 19th century origins of the American game of baseball. Recognition and lionization were present aplenty among spectators and on the field opponents.[22]

Something else of some significance was present as well. Those Negro teams and those players were preparing to effect shortly what is arguably the most important baseball moment in the history of the game — namely the integration of America's major leagues, with the significant impact connected with that integration on society as a whole.

We remember the first generation of Black major leaguers by the great skill and great joy that marked their playing, and by the numerous records they set. What we sometimes forget is that Robinson, Newcombe, Campanella, Mays, Irvin, Banks, and Aaron all learned the skills they brought to the majors during their years in the Negro Leagues. So did Luke Easter, Junior Gilliam, Larry Doby, and Satchel Paige, each of whom we find in box scores from Cardines. If the times had been different — if the assault on baseball segregation had come just a bit earlier — or when it finally came if it had come more fulsomely than it did — the likes of Mahlon Duckett, Stanley Glenn, Bill "Ready" Cash, Dick Seay, and a host of other Negro Leaguers who showcased their major league caliber skills at Cardines, would have done so in the Bigs as well. In baseball terms it is certainly not a small thing that some of their learning of their game, and the witnessing the Negro Leagues gave to the lie that supported American segregation, was done in glorious style on the playing fields of Cardines and Wellington and Freebody Parks in Newport Rhode Island.

John Buck O'Neil, great first baseman and manager for the Kansas City Monarchs of the Negro American League, in recollecting what his Negro League playing days meant to him, tells us that "there is nothing like getting your body to do all it has to do on a baseball field. It is as good as music. It is as good as sex. It fills you up. Waste no tears for me. I didn't come along too early. I was right on time."[23]

Buck O'Neil's sentiments about the meaning of playing America's national game were echoed recently in the recollection, memories, and camaraderie of veteran Sunset All Stars Gordon Ross, Ed Pado, and Bernie Kane who gathered for a reunion and panel discussion at The Scholar Athlete Hall of Fame at Kingston, Rhode Island's Institute for International Sport in January, 2000. They were reunited on that occasion with Stanley Glenn and Mahlon Duckett from the Philadelphia Stars whom the Rhode Islanders had last seen in a Sunset League game at Cardines Field on July 21, 1948.

Those Buck O'Neil sentiments go beyond what was experienced on the playing fields of the 1940s, and beyond as well the reminiscing of aging veteran ball players. They are clearly present in the record crowds that filled Cardines bleachers and sometimes spilled beyond the grandstand when those great Negro League clubs came to Newport in the post-World War II years.

Those same sentiments are evidenced in the obvious verve and joy that exude from the columns of the Newport News reporting on those wonderful summer evenings under the floodlights at Cardines.

They are present too in Katie Grovell's treasured memory of having warmed up the incomparable Satchel at what is arguably the oldest baseball site in America.

They continue to be present in the baseball ghosts who roam Cardines today, in the throws from center to cut down a runner on a close play at home, and in the suicide squeeze that brings in the winning run from third in the bottom of the ninth.

And we can hope Buck's sentiments will continue to dwell in the hearts and minds and spirits of each new generation that makes of that aged and hallowed ball yard on Billy Bull Way their own field of dreams.

Buck O'Neil's "right on time" Negro League fellas came in glorious baseball ways to Newport, Rhode Island, between 1946 and 1948. It seems very right to say that Newport, Rhode Island, Bernardo Cardines Field, and Gordon Ross, Ed Pado, Bernie Kane, and their like were not found wanting in being right alongside Buck and his "good as music, good as sex, it fills you up" baseball experience.

Notes

1. Bill Cash comment from interview for the video documentary *Before You Can Say Jackie Robinson*, Thomas Guy, producer/director; Lawrence Hogan, executive producer, available from John Henry Pop Lloyd Committee, Atlantic City, New Jersey, (609) 927-8914.

2. Robert Peterson, *Only the Ball Was White* (New York: Oxford University Press, 1970). Other important books on Negro professional baseball include: several works by John Holway; James Riley, *Biographical Encyclopedia of the Negro Leagues*; Dick Clark and Larry Lester, *The Negro League Book*.

3. The fellow researcher is James Overmyer, author of the excellent monograph, *Queen of the Negro Leagues: Effa Manley and the Newark Eagles*.

4. The International Institute for Sport, with its magnificent Scholar Athlete Hall of Fame, and the sports values programs and international youth games it runs from its home at the University of Rhode Island in Kingston should be singled out for its role in the inception of the research for this paper, as well as for the wonderful ideals it promulgates.

5. Providence *Daily Journal*, August 1, 1886; Providence *Evening Telegram*, September 21, 1886.

6. Providence *Journal*, June 3, 1888.

7. Newport *Daily News*, May 4, 1946.

8. Information on Arthur "Daddy" Black is found in the Providence *Journal*, September 25, 1932, account of his murder, and subsequent issues of the *Journal* reporting extensively on his trial.

9. Providence *Journal*, September 25, 1932.

10. Roster of Providence Colored Giants provided to author by Richard Clark, chair of Society for American Baseball Research Negro Leagues Committee.

11. Malden newspaper for May 9, 1930; Woonsocket *Call*, September 25, 1933.

12. Jeffrey Statts, Portsmouth, Rhode Island, architect and baseball historian researched and authored an excellent study of the history of Cardines Field, and of baseball in Rhode Island as part of his work to refurbish the stadium and to see that its special baseball history legacy is commemorated and preserved. I have drawn extensively on his work through this section to such a degree that he merits co-authorship designation. SABR member, baseball historian, and Director of the Rhode Island Baseball

Project, Richard Harris made a significant contribution to the early stages of the research for this paper.

13. Newport *Daily News*, May 4, 1946.

14. Interviews conducted by the author with Gordon Ross and Katherine Grovell.

15. Newport *Daily News*, June 14, July 19, August 23, September 4, 6, and 13, 1946.

16. Newport *Daily News*, September 6 and 12, 1946.

17. Newport *Daily News*, September 24, 1947.

18. Newport *Daily News*, July 14 and 21, 1947.

19. Newport *Daily News*, July 3, 1947.

20. Newport *Daily News*, July 22, 1948.

21. Interview with Clement Price for video documentary *Before You Can Say Jackie Robinson*.

22. Published attendance figures in Newport *Daily News* stories reporting Floodlight games put the total attendance for games at Cardines involving Negro professional teams to over 20,000 for the 1936 to 1948 period.

23. John Buck O'Neil choose as a title for his autobiography the phrase *Right on Time*.

"She Loved Baseball": Effa Manley and Negro League Baseball

Amy Essington

An obituary in the *Los Angeles Times* said Effa Manley was "thought to be the last surviving owner of a franchise in the black baseball leagues."[1] Eighty-one years old at her death, Manley was buried in a simple grave in Culver City, California in 1981.[2] Contemporaries consistently remembered her glamour, style, and beauty. Her intelligence and spirit, however, made Effa Manley a successful business manager and co-owner of the Newark Eagles Negro League baseball team from 1935 to 1948. Even beyond her self-taught business sense, Effa Manley defined every aspect of her life: as a white woman who identified culturally and socially as black, as a woman in the front office of a baseball team, as a life-long outspoken supporter and defender of the value of the players and institution of the Negro Leagues. While her place in Negro League baseball history as a co-owner and business manager are significant, Effa Manley was a white woman whose greater importance comes from her ability to transform her racial identity and challenge gender roles. This paper examines the life of Effa Manley as an independent woman whose career was in baseball.

Racial Confusion

During the first part of her life, Effa Manley experienced conflicting messages about how others saw her and how she saw herself. In the spring of 1900, Effa, the fifth child in the Brooks family of Philadelphia, was born.[3]

Effa's mother Bertha, a white woman, was married to Benjamin Brooks, a black man. Bertha Brooks believed, however, that the biological father of her daughter Effa was not her husband, Benjamin Brooks, but John Bishop, her white employer. While paternity has never fully been determined beyond Effa's information from her mother, throughout her life Effa Manley believed that John Bishop was her father. After her birth, Benjamin Brooks sued John Bishop for alienating his wife's affections and won.[4] John Bishop paid Benjamin Brooks $10,000, and Benjamin and Bertha went their separate ways.[5] Effa's gravestone reads Effa Bishop Manley.[6]

For the first part of her life, Effa Manley lived between two racial worlds. Effa Manley experienced several incidents where there was confusion about her racial identity. She remembered one incident from the first grade.

> The principal sent for me. At that time Negroes and whites weren't supposed to mix ... she sent for me to ask why I was always with these colored children ... I didn't know what to say to her, I went back and told my mother ... I've always felt stupidly about how mother reacted. I felt she should have made some effort to talk to the principal something, explain things. But Mother said to me, "You go back and tell her you're just as white as she is."[7]

Effa's mother told her she was white, although Effa lived and played with her black siblings. Because she associated with blacks, people assumed that her olive colored skin belonged to a black woman.

> Mother's mother was a German woman and her father was an Indian, so my skin is kind of olive if you look at me, if you look close, and I think that is probably from Mother's dad.[8]

Her racial identity appeared under suspicion. Effa may have explained away suspicions with this story of her parentage.

Before her marriage, Effa choose to move between her black and white identities. Frequently she worked and traveled as a white woman. Effa held several positions in which she portrayed herself as a white woman. On at least one occasion, when with her black fiancé, Abe Manley, she was thought to be white. When the couple went to Tiffany's to purchase a ring, Effa Manley believed the salesclerks thought her to be a white woman.

> When we decided to get married, he took me to ... Tiffany's in New York, to pick out the setting I wanted for the ring. He picked the stone, of course, and I picked the setting. When we went back a few days later to pick up the ring, every clerk in Tiffany's was in there taking a look. There was this young white woman and this old black man ... and he was buying her this beautiful ring, and it was a 5-carat beautiful ring. So every clerk in Tiffany's was there taking a peek. I got a kick out of that.[9]

Whether or not the clerks saw her in this way, Effa Manley was very perceptive about her appearance and how others perceived her. Into her early 30s she was thought of as both black and white. Historically, race in America has never been simple. While proving the paternity of Effa Manley is not the purpose of this paper, how she chose to portray herself is central. Arthur G. Rust, a black sportswriter, believed:

> Identification is so difficult to pinpoint in this basically racist society we live in that whether Effa was really white or black seems ludicrous. After all, being black is also a state of mind, and apparently Effa thought so too.[10]

On the surface, her conflict ended when she chose to live as a black woman after her marriage to Abe Manley.

Making a Choice

After racial confusion in her childhood, Effa Manley made a choice about her racial identity: she chose to live publicly as a black woman. Although she was not at Babe Ruth's infamous "called shot" at the third game of the 1932 World Series in Chicago, Effa Manley attended the Series in New York. Generally, Effa enjoyed baseball, but she was a fanatical fan of Babe Ruth. In an interview in 1980, she recalled:

> I didn't know the game as well as I do today, of course, but I was crazy about Babe Ruth. I lived in Harlem, which was close enough to Yankee Stadium for me to walk.... So I used to go see all of the Yankee games just to see Babe Ruth come up to bat and hope that he'd hit the ball out of the park. I was a definite, 100-carat Babe Ruth fan.[11]

At the Yankees-Cubs series, on either September 28 or 29 in New York, Effa met her future husband Abe Manley, a black man from the South. At least fifteen, and possibly twenty years her senior, Abe was successful in the gambling business as a "numbers banker."[12] Their marriage certificate, dated June 15, 1933, describes Abe Manley as a "colored, divorced, real estate broker from Hertford, North Carolina," and Effa Manley a "colored, divorced, woman from Philadelphia, Pennsylvania."[13] Although she believed John Bishop to be her real father, Effa listed her parents as Bertha Ford and Benjamin Brooks, her stepfather. By claiming Benjamin Brooks as her father, Effa Manley's legal identity as colored would allow her to legally marry Abe at a time when interracial marriage was restricted.

From this point on, after her marriage to Abe, Effa Manley chose to present herself publicly and privately as a black woman. Effa no longer moved between white and black as openly. While it may seem a strange choice to live as a black woman in a segregated society when she had the option of not having to experience segregation, the influence of love for her husband on this decision is difficult to gauge. At some points the marriage seemed to be a business decision and at others Effa appears a woman in love. Her choice of racial identity does not appear in any one quote or interview, but in pieces of her recollections. In her reminiscence, Effa Manley remembered her upbringing in a black household.

> I have come up entirely in a Negro atmosphere ... I was very fond of these half brothers and sisters ... I know that even you must have been thinking that all this conversation, I'm always talking about the Negroes and I guess you figured, "What's this white woman doing so concerned about the Negro?" So that's what happened. I've just come up entirely in this Negro atmosphere.[14]

Throughout her life Effa Manley chose black sexual partners. This may be another indication of her cultural identification, or it may just have been a personal preference.

> I've often wondered what it would be like associating [chuckling] with white people because ... is it ... and ... and since Abe died I've married twice; again, both of them Negroes. [Laughs] It does seem funny that at some time I wouldn't have gotten involved with some white per- ... man, you know. But n- ... n- ..., in ... in my long and unusual life history, and even being involved with baseball and everything, I never ... there was never any Caucasian. It was the darndest thing.[15]

She was married four times, all to black men, and had several, if not many, relationships with others.

On her later travels with the Newark Eagles, Effa Manley stayed in the segregated hotels with her husband and the players. She chose to live as a black even if that meant segregation.

> The hotels positively, I never found anything wrong with any of them, and I always stayed with them ... I could have stayed at any white hotel in the world. I always went where the ball players went, and Abe stayed right with them every game, every day.[16]

However, Effa Manley had a choice the others did not. Since she had the ability to travel in society as a white woman, as others believed her to be when she presented herself as such, Effa did not have to stay in segregated hotels. None of the players or her husband had that ability. Before her marriage, she applied for positions as a white woman because of the better financial opportunities.[17] After her marriage, she defended the right of blacks to be recognized equally. Converts to a group are often more enthusiastic about it than those born into it. Effa Manley had chosen a black identity and remained an ardent supporter of blacks and the baseball leagues they created until her death.

Owning and Managing

In 1935, Abe Manley organized the Brooklyn Eagles baseball team in the Negro National League. The wealth from his business enterprises allowed Abe to own his own baseball team. Initially, the team played in the Brooklyn Dodgers' Ebbets Field; then, in 1936, for financial reasons, the team moved across the river to Newark, New Jersey. The Newark Eagles were a successful Negro League team that won a championship in 1946 and sent several players to the major leagues after integration in 1947, including Larry Doby, the first black player in the American League.[18] The team was central to the community of Newark and Effa was central to the team. Her players and fans assumed she was a light skinned black woman.[19] One black woman, Harriet Everett, who was a teenager in Newark in the 1930s, recalled: "I can never remember was she black or white? She was very fair...."[20] Manley did not reveal her racial history until well after the death of Abe and long after her baseball career had ended. In the 1970s, she gave several interviews in which she discussed her racial background. By this time, the civil rights movement had changed the way the country thought about race.[21]

In addition to her race, Effa Manley revealed her active role as a business manager during her interviews in the seventies. In the 1950s, after the death of her husband, Effa claimed not to have been an active manager of the team. A 1956 article read:

> Mrs. Manley steadfastly denies that she ever tried to run the Eagles emphasizing that her role was that of secretary to her husband. However, in this capacity Mrs. Manley picked up some factual insides of the integration of the Negro in organized baseball.[22]

This description is in contrast to her image in the 1930s and 1940s, both decades during which Effa Manley held a central and active influence on the team. An article in 1943, by Wendell Smith for the *Pittsburgh Courier*, painted a different portrait.

> When Mr. Manley moved his Eagles' nest from Brooklyn to Newark a few years ago, Mrs. Manley left the kitchen and moved right into the front office with her husband. Since that time she has been the No. 1 thorn in the vulnerable side of the other owners, simply because she is a woman with ideas and aggressiveness.[23]

When she did discuss her role as business manger, she did so proudly. Frequently, Effa Manley thought of the players as if they were her family. Her players remembered, "She had some people who were her favorites, she'd mother them,"[24] and, "We were Mrs. Manley's boys."[25] Appearance of the team particularly concerned her. Pitcher Max Manning recalled:

> Effa would rule the roost. The whole women's approach to things is entirely different from a man. She was interested in appearances — uniform neat, shoes shined. She was particular about that.[26]

In 1946, Effa purchased a new top-of-the-line $16,000 bus for traveling. Since buses were the main mode of transportation for the Negro Leaguers, who spent many nights sleeping while moving toward their next destination, the quality of the bus was important; it was a showpiece in the community. Effa was very proud to give her team a new bus.[27]

From a player's point of view, Effa Manley may have attended to unnecessary detail. It was her attention to detail, however that helped make her club a successful one. After winning the Negro League World Series in 1946, Effa Manley celebrated as a victorious owner and manager. One of her players, Monte Irvin, recalled:

> I've never seen a woman so happy as Mrs. Manley. She gave a big party for the team. You *know* all of Newark celebrated. I think for winning the Series, we each received a hundred bucks. It was great for us because it was the first time that Newark had won a championship. Mrs. Manley strutted around Newark all winter and the press published pictures of her accepting the Championship trophy. One of the local politicians even gave us a big party because her picture had appeared in the newspapers.[28]

Effa Manley was at the top of the world, enjoying a victory she had helped create.

When the team did not win, Effa Manley became unhappy about their failures. James Overmyer connected her reaction with her "growing personal attachment to her role as a baseball executive."[29] One of her players, George Giles, recalled her actions on Opening Day in 1935.

> When she was displeased, the world came to an end. She'd stop traffic ... Mrs. Manley loved baseball, but she couldn't stand to lose. I was a pretty hard loser myself, but I think she'd take it more seriously than anybody.[30]

Over time, Effa Manley was responsible for the business aspects of the Eagles. Abe scouted talent for the team, but Effa made almost all of the decisions.

> I surprised even myself with my rapid progress in absorbing the lessons so vital to the successful operation of a modern day baseball organization.... Abe needed all the help he could get — and immediately ... I found that I could be of a genuine assistance, by performing a growing number of front office duties, along with the thousand and one other details relating to the business ends of matters.[31]

Pat Patterson, a player, recalled, "Her husband was supposed to run the team ... but she ran it."[32] Her attention to the Yankees and her marriage to Abe made it possible for Effa to assume the role of business manager. First, Effa was a baseball fan. She already understood the fundamentals of the game. Second, by marrying a wealthy man, Effa had the opportunity to worry less about earning an income and more about supporting her husband's interests. It does not appear that Effa had a role in purchasing the baseball team in 1935,[33] but she certainly made the most of the business decisions as the enterprise expanded.

> For the first two years, Abe wouldn't let me have a word to say.... Then it got to a place where he would let me make a suggestion or offer a criticism, and finally right out of the clear sky one day, he said, "Honey, I think I'll let you take over now."
>
> It thrilled me, but I wasn't sure of myself. I was scared I'd do something wrong, but he soon got rid of that fear for me. Whenever I'd show signs of hesitating about making a move, he'd simply put on his hat and coat and go out and get in the car and drive off.[34]

Abe's voice in the history of the team and his perspective on Effa's role is nonexistent. Most of the information given by Effa comes from interviews done in the 1970s and 1980s, long after Abe's death. The accuracy of Effa's memories cannot be compared to Abe's version of the story because he did not leave one. In the 1950s, at the time of Abe's death, Negro League baseball was a dead industry that had not yet captured the attention of historians. His story was not recorded before his death.

There are many cases from the 1930s and 1940s that illustrated that the players knew Mrs. Manley was in charge. One instance occurred when George Giles, a player, was hired as manager.

> [Abe] Manley met me in his apartment and offered me the manager's job.... He said, "My wife wants you to manage the ball club." He didn't say he wanted me; he said "my wife" wanted me.[35]

Credit for the success of the team was often given to Effa Manley. Players deferred to her for contract negotiation and on payday. Monte Irvin recalled:

> I went to Mrs. Manley and told her about his great offer and that I was going to be married. She [Effa Manley] asked, "Well, how much are

they [a Mexican team] going to give you?" I told her and she said, "I can't afford that." "Just give me a twenty-five dollar raise," I said, "and make it one hundred seventy-five dollars a month." She said, "Well, I can't pay you that much because I'm paying these other guys." "Mrs. Manley, they're not getting married — I am," I said. "You can find twenty-five dollars more a month anywhere." She said, "Well, it's just not in the books and I can't do it." "Well, if you don't do it, then I will just have to accept the offer ... to go to Mexico." ... But Effa said, "Well, I just can't do it. You'll just have to go Monte because I can't afford it."[36]

Effa Manley was a shrewd negotiator and tried to call Monte Irvin's bluff. However, the next day, Effa went to Irvin's home, tried to re-negotiate. In the end, Irvin got his raise. Johnny Davis remembered:

Abe Manley was kind of easy-going. Ms. Manley was the toughie, 'cause she handed out the money on payday.[37]

In addition to financial decisions, Effa made decisions about the action on the field as well. Author Brent Kelley remarked:

Effa Manley ... recognized [Red] Moore's ability.... When Moore joined Newark, Mrs. Manley had Suttles shuffled to outfield so Moore could play first base.[38]

When scouts for the Mexican leagues expressed an interest in her players, Effa was quick to claim her territory. A journalist described the scene:

Her eyes suddenly narrowed, her frame grew taut like a chicken making ready to pounce on a worm, a slow flush of deep anger spread from her neck to the roots of her hairs. Up she jumped and down the aisle she flew, as surprised fans on either side looked apprehensively behind her, sure that somebody must be chasing her for robbing a bank or putting a firecracker on a streetcar track. Down behind the home plate box seats, she stopped, rushing into a clot of foreign-looking gents.... "What are you doing, talking to my ballplayers?" She shrilled as the foreign looking hombres fell aback. "...Now, you fellows should be ashamed of yourselves trying to steal my ballplayers right under my eyes."[39]

Effa Manley did not just support Abe. As she claimed in the years after his death, she was, without a doubt, the business manager of the team.

Effa Manley worked to organize the Negro League owners to improve the overall situation of the entire Negro Leagues. One issue involved booking agents. Negro League teams paid Major League owners to rent their fields while the Major League teams traveled out of town. A Negro League owner had to work with a booking agent to secure fields, a practice that frequently worked against owners such as the Manleys. Monte Irvin, a Newark Eagle, recalled:

Mrs. Manley was a very astute businesswoman and she became very knowledgeable about baseball affairs. This practice of having to go through booking agents was one of the things that stuck in her craw. I think she tried to get the other owners to organize and fight this practice somehow, but she was not successful. It was that way through the country, except for the ball parks owned by black teams.[40]

Even for the great East-West game, a popular All-Star game, the Negro Leagues rented out Comiskey Park in Chicago every year. Although she was not successful in changing stadium rental terms, Effa Manley's efforts did improve umpires' pay at the East-West game. A journalist wrote:

Mr[s]. Effa Manley of the Newark Eagles seems to be about the only owner in the N.N.L. who can see the disparity of pay and treatment of umpires, especially since Negro baseball is having a banner season in gate receipts. It was she who broke up the sorry spectacle of umpires running from club owner to club owner after each game trying to collect their pay, or standing on the sidewalk late in the night to get their measly salary, while the boys in the back room told tall tales of the days when they were young and otherwise took plenty of time before paying off.[41]

Effa also participated in the Negro National League (NNL) administration. Effa joined Abe at the business meetings of the NNL; however, her opinions were not always appreciated. An article by Frank A. Young dated September 9, 1939, said:

Mrs. Abe Manley, who owns the Newark Eagles with her husband, usually does a lot of talking. While in Chicago [at an East-West game business meeting], she opposed and argued against every move that helped put 32,000 paid admissions in Chicago on Sunday, August 6. But the fortunate part of Mrs. Manley's arguments was that the other club owners ignored her.

Some of Mrs. Manley's objections, as well as some of her arguments are, as Shakespeare said in *The Merchant of Venice*, "like two grains of wheat lost in two bushels of chaff, you may seek all day ere you find them — and when you have found them they are not worth their search."[42]

Another article in 1942 described an annual meeting of the Negro National League.

Effa Manley has long been a sore spot in the N.N.L. setup in that the rough and tumble gentlemen compromising its inner sanctum have complained often and loudly that "baseball ain't no place for no woman. We can't cuss her out." However, Mrs. Manley can't be blamed for standing for her convictions and for the protection of the investment she and her husband have in the baseball franchise in Newark.[43]

They may not have approved of her role in league politics, but Effa Manley was credited with a strong opinion and her convictions.

Reversing Roles

Effa Manley also thought of her players as opportunities for personal relationships. Rumors about sexual relationships with her players appear in several sources. Monte Irvin, one of her favorite players on the Newark Eagles, says:

> She was quite a sexpot. When they [Abe and Effa Manley] first got married, everything was okay but later on, I understand Abe got sick somehow and wasn't able to satisfy her sexually. So Effa started to look for sex wherever she could find it.[44]

The accusations were more than generalizations, as they included specific incidents.

> Effa developed a fondness for our star pitcher, Terris McDuffie, and there's no way to keep a thing like that quiet. I guess everybody knew it a long time before Abe did. When he found out, he called a meeting and told McDuffie that he had been traded to the New York Black Yankees for two broken bats and an old pair of sliding pads.
> Then Effa started to date another fellow. His name was Ham Jones.... She went with him a long time, and then came along Lennie Pearson.... Effa fell in love with Lennie and they went together for quite a long time.... Effa tried to keep him happy by giving him a watch and other expensive gifts, but never much money.[45]

In an interview with James Overmyer, Eric Illidge, the traveling secretary for the Newark Eagles, hinted at a possible relationship between Effa Manley and McDuffie. Illidge once heard Abe Manley on a bus ride say:

> When I get there, I'm going to trade that son of a bitch McDuffie to [Cumberland] Posey [owner of the Negro League team the Homestead Grays].[46]

That trade was not made, but Abe sent McDuffie to the Black Yankees in 1938. While there is no conclusive evidence to support whether or not Effa and McDuffie had an affair, there are examples of Abe's dislike for McDuffie. In addition to information about Effa's affairs with others, Monte Irvin also experienced her sexual advances first hand.

> Mrs. Manley was tough to deal with. She always wanted to give you something besides money ... in 1946, I went to her house to talk contract with her and Abe. When I got there, she came to the door in her

negligee. I asked her where Abe was, and she said he had to go out of
town and would not be back until tomorrow. She invited me in so we
could sit and talk. I sat right across from her and, as we talked, the negligee got higher and higher until, all of the sudden, I noticed it was up
around her navel.

This made me very uncomfortable because I had a lot of respect for
Abe and I had a lot of respect for her. I just thought that her acting that
way wasn't the right thing to do. "Mrs. Manley," I said, "I don't think
you have contract talk on your mind today. Maybe I had better come
back another time when Abe is here." She assured me that it was O.K.
to continue the discussion and not to be uncomfortable because she
was just a little warm and wanted to air things out a bit. But I got up
and went to the door. "Well, I'll come back sometime," I said and
closed the door as I left.[47]

Ray Dandridge told Monte Irvin "you're about the dumbest guy I know.
You could have probably gotten your raise and anything else you wanted."
Maybe there was a reason Monte Irvin titled his autobiography *Nice Guys
Finish First*.

In addition to Monte Irvin's detailed description, there is a story about
the Manleys trying to sign the great pitcher Satchel Paige to the Newark
roster. In 1937, Paige's contract was sold to the Eagles, but Paige went to
Latin America instead. Effa claimed that before Paige left he said he would
come to the Eagles if she would be his girlfriend. Her response was, "I didn't
know what to say ... so I threw it [Paige's letter] away."[48] Whether or not
Effa Manley had relationships with her players, she did not publicly admit
to any before her death.

Changing the Community

In the 1930s, Sugar Hill in Harlem was home to the elite in black soci-
ety, including Abe and Effa Manley. With the success of their team in
Newark, the couple held a high status. Max Manning, a pitcher for the
Eagles, believed that "The Eagles were to (black) Newark what the Dodgers
were to Brooklyn."[49] If the Eagles were at the center of the community, Effa
Manley was at the center of fostering that relationship. A long time member of the National Association for the Advancement of Colored People
(NAACP) and a treasurer for the New Jersey NAACP, Effa used game days
for fundraising opportunities. In 1943, the NAACP Youth Council raised
$143 at a game in May. In 1945, $215 was collected on Opening Day. The
next year's Opening Day included volunteers with NAACP banners solic-
iting fans.[50]

Another cause Effa Manley fought for was a successful boycott of

Blumstein's department store in Harlem in 1934. Blacks gave the store seventy-five percent of its business, yet employment was denied to them. The protest, organized by the Citizens League for Fair Play, an organization co-founded by Effa and the Reverend Johnson,[51] surrounded the store with pickets holding signs that read "We Don't Trade Where We Can't Work." Blumstein's caved to the pressure. The Citizens League won the hiring of black clerks after six weeks of picketing.[52] A year later, 300 black employees worked in the store on 125th Street where none had worked before.

Fighting Integration

After Abe Manley's death, Effa Manley became a vocal supporter of the Negro Leagues. She became one of the loudest voices to save the Negro Leagues as integration progressed. Caught between integration and loss of her business, her advocacy began in earnest in 1948. In response to Jackie Robinson's article published in *Ebony* in 1948, "What's Wrong with Negro Baseball," Manley wrote an article of her own. "Negro Baseball Isn't Dead!" was her response to one of the most celebrated sports figures of the time.[53] Robinson noted all of the problems with Negro League baseball: low pay, long bus rides, segregated hotels that were inherent in a segregated society.

In contrast, Effa placed the focus on the positive role the Negro Leagues played in the lives of individuals and in the black community. Challenging Jackie Robinson was not an insignificant choice. Like some of the other Negro League players, Effa Manley did not think as highly of Jackie Robinson as Branch Rickey did. Branch Rickey, owner of the Brooklyn Dodgers, chose Jackie Robinson to integrate Major League Baseball. Effa said, "Robinson was never really much of a superstar."[54] Robinson, a rookie from the Kansas City Monarchs, was quickly vaulted to the top of the list of heroes in the black communities. Although viewed by many in the Negro Leagues as not the best first choice for integration, many respected and supported Robinson as an individual.

Effa Manley had always supported her Negro League players, even if it meant signing them over to Organized Baseball.[55]

> He [Branch Rickey, who signed Jackie Robinson in 1945] had us over a barrel in a way. The fans would never have forgiven us plus it would have been wrong to have prevented [the players] from going to the major leagues.[56]

Her campaign against Branch Rickey lasted several years. Rickey's decision placed him on the bridge of the integration ship. Wendell Smith included her feelings in an article in 1948.

> Negro baseball's self-styled "Carrie Nation," fast-talking Effa Manley, woman owner of the now deceased Newark Eagles, carried on her violent campaign against Brooklyn's Branch Rickey yesterday at a joint meeting of the Negro American and National Leagues here [Chicago]. Vitriolic Mrs. Manley declared that the Brooklyn boss ruined Negro baseball when he "stole" Jackie Robinson and Don Newcombe.... "He just took those players without giving us any compensation..."[57]

The loss of her players and the Negro Leagues was a bitter pill for her to swallow, even thirty years later.

> Every time I see the Dodgers get beat ... I say they don't deserve to win for what they did to Negro baseball.[58]

Effa Manley had always supported black people, despite her belief that she was white.

> The Negroes always suffered with a terrible inferiority complex. With Jews, Italians, Spanish, Irish — in everything they did, they stood together and did things and were proud of themselves and their accomplishments. The minute you say "Negro," it was Jim Crow, segregated, inferior, and I haven't been able to understand it. And in my book [*Before Integration*], Negroes have never been inferior. They have always had an awful lot on the ball.[59]

To support the Negro Leagues players' move into the segregated major leagues seemed like an easy choice. However, it sealed the fate of one of the most successful black businesses that had ever existed in the United States.

> As early as the year 1944 ... we in organized Negro baseball could see quite plainly the proverbial handwriting on the wall. The gathering storm of inevitable baseball integration was approaching rapidly, ever more relentlessly.[60]

Negro League team owners felt the impact of integration immediately. Attendance for the Newark Eagles decreased from 120,000 in 1946 to 57,000 in 1947.[61] Effa Manley understood the magnitude of Branch Rickey's decision very early.

> The livelihoods, the careers, the families of 400 Negro ballplayers are in jeopardy ... because four ballplayers were successful in getting into the major leagues.[62]

Effa called the signing of Negro League players to Major League contracts a "bargain basement rush."[63] She responded with the calculated move of a business manager. If players received major league offers, she would demand payment for their contracts.

Effa Manley's team lost three players to major league ball in three years. Between 1947 and 1949, Larry Doby, Monte Irvin, and Don Newcombe signed contracts with the Cleveland Indians, the New York Giants, and the Brooklyn Dodgers respectively.[64] The first two were eventually inducted into the National Baseball Hall of Fame. When Bill Veeck, owner of the Cleveland Indians, approached Effa Manley in 1947 about signing Doby to the Cleveland Indians, she negotiated the sale of his contract, a precedent-setting act[65] with the following exchange: Veeck first offered $10,000 for Doby.

> Mr. Veeck, you know if Larry Doby were white and a free agent, you'd give him $100,000 to sign with you merely as a bonus.... However, I am in no position to be bargaining with you. If you feel you're being fair by offering us $10,000, I suppose we should accept.

Veeck responded.

> Mrs. Manley ... I'll do this much in your case: If we keep Doby 30 days from the time we sign him up, I'll send you an additional five grand, which will make the total come to $15,000.

Not to be outdone, Effa had one more clause.

> Mr. Veeck there is just one more thing. We're paying Doby $4,000 a season right now. If he goes with you, I want you to assure me that he won't get less than $5,000 a year. I don't want this youngster kicked around.[66]

Getting any money for a Negro Leaguer was unusual, but Effa Manley knew the value of her players. As more of her players left, she became increasingly unhappy.

> They paid me 5000 lousy dollars for Monte Irvin. If he'd have been white they'd have given me $100,000.... But I was glad to get it.[67]

Effa Manley also stood up for the skill and experience of her players. Negro League player Willie Grace remembered:

> They [white ball] can't say they trained these ballplayers because Miss [Effa] Manley, the way I got it, she told Cleveland, "I'll sell you Larry Doby but you ain't gonna send him out to no farm team." They said "We was wantin' to send him down to brush him up." She said, "He's better 'n anybody you got on your ballclub now. He's not goin' to no farm team." She told the New York Giants the same thing about Monte Irvin at the same time so they couldn't get no credit for developin' them.[68]

When in contract negotiations over Monte Irvin, Effa Manley hired a lawyer, especially after she had lost Don Newcombe to the Dodgers without compensation. Monte Irvin recalled:

> ...from a purely business standpoint, Mrs. Manley felt that Branch Rickey was obligated to compensate her for my contract. That position probably delayed my entry into the major leagues.... Mrs. Manley told Rickey that he had taken Don Newcombe for no money but she wasn't going to let him take me without some compensation. Furthermore, if he tried to do it, she would sue and fight him in court.... Rickey contacted her to say he was no longer interested and released me ... the New York Giants picked up my contract....[69]

Effa's legal maneuverings delayed Irvin's entrance into Organized Ball. Even though fans and the black press did not agree with her stand, Effa adhered to her position. Whether driven by financial gain, personal pride, or concern for future Negro Leagues teams whose players entered the major leagues, Effa Manley maintained her convictions.

Defending the Past

After Abe's death in December 1952, Effa Manley's support of the declining Negro Leagues included fighting for national recognition. Throughout her career, Effa wrote and published articles about the Negro Leagues. In 1941, an article written by Effa promoted the development of the Negro National and American Leagues.[70] In 1946, Effa Manley, Alex Pompez, and Curtis Leak met with Louis F. Carroll, a lawyer for the National League, to discuss integration. The three representatives of the Negro Leagues wanted "to petition the Major Leagues for recognition, protection of Negro National and Negro American League players, and find the best way to go about 1 and 2."[71] Officials from the Negro Leagues worked to save their franchises and their livelihood.

In 1949, Effa wrote a statement to the Negro Publishing Association in Washington, D.C. Negro League baseball had not yet collapsed, but its integration had weakened the foundation. In her statement, Effa Manley stressed the importance of developing a relationship between the Major Leagues and the Negro Leagues so organized black baseball could survive.

> Unless something is done we are now seeing the last crop of Negro players in the big leagues. They have killed themselves off, because at the same time, Negro professional baseball is being killed ... The Negro press has a very definite responsibility in helping to preserve the leagues. If [only] the sports writers on your publications will evidence the same enthusiasm toward our Negro baseball leagues and our colored boys playing in these organizations....[72]

Utilizing every means possible to save the leagues in which she spent fifteen years of her life, Effa Manley became one of the voices to save the Negro Leagues during a time in which popular support was for integration.

In 1976, Effa Manley co-authored *Negro Baseball ... Before Integration* with Leon Hardwick. She dedicated the book to Abe Manley, "A wonderful individual, whose farsightedness, steadfast spirit and tremendous organizational ability provided a source of inspiration for all who were privileged to know him."[73] The book is Effa's version of the Negro League during its peak period between 1935 and 1960. It is sometimes heavily autobiographical, but the elements of what she said were true. Throughout the text are references to Effa and Abe and the former players of the Eagles, such as Larry Doby and Don Newcombe. Writing mostly in the third person, Effa portrayed herself as an influential figure in the success of the Negro Leagues. A section of the introduction said:

> All of this is described in colorful detail by Effa Manley, who — during those topsy-turvy, momentous times — served in the dual capacity of co-owner and business manager of the Newark Eagles, one of the most famous teams of that era ... Effa Manley, in her own right, is a woman who through dedication and sparkling personality influenced — as much as any other single factor — the course of Organized Black Baseball throughout this second (and final) stage.[74]

In addition to promoting the memory of the Negro Leagues, and her role in their success, Effa Manley consistently evoked the memory and importance of her husband.

> Abe Manley who was largely responsible for rebuilding of the defunct Negro National League in 1935, serving as league treasurer during that loop's rather hectic 14-year existence.[75]
>
> Little did I dream at the time that vast changes were about to take place in Negro Baseball — and that my husband was destined to play a vital role in helping to bring about this Great Transformation![76]

It is true that Abe Manley was an owner of a successful team during the height of the Negro Leagues. What is not as certain is his centrality in changing the League. Abe Manley's friend, Gus Greenlee, a fellow numbers man, founded the Pittsburgh Crawfords in 1931 and persuaded several of his wealthy friends to do the same. Abe was one of these men. His influence appears to have come more through his marriage to Effa and her role in Negro League politics than anything he may have done personally.[77]

She appeared to downplay her efforts as a businesswoman in the 1950s, acting as a dutiful, supportive wife without a central role, but by 1976, Effa Manley played an important role in recalling the Negro League past and the need for remembering and recording. One of Effa Manley's missions was to get the National Baseball Hall of Fame to recognize and include Negro League ball players. The first section of *Negro Baseball ... Before Integration* was devoted to creating a list of qualified candidates for election to the Hall of Fame. Position by position, the authors listed possible contenders. Manley and Hardwick included players such as Luke Easter, John "Buck" O'Neil, Lorenzo "Piper" Davis, Ernie Banks, Willie Wells, Judy Johnson, Henry Aaron, James "Cool Papa" Bell, Martin Dihigo, Willie Mays, Leroy "Satchel" Paige, Roy Campanella, and Josh Gibson on the list. Several of the players would have made it into the Hall of Fame based on their Major League career alone. The focus was not only on the players of the past, but also contemporary black players.

Inclusion of Negro League stars into the Baseball Hall of Fame was also on Effa Manley's agenda. In 1971, Commissioner Bowie Kuhn appointed a special committee to "vote on outstanding players who were active in the Negro Leagues during the period and up to and including 1946."[78] The committee was to elect one Negro League player each year. Controversy surrounded the process because Hall of Fame intended to place the plaques of the elected Negro Leaguers in a separate location that appeared to many as segregation. The committee disbanded after electing nine players to the Hall of Fame. Effa Manley's response was that of a "Furious Woman." She wrote:

> The committee was supposed to atone partially for Organized Ball's past sins of omission and commission ... but instead of doing that, they piled insult upon insult by ignoring so many truly outstanding Negro baseball figures.... Everyone connected with the Negro League Hall should be ashamed.... They were guilty of miscarriage of justice. They selected only nine Negro league players for the Hall of Fame. I probably would have settled for 30, but I could have named 100.[79]

The Hall of Fame currently has sixteen Negro League players in the Hall of Fame.[80] Election of the players became the charge of the Veterans Committee.[81] The plaques were never placed separately, and today they are integrated in the gallery with those elected by the Baseball Writers Association of America.

In addition to publicly voicing her sentiments about the Hall of Fame elections, Effa Manley wrote to Major League Baseball. In 1972, Effa's original purpose was to make sure that major league baseball did not forget anyone on her list of candidates, especially qualified Newark Eagles. In a letter to Joseph Reichler, Effa urged:

> There is a great deal of interest now in the Negro Ballplayers being named to Baseballs [sic] Hall of Fame, but I am afraid some of those

most deserving will be bypassed because a couple of members of the committee picking them has [sic] a real hatred for Abe Manley and I am afraid his team the Eagles.[82]

Her lifelong commitment to Negro League baseball did not decrease over time. Effa Manley continued to support the organization and its players that occupied her life for almost fifty years until her death.

Conclusion

Effa Manley was a woman who defined her place in society by choosing her own racial identity and gender roles. A strong-willed businesswoman, Effa Manley did not always fit into traditional categories. Her life was at times conflicted, at times against societal norms, but always a creation of her own. She is worth remembering not only for her baseball contributions, but also for her independence in how she chose to live her life.

Notes

This paper is for Sean who gave me baseball and my parents who have always given me their love and support. Thanks to the people who read and commented on this paper: Janet Farrell Brodie, Robert Dawidoff, Eric Enders (thanks to Eric also for his answers to research questions), Clem Hamilton, Jim Overmyer, and members of my research seminar at Claremont Graduate University. Thanks also goes to the staff of the National Baseball Hall of Fame Library in Cooperstown, New York, for assigning me to work on the Negro Leagues for my project as a summer intern, a project that increased my interest in Effa Manley and the Negro Leagues.

1. "Manley, Black Baseball Club Owner, Dead at 84," *Los Angeles Times* (April, 18, 1981), Part III, page 9.

2. She was not buried next to Abe, her late husband, who died December 9, 1952, and was buried in the Fairmount Cemetery in Newark, New Jersey.

3. The 1900 birth date is taken from her grave. The *Los Angeles Times* obituary lists her year of birth as 1897, which is the same as the Social Security Death Index. Thank you to James Overmyer for this information. Her birth certificate is not available.

4. William Marshall, "Effa Manley interview" (October 19, 1977, Los Angeles, CA), University of Kentucky Library, A.B. "Happy" Chandler Oral History Project, 69. Benjamin Brooks' victory in court lends to the belief of proof for a relationship between Bertha Brooks and John Bishop. Paternity is still uncertain and cannot be concretely established without more evidence.

5. Bertha Brooks later married B.A. Cole and had two more children. James Overmyer, *Queen of the Negro Leagues: Effa Manley and the Newark Eagles* (Lanham, MD: Scarecrow Press, 1998), 6.

6. Holy Cross Cemetery and Mausoleum, Culver City, California.

7. Marshall, 71. The majority of the sources for this paper are oral histories.

Interest in preserving the history and recognizing the players became popular publicly in the 1970s and 1980s when former players, baseball enthusiasts, and historians began writing about the history and conducting oral histories. The oral histories are valuable since the records of Negro baseball are not always complete.

8. Marshall, 72.

9. Allen Richardson, "A Retrospective Look at the Negro Leagues and Professional Negro Baseball Players" (MA Thesis: San Jose State University, 1980), 193.

10. Arthur G. Rust, *Collections of a Baseball Junkie* (New York: William Morrow, 1985), quoted in Overmyer, 8.

11. Richardson, 158.

12. Overmyer, 9. A "numbers banker" was the career for many of those starting Negro League teams since they had money during this period. As Overmyer explains, the business was highly illegal and extremely popular in black society during this period. Players could place bets on almost anything with any amount of money. Occasional wins kept the poor playing and the bankers wealthy.

13. Certificate of Record and Marriage, "Abe and Effa Manley" Officials File, National Baseball Hall of Fame Library, Cooperstown, New York. Abe was her second husband and that marriage lasted the longest.

14. Marshall, 71–72.

15. Marshall, 71.

16. Richardson, 175.

17. Overmyer, 7.

18. The Negro National League began in 1920 when Rube Foster, a black pitcher, organized professional baseball for blacks. Major League Baseball was closed to blacks due to an unofficial gentleman's agreement by the owners for segregation. The Negro Leagues were one of the most successful black businesses in the country until integration in 1947 began its demise.

19. There is a story, most likely apocryphal, that Effa was the inventor of the batting helmet. One day, when sending Willie Wells the bunt signal, crossing and uncrossing her legs, Wells was looking at her legs and did not look up in time to miss the pitch as it hit him in the head. Donn Rogosin, *Invisible Men: Life in Baseball's Negro Leagues* (New York: Atheneum, 1985), 74. Wells is, in fact, credited with inventing the batting helmet by wearing a coal miner's helmet because of how pitchers threw at him. John B. Holway, *Voices from the Great Black Baseball Leagues* (New York: Da Capo, 1992), 219.

20. Overmyer, 7.

21. Overmyer, 7.

22. Marion E. Jackson, "Sport of the World," *Atlanta Daily World* (Wednesday, September 5, 1956), found in Effa Manley's Scrapbook File, National Baseball Hall of Fame Library, Cooperstown, New York.

23. Wendell Smith, "Smitty's Sport's Spurts," *The Pittsburgh Courier* (Saturday, January 30, 1943), found in Effa Manley's Scrapbook File.

24. John Holway, *Black Diamonds: Life in the Negro Leagues from the Men Who Lived It* (New York: Stadium Books, 1991), 1991.

25. Holway, *Black Diamonds*, 162.

26. Holway, *Black Diamonds*, 124.

27. Rogosin, 77.

28. Monte Irvin with James Riley, *Nice Guys Finish First: The Autobiography of Monte Irvin* (New York: Carroll and Graf, 1996), 107.

29. Overmyer, 35.

30. Quoted in Overmyer, 35.

31. Quoted in Overmyer, 35.

32. Rogosin, 109.

33. Richardson, 156.

34. Quoted in Overmyer, 74.

35. Quoted in Overmyer, 35.

36. Irvin, 89–90.

37. Holway, *Black Diamonds*, 162.

38. Brent Kelley, *Voices from the Negro Leagues: Conversations with 52 Baseball Standouts of the Period 1924–1960* (Jefferson, NC: McFarland and Co., 1998), 49.

39. Dan Burley, "The Senors Get in Mrs. Manley's Hair," article in Jim Reisler, *Black Writers/Black Baseball: An Anthology of Articles from Black Sportswriters Who Covered the Negro Leagues* (Jefferson, NC: McFarland and Co., 1994), 138–9. Despite the racism, which is extremely apparent in sections not included, this article illustrates Effa Manley's possessiveness of her players as any owner would.

40. Irvin, 64.

41. Reisler, 135.

42. Reisler, 59.

43. Dan Burley, "Confidentially Yours," *Amsterdam New York Star-News* (February 21, 1942): Section 2, 14.

44. Irvin, 44

45. Irvin, 44.

46. Overmyer, 81.

47. Irvin, 44.

48. Donn Rogosin, *Invisible Men: Life in Baseball's Negro Leagues* (New York: Atheneum, 1985), 110.

49. Quoted in Overmyer, 58.

50. Overmyer, 59.

51. Gai Ingham Berlage, "Effa Manley, A Major Force in Negro Baseball in the 1930s and 1940s," *Nine* 1(2) (Spring 1993), 164.

52. Articles on Boycott in Effa Manley's Scrapbook File and Officials File, National Baseball Hall of Fame, Cooperstown, New York. Effa Manley was secretary of the Citizens League for Fair Play.

53. The article in the Hall of Fame Abe and Effa Manley Officials file is subtitled "But It Is Pretty Sick."

54. Quoted in Jules Tygiel, *Baseball's Great Experiment: Jackie Robinson and His Legacy*, Expanded Edition (New York: Oxford University Press, 1997), 78.

55. Since the Negro Leagues were also considered to be professional baseball leagues, major league baseball is commonly referred to as organized baseball when contrasted with the Negro Leagues.

56. Tygiel, 88.

57. Wendell Smith, "Woman Magnate Rips Rickey for Raids on Negro League," article in Effa Manley's Scrapbook File, National Baseball Hall of Fame, Cooperstown, New York. Wendell Smith, along with other black sportswriters such as Joe Bostic, Sam Lacy, and Frank A. Young, strongly supported the integration of the major leagues.

58. Quoted in Tygiel, 147.

59. Richardson, 174.

60. Rogosin, 187.

61. Tygiel, 240. The Manleys sold their team to a Houston buyer in 1948.

62. Tygiel, 240.

63. Tygiel, 301.

64. Larry Moffi and Jonathan Kronstadt, *Crossing the Line: Black Major Leaguers, 1947–1959* (Iowa City: University of Iowa Press, 1994), 15, 39, 45.

65. Rogosin, 216.

66. Effa Manley and Leon Herbert Hardwick, *Negro Baseball ... Before Integration* (Chicago, IL: Adams Press, 1976), 75–76.

67. Rogosin, 217. Rogosin notes "In the deepest irony of all, Monte Irvin took a pay cut to join the major leagues, dropping from $6500 to $5000 a year."

68. Kelley, 142.

69. Irvin, 119–120.

70. Effa Manley, "Baseball Leagues Spend Half Million," *The Afro-American* (July 26, 1941), 20.

71. From document in "Newark Eagles" File, National Baseball Hall of Fame Library, Cooperstown, New York.

72. "Statement of Effa Manley to The Negro Publishers Association," in Effa Manley's Professional File, Ashland Collection, National Baseball Hall of Fame Library, Cooperstown, New York. The last page of this statement is missing.

73. Manley and Hardwick, 3. Effa had the baseball knowledge and Leon Hardwick was a newspaper editor and magazine editor-publisher.

74. Manley and Hardwick, 7–8.

75. Manley and Hardwick, 8.

76. Manley and Hardwick, 41.

77. Most recollections of Abe note his abilities as a talent scout, although some do not even give him credit for that. Effa most likely did any other role listed as his, such as National Negro League Treasurer and Newark Eagle management.

78. "Place for Ex-Negro Stars in Shrine" in "Negro Leaguers in the Hall of Fame" Subject File, National Baseball Hall of Fame Library, Cooperstown, New York.

79. "A 'Furious' Woman," article by C.C. Johnson Spink dated June 20, 1977, in "Abe and Effa Manley" Officials File, National Baseball Hall of Fame Library, Cooperstown, New York.

80. The sixteen were elected solely on their careers in the Negro Leagues. Other players have been elected based on their Major League career, but played in the Negro Leagues.

81. The Veterans Committee election of Negro League players was limited. Elected in 1999, "Smokey Joe" Williams would have been the last Negro League player if the rules had not been revised. On October 6, 1999, the Hall of Fame announced "...the Board has extended an amendment made to the Veterans Committee rules of election in 1995. The amendment call for two special elections — one exclusively for 19th century players and the other for Negro League players — to be held in conjunction with the regular election from 1995 through 1999. Both elections will be held for two more years. From National Baseball Hall of Fame Press Release, October 6, 1999.

82. Letter from Effa Manley to Joseph Reichler in "Abe and Effa Manley" Officials File, National Baseball Hall of Fame Library, Cooperstown, New York.

Black Players on the Field of Dreams: African American Baseball in Film

George Grella

The rather fanciful and, frankly, inaccurate title of this paper, as we all must know, suggests some of the familiar mythology and outright false-hood in the complicated and neglected subject of the African American baseball player and his representation in motion pictures: in the two most famous and popular baseball movies, *The Natural* (1984) and *Field of Dreams* (1989), after all, no black players appear. In fairness, *The Natural*, both as film and novel, despite its remarkable connections with some his-torical occurrences in baseball, apparently takes place in some vague, unspecified, even mythic time in the nation's memory, before the integra-tion of the sport, which may justify or at least explain its neglect of that important presence. In *Field of Dreams*, however, which magically and rather mawkishly resurrects whole teams of dead athletes, surely some of the most famous black ballplayers — Jackie Robinson and Josh Gibson come immediately to mind — deserve to participate in those supernatural contests in that mystical cornfield out in Possum Droppings, Iowa, par-ticipating in that often bathetic but also admittedly often lovely pageant of the past.[1] (That problematic movie earned the usual tired responses from the reviewers, many of them fans of the most sentimental persua-sion — "heartwarming" and "not a dry eye in the house," but heartwarm-ing for some can mean heartburn for others and those wet eyes sometimes resulted from upset stomachs.) The presence of such players on the generic field of dreams, that green expanse we all know so well and love so much, however, took a long time to occur in what we all like to regard as real life, in actual baseball, and consequently, in the cinema of baseball. Investigating the subject of that integration, in the larger arena of American life as well as in the national pastime, along with the related matter of black cinema, opens up a long, rich, tangled history of the nation, of baseball, and of film itself.

In the considerable work I have done and continue to do on baseball, cinema, and the special nexus that joins those two complex and fascinating activities, I am continually struck by the parallel metaphors these powerfully entwined subjects provide for what we may like to think of as the American experience. Both endeavors, separately and together, reflect something of the nation's history and the nation's collective spirit, its essence, its soul; the subject of the African American baseball player in film illustrates at least a few of the many ways in which the two combine and perhaps, as well, the possibility of at least a measure of redemption for that soul. The integration of both baseball and the armed forces at virtually the same moment in history, for example, results most directly and obviously from some of the lessons of World War II, in which millions of innocent human beings died for no reason beyond their ethnic identity. Black soldiers fought the same enemies as their white brothers, and whatever the color of their skin, bled the same red blood. Baseball and the baseball film, in effect, record the events in their own fictional constructs, thus making them permanent and immortal in the related realms of sport and art. In telling their familiar stories of racism, injustice, and exclusion within the framework of the sport, the films clearly inform the public about the history of those concepts in the broader culture. They demonstrate some of the unchanging attitudes toward race, many of them entirely unpleasant and obnoxious, that dominate American discourse and behavior throughout the dynamics of separation and acceptance, segregation and integration; further, sometimes perhaps quite inadvertently or even now and then out of good intentions, they also reiterate the tired liberal pieties and shallow patriotism that often gloss over that sad and painful history.

Initially it seems apparent that cinematic representation of black athletes in the sport simply could not occur until they were permitted to participate in that entity we know as organized, professional baseball. Harold Seymour and other historians point out, however, that black people had been participating in ball games well before the Civil War,[2] and later formed numerous amateur clubs that laid the foundations of the Negro Leagues. Whatever the particular conditions of any definite historical period, whether of slavery, servitude, or various levels of segregation and discrimination, black people created their own special, identifiable culture, after all, which of course included a wide variety of games. Those games in turn undoubtedly included baseball — how could they not? Dating all the way back to the silent era, moreover, the film industry has produced works aimed specifically at black audiences — what the demographic folks these days call niche marketing — so it seems entirely likely that black teams, organized or not, also played their games on the screen, and even more likely that baseball appeared at least incidentally in some movies,[3] but since the majority of silent motion pictures of all kinds, let alone the black-oriented works, are now considered "lost," those obscure contests, despite the existence of their titles in archives and filmographies, will probably remain forever unseen, conducted only on the boundless fields of memory, fantasy, and imagination.

The great breakthrough in showing black players in the cinema, of course, follows in the wake of the first steps toward racial integration in organized baseball, in short, with Jackie Robinson's signing with the Brooklyn Dodgers. Naturally, a movie followed to exploit the event — hey, this is America, isn't it? — *The Jackie Robinson Story* (1950), in which Robinson played himself, not always so easy a task as it sounds, particularly with the picture's sentimental script. Reasonably relaxed for an amateur, handsome as a movie star — probably one of the reasons he filled the role of pioneer so appropriately — Robinson obviously could impersonate a great athlete, i.e., himself, without the implausible awkwardness of most actors attempting to look athletic. The movie presents, in a crudely linear fashion, some of the familiar details of his public life and athletic career, from childhood through his triumphs in college football, concentrating especially, of course, on his progress through baseball. He plays for a Negro League team called the Black Panthers (!) before signing with the Dodgers, playing for Montreal and then Brooklyn, endures the taunts of fans and opponents — not so well known then as now — and becomes the star we all know. Most such film biographies — biopix to the initiated — tend towards hagiography, and *The Jackie Robinson Story* upholds that sacred tradition, not only showing the several inspiring colloquies with Branch Rickey, who serves as the Wise Old Man and benevolent patriarch of the film, but also sending its star to Washington, as he did in what we like to think of as real life, to appear before the notorious House Un-American Activities Committee. There Jackie speaks about equal opportunity, truth, justice, and the American Way, his face and his remarks superimposed over the Statue of Liberty in the background, while appropriate patriotic music plays on the soundtrack. Although no one can question Robinson's athletic ability and extraordinary qualities of character, he surely deserves something more than the sentimental apotheosis of this purported biography.

The Jackie Robinson Story demonstrates some useful and enduring truths about the public voice of America — the self congratulatory smugness of politicians, society, and Hollywood, the hypocritical exploitation of its subject, and the condescending triumphalism that so often operates in films about black athletes or heroic black figures in general. In retrospect, the movie also emphasizes that, more than a biopic or a baseball flick, it participates in that crowded and ignoble collection of fake patriotic, anti-Communist propaganda pictures of the 1950s, which themselves masqueraded as family dramas, thrillers, cop flicks, science fiction movies, and Westerns. Hollywood joined the innumerable jingoistic voices endorsing the Cold War status quo, the loud, plangent repetition of platitudes about capitalism, nationalism, militarism, Western values, and other fashionable illusions of a dark and shameful time. Ultimately, beneath its superficial representation of an inspiring personal story, of a great step forward in baseball, of a grand development in the important connection between American sport and society, it actually reveals the political establishment and the film industry collaborating in yet another exploitation of the African American.

Somewhat different in tone, *Don't Look Back* (1991), another biopic, this one made for television, shows the life and career of Satchel Paige, charting again the familiar progress of a black ballplayer of his and Jackie Robinson's generation. The movie opens with an exhibition game between the Paige All Stars, a team that includes such legendary names as Cool Papa Bell, Buck O'Neil, and Josh Gibson, and the Dizzy Dean All Stars, with, among others, Lou Gehrig, Rogers Hornsby, and Charlie Gehringer; the essential action unfolds in a long flashback as Paige recalls his baseball career up to that point. When the Paige team wins, the black players celebrate at least for a while, knowing they are as good as the big leaguers, but ultimately realize that they have won only a meaningless victory in a mere exhibition, that they are excluded from the highest levels of the sport they play so well. Seemingly longer even than an American League game and not terribly convincing in its portrayal of athletic ability, the picture shows the familiar struggles of players in the Negro Leagues — talented, dedicated athletes who loved the game but never won the recognition they deserved, and of course, never ascended to the major leagues. Like most such films, it shows the disappointment, frustration, and heartbreak the color barrier created for some great individual players, and indicates some of Satchel Paige's own bitterness at the selection of Jackie Robinson, whom he had played with on the Kansas City Monarchs, instead of himself, as the first black player in the majors. Although the baseball itself, like the games in the previous film, follows a predictable pattern, it generates even less vivacity and energy than the similar repeated moments in *The Jackie Robinson Story*. One of its few instances of relatively efficient visual narrative nicely indicates the instability and fluidity of a player's career in the Negro Leagues, as Paige pitches for a whole series of teams in a lyrical montage, with rapid lap dissolves, going through his pitching motions in a number of ball games while his uniform keeps changing, a rare sequence with at least a modicum of beauty and wit in an otherwise dull and dutiful work of cinema. Like *The Jackie Robinson Story*, *Don't Look Back* also displays its real life subject, as Satchel appears in a coda, talking more or less philosophically about the struggles of his youth and the achievements of his storied past.

An accidental trilogy of otherwise very different movies, set in the time frame just before Jackie Robinson's entry into the big leagues, suggests some of the various ways in which baseball's rigid policy of racial segregation conditions some contemporary cinema. Occupying themselves with roughly the same period of what now seems the ancient past, from about 1939 to about 1944, *The Bingo Long Traveling All-Stars and Motor Kings* (1976), *A Soldier's Story* (1984), and *A League of Their Own* (1992) dwell in varying ways on the exclusion of African Americans, generating a range of emotion, meaning, and artistic possibility from the common, essential experience of that historic denial. No matter how occasionally sentimental, falsified, or slick, each film hints at the complexity of the racial situation in America, then or at any other time, showing the separation of the races as not only cruel, unjust, and of course regrettable, but also at one point, for its victims a cause of shame and ultimately even a bitter self hatred. Whether accidentally or not, moreover, even the most upbeat and positive work of the trio exaggerates the clownish characters and behaviors of its people, trading on stereotypes of the shuffling, dancing, happy Negro.

Employing an ensemble cast of prominent black performers, including James Earl Jones, Billy Dee Williams, Richard Pryor, and Stan Shaw, *Bingo Long* creates a kind of collective picaresque, as the barnstorming All-Stars travel through pre-war America in a series of generally comic adventures, staying a step or two ahead of the law, the white community, and their enemies among the owners. Jones and Williams play versions of Josh Gibson and Satchel Paige, the two great recurring legends of Negro ball, while Pryor's foolish attempts to "pass" as a Cuban or an American Indian duplicate some of the common deceptions black players (and apparently some white owners) allegedly practiced so that a particularly light-skinned athlete might be accepted into the mainstream of the game.[4] The movie avoids the usual pious falsehoods and sentimental self pity by showing some of the internal political machinations of the Negro League ownership, who often behave very like their white counterparts, the major league owners, in their dishonesty, manipulation, and greed — whether their conduct reflects historical accuracy or not, at least it touches on one area of racial equality and perhaps even brotherhood, the common exploitation of players by owners. Although the movie confronts the familiar situations of racism, it generally avoids the easy, self serving clichés of the poor, downtrodden black baseball player suffering under the yoke of athletic slavery, celebrating instead the joy and exuberance, the sheer fun of participating at any level in the greatest game of all. In a sequence that offended many veterans of the Negro Leagues, including Buck O'Neil,[5] the All-Stars cakewalk through a Southern town; in one of the most exaggerated versions of the behavior that disgusted O'Neil and his colleagues, the camera focuses on their dancing feet, a shot that then dissolves into those same feet running the bases, sliding, going through the actions of the baseball game. Like it or not, and despite its own racial stereotyping, the sequence at least captures visually some of the grace and joy of the players, a rare enough event in any film dealing with the plight of the black ballplayer. We should not forget that players in the Negro Leagues did not necessarily regard their activity as a political gesture or a crusade, nor while away those long hours on the team bus brooding incessantly over their lot in life, but believe it or not, just like their white brothers, these guys loved the game. It may constitute a somewhat more refined form of racism to claim otherwise and, concentrating on segregation and injustice, deny that special dedication and love.

A much more complex and subtle picture, *A Soldier's Story* (1984) examines racial divisions in the nation in 1944 through those two rigidly segregated institutions introduced earlier in the paper, American baseball and the United States Army. A military film, a murder mystery, a baseball movie, *A Soldier's Story* deals with a young black officer investigating the shooting death of a cruel martinet, the sergeant in charge of a unit of black soldiers whose real duties consist of playing baseball. The sergeant's own social and professional ambitions, his bitterness, his boundless hatred of everyone, including himself, condition his contemptuous treatment of the black soldier-ballplayers, especially the Southerners, who serve under him; the men, most of whom played in the Negro Leagues, display a range of attitudes about the war, the army, and baseball, which operates here metaphorically to comprehend all of the problems associated with a segregated society.[6] One scene of many indicates the character of the sergeant, his attitude toward his troops, and some of their reactions to his behavior — no wonder one of them, not some Southern redneck, killed him. He upbraids his soldiers for what he conceives as their sloppiness, laziness, and ignorance, emphasizing a hostility between Northern and Southern blacks, and while insulting them, betrays some of his own complicated and conflicted feelings about race. Its central confrontation also emphasizes the distinctions between military attire and baseball uniforms and therefore between authority and individuality, discipline and freedom, the business of death and the game of life, that frequently pop up in the war movie, underlining the fascinating cinematic connection between war and baseball.[7]

One particularly affecting and perhaps double-edged moment in *A League of Their Own* (1992) creates, with an unwonted subtlety and understatement for a baseball film, or a film directed by Penny Marshall, the simple sadness of racial exclusion in the game. In exactly the kind of purely visual moment that the cinema at its best should always demonstrate, the movie epitomizes the complex social and emotional price of that separation. During a practice of the Rockford Peaches, when a ball gets away, a young black woman retrieves it and pegs it back, making one of the best throws in the film. Appropriately, she appears on the field itself, though not of course in uniform, but in street dress in the fashion of 1944, and demonstrates in that single gesture her suitability to play for the Peaches. Geena Davis's silent acknowledgment of the throw and the young woman's own quiet but obvious pride in her ability shows precisely, in just a few seconds of screen time, the personal loss, the peculiar poignancy in the segregation of baseball at any level, the antiquated, unjustified, meaningless refusal to accept the right of perfectly competent players to participate in the game, the sheer sadness of racism. The brief sequence also underlines the sad reality that even among the excluded — the women who play under and chafe at some stuffy and ridiculous regulations and conditions in the All-American Girls Professional Baseball League — other discriminations still exist; in this instance, as a result, the title takes on an additional, not entirely pleasant meaning — a league of their own, indeed.

In movies dating from and concerned with the post-Robinson era, naturally, black ballplayers finally begin to suit up and play the game. Two of the more entertaining films of that period, both of which figure prominently in some of my own previous discussions of the sport,[8] *It Happens Every Spring* (1949) and *Angels in the Outfield* (1951), strangely and inexplicably, show only white members of their respective teams, the St. Louis Cardinals and the Pittsburgh Pirates.

The 1994 remake of *Angels in the Outfield*, however, as one might expect, redresses that balance, so that the team receiving supernatural assistance, the California Angels (naturally), resembles a contemporary major league baseball team. The athletes, the supernatural figures who help and inspire them, and most important, the manager, reflect some of the realities of baseball today—he California Angels and the heavenly angels are fully racially integrated, which promises something positive at least about the afterlife, and the team's manager is a black man: one sequence, when an outfielder receives divine assistance and makes an impossible catch, comprehends all that progress. The final shot of the sequence also conflicts, perhaps more dramatically than any others, with the history of blacks in baseball films, because it shows not only the black players, manager, and angels, but amazingly, even that largely absent presence in the cinema of baseball, black fans in the stands.

When baseball film moves into our time, as the newer version of *Angels in the Outfield* demonstrates, the fact of the African American presence becomes commonplace, or at least a regular feature within certain defined limits. A kind of benign quota system may operate either by design or accident, which ensures that some acceptable, essentially inoffensive number and percentage of various ethnic groups appear on screen, so that the contemporary baseball movie fulfills the functions of yesterday's war flicks, and in another instance of a connection between baseball and warfare, the baseball team supplants Hollywood's historic bomber crews and infantry platoons. In the past those groupings consisted of some variation on an assortment of young men of several geographic and ethnic backgrounds, including, for example, perhaps an Irish or Italian or Jewish soldier from Brooklyn, mixed in with good *ole* country boys from the South, farm lads from the Midwest, cowboys from Texas, and a clean cut officer from the suburbs of some large city. In accordance with the progress of recent history and the changing ethnicity of both baseball and America, Hollywood teams now include not only the usual identifiable Caucasians and African Americans, but also Latinos and even Asians—who knows, perhaps even those more exotic transplants to the Major Leagues, the Australians, who now play the game may soon be showing up on the screen.

In the generally charming and entirely traditional *Rookie of the Year* (1993), the presence of black players, some of them actual major leaguers in another tradition going back to the 1950s, appears the ordinary state of things; the movie also indicates how times and the baseball film have changed in the inclusion of an exaggeratedly loony coach on the Cubs roster. When 12-year-old Henry Rowengartner first enters the Chicago Cubs clubhouse, the camera routinely shows of course both black and white players mingling in the background. Once again, like the team in the remake of *Angels in the Outfield*, this one boasts a black manager, possibly a prophetic anticipation of the hiring of Don Baylor (though, given the ephemerality of that position in baseball, both will of course be fired sooner or later), whose white pitching coach, addled by a beaning in the minor leagues (by the manager, not incidentally) becomes the shuffling clown formerly played by black actors. The character demonstrates the enduring powers of an archetype, itself derived from the inherent irrationality of a magical sport and an equally magical art, that I like to think of as the baseball goof; he appears in scores of baseball films dating back to the infancy of the form, sometimes as the moronic sidekick, sometimes as a minor source of comic relief, sometimes as the bumbling protagonist who develops into a mature player and person. One of the striking innovations of *Bang the Drum Slowly* (1973), incidentally, occurs in its transformation of the baseball goof played by Robert De Niro into a figure of a sort of heroic pathos. The baseball goof first shows up in a film featuring a black player way back in — where else? — the grand original and template for all these movies, *The Jackie Robinson Story.*

In *The Sandlot* (1993), a weak film liberally sprinkled with both the customary sentimentality and the obligatory touch of fantasy, a group of kids who exemplify the Our Gang style of ethnic variety play an endless game of baseball all summer long, which becomes the means by which they learn all the usual lessons of life. More important, James Earl Jones appears once again, this time as an elderly blind man, a former baseball player himself, who once played ball with the great Babe Ruth, who turns up in a dream sequence. (Jones generously allows that the Babe was nearly as good as he was.) When the kids enter his house, they see a photograph of him and Ruth together in uniform, a perfect and really rather sad example of an integration that of course only occurred in exhibition games and in the arena of desire. The presence of Jones reminds us that his career just might include more links with baseball and reveal more possibilities in the personality of the ballplayer than any other actor's performances — even if no actual black players appear in *Field of Dreams*, his character, the surly writer Terrence Mann, delivers the famous and eloquent set speech on the enduring meaning of baseball for the nation. Interestingly, his first appearance in a baseball uniform occurs in a boxing movie, *The Great White Hope* (1970), where he plays an angry, arrogant, "uppity" black heavyweight champion obviously based on Jack Johnson; as a ruse to deceive the authorities and escape a fraudulent conviction, he dresses as a member of a Negro League team and jumps bail; since as he points out, to the white cops all black men look alike, he can walk out in uniform with the team while another man stands in the window of his mother's apartment, impersonating the champ. The waiting policemen simply see a line of black men dressed in identical baseball uniforms and, of course, the champ escapes.

Sandlot comes near the end of a surprising career in baseball cinema, which takes him from *The Great White Hope* through *Bingo Long's Traveling All-Stars and Motor Kings* and even *Matewan* (1987) to the grandiloquent utterance of *Field of Dreams*. Now, metamorphosed through the magic of baseball and cinema and transformed by the passage of time, he has become the Wise Old Man, repository of memories, dispenser of advice to the young, perhaps even blind seer of visions and dreamer of dreams, the erstwhile excluded spokesman for the glories of their times, those segregated days of the past. Blind like Tiresias, his bat his staff, he now imparts the wisdom of his years and the lore of the game to youngsters, who will learn from him, as the movie promises, the proper conduct of the game and of life.

Finally, as the sport and the art achieve something like a state of integration — though some commentators question the success of that appropriate and inevitable endeavor — the baseball film moves to other racial and ethnic groups for stereotyping. In both *Bull Durham* (1988) and *Major League* (1989), the first a gritty, reasonably authentic, and possibly even the best baseball film of them all, the second a predictable, silly, but mildly entertaining farce, the African American players generally appear to coexist normally with their white teammates and to receive the same cinematic treatment on and off the field, which probably continues the relatively positive and progressive movement of society, baseball, and film. A new ethnic group, however, identified in both movies as Latin, and in one case, specifically Afro-Cuban, now appears for comic purposes. In one of several shots and sequences from each film, a baseball player mingles Catholicism, superstition, and paganism in some semblance of Voodoo to make his bat more potent, in one case to hit the curve ball; later, as the rituals and prayers also assist in the field, to take the curse off his glove.[9] Somehow the comedy appears less threatening and offensive than in other manifestations in other movies, perhaps in part because both teams are already well stocked with fools, clowns, and buffoons of all races and yes, baseball goofs — the new version of the Hollywood infantry platoon — and neither the African American nor the Latin American players stand out from the rest of the comic troupe.

Those last two motion pictures, whatever their merit, may however indicate something of what the future holds for baseball movies. They may represent the first tentative steps toward transforming the African American ballplayer into a major character in films that otherwise choose to exploit other sources of difference, either for comic or serious purposes, fixing on the religious rather than the racial minorities, especially focusing on the Latin Americans — from Puerto Rico, the Dominican Republic,

Mexico, Venezuela, Nicaragua — who have risen so rapidly to prominence in organized baseball. (Both films, incidentally, present the aggressive Christian fundamentalism that exists in so many major and minor league clubhouses as something of a joke, with on the one hand a foolish religious lad who marries the town tramp and on the other an obnoxious veteran who takes offense at the Afro-Cuban's comic religious ceremony.) The great waves of foreign immigration that brought, in Emma Lazarus's unkind phrase, the "wretched refuse" of the world to this continent (including my grandparents, I hasten to state), and the consequent development that baseball reflects throughout its history, continue to emerge in the game. After the many Irish, German, Italian, Polish, and Jewish ballplayers, the Hispanics represent the largest immigrant group to thrive in the sport, and in years to come, the increasing number of Asian players — several well known Japanese and Koreans already play in the Major Leagues — may find themselves generating the laughs that quite properly arouse resentment in other minority fans and viewers. Sadly and ironically, of course, African Americans predated all those ethnic groups as residents, albeit unwilling ones, of the country, but were forced to wait the longest for their own day in the sun of the Major Leagues. At some date, many years from now, perhaps the pendulum will swing in another direction, and Caucasian Americans themselves may constitute a new minority, as they do in basketball and football, and perhaps our African American brothers and sisters will be commenting on the history of our representation in baseball and baseball cinema. But then perhaps also Jackie Robinson's noble speech will more correctly describe the state of American society. To paraphrase in a different context an eloquent utterance from William Faulkner's great novel *Absalom, Absalom!*, then I who regard you will also have sprung from the loins of African kings.

Notes

1. For a fuller exploration of religion and resurrection, see, e.g., my paper, "The Church of Baseball, Baseball and the Church," delivered at the Cooperstown Symposium, June 1996.

2. Harold Seymour, *Baseball: The People's Game* (New York: Oxford University Press, 1990), p. 541.

3. Organized baseball implicitly promotes the notion that the sport exists under the custody of the Major Leagues, while in actuality, it truly belongs to the people and its truest versions — in film and in life — play out in the most informal and unorganized ways. See, for example, George Grella, "The Baseball Moment in American Film," *Aethlon: The Journal of Sport Literature* XIV: 2 (Spring, 1998), pp. 7-16.

4. See, for example, William Brashler, *The Story of Negro League Baseball* (New

York: Ticknor & Fields, 1994) for the story of John McGraw's attempt to sign Charlie Grant, star of the Chicago Columbia Giants, as an Indian named Chief Tokohama (p. 21).

5. Howard Good, *Diamonds in the Dark: America, Baseball, and the Movies* (Lanham, Md.: The Scarecrow Press, 1997), p. 148.

6. For a slightly different view of the film's themes, see Ed Guerrero, *Framing Blackness: The African American Image in Film* (Philadelphia: Temple University Press, 1993). Guerrero suggests (p. 135) that the "varied personalities and social outlooks of the platoon members construct a contest of black ideologies that leads to the sergeant's death and the eventual exposure and capture of his killer," and sees the sergeant as a "black parody of Hitler," whose ideas conflict with the "range of black philosophical perspectives from a rural survivalist blues ideology to the militant black activism of ... Peterson (Denzel Washington)."

7. See my paper, "Uniforms and Uniforms: Baseball and the War Movie," Cooperstown Symposium, 1997.

8. See my paper, "Baseball Mystery, Cinema Magic," Cooperstown Symposium, 1995.

9. See "The Church of Baseball, Baseball and the Church," *op. cit.*, for a discussion of religion in baseball and baseball movies.

"I Haven't Got Ballplayers. I've Got Girls": Portrayals of Women in Baseball Film

Robert Rudd and Marshall G. Most

Early in the 1992 film *A League of Their Own*, former major league slugger Jimmy Dugan (played by Tom Hanks), makes no secret of his feelings about women in baseball. Drunk and angry at what he considers the humiliating task of managing the Rockford Peaches of the All-American Girls Professional Baseball League, he confronts his boss and thunders, "I haven't got ballplayers. I've got girls. Girls are what you sleep with after the game, not what you coach during the game." Dugan's opinion of the limited role of women in baseball is one shared by many in American culture.

Later in *A League of Their Own*, Dugan's view undergoes a profound change, a transformation, some might say, that is symbolic of the shift in American culture's attitudes toward the roles women might play in professional baseball. However, as we examine the portrayals of women in Hollywood films about baseball, produced over more than sixty years, it becomes clear that little has changed. The reality is that the role of women within baseball's cultural vision remains extremely limited.

Baseball Ideology, American Culture, and Hollywood Film

Baseball, "the National Pastime," is said to embody those basic values which underlie the nation itself, reflecting the wholesome, rural values upon which the nation was presumably founded. In his history of the development of baseball's ideology, Steven Riess (1980) observes that ideology was largely the product of sportswriters and publicists in the Progressive Era promoting, for their own purposes, an idealized vision of the game. Their vision found favor with other interests in American culture, and together they endorsed it as a way to "provide the symbols, myths and legends society needed to bind its members together" (p. 5), particularly during a period of social strain caused by an increasingly industrialized, urbanized society. As Riess' analysis makes clear, the game of baseball has been viewed by its proponents not simply as a *reflection* of traditional American values, but also as a *means of cultivating* those values in a modern industrial society.

Of particular importance to this process of socialization was the rise of the sports hero. The baseball hero, according to the game's ideology, should serve as an ideal role model for American youth, teaching through example such values as hard work and moral virtue (Lipsky, 1981).

The ideology of baseball, especially the idealized image of the baseball hero, was constructed with some enthusiasm throughout the 20th Century by Hollywood filmmakers. As Berman (1982) noted, American baseball films have been especially pure in reflecting an idealized vision of the game and in keeping the mythology of baseball intact. But these films are more than simple reflections of an idealized view of the game. They are also reflections of an idealized view of American culture. The popular baseball film constructs images of a larger moral order, and defines the characteristics of the ideal baseball hero/citizen within that order.

In her analysis of the construction of gender in baseball, Ferrante (1994) contends that baseball is "an expression of the naturalness of a patriarchal order that regularly associates positive meanings with men and negative meanings with women" (p. 9). "Baseball," she continues, "embodies a nostalgia for a pure and perfect experience of individual, masculine achievement and that the sacredness of that ideal is protected against the mundane by a taboo against women." Women, according to Ferrante, have traditionally been restricted to auxiliary roles in baseball, primarily as providers of comfort and support to men. Even such limited roles might have been denied women had they not been included in the community of baseball as spectators. During the Progressive Era, women were encouraged to become involved as observers of the game, largely because it was believed a feminine presence brought greater respectability to professional baseball (Riess, 1980). In the idealized community constructed within baseball's cultural vision, the positions assigned to women remain anything but ideal.

In his review of the roles of women characters in baseball literature, Solomon (1985) found that women generally do not appear in baseball novels, or are portrayed as "either complaisant wives, stupid bimbos–or sexual threats" (p. 19) when they do appear. As we shall see, however, in baseball films, women are central, and frequently positive characters, often playing significant roles in constructing the ideal community and moral order envisioned in baseball's ideology. Nevertheless, the nature of those roles remains narrowly defined.

Dickerson (1991) identifies two principal roles for women in baseball films. The first is the evil "vamp" who interferes with and threatens the hero's success. The second is the loyal, wholesome hometown girl who serves as a source of strength and power for the male hero, and with whom the hero eventually settles down. Together, these two representations construct a vision of the proper role and place for women within baseball's cultural vision.

Temptresses, Vamps, and "Good Time Girls"

Although not as typical as women who serve as sources of strength and support for their heroic counterparts, women as a threat to the baseball hero are not uncommon in baseball films. The threat posed by these women can range from distracting the player, to literally endangering his life. Occasionally, this theme has been treated lightheartedly, as in the 1943 comedy *Ladies' Day*. In this film, pitcher Wacky Waters tends to lose his focus — and his control — every time he falls in love, which is quite frequently. When he falls in love with and marries the alluring Pepita Zurita late in the season, thus threatening the Sox' chances in the World Series, a group of the Sox wives conspire to keep the two apart until after the Series, even kidnapping Pepita and holding her hostage in a hotel for a week. Ultimately, however, the value of true love and marriage is upheld. In a sudden switch, Wacky falters in the final game of the World Series, until Pepita escapes and makes her way to the ballpark. Her sudden appearance, rather than distracting Waters, revives the struggling star, who not only regains his pitching form, but even drives in the winning runs. Thus, the "threat" posed by women to the Sox' star pitcher is, in the final reel, dissolved in favor of the more common role of women as supporters and nurturers.

More typically, however, women who threaten the success and well-being of the baseball hero are portrayed as more sinister. In *Rhubarb* (1951), for example, the sole human survivor of Brooklyn Loons owner Thaddeus

J. Banner, daughter Myra, is portrayed as so evil that, upon his death, Banner leaves the team to his cat Rhubarb, rather than his spoiled, disagreeable daughter. She responds true to character by trying to kill the cat, among other schemes.

This selfish pursuit of their own material interests is the common thread characterizing the "evil" women of baseball films. In *Bang the Drum Slowly* (1973), "mercenary good time girl Katie" (Erickson, 1992, p.68) convinces the dying and gullible Bruce Pearson that she loves him, in hopes he will make her the beneficiary of his insurance policy; a plan thwarted by Pearson's best-friend, roommate, and insurance agent, Henry Wiggen. Even though she has fallen in love with New York Knights' star Roy Hobbs, Memo Paris eventually poisons him, at the behest of her keeper, gambler Gus Sands, to try to prevent Hobbs from playing in the championship game (*The Natural*, 1984). In *Major League* (1989) owner Rachel Phelps does not resort to quite such drastic means, but still does everything within her power to destroy the Cleveland Indians, so she can break her stadium lease and move the team to Florida. And, in *Major League II* (1994), pitcher Rick Vaughn allows himself to be transformed into a selfish jerk by his agent/lover, Flannery, who then callously makes plans to dump him when his career begins going downhill — only to return once his career begins taking off once again.

In these films, the baseball hero is confronted by the traditional temptress; the woman who seeks to use him solely for her own, selfish interests and who, in doing so, threatens not only his career, but even his life. Contrasting with the greed and selfishness of the Myra Banners and Memo Parises, however, is the much more dominant stereotype in baseball films; the supportive, nurturing savior of the baseball hero. Where the vamp provides a negative example of the actions of women in baseball's moral order, the nurturer and redeemer represents the proper role of women within baseball's cultural vision.

Supporters, Saviors, and "Companions for Life"

The Lou Gehrig of *Pride of the Yankees* (1942) is the epitome of the ideal baseball hero — humble, hardworking, morally virtuous, and one of the game's greatest players. But while it is Lou's talent and character which make him a baseball hero, it is Eleanor Gehrig's nurturing and support which, in the film, enable him to fulfill that role. Eleanor Gehrig's presence, from the very beginning of his career, ensures Lou will be a "hero of the peaceful paths of everyday life," rather than an ordinary, rough ballplayer. And she will become the prototype for the woman behind every good baseball hero.

Eleanor ensures Lou's virtue by being everything this baseball hero could want. When Lou reminds her that they honeymooned in Yankee Stadium, Eleanor replies, "We've never had anything but [a honeymoon]". After he is honored for playing in his 2000th consecutive game, Lou thanks Eleanor for "being the greatest fan a man ever had," for not letting him quit, and for nursing him through injury and illness. As he recounts the reasons he considers himself "the luckiest man on the face of the earth" in his farewell appearance at Yankee Stadium, none is more prominent than Eleanor, whom he calls his "companion for life." She is the perfect wife of traditional marriage vows: she loves, honors, and cherishes Lou for better or worse (richer and poorer are never an issue for the Gehrigs), in sickness and in health, till death does them part. The Gehrigs, in baseball cinema's cultural view, are the ideal — the perfect hero and his perfect wife, the model relationship, and moral order to which other couples in baseball cinema will aspire.

The early Babe Ruth of *The Babe Ruth Story* (1948), on the other hand, is not remotely as virtuous as the cinematic Lou Gehrig. Much of this film's narrative follows Babe's attainment of the moral characteristics of the baseball hero, which were so much a part of Lou Gehrig's essential character. The Babe and his future savior/wife, Claire, meet early in the film in a restaurant, when Claire proves to a struggling Ruth that the reason he has lost four in a row, and been knocked out of the game early in his last five pitching starts, is that he is telegraphing his curve ball to opposing batters by sticking his tongue out during the windup. As a result of this knowledge, she saves Babe Ruth's baseball career. And it is in this early scene that a central subplot of the film is established — the great Bambino's pursuit of the love of his life, Claire.

Winning Claire's affections is not an easy task for the Babe, an arrogant, self-indulgent individual who likes to spend his evenings throwing money around in nightclubs. A number of early scenes depict Claire's continual rejection of Babe. The reason for Ruth's failure to impress Claire, these scenes suggest, is that at this stage in his life/career he has not yet acquired the qualities of humility or moral virtue that are characteristic of the true baseball hero. As a result of his conceit and his lack of moral discipline, Babe not only fails to win over the object of his affections, but his life on and off the field begins to decline. He is suspended by the Yankees for two weeks for being a constant discipline problem. His playing has begun to slump. And there is also the matter of his drinking. It is at this point in Babe's life that Claire intervenes again, this time, not simply as a source of baseball knowledge, but as a source of moral virtue. It is Christmas Eve, and a roundly inebriated Ruth, dressed as Santa Claus, is preparing to enter a children's hospital to distribute presents. As fate would have it, he runs into Claire who is just leaving the hospital. To this point, Claire has been avoiding the immature and irresponsible Bambino, but now she prevents him from entering the hospital, confronting him about his bad behavior. After telling him the story of a young urchin who had begged her for a quarter on the street, so he could buy a Babe Ruth hat, just like all the other kids have, she reminds the Babe of his position as role model for America's youth. "How you act, they act," she tells him. This moment is a turning point in Ruth's life and career. The contrite, humbled Ruth allows Claire to take him home, and begins the transition from great ballplayer to true baseball hero (*The Babe Ruth Story*, 1948). She imparts to Babe Ruth the moral virtue he has so far lacked.

In *The Babe Ruth Story* (1948), Claire Ruth serves as a source of knowledge, virtue, and inspiration for the great Bambino. Babe Ruth might have saved baseball, but it was Claire who saved Babe Ruth — as the source of knowledge regarding the telegraphing of his curve ball, as the source of moral virtue in convincing Babe to reform his personal life, and as the source of inspiration, whose love gives Babe the strength and determination to redeem both his career and his life. While perhaps not quite as dramatically as the original, the Claire of the 1992 production of *The Babe* performs a similar role over 40 years later, serving once again as a source of knowledge, support, and virtue for baseball's best-known hero.

Claire Ruth is not a unique figure in baseball cinema, a mythic realm in which saviors abound. In baseball films, at least, it is often women who perceive what the hero needs at any given moment in his life, and fulfills that need. It is Adam Paluchek's romantic interest Christy Lobert, who is also the daughter of the Giants' tryout camp director, Hans Lobert, who delivers the crucial lecture at the crucial moment in *The Big Leaguer* (1953). When top prospect Adam Paluchek, feeling guilty about deceiving his father, who believed Paluchek was at law school, decides to leave camp in the middle of the night, Christy tells him that "running out on your father is not as bad as running out on yourself." Paluchek learns the lesson of being true to himself, and ends up being signed by the Giants. In a similar vein, when, in the early Joe E. Brown comedy *Elmer the Great* (1933), Gentryville's star pitcher, Elmer Kane, is offered a contract by the Chicago Cubs, he declares he does not intend to go to Chicago, but plans to remain in Gentryville to be near his beloved Nellie. Nellie, recognizing that being signed by the Cubs is the greatest opportunity in Kane's life, professes that she has no similar feelings for Kane, and fires him from his job as a deliveryman for her general store. Kane, of course, becomes a star pitcher for the Cubs. But, her role, as Kane's guardian angel, does not end there. Later in the season, when the naive Kane becomes involved with gamblers, she pays off his debts, bails him out of jail, where he landed after punching out one of the gamblers, and convinces him to return to the Cubs for the final game of the World Series against the Yankees, which Kane wins. He and Nellie are, of course, married at the end of the film.

In *The Monty Stratton Story* (1949), Ethel Stratton not only remains devotedly and lovingly by her bitter husband's side, following the hunting accident which ended his career, but inspires him to begin rebuilding his life by reminding him of his own words, "a man's got to know where he's going." Similarly, in the 1999 release *For Love of the Game*, aging Detroit Tiger pitcher Billy Chapel's love interest Jane Aubrey is instrumental in Chapel's recovery from a terrible injury to his pitching hand. Chapel, frustrated by a lack of progress in his rehabilitation, accuses those around him of giving up on him. Jane, a single mother struggling up the career ladder in the New York publishing industry, tells him, "You need to let me teach you something about what I know. About how sometimes life seems like it's slamming you down, but it's really giving you a gift." It is one of the few scenes in which Jane, portrayed in much of the film as insecure and weepy, is shown as a strong, capable character. In *The Winning Team*, Aimee Alexander, who walked out on her husband, Grover, because of his drinking, learns that he actually suffered from a neurological disorder. She searches the country for him, finally tracking him down in a seedy carnival. With the aid of friend and Cardinals manager Rogers Hornsby, whom she had called on for help, she helps Alexander rebuild his life, marriage, and his career. Alexander credits his wife as being the source of his strength and inspiration, telling her, "without you, I'm just half a man, waiting to black out" (*The Winning Team*, 1952).

The Natural's (1984) Roy Hobbs is not unlike the Babe Ruth of *The Babe Ruth Story* (1948): a basically good man who succumbs to temptation but returns to virtue with the help of a good woman. It is not until the reappearance of Iris Gaines — Roy's childhood sweetheart and the woman he had proposed to sixteen years before — that Roy can achieve the mythic stature and virtue required of a baseball hero. After sixteen years, unable to watch him fail she later confesses, Iris attends a game at Wrigley Field where Roy and the Knights are suffering a typically dismal day. Roy strikes out three times. But during his final at-bat Iris, wearing a bright white dress and hat, backlit from the sun in an angelic glow, stands up in the crowd. Roy catches a glimpse of her through the late afternoon sun and returns to the batter's box to hit a massive game-winning home run that shatters the scoreboard clock. The following day Roy hits four home runs. Iris' reappearance is the inspiration for Roy's almost supernatural effort during the remainder of the season.

Later in the film, after Roy is poisoned by the evil Memo Paris (the classic Hollywood vamp stereotype juxtaposed against the angelic Iris), it is up to Iris again to provide inspiration and wisdom. She must provide Roy the strength to triumph over evil (as well as the Pirates) in the final playoff game for the pennant. As Roy lies in the hospital, trying to decide whether to risk his life by playing in the deciding playoff game against Pittsburgh, it is Iris Gaines who transforms Roy Hobbs into a true baseball hero, supplying the knowledge and wisdom Roy needs to emerge as moral exemplar. "I believe we have two lives," she tells him, "the one we learn with and the life we live with after that." And, reminiscent of Claire's speech to Babe, she tells him, "With or without the records, they'll remember you. Think of all those young boys you've influenced. There's so many of them." When his silent reflections lead him to summon the memory of his father and his love for baseball, rather than producing another statement of self-pity, we know Iris has taught the lesson well. Roy Hobbs has acquired the insight that leads to humility — a crucial characteristic of a true baseball hero. With the words "God, I love baseball," Roy vows to play, and blasts a spectacular game-winning home run in the bottom of the ninth inning to win the pennant.

The savior role assigned to women continues into the 1990s. In *Mr. Baseball* (1992), it is Hiroto, daughter of the Chunichi Dragons manager and future wife of American slugger Jack Elliot, who provides the wisdom, and the discipline, at times, necessary for Elliot to rebuild his character and his career, and finally achieve happiness and fulfillment both on the field and off. And in the 1996 film *Ed*, it is Jack Cooper's love interest, Lydia, who delivers the wisdom and insight into his character flaws that enable Jack Cooper to succeed in both the game of baseball and the game of life. When Cooper's roommate and team mascot/third baseman, the chimp Ed Sullivan, is sold to another team by the owner's greedy son, Lydia convinces Jack he should steal him back, and forces Cooper — who has a tendency to be concerned solely with his own pitching performance — to recognize his responsibility to others. "When Jack Cooper is in trouble, you work twice as hard. When it's someone else, it's just too much trouble," she tells him. "If your best friend can't count on you, who can?" Lydia's daughter Liz reinforces the lesson, telling him, "Don't choke now, dude." Cooper finally learns the true meaning of community, and the value of being willing to sacrifice for others. He rescues Ed from his abusive new owners, wins the final game, is signed by the Los Angeles Dodgers (Tommy Lasorda says to pay him whatever he wants), and in the final scene drives off to Los Angeles with new wife Lydia, daughter Liz, and Ed.

The ideal baseball hero, according to the "official" ideology of baseball, is humble, possesses a strong work ethic, and is the epitome of moral virtue, refraining from such vices as smoking, drinking, and womanizing (Riess, 1980). It is a conservative, puritanical moral order which is constructed and endorsed in baseball films. And the transformation from simply being a great player to the status of true baseball hero is, in baseball films, portrayed principally as a process of developing these characteristics. It is often the role of women, these films suggest, to bring about that transformation and to establish a moral order which reflects these characteristics of the idealized baseball hero. And although the ways in which the central female character functions to bring about this ideological vision varies somewhat from one film to the next, the nature of that order and the place of women within that order are quite consistent. In the end, the "ideal" order envisioned in these popular films is one in which the woman settles comfortably into her place by her hero's side, providing the love and support he needs to become all that he can be. The message is quite clear. Behind every good baseball hero, stands a good woman.

The Conundrum of Annie Savoy

One film which, on the surface at least, appears to challenge many of the gendered assumptions of earlier baseball films is *Bull Durham* (1988). Consistent with earlier films, *Bull Durham* (1988) offers a similar, though considerably more subtle and less mythic transformation of the male hero by a female savior. In this film, the independent loner Crash Davis, who has moved from one minor-league ballpark to the next for the past twelve years, is tempered and domesticated by the film's female lead, Annie Savoy. Indeed, throughout the film she is portrayed as the only person who has anything to offer the aging loner. And it is Annie Savoy who emerges to provide a sense of purpose to his life at a most critical time for a baseball hero—the end of his playing career. After hitting the home run which gives him the record for minor league home runs, Crash returns to Durham and to Annie Savoy. He tells her that he has quit playing baseball. It is evident that, for the first time, there is more to life for Crash Davis than playing baseball. He is ready to settle, and to move on to the next stage of his life, hopefully as a manager, and clearly with Annie Savoy. Just as Claire served to help Babe Ruth "grow-up," so too does Annie Savoy serve to teach Crash Davis that there is more to life than playing the game. By the end of the film, we see a more mature Crash Davis; for the first time, he seems to need what someone else has to offer, and commits himself to something more than just finishing out the season.

What seems to separate *Bull Durham* (1988) from the earlier stories of such epic heroes as Lou Gehrig, Babe Ruth, and Roy Hobbs, however, is the initially feminist character of Annie Savoy. On the surface, *Bull Durham* seems to counter the patriarchal order of these earlier films with an affirmation of feminist values of strength, independence, empowerment, and the control of women over their own sexuality. The film begins with Annie Savoy explaining that at the beginning of every baseball season she chooses one Bulls player to hook up with during the season. She gives the boys an education and makes them feel confident, she says, and in return they make her "feel pretty." It is Annie Savoy who assumes the lead both in choosing her sexual relationships, as well as in directing the nature of her sexual encounters.

In addition to her sexual independence and empowerment, Annie Savoy is seen as economically independent, living alone in a large older home in Durham. A part-time teacher at the local junior college, it is evident she is not dependent upon anyone for her financial support. Finally, Annie Savoy is portrayed as knowing a great deal about the game of baseball. In an early scene, during rookie sensation Nuke Laroosh's first pitching start with the Bulls, she sends a note to him in the dugout telling him he is not bending his back on his follow-through. This piece of advice enables the wild Laroosh to regain his control. Throughout the film her advice to Laroosh, from teaching him to breathe through his eyelids to having him wear garters to distract him and keep him from thinking too much about his pitching, dramatically improves his pitching performance. It is clear in the film that Annie Savoy knows a great deal about both the mechanics and the psychology of baseball.

Such images of an independent, knowledgeable, and empowered woman are, however, only surface images. In the end, the independent Annie Savoy, in the mold of Eleanor Gehrig, Claire Ruth, and Iris Gaines, devotes herself fully to the male hero of the film, Crash Davis. Indeed, the central story line of the film centers around the romantic attachment of Annie Savoy and Crash Davis, and the domestication of them both. And despite the tempering and maturing of Crash Davis by Annie Savoy, the most striking transformation within *Bull Durham* is that of Annie herself. At the end of the film, sitting on the porch with Crash, who has just announced he has quit playing baseball, Annie Savoy announces she has given up boys. When Crash asks if she thinks he could make it as a manager, she is quick to assure him he could, and begins to expound on the non-linear nature of baseball. Crash cuts her off, saying that he wants to hear all of her theories about baseball, and he will, but for the moment, he just wants to be. Tearfully, wide-eyed, Annie Savoy responds, "I can do that, too." The strong, independent Annie Savoy, who at the beginning of the film made it clear that she did the choosing, is no more.

Granted, the role of Annie Savoy in *Bull Durham* is considerably more complex than that of the central female characters in the other three films. In *The Babe Ruth Story* (1948), for example, it is Babe Ruth who was "redeemed," with Claire Ruth serving as the redeemer. In *Bull Durham* (1988), it is not only the male hero Crash Davis who is brought within the desired moral order by Annie Savoy, but Annie herself is "redeemed," and also returned to the preferred moral order within the film. While films such as *The Babe Ruth Story* (1948) and *The Natural* (1984) serve principally to temper the excesses of masculinity in the male hero, and to reclaim him into a moral order more consistent with the needs and values of the modern industrial state, *Bull Durham* (1988) serves also to reclaim what contemporary patriarchal values perceive as the excesses of feminism into that same moral order. Like other Hollywood films of the 1980s (Ryan and Kellner, 1988), *Bull Durham* appears as a reaction against feminism; a conservative return to a patriarchal vision of romance.

In the end, the moral order which emerges in *Bull Durham* is very much the same as that which has emerged in baseball films before it. In the final scene, it is Annie Savoy, in the tradition of Eleanor Gehrig, Claire Ruth, and Iris Gaines, who offers support and encouragement to Crash Davis as he prepares to pursue his managerial career, and who gives up her career to commit to the relationship. It is Annie Savoy who tearfully assures Crash Davis, "I can do that, too."

Shifts in the Portrayals of Women

The foregoing analysis of Bull Durham should not suggest that there have been no changes in the portrayal of women in baseball films through the years. In several ways, contemporary films reflect changing roles of women within our culture, and offer — on the surface at least — a critique of some of the traditional, patriarchal values which have dominated our culture, as well as cinematic representations of women in earlier eras.

The first notable change is in the representation of women baseball players. As Ferrante (1994) notes, until only recently historical records of the game have virtually ignored the fact that women have, since the Victorian era, played professional baseball. The tendency to ignore the role of women in baseball as *players* of the game has, obviously, been characteristic of baseball films as well. Two films in the 1980s and 1990s, however, actually feature women as professional baseball players. The 1983 film *Blue Skies Again* tells the fictional story of Paula Fradkin, who becomes the first woman player to make it to the major leagues, and purports, in the process, to confront the range of sexist values which have inhibited women from achieving success not just in baseball, but throughout American culture. Unfortunately, as Erickson (1992) rather generously observes, the film's excellent premises are "laid low by muddled execution." Far more successful is *A League of Their Own* (1992), a fictionalized account of the All-American Girls Professional Baseball League during the Second World War. This film not only portrays women as good baseball players worthy of professional status, it also ridicules some of the absurdities these players were forced to endure (e.g., attending charm school, and wearing short skirts while playing) in order to assure the American culture that, even though they were playing baseball, they were still "ladies."

Beyond these two portrayals of women as professional baseball players, there has also been a slight change in the representations of other women's roles. For example, *The Fan*, a 1996 film, features a tough, aggressive sports reporter named Jewel Stern, known for asking hard questions and doing tough interviews. While the reporter featured in the 1951 version of *Angels in the Outfield* normally reported on household hints for her paper, and knew nothing about baseball, Stern is extremely knowledgeable about the game and the contemporary athlete. And even though Stern, like so many women before her, provides struggling Giants' star Bobby Rayburn with some much needed insight into his own character which helps him pull out of an horrendous slump and become a bit more of a human being (telling him he is putting too much pressure on himself and that no one could live up to the expectations he has set for himself), she does not become romantically involved with the star and does not, like Jennifer Page (*Angels in the Outfield*, 1951) or nearly all the other women who serve as a source of support and growth for baseball heroes, end up marrying him. *The Fan* stands out as the one film that acknowledges it is possible for women to know a great deal about the game, to work as talented and successful professional sports reporters, and even offer some wisdom and insight to the baseball hero as a professional herself, without becoming romantically involved.

Another subtle change in the representation of women has occurred in the portrayal of single mothers. *Rookie of the Year* (1993), *Little Big League* (1994), *Ed* (1996), and *For Love of the Game* (1999) all feature single mothers in strong, positive roles. Most striking in comparison with an earlier portrayal of a single mother in the 1950s in *Roogie's Bump* (1954) are the portrayals of the mothers of Cubs child/pitcher Henry Rowengartner in *Rookie of the Year*, and of 12-year-old owner/manager of the Minnesota Twins, Billy Heywood, in *Little Big League*. Whereas Roogie Rigsby's mother in *Roogie's Bump* essentially turned her son over to Boxey, the manager of the Brooklyn Dodgers, once the child became a baseball player, and continued to defer to Boxey's judgment regarding what would be best for Roogie, both Mary Rowengartner (*Rookie of the Year*) and Jenny Heywood (*Little Big League*) play strong and important roles in the development of their sons' careers, and lives. Mary Rowengartner, for example, gets rid of her boyfriend, who was also Henry's agent, when it turns out he is simply trying to exploit the boy — flattening him with a right hook in the process. We also learn at the end of the film that she was once a baseball player herself. It is her old glove, not his father's, that Henry is wearing. And, all the stories she told him about his father as a baseball player were really about her own playing days. It is she who tells Henry what pitch to throw to get the final out in the division-winning game against the New York Mets. When Billy Heywood begins to take himself too seriously, Jenny Heywood grounds him for a day, forcing him to miss a game, for swearing at an umpire. It is Jenny Heywood who helps her son understand what he is becoming, and to return to being the manager who told his team the only thing that mattered was that they have fun.

The third notable change in the representation of women in recent films is that in three of the contemporary films there is some attention given to the ways women have been victimized by those patriarchal values which earlier films have consistently endorsed. In the 1992 version of the life and career of Babe Ruth (*The Babe*), for example, Ruth's first wife, Helen, is presented as a tragic victim of the early Ruth's immaturity and self-centeredness. Unable to play the role of dutiful, supportive wife to an unfaithful, carousing, sometimes abusive husband, Helen finally leaves Ruth. At the same time, however, the film, through its later redemption of Ruth, suggests that Helen was not victimized by "true" patriarchal values, but rather by Ruth's failure to live up to the genuine values of the idealized baseball hero. In other words, the expectations of women within a patriarchal order are not seriously challenged, as Ruth's cruel treatment of Helen is attributed not to the unquestioned, and often unstated, values of patriarchy itself, but rather to Ruth's individual deviancies within what remains a conservative, patriarchal, moral order. Similarly, although audiences learn in *Major League* (1989) that Jake Taylor's wife, Lynn, left him as a result of Taylor's immaturity and infidelity, they also see her return to Taylor, resuming her rightful place as cheering supporter in the stands, when it is clear that Taylor has grown up, and forsaken his earlier ways.

Perhaps the most explicit challenge to the expectations of a woman's role in the life of the baseball hero which characterize most baseball films, comes in a 1985 film, *The Slugger's Wife*. Like Grover Cleveland Alexander in *The Winning Team*, over 30 years before him, Atlanta Braves slugger Darryl Palmer receives his inspiration and power from his wife Debbie sitting in the stands. The problem is, Debbie has her own career as a pop singer. Smothered by Palmer's possessiveness and insistence that she sacrifice her professional life for his, Debbie finally leaves him. Although they do not completely reunite at the end of the film, audiences are left with the likely possibility of a reconciliation, as Palmer has evidently learned love means allowing one's partner the freedom to live her life as well.

Discussion

Despite these subtle changes in more recent films, the role of women within baseball's cultural vision remains essentially the same. As Degler (1980) observed, the proper role of women within the patriarchal value system is to nurture and care for their husbands and children, as well as to shape and direct their husbands' moral behavior. That role is well defined within baseball's value system as well. "Baseball as a cultural icon constructs woman as the Other, whose function is to bring comfort, meaning and identity to the One" (Ferrante, 1994, p. 247). And such is the role of the women in these films. The transformation from baseball player to baseball hero is, in these films, a process of tempering the excesses of masculinity — of containing the undisciplined dimensions of individualism and of redefining masculinity within a moral order more consistent with the needs of the modern bureaucratic and industrial society. Like women/saviors in other genres of Hollywood films, the central role of women in these films is to "civilize" the male hero (and, in the case of *Bull Durham* [1988], to at the same time be "civilized" by him), to temper his unbridled masculinity with the more "feminine" characteristics (at least according to cultural gender definitions) of moral virtue and humility and thus assure his salvation. Their primary function is to inspire, to support, to nurture, to guide the baseball hero so he can achieve greatness on the field while maintaining a virtuous existence off the field (and after baseball).

Having thus completed the tasks of tempering the male athlete's swaggering masculinity with a fierce moral fire, while inspiring his play and supporting his aspirations, the savior then fades into relative obscurity and decided subordination, a mere spousal spectator to the continuing saga of a man now ready to assume the mantle of Baseball Hero. Eleanor Gehrig (*Pride of the Yankees*, 1942) establishes the precedent for other women of baseball cinema to follow. Although she is a central facet of Lou's life, she has no life beyond his. Her function in the film is to maintain the ideal romantic marriage. After Claire marries Babe (*The Babe Ruth Story*, 1948) she abandons her own career on the stage, and we see her only in her role of caring and devoted wife — rooting for the hero at ball games, offering encouragement when he is down, and crying at his bedside as he is dying from cancer. And, to cite two more examples, this is the role that Iris Gaines (*The Natural*, 1984) and Annie Savoy (*Bull Durham*, 1988) seemed destined for at the conclusion of their film sagas as well: Iris watching approvingly as father and son play catch, Annie sitting teary-eyed on the porch swing with Crash Davis.

What is particularly noteworthy in many baseball films is the power of the central female characters. Each plays a prominent role in building the type of world envisioned in baseball's cultural ideology. Despite the influential role of women in transforming the male hero, however, these films serve not as expressions of feminist values or a challenge to traditional patriarchal gender definitions, but rather as reflections of those values. These women serve not to challenge or redefine masculinity in a way which reflects feminist values, but rather in a way which adapts masculinity to the needs of the modern industrial culture while preserving dominant, traditional patriarchal values. Indeed, when feminist values are present, as in *Bull Durham* (1988), they are incorporated back into the preferred moral order, just as the undisciplined excesses of masculine individuality are contained within these films.

A central function of ideology, of course, is to foster not only the illusion that the dominant social, political, economic, or, in this case, moral order serves the interests of those whom it actually dominates, but also the illusion that this order is one which all have accepted freely, and which all have a voice in shaping. Baseball films serve as significant examples of this legitimizing process and function of ideology. In many cases, the world established in these films is presented as one which reflects feminine values and as one which is willingly acceded to and even constructed by women. It is a double twist that Hollywood's mirrors of illusion have offered to women here. Not only does this world serve your needs, they are told, but it is one which you have helped build, and which reflects your values.

From the 1930s through the 1990s, baseball films expressed a set of values that permeated our culture. The continued expression of these values, and the continuing popularity of these films, reflects how deeply ingrained these values remain. However, just as all media serve not only to reflect but to shape culture as well, so too do these films work to legitimize, naturalize, and perpetuate a moral order which embraces puritanical and patriarchal values. What is most striking when these cinematic visions of American culture, which span more than 60 years, are placed side by side is the realization of how little distance we have traveled.

Filmography

Chronological Listing

Elmer the Great	1933	The Slugger's Wife	1985
Pride of the Yankees	1942	Bull Durham	1988
Ladies' Day	1943	Field of Dreams	1989
The Babe Ruth Story	1948	Major League	1989
The Monty Stratton Story	1949	A League of Their Own	1992
Angels in the Outfield	1951	Mr. Baseball	1992
Rhubarb	1951	The Babe	1992
The Winning Team	1952	Rookie of the Year	1993
The Big Leaguer	1953	Little Big League	1994
Roogie's Bump	1954	Major League II	1994
Bang the Drum Slowly	1973	Ed	1996
Blue Skies Again	1983	The Fan	1996
The Natural	1984	For Love of the Game	1999

Alphabetical Listing

Angels in the Outfield	1951	A League of Their Own	1992
The Babe	1992	Little Big League	1994
The Babe Ruth Story	1948	Major League	1989
Bang the Drum Slowly	1973	Major League II	1994
The Big Leaguer	1953	The Monty Stratton Story	1949
Blue Skies Again	1983	Mr. Baseball	1992
Bull Durham	1988	The Natural	1984
Ed	1996	Pride of the Yankees	1942
Elmer the Great	1933	Rhubarb	1951
The Fan	1996	Roogie's Bump	1954
For Love of the Game	1999	Rookie of the Year	1993
Field of Dreams	1989	The Slugger's Wife	1985
Ladies' Day	1943	The Winning Team	1952

Note: The definition of a baseball film is not precise. For this research, we have adopted Dickerson's (1991) definition of baseball films as films in which the narrative is principally about baseball, and in which the principal characters are more than casually involved in the game of baseball in some way. Although subtle and subjective at times, the distinction between films which are principally about baseball, and those in which the game is played in one or two brief scenes, is important. There are hundreds of films in which people are seen playing baseball. This is not surprising, given the embeddedness of the game within our culture. Our focus, however, is on those theatrical films which are primarily about baseball players and the game of baseball. It is these films, in which baseball is the central focus, that baseball's cultural vision emerges most profoundly. These films, which are centrally about baseball, are also about baseball's vision of the way the game of baseball, and American culture, should be. Even with this definition, however, the boundaries between "baseball" and "non-baseball" films are not always clear. While Erickson (1992) includes the 1988 film Stealing Home *as a baseball film, for example, Wood et al.(1994), categorize this as a "secondary," rather than "primary" baseball film. Despite the occasional ambiguities involved in such borderline cases, however, the above definition does serve to establish the general boundaries separating the genre of baseball films from other types of films.*

References

Berman, R. (1982). *Sports in the Movies.* New York: Proteus Books.

Degler, C.N. (1980). *At Odds: Women and the Family in America from the Revolution to the Present.* New York: Oxford University Press.

Dickerson, G. (1991). *The Cinema of Baseball.* Westport: Meckler.

Erickson, H. (1992). *Baseball in the Movies.* Jefferson, NC: McFarland.

Ferrante, K. (1994). "Baseball and the Social Construction of Gender," In P.J. Creedon (ed.), *Women, Media, and Sport: Challenging Gender Values,* (pp. 238-256). Thousand Oaks, CA: Sage.

Lipsky, R. (1981). *How We Play the Game.* Boston: Beacon Press.

Riess, Steven A. (1980). *Touching Base: Professional Baseball and American Culture in the Progressive Era.* Westport, CN: Greenwood Press.

Ryan, M., and Kellner, D. (1988). *Camera Politica.* Bloomington, IN: University of Indiana.

Solomon, E. (1985) . "'The Bullpen of Her Mind': Women's Baseball Fiction and Sylvia Tannenbaum's *Rachel, the Rabbi's Wife*." *Arete, 3:1,* 19–31.

Wood, S., Pincus, J.D., DeBonis, J.N., and Mastroianni, G. (1994). *Baseball Symbols in Non-Baseball Films: Reflections of American Culture.* Paper presented to the 6th annual Symposium on Baseball and the American Culture, Cooperstown, NY.

Index